SEX AND THE SCIENTIST

Sex and the Scientist

The Indecent Life
of Benjamin Thompson,
Count Rumford (1753–1814)

Jane Merrill

McFarland & Company, Inc., Publishers
Jefferson, North Carolina

ALSO OF INTEREST

Jane Merrill and John Endicott,
*Aaron Burr in Exile: A Pariah in Paris,
1810–1811* (McFarland, 2016)

Frontispiece: *A Country Walk* (1791)
by Johann Georg von Dillis (Munich, Private Collection).

LIBRARY OF CONGRESS CATALOGUING-IN-PUBLICATION DATA

Names: Merrill, Jane, author.
Title: Sex and the scientist : the indecent life of Benjamin Thompson,
Count Rumford (1753–1814) / Jane Merrill.
Description: Jefferson, North Carolina : McFarland & Company, Inc., 2018. |
Includes bibliographical references and index.
Identifiers: LCCN 2017052162 | ISBN 9781476665924
(softcover : acid free paper) ∞
Subjects: LCSH: Rumford, Benjamin, Graf von, 1753–1814. |
Rumford, Benjamin, Graf von, 1753–1814—Friends and associates. |
Rumford, Benjamin, Graf von, 1753–1814—Relations with women. |
Physicists—Great Britain—Biography.
Classification: LCC Q143.R8 M47 2018 | DDC 530.092—dc23
LC record available at https://lccn.loc.gov/2017052162

BRITISH LIBRARY CATALOGUING DATA ARE AVAILABLE

ISBN (print) 978-1-4766-6592-4
ISBN (ebook) 978-1-4766-2917-9

© 2018 Jane Merrill. All rights reserved

*No part of this book may be reproduced or transmitted in any form
or by any means, electronic or mechanical, including photocopying
or recording, or by any information storage and retrieval system,
without permission in writing from the publisher.*

Front cover: *Sir Benjamin Thompson, later Count Rumford (1753–1814),*
by Thomas Gainsborough, 1783. Oil on canvas. Dimensions 75.7 × 62.7 cm
(29^{13}⁄$_{16}$ × 24^{11}⁄$_{16}$ in.); framed 99.8 × 88 cm (39^{5}⁄$_{16}$ × 34⅜ in.). Photograph by Imaging
Department © President and Fellows of Harvard College (courtesy Harvard Art
Museum/Fogg Museum, Bequest of Edmund C. Converse, 1922.1).

Printed in the United States of America

*McFarland & Company, Inc., Publishers
Box 611, Jefferson, North Carolina 28640
www.mcfarlandpub.com*

Table of Contents

Acknowledgments — vii
Dates in the Life of Benjamin Thompson — ix
Author's Note — xi
Preface — 1

1. The Apprentice (1753–1770) — 7
2. The Young Schoolmaster (1770–1776) — 15
3. Thompson and the Wentworths (1772–1775) — 25
4. The Royalist and the Printer's Wife (1776–1779) — 33
5. The Affair of the Letters and Dr. Jeffries' Wife (1776–1779) — 45
6. Advice from General Burghausen's Wife (1784) — 59
7. Honors and Enterprises (1784–1790s) — 66
8. The Highborn Sisters (Mid–1780s) — 79
9. An Italian Idyll on Which He Met Lady Palmerston (1793–1794) — 89
10. Educating Sally (1794–1796) — 102
11. With Sally in Munich (1796–1798) — 112
12. The Stories Portraiture Tells (1800s) — 127
13. Leaving London and Paris Opens Its Arms (1801–1802) — 137
14. Pursuing Madame Lavoisier (November 1801) — 148
15. Engaged (circa February 1804) — 155
16. A New Method of Spending Time (October 1805) — 161

17. Boiling Over (1806–1809)	168
18. Single Again (1809)	174
19. Victoire (Circa 1809)	183
20. Children on Both Sides of the Atlantic (Mid–19th Century)	200
Epilogue: "The Most Sublime of All Affections"	213
Afterword: Experiments and Inventions	223
Chapter Notes	233
Bibliography	241
Index	243

Acknowledgments

About the same time I finished my book on Aaron Burr's self-exile in Paris, two of my friends with a moving business brought me 15 cartons of books that had belonged to a professor at MIT. One friend told me, that while looking at the books piled up in the professor's garage, they said, "Who would want these? Jane likes books."

It is engrossing to browse in someone else's library, and I set out to read and reread some of the professor's books, appreciating the interests of the collector I will never meet, and sharing them with my son, also at MIT, whose paternal grandfather claims patents for a banjo capo, a mechanized sharpener for sawmill saws, and a compressed air coal-mining machine that replaced explosives.

This was when I became obsessed. In the trove was Sanborn Conner Brown's biography *Benjamin Thompson, Count Rumford* (1981). Brown, professor of physics at MIT, wrote the signal scientific biography from which many quotes and facts in this book are drawn. The 18th-century gentleman on its cover, elegantly dressed, including a suit jacket with standup French collar and natty foulard, had a penetrating glance, humorous mouth and high cheekbones. What did MIT Press have to do with him? When I found out, my son, who is also an inventor from a family on both sides of engineers and inventors, helped me seek out the birthplace of Thompson, not far from where Burton and his family live. Here in Woburn, Massachusetts, I felt the parallels between the inventor types in our family and this man. My rationalist son says that all people are interesting once you to get to know them, but agreed that Benjamin Thompson is extraordinarily interesting.

Thus the adventure of going places to do this book began when Leonard Harmon, president of the Rumford House, gave us a tour. A year into the project it seemed a miracle when Josiah Pierce, direct descendant of Thompson's half-brother, invited me to his and his wife Kathleen's farm in Baldwin, Maine, where Thompson's mother and stepfather lived in their later years (Josiah's great-great-great-grandfather having established a sawmill operation on the farm in 1785). Some New Englanders have long memories. The next year in Concord, New Hampshire, I met another individual who conveyed lore, this time of Thompson's first wife's family. I am thankful for these fruitful trips.

There was more adventure ahead at archival collections, unfolding long-hidden layers of Thompson's life, for which I would like to thank the following archivists and librarians: the staff at the Rauner Special Collections Library of Dartmouth College; Daniel Hinchen at the Massachusetts Historical Society; Lynn Catanese and Lucas Clawson at the Hagley Museum; Karen Robson, Pearl Romans, and Susan Worrell at the University of Southampton, UK; Malia Ebel and Douglas Copeley at the New Hampshire Historical Society; Michele Lavoie and Caitlin Sanders at the American Academy of Arts and Sciences; the Phillips Library of the Peabody Museum, Salem, Massachusetts; Susan Halpert at Houghton Library of Harvard University; Phillips Library of the Peabody-Essex Museum; and the Clements Library of the University of Michigan. For year-after-year reference service and a place to work I thank the public libraries of Westport, Connecticut, and Weston, Massachusetts.

I would also like to thank the scholars who provided extensive help, some to a stranger they met virtually: Paul H.D. Kaplan, professor of art history at Purchase College, SUNY; Nicholas Dames, professor of English at Columbia University; Erik Goldstein, curator of Mechanical Arts and Numismatics, Colonial Williamsburg Foundation; Neil Chambers, research fellow, Nottingham Trent University; Marco Girardi, archivist at the Biblioteca Civica of Verona; Nichole Chalfant, collection manager of the Rundlet-May House, Portsmouth, New Hampshire; Ralph Baylor and Stephen Bury, Frick Museum Art Reference Library; Hubert Demory, vice president of the Federation of Historic and Archeological Societies of Paris and the Ile-de-France; Natalie Bonamy of the Department of Hauts-de-Seine; Brigitte Muller Konrad; Hinrich Sieveking, art historian, Munich; Christina Resch, Regensburg, Germany; Michel Petit, president of the Association Patrimoine de Linas; Brynn E. White, archivist, American Kennel Club, New York City; Tom Doyle, archivist, Woburn Public Library; antiquarian bookseller Joseph Luttrell and Michael Scammell; Harald Stockert, historian, Mannheim; Thomas Weidner, senior curator of the Munich City Museum; and scholar of international law, Jedidiah Kroncke. Karin Flynn bolstered my German and Jeri Quinzio, historian of food, clarified the nature of Rumford soup.

I loved the subject so much I boldly enlisted the help of family members as never before. They lent energy and intelligence and mostly got hooked. My heartfelt thanks goes to E. Christian Filstrup for canny research and valued repartee, Laurie Filstrup for genealogy help, Burton Filstrup for enthusiastically keeping images "after hours" with his family, Julia Merrill for computer arranging, Rosalind Parry for scrutiny of my thoughts, and Diane Glynn and David Arnheim for what authors need: supportive persons to read the book in process.

Dates in the Life of Benjamin Thompson

1744—Loammi Baldwin was born in Woburn

March 26, 1752—Benjamin Thompson was born in Woburn, Massachusetts

1756—Ruth Thompson married Josiah Pierce, Jr.

1760—George III succeeded to the throne of England

1766–1770—Benjamin Thompson served as an apprentice in Salem, Boston, and Woburn

December 1771–Feb. 1772—Taught school

November 14, 1772—Married Sarah Walker Rolfe

1773—Commissioned in New Hampshire militia by Governor Wentworth

Summer 1774—Summoned by People's Committee of Safety

October 1774—Sarah "Sally" Thompson was born

Late fall 1774—Thompson fled to Woburn, temporarily leaving his wife and baby

Early 1775—Began to operate as a secret agent for General Gage

February 1775—Took a trip with Mary Dill Thomas

March 1775—Baldwin deflected Minutemen from arresting him

March 24, 1776—Evacuated with Loyalists

April 1776—Lord Germain gave him appointment as secretary

May 27, 1777—Isaiah Thomas and Mary Dill Thomas divorced

April, 1779—Gave letters of Benjamin Franklin to King George

1779–1781—Made under-secretary of state by Germain

Fall 1781—Departed for America to recruit the American Dragoons

Late 1783—Returned to London and was made a full colonel

1784—Met General and Mrs. Bourghausen in Vienna

1784—Hired by Karl Theodor, Prince Elector of Bavaria

1788—Made major general of the cavalry and privy councillor by the prince

March 1791—Mozart wrote an aria for Countess Baumgarten

1792—Holy Roman Emperor ennobled Thompson as Count Rumford

January 1792—Death of Sarah Thompson

Spring 1793–Spring 1794—Took a year's holiday in Italy

Fall 1795—Prince allowed him to spend six months in London

January 1796—Sally sailed in the *Charlestown* from Boston

Late 1796—Averted Munich's destruction; published on chimneys

1798—Sally returned from London to Concord, New Hampshire

1799—Thomas Jefferson put in Rumford fireplaces at Monticello

November–December 1801—Rumford visited Paris for the first time

1802–1803—Toured Switzerland with Anne Lavoisier

May 1803—Napoleon allowed him to live in Paris

October 24, 1805—Married Anne

June 30, 1809—Separated from Anne

circa June 26, 1810—Death of Countess Nogarola

October 11, 1813—Victoire Lefebvre gave birth to his son Charles

August 21, 1814—Died suddenly (buried at Auteuil)

1836—Anne-Marie Lavoisier Rumford died

1838—Lefebvres offered Sally hospitality in Paris

September 8, 1855—Charles married Marie Louise Pauline de Tauzier

1852—Sally made extractions from, and then burned, her father's letters

January 1853—Charles reclaimed the name Rumford; died at the Siege of Sebastopol

December 29, 1887—Amedée-Joseph Lefebvre, major of the 138th Regiment, died in battle

Author's Note

Throughout this book I call certain people (who are mentioned many times) by their first names. Most of them are women, which is practical, as they are in the story because of their relations to the protagonist. Other choices of first versus last name or title are made to keep the reader from frowning. Thus Isaiah Thomas is "Isaiah" to avoid confusion between "Thompson" and "Thomas" while Mrs. Thomas is "Mary Dill" to distinguish her from their houseguest Mary. Lady Palmerston is called that as her given name was "Mary," but so was Countess Nogarola's and they appear in the story at the same time. To distinguish between Thompson's wife Sarah and his daughter Sarah, the latter is called "Sally," her nickname as a girl.

After becoming a married man, "Benjamin" in the text cedes to "Thompson." When he was made a count, that allows me to call him "Thompson" or "the Count" or "Rumford," three variations of nomenclature. I have done this on the one hand because I could—sheer authorial license. Also, though, my continuing to call him Thompson at times indicates that he did not go through a total identity change when made a count of the Holy Roman Empire anymore than when he received knighthood in England or any of his ranks in Bavaria—speaking of which, the Bavarian prince Thompson worked for the longest, "Karl Theodor," signed his first name with a *C*, apparently preferring the French version of his name (for the sake of consistency, he is referred to in this book by the German version of his name, Karl Theodor).

Preface

Benjamin Thompson had a particular charisma based on the circumstances of his background. He was from rural New England where people were thrown on their own ingenuity by cash limits, long winters, and the self-examined conscience. Self-reliance bred natural inventors, or as one of my neighbors in Maine quipped speaking of his life partner, Linda, who has a horse farm, "If she won't call me handsome she can call me handy."

Today relegated to obscurity, Benjamin Thompson was about the handiest American who ever lived. This explains why when Franklin Delano Roosevelt was a candidate for the presidency he named in response to an inquiring interviewer the characters in history he most admired: Benjamin Franklin, Thomas Jefferson and Benjamin Thompson. On the eve of Roosevelt's sixtieth birthday, the same interviewer, still curious, ventured to recall to the president that ten-year-old question. Without hesitation or prompting, although he presumably had not thought of the matter since, Roosevelt named the same all–American list: Benjamin Franklin, Thomas Jefferson, and Benjamin Thompson (a little-known genius of Revolutionary times), as well as Theodor Roosevelt.[1] But whereas the reason he gave ten years earlier for his admiration was that his heroes were versatile men, of wide-ranging and universal minds, this time he added another reason. They were all happy men, he pointed out, happy because they were always interested, eager for new experience. Any one of the four would have found plenty to excite him on a desert island.

While Benjamin Franklin championed freedom from the tyranny of the Old World, Benjamin Thompson, widely known by one of his titles, Count Rumford, was a Royalist whose ideal government was the Chinese rule by brainpower (as imagined in the West). Both men were iconized in Europe for their humanitarianism and diplomacy, Franklin capturing the public imagination for harnessing electricity and Thompson for curing smoky chimneys. Charles William Elliott (1834–1926), president of Harvard for 40 years, considered Count Rumford to be the greatest of American-born scientists. Had Thompson not spied on General Washington's army, his story would be a staple in American schoolbooks.

Thompson invented, for starters, the drip coffeepot, the double boiler, the *sous-vide* method of cooking, and the smoke-free fireplace; Jefferson invented the dumb waiter and the wine cooler; and Franklin invented bifocals and swim fins. All three men, in the eyes of their contemporaries, had immense glamor. While publications on Thompson's life occupy a short shelf compared with the libraries on Jefferson and Franklin, there have been significant biographies and other secondary sources on him since the Victorian era. Yet the original documents relating to Thompson's personal life I found had been lightly investigated and often passed over.

One-half of my research material is from archives, especially but not exclusively, of the American Academy of Arts and Sciences, Dartmouth's Rauner Library, Houghton Library of Harvard University, New Hampshire Historical Society, the Massachusetts Historical Society, and the University of Southampton (UK).

The second half of this book comes from published works, especially two. Boston clergyman and author George Edward Ellis presented Thompson's life story in a so-called *Memoir* in 1871.[2] While there were short tributes preceding it this was the first full-length biography, and since Ellis had access to many documents now lost it has special significance. The acknowledged major study of Thompson's life is by Sanborn Conner Brown, published by MIT Press in 1980. My own book covers some of the same grounds as this outstanding study but with a special emphasis on the character of the inventor and his relations with women.

Nuggets of unique material complementing my book with information on science are several entertaining books in English by Bence Jones (1871), Edwin E. Slosson (1910), Egon Larson (1953), W.J. Sparrow (1964), and G.I. Brown (2000), enumerated in the bibliography. Revisiting Thompson's private life through these sources is a quest of separating rumor from fact, which I have endeavored to do. The French writers have tended to write about the person as opposed to the career. Denis I. Duveen (1952) and Robert Campeix (1996) wrote perceptive articles and had access to materials not entirely sourced elsewhere. Thomas Weidner's *Rumford: Rezepte für ein besseres Bayern*, which accompanied an exhibit at the Munich State Museum (October 2014 to April 2015), is a gorgeous book that Rumford deserved and contains information of great value.

On the *Memoir*'s first page, Ellis linked "two men [who were] the most distinguished for philosophical genius of all that have been produced on the soil of this continent. They were Benjamin Franklin and Benjamin Thompson. They came into life in humble homes, within twelve miles of each other [from Franklin's birthplace on Milk Street in Boston to Thompson's in Woburn], under like straits and circumstances of frugality and substantial thrift." Both came from farm families and were "cast, as their progenitors had been, upon their own exertions, without dependence upon inherited means, or patronage, or even good fortune."

Neither eminent *philosophe* conformed, especially in Europe, to lifelong marriage, monogamy, or the prescribed rules of sexual behavior of mainstream early American culture. Neither was sanctioned for this. Both thrived on female companionship, put reasoning and personal ambition before human relationships, from early manhood were attractive to women, and neatly bypassed social-sexual proprieties. They both had illegitimate children and did not arrive at or stoop to conventional marriages, being perfectly happy to live across the ocean from wives. They shared the beds of women who asked of them what they could give, their brilliant company and no ties.

Ellis continued with this circumlocution: "Neither of them had in his early, nor even in his later, years that rigid purity of principle which insured that all his domestic relations should be such as would admit of record, according to the good New England usage, on the few blank leaves between the Old and the New Testament in the family Bible. There are details concerning both these Benjamins of a sort which their biographers must pass unmentioned, thankful if only they can be referred to foreign soil and foreign customs."

Pierce Farm, Baldwin, Maine (courtesy Kathleen Pierce).

The advent of both fascinating men would have eroded marriages that were short on love, yet neither man was a seducer who disrespected women. Part of their attraction was how signally their friendships with the opposite sex counted for them.

A display of idle refinement was key to the role of an 18th century aristocratic woman. Since she probably married in her teens, she had satisfied the first prerequisite of providing children while she was a young adult. As for work, that was what commoners did. A royal, if he did anything, rode to war. His wife's job was to be a figurehead of the ruling class (the girl in *The Princess and the Pea* passes the test of high birth by her physical sensitivity). Aristocratic girlhood had wrapped the lady in cotton candy, requiring she sleep on an exceedingly soft bed. From the first elite woman 20-year-old Thompson encountered—the royal governor's wife on his honeymoon with his first wife to Portsmouth, New Hampshire—through almost all his mistresses, to Anne Lavoisier, his second wife, when he was 50, nearly all the liaisons he had were with bright women who expected to be pampered.

When Benjamin Thompson arrived in London from America, Europe's social order was being challenged. Denis Diderot had produced the last volume of his *Encyclopedia* pervaded by rationalism and skepticism, and ideas of republicanism and freedom were cracking the ice of tradition. An intelligent woman in the elite would be reflecting on her society and asking, as in Amy Lowell's poem *Patterns*, "What are patterns for?" as she walked up and down the garden paths. In fact, as for her body's being "guarded from embrace by each button, hook, and lace," the stylish European was letting out her stays, literally. The Empire chemise that hid next to nothing would soon replace a high-waisted frothy negligee à l'anglaise. Fashion and government were breaking patterns, which supported women looking outside the garden walls and thinking, "I too am a rare pattern."[3]

The rococo put an accent on play, the bubbly appearance of having not a care in the world. The first noble mistress Thompson had was a blithe countess, while his closest two intimate women friends met him more on common, serious ground. They were impressed by, and encouraged, his charitable enterprises and his experiments. Thompson epitomized a new dream of the ideal man they had within.

Infidelity among aristocrats had long been part of their lifestyle but, during the Enlightenment, society tolerated greater permissiveness for the woman than ever before. Typically her husband was away for long periods serving his liege lord, they had several homes they often occupied at different times from each other, and the husband took pride in having a cultivated wife. Once he had several children it wasn't vital she be sexually faithful; a faithful wife would make more trouble about one's mistresses. If the wife had artists and musicians visit and discussed ideas, it enhanced his prestige. He was discreet and walked carefully on the garden paths and marble parterres of aristocratic life, as did she.

Traditionally men and women had different spheres and the women didn't do anything outside their sphere, whatever their class. There weren't free spaces to interact as unattached people. Now the top of the social order allowed men and women to mingle in salons, on rustic walks and during country visits. Thompson liked to ride and hunt with the men and spend long convivial hours in the realm of women. He talked out his ideas with the women and got along with their children. He was an outsider harmless to the men, a friend of the family.

The intimate friendships Thompson enjoyed with women in Europe tended to be not romps but lasting meetings of minds. This happened between him and women of aristocratic rank because of their very idleness, which made them cry out emotionally for more. Thompson was a man of cultivation, a modern man trying to make the world better through technological change, offering an immaterial sort of friendship that was itself an innovation for the European woman. In terms of sexual liaisons, this eminent inventor was an adulterer many times over. But in this book I will present the subtler truth of his relations with women of his mature years in Europe in terms of the light they brought to a reserved person with an intense expatriate life.

> I would be the pink and silver as I ran along the paths,
> And he would stumble after,
> Bewildered by my laughter.
> I should see the sun flashing from his sword-hilt and the buckles on his shoes.
> I would choose
> To lead him in a maze along the patterned paths,
> A bright and laughing maze for my heavy-booted lover,
> Till he caught me in the shade,
> And the buttons of his waistcoat bruised my body as he clasped me,
> Aching, melting, unafraid.[4]

At the conclusion of work on this book no more than at the beginning do I comprehend why this great inventor and social reformer has had his character vilified by those who have taken up their pens to write about him.

1

The Apprentice (1753–1770)

Faber quisque ingenii sui [Every man is the architect of his own character].—Francis Bacon

Benjamin Thompson was born on March 26, 1753, at 90 Elm Street, North Woburn, Massachusetts (Thompson would write it "Wooburn" as it is still pronounced). The 2½ story clapboard house, with gambrel roof and central chimney, once near the town's meeting house, is now a historic site and museum.

Thompson was the sixth generation in America, of farming stock, and his 26-year-old father, as well as his paternal grandfather, who built the house in 1714, died before Benjamin was two years old. The low, sturdy cradle where the future physicist lay as an infant remains today in the west end of the house, where his parents had lived after their marriage. A descendant of one of Woburn's first settlers, James Thompson, who came to New England with Governor John Winthrop in 1630, Benjamin's grandfather Ebenezer Thompson had property in Woburn and Wilmington, of which Benjamin was left 50 acres of woods and farmland within the year after his father died. Cutting, stacking and selling firewood from his grandfather's property would provide a major source of income during his teenage years.

Ebenezer's will specified the rights of Benjamin's mother, Ruth, in terms that seem cool but speak for the elemental nature of 18th century rural New England households. Ruth had permission to garden a part of her former father-in-law's property, "one half of the garden at the west end" and "the privilege of land to raise beans for sauce." As long as Ruth was a widow, her brother-in-law, Benjamin's Uncle Hiram, was instructed to help her with provisions to "give the said widow eighty weight of beef, eight bushels of rye, two bushels of malt, and two barrels of cider for the present year," while she also had the "liberty of gathering apples to bake, and three bushels of apples for winter, yearly and every year."[1]

By Ebenezer's instructions, Benjamin himself would have a certain number of shillings a week until age 13. The young widow remarried in 1756; she and Josiah Pierce, Jr., moved down the road, opposite the Baldwins, whose house, the finest in town, dated from the 17th century. Loammi Baldwin, born in 1744, formed a lifelong friendship with Benjamin. As men the two would be on opposite sides in the Revolutionary War; Loammi Baldwin resigned his commission before its close and was then appointed high sheriff of Middlesex County. The Pierce, Baldwin and Thompson families intertwined at least from the point of the remarriage of Benjamin's mother, Ruth.

Count Rumford Birthplace. Built in 1714 by Ebenezer Thompson (Woburn Public Library). The count was born there in 1753, and his parents had lived there since their marriage. The long pivoted pole is part of a well sweep, which had a bucket attached to one end by a long rope.

Ruth had four more children with Josiah (having two or three spouses then was common, chiefly because of death) and eventually moved to Maine with him. For a time, Loammi Baldwin and Josiah Pierce had a store in North Woburn. They became business partners in the firm of Baldwin & Pierce. The old part of the present Pierce farm in Baldwin, Maine, was built by their firm and has remained in the Pierce family since the late 18th century. It was also partly a store, a common enough diversification in colonial times (as evidenced by both Hepzibah Pyncheon and one of her ancestors in *The House of Seven Gables*). Josiah Pierce, a direct eighth-generation descendant of Benjamin Thompson's stepbrother, and his wife Kathy own and farm the property in Baldwin now, acting as stewards keeping it in the family. Benjamin's mother and stepfather are buried in a cemetery on the beautiful grounds.

Farming families in early America lived differently from their English counterparts. Historian David Freeman Hawke wrote, "The semi-isolated farm ... forced men to do for themselves what they had once depended on village craftsmen to do for them."[2] Specialization, in other words, had not occurred and generalization of know-how typified the mid–18th century New England yeoman. Benjamin Thompson, who would come to love fine clothes and horses, fancy balls and chamber music, split and hauled wood, growing up to pay for his education; and when he wanted to address a scientific problem, throughout his life he designed his own instruments.

The history of 18th century science is noted for such individuals with diversified, experimenting intelligence and self-schooling: Joseph Priestley, the discoverer of oxygen, and Henry Cavendish of hydrogen, Alessandro Volta, inventor of the battery, and Benjamin Franklin all sharpened their wits and applied their genius, mostly by informal studies out in the world. The great chemist Sir Humphry Davy was a protégé of Thompson's. A teacher speaking of Davy as a lad remarked, "I could not discern the faculties by which he was afterwards so much distinguished." Davy, however, had self-knowledge and said, "I consider it fortunate I was left much to myself as a child, and put upon no particular plan of study."[3]

Woburn, Massachusetts, in the mid–18th century was a community of only 1500 persons yet it spawned, within six years of each other, Thompson and his lifelong friend Loammi Baldwin, America's first civil engineer and builder of the Middlesex Canal. As young men in the tradition of walkers—for instance Herman Melville and Nathaniel Hawthorne in Lenox—they had passionate talks about science while they stretched their legs. The Baldwin apple—a good keeper, a variety they found on a hillside—was eventually named after Loammi.

The fleeting moments of parent and child companionship in colonial America were built around shared labor but Benjamin did not care for his forebears' and Josiah's métier of farming. Indications are that through young adulthood, Thompson gravitated to father figures who shared his intellectual interests in science and mathematics. After he became famous in Europe, Thompson would encapsulate his childhood in a chimerical narrative, useful for him because he put a premium on efficiency. The curious in Europe must have asked him over and over about his background. His family had once owned an island in Boston Harbor, he fibbed, and his childhood was blighted.

Report of a troubled childhood comes through from a report of Marc-Auguste Pictet, a Swiss professor and science writer who admired Thompson. On a visit to England in 1801, Pictet spent several days at Thompson's home in London and wrote particulars in a biographical entry in the *Bibliothèque Britannique*. Pictet cited Thompson as having said that the mother's second marriage "proved for her a source of misfortunes. A tyrannical husband took me away from my grandfather's house with her.... I was then launched at the right time upon a world which was almost strange to me, and I was obliged to form the habit of thinking and acting for myself, and of depending on myself for a livelihood."[4] These sources that seem to compound something about his childhood actually compound Thompson's attitude towards his past, which was essentially that he did not find himself in America and when he was ejected he formed a concerted attitude that he had a better life abroad.

Thompson, though, loved his mother with devotion that he expressed more, namely in his correspondence, as the years progressed. In the day when a portrait was understood to have a mystical connection with a person, carrying one's spirit, the back of an oval portrait of Thompson in the home of the descendant of his stepbrother Josiah Pierce says it was for her, copied in 1799 from a portrait by "Mr. Kellerhofer of Munich" in 1792. Every human life, from the inside as well as in the eyes of others, is a story. Fashioning one's story into a fairy tale results in having less psychic work to do, either to inform others about or to reflect about. It is also characteristic of those who, many inventors among them, look ahead and not behind.

That Thompson owed his drive and chance in life to early misfortune also appears in a biographical sketch that the 19th century Frenchman Baron Cuvier included in his *Récueil des Éloges Historiques*. Cuvier appended his own fairy tale, inserting a facetious note in this eulogy that a cause of Thompson's death was his "rigid observation of order," a quality surely typical of many a great scientist.[5] Another way to understand the description and self-description of a deprived childhood is that on the Continent people were casting Thompson as another Benjamin Franklin, who emphasized his humble origins and dressed like a simple rural person abroad. The luster of Franklin must have prepared Continental Europe for another American star of resourceful gravitas.

In terms of the historiographical press, one of the worst things an early American luminary could do was flout the sexual mores of Protestant America. In essence Thompson forgot them when no longer paying Uncle Hiram rent for his church pew, and living in Europe. If the transnational perspective could corrupt, how strong were the ramparts? To take one instance of a scolding biography, 19th-century journalist and Vassar graduate Frances M. Abbott, wrote that the careers of the two Benjamins presented many points of similarity: "Although devoting their lives to benefiting their fellow-beings, neither appears to have been remarkably warm-hearted nor a great lover of his kind. There are blemishes in the private life of each. Cold, prudent, calculating, they pursued the relation between cause and effect with an assiduity and singleness of purpose that amounted to genius."[6]

The parallels stand out like checkpoints. Franklin pretended to have got a girl pregnant to take his leave of Boston, was rather dismissive of marriage, was never forthcoming about his progeny, and brought two grandsons to Paris. Benjamin Thompson left his wife and baby in America when forced into exile, took an avuncular interest in his out-of-wedlock second child, and brought his first daughter to Europe when she was 22 to educate her. Thompson showed fondness for his natural son by keeping him in his home, which was unconventional.

By the age of 13, Benjamin had attended three schools, Master Fowle's in Woburn, a grammar school in Byfield, and Mr. Hill's in Medford. Next came an apprenticeship, which served then as an experience of general education as well as instruction in a trade. Meanwhile, Loammi Baldwin stayed in Woburn. Loammi had an apprenticeship (cabinetry) that wasn't quite his calling and turned to surveying and engineering. He was always ready to dialogue on science and try an experiment. Loammi and Benjamin shared an interest in mechanics, physical processes, and learning. To apprentice with a merchant, Thompson was sent in 1766 to Salem. He was participating in what Roy Porter, writing of contemporaneous English society, has called "a local migration, creeping caterpillar-like towards the larger towns."[7] His family indentured him to John Appleton, a merchant who sold imported dry goods. The considerable distance of 15 miles from Woburn indicates that Benjamin's family thought he was truly best placed there. Appleton often advertised in the *Essex Gazette*, such as in December 20–27, 1768, the first year of its publication, the sale of goods from England and Scotland including "cardinal silks, fur and snail trimmings [apparently decorations of snail shells]."[8]

Benjamin Thompson had good fortune in apprenticeships. It is likely that his uncle or stepfather was instrumental in the first. In the thriving coastal town of Salem, he was living in an established merchant's home. Appleton was a Harvard graduate and son of the Rev. Nathaniel Appleton of Cambridge. Benjamin attended church with the Appleton family and became friends with the younger son of the minister. The Rev. Thomas Barnard tutored Benjamin in mathematics and astronomy. Benjamin cut his name into his slate while at Appleton's in very big letters. When he was 14 there occurred a solar eclipse. He was able to calculate the moment it would occur and was off only four seconds, a feat he would recall with pride. He liked to draw and made a fanciful heraldic plate for himself figured with books, swords, ship, compass, lion and rays of the sun emitted from a human eye. For other boys he did engravings of devices and names on their knives and other implements. He played the fiddle in the store when he was sure the sounds would not call in Mr. Appleton.[9]

One night, Benjamin walked all the way to Woburn from Salem to show Loammi a contrivance he thought would solve the problem of perpetual motion. Edwin E. Slosson, a physicist writing in 1910, observed that Thompson "was no exception to the old saying that no man ever became a great physicist who did not attempt to invent a machine for perpetual motion in his youth."[10] The ardor of the budding scientist can be seen in Benjamin's letters to Loammi, asking the older friend about matters such as why fire changes the color of clay, the "Beginning of Existence, and Rise of the Wind in General," and "how the Great Creator formed the matter thereof."[11]

During Benjamin's apprenticeship, certain merchants of New England protested the taxes levied on them. Previously, the British parliament had levied a tax on paper to help pay for the French and Indian War. This might seem logical, as the colonies were being defended. In Woburn, from the time the conflict with the French began in 1755 through the signing of the peace treaty in 1763, one in five men were drafted for active military service. Yet the Stamp Act lit a fuse of protest and was repealed in 1756. Appleton's business depended on imports, and the fact that the English suppressed manufacturing in the colonies meant that imports were not just luxuries. In a 1769 issue of the *Essex Gazette*, Appleton advertised the sale of "Ruffia and Ravens Duck, best Bank Cod-Hooks" and a "good Assortment of English Piece Goods."[12] He hoped his customers would not neglect his shop because of the lack of a full assortment due to the import agreement. The business would have recovered except that, despite the repeal of the Stamp Act he was a signer, in response to the Townsend duties, of the nonimportation agreement for no more goods from Great Britain. Benjamin remained a merchant's apprentice in Boston for 2½ years, until 1769.

Young Benjamin also took an interest in guns and gunpowder and heat and astronomy and read all the science he could put his hands on. He used his shillings and pennies to buy materials to do experiments and also made fireworks. As he noted in his daybook, he was making at least four types of skyrockets: serpents, stars and other configurations included. The fireworks were being prepared for a red-letter day. This might have been Guy Fawkes Day, or the English November holiday marking the end of the Gunpowder Plot, or the anniversary of the first repeal of the Stamp Act. There is a likelihood of another possibility, not an anniversary or holiday but an on-the-spot event. The recall to England of the much-resented Governor Francis Bernard, whose intransigence helped along the forces of revolution, occurred just at the time of the accident discussed below.

When Bernard left, in about August 2, 1769, a Boston newspaper reported that there was much rejoicing including bells, bonfires and cannons, which "soon diffused through the neighboring Towns, who gave Similar Demonstrations of it."[13] (Bernard's son Thomas would in the late 1790s be a big supporter of Benjamin Thompson's enterprises to found poorhouses and the Royal Institution in London). Egon Larsen in *An American in Europe* stated "the people of Salem asked Mr. Appleton to supply the necessary fireworks, and Thompson claimed that he could arrange them in the required style of 'extraordinary and unparalleled brilliancy and impressiveness.'"[14] Benjamin overreached himself in making the skyrockets. In grinding together the ingredients in a mortar, he became careless and the mixture exploded. It is said he damaged the shop and himself, burning his head, chest and hands and nearly losing his eyesight. The accident concluded his apprenticeship for Mr. Appleton. Benjamin returned to Woburn at the beginning of August, where for two months he recuperated. The linen notebook the apprentice kept at the time recording expenses put directions for the fireworks, ending one (entered at 16) with, "LOVE is a noble passion of the mind. LOVE."[15]

Now he found himself in his rural hometown, chopping and carting wood like a college kid who had dropped out of school. He had transactions in fuel with his stepfather and his uncle for small loads and made a contract with one Abraham Alexander to "cut and cord for him seven or eight cords at nine shillings per cord," all of which calculations went into his memorandum book. At 16, he had the responsibility to pay for his share of the family pew. Some of the wood was his own and came from the property he inherited from his grandfather. While home, Benjamin pelted Loammi with questions of a scientific nature. It is clear from their correspondence how fired up he was to learn:

Woburn, Aug 14, 1769
Mr. Loammi Baldwin,
   Sir,—Please to give the Direction of the Rays of Light from a Luminous Body to an Opake, and the Reflection from the Opake Body to another equally Dense and Opake; viz. the Direction of the Rays of the Luminous Body to that of the Opake, and the direction of rays by reflection to the other opake Body.

Yours, &c.
BENJ. THOMPSON

N.B. From the Sun to the Earth, Reflected to the Moon at an angle of 40 Degrees.[16]

The following fall, Benjamin himself initiated his next apprenticeship. Hopestill Capen, proprietor of At the Sign of the Cornfields, near Faneuil Hall in Boston, asked Appleton on October 11, 1769, for a letter of character reference because a "young Ladd … offers himself to live with me."[17] Mr. Capen, at this juncture a Royalist shopkeeper, had been a carpenter and married a woman who had a dry goods store and joined her in the shop.[18] Benjamin was dreaming of the opportunities of the city. A week later, he wrote again thanking Appleton and asking that his things be packed and sent to Boston. Thus the outbreak of revolution found Benjamin living at 41–45 Union Street, in the house of Hopestill and Patience Capen. The house is now the Union Oyster House and on the Freedom Trail. Capen held the elected town offices of fence viewer (1764), warden (1768), and scavenger (1770) and served as a sergeant in the Ancient & Honorable Company.

From 1771 until the Revolution, the *Massachusetts Spy* (further discussed in Chapter 4) was published in the upper part of the building at the same address. It reconciles with difficulty that the key newspaper of revolt was published where Benjamin apprenticed at the Sign of the Cornfields, if a year too late to put his ear to the floor of his garret to listen in.

At an age to take sides in the fomenting unrest of colonial America, Benjamin had no personal qualms that would cause him to sympathize with the Sons of Liberty. Despite being fiercely ambitious he had not a political bone in his body. The rhetoric that incited many colonists, as well as grievances of the powerful merchants who smarted at tariffs, passed over his head. As Silas Deane said, "Americans will smuggle."[19] After all, the Stamp Act had been repealed. Britain was unbending about ruling the seas but flexible about the means of revenues. Lord North's ministry came to power in 1770, and all taxes were removed except on tea, thus keeping to the principle of taxation. North said if the Americans resisted these tariffs, the Crown would try others. In short, Benjamin in his teens went with the Loyalist flow. In a few years the Loyalists would diminish in number in the colonies, having little choice but to join in the revolt or depart.

If Benjamin did not have a self-conscious sense of national identity, neither did, as yet, many around him. Colonists were only beginning to think of themselves as Americans, a sense of cohesion that occurred over the quarter-century between 1750 and 1775. In his 1775 *The Farmer Refuted*, Alexander Hamilton formulated a very popular argument in the colonies at the time: parliamentary law bound them unfairly but George III was the King of America "by virtue of a contract between us and the Kings of Great Britain."[20]

Domed brass button made in England circa 1775, bearing the numbers 22 for the regiment for which the clothing was intended (Mount Vernon Ladies' Association).

Hamilton was reflecting the sense that for many colonials the problem was parliament not the king. Young Benjamin Thompson, concerned only with his own needs and wishes, stopped his thinking on the burning questions of the day with a position of giving loyalty to the king. He would not have become exercised about current events no matter how big the topic. His emotions burned low; if they burned high he tended to be sick. Being a courtier as well as a dispassionate scientist, smoothing people's discord and not being swayed by others' emotion would come to him naturally. Despite his interest in cannon and gunpowder, military uniforms and provisions, and warships, he was not a fighter. Years later, he would speak of how the point of soldiering was to help the citizenry and soldiers should be citizens and citizens soldiers. He was loyal to England and the king, like many Bostonians, before a wave took them with it.

Young Thompson was living, as he had at Salem, in a port town, where men and women wore the latest look in periwigs, ate with forks, and followed the fashions from England. Class distinctions were more prominent than in Woburn, a fact that provoked aspirations to rise.[21] At the Sign of the Cornfields was in the heart of town near the harbor and gave Benjamin a lookout on goings on from his dormer in the garret of the two-story shop (today extending one floor higher). He was able to take fencing and French at one of Boston's private night schools. He drew a cartoon of fencers in his notebook and perhaps was imagining himself a soldier as Benjamin Franklin and John Adams did when they were boys. Then again, he aimed to rise to a higher station and swordsmanship was a gentleman's sport.

As for his study of French, the French and Indian War left no hostile residue in the mind of this young man intent on learning the language of many scientific works and of one day conversing with learned foreigners. It is recorded in his piece book (at the New Hampshire Historical Society) that he started French on October 27, 1769, and planned to go every evening except Sunday; but he went only half that often. The Boston Massacre occurred close by on March 5, 1770, during his time with Capen. He probably saw the taunting crowd and would not have been shocked when John Adams defended two of the soldiers. In 1770 unrest was becoming rebellion. The revolutionaries drew up a list of those with inimical views, and Capen's name was on it. In the same year, he was listed as an "addressee" to Governor Hutchinson and a protestor against the activities of the Whigs (separatists).

Capen thought well enough of Benjamin not to punish the apprentice for ducking under the counter to read and do science. Capen stated genially after the fact what Baldwin recalled: "He employed as much of his time, as he could by any means steal from the duties of his station, to amuse himself with study and little, ingenious, mechanical recreations, and would be more frequently found with a penknife, file and gimlet under the counter, than with his pen and account books in the counting room." Benjamin's employment ended after two years, when Hopestill Capen signed the nonimportation treaty discussed above. For a half-year, ending in early June 1771, Benjamin studied medicine under Dr. Hay in Woburn.

Intermittently he was back with family in Woburn. He borrowed books and studied continuously through the various shifts in his living situation. He wrote up daily programs of the schedule he set from himself, of which this was one: "From eleven to six, Sleep. Get up at six o'clock and wash my hands and face. From six to eight, exercise one half and study one half. From eight till ten, Breakfast, attend Prayers, etc. From ten to twelve, Study all the time. From twelve to one, Dine, etc. From one to four, study constantly. From four to five, Relieve my mind by some diversion or Exercise, From five to Bedtime, follow what my inclination leads me to; whether it be to go abroad, or stay at home and read either Anatomy, Physic or Chemistry, or any book I want to Peruse."[22]

Societies since the time of Cotton Mather had existed in New England for intellectual discourse and Benjamin and Loammi formed a society of two. In June 1770 they had walked to Cambridge to attend the Natural Philosophy lectures at Harvard given by John Winthrop, a star professor who was John Adams' favorite.[23] Natural philosophy was the rubric for most every line of study of the rationalist Enlightenment, as opposed to religion, the classics, mathematics or languages. It included science from chemistry and physics to mechanics, meteorology and biology. Benjamin and Loammi would have looked at the satellites of Jupiter when they gazed through Professor Winthrop's 28-foot refractory telescope from the roof of Harvard Hall. This was the type and the same approximate size as the telescope Christiaan Huyghens invented and through which he was able to describe the rings of Saturn. Benjamin and Loammi went the round-trip on foot or possibly stayed in Cambridge. Winthrop on electricity, weather or astronomy was a breath of rational fresh air worth the walk. Neither young man had the benefit of a college education yet Loammi became a pioneering civil engineer and Benjamin a prominent inventor.

This was the time Harvard trained ministers and the elite, and lists of students were published by prominence; to apply on merit would have been preposterous. Yet Harvard had separate and endowed professorships of mathematics and science beginning in 1738, and Winthrop taught science supported by many microscopes, telescopes, and the like. Although not slated for an advanced formal education, Thompson would write that he made sufficient progress in natural philosophy "under that excellent and happy teacher."[24]

Loammi, probably in league with Benjamin, repeated Franklin's kite and key experiment to conduct electricity from lightning in thunderclouds. The kite in a storm inspired them as an early form of empirical research. Franklin was not working out answers from books but in the field, by observation, even at the risk of his life. After repeating the experiment, Loammi would recall feeling dazed and weak-limbed, and he appeared to spectators in a bright flame as he brought flashing lights of static electricity to his conductor during a storm.

2

The Young Schoolmaster (1770–1776)

> That out of sight is out of mind
> Is true of most we leave behind.
> —Arthur Hugh Clough (1819–1861)

Commerce did not hold interest for Hopewell Capon's apprentice. Benjamin Thompson had learned the basics of French, dueling, and customer service, and had studied privately. A cheerful sketch he made of the Sign of the Cornfields, with his room prominent in it, suggests he liked city life. It was at 17, he declared medicine his bent and returned to Woburn for a third apprenticeship.

Benjamin boarded with Dr. Hay at 40 shillings a week, and did dissections in his spare time. It was a work and study situation, so he did stints of teaching and odd jobs to pay the board. Local custom reinforced his native frugality. Dr. and Mrs. Hay discounted his fees during his periods of absence to teach or audit classes at Harvard, including the time "my mother washed [did laundry] for me."

Massachusetts had a law requiring that each town provide a school. It was feasible for townspeople to reduce the weight of this expense by engaging a teacher but paying him only seasonally. Benjamin fulfilled teaching assignments in Wilmington from December 1771 to February 1772 and then in the spring at Bradford. He would be remembered for his energetic and dramatic teaching methods as well as his vaulting and acrobatics. A judge who taught school in Wilmington during college about 1820 recalled that the oldest people spoke of their "distinguished and eccentric master" of the former age and that "strange stories were told of certain athletic and gymnastic performances and feats, not to say tricks, in which he sometimes exercised himself and his scholars, within the walls as well as outside."[1]

Teaching and bartering took care of Dr. Hay's fees and paved the way to better fortunes. While keeping school in Bradford, Benjamin became the boarder one summer of the young Reverend Samuel Williams, who became his inspiring teacher of mathematics and astronomy. Williams had an unusual background. When his father, Warham Williams, was four he and his entire family were captured by a party of French and Native Americans in the Deerfield Raid of 1704. The boy was purchased by a French businesswoman in Montreal and ransomed a few years later. An older brother became the leader of counterattacking colonist raiders. Samuel's Aunt Eunice, who like his father had been captured in the Deerfield raid, married a Mohawk and returned to the white world only to visit relatives, with her husband, Arosen. She converted to Catholicism and one of Samuel's brothers left the Congregational fold. Warham's uncle Increase Mather got him a scholarship to Harvard. The diversity of his background as well as his inquiring scientific mind made Samuel Williams an outstanding and liberal teacher. Williams suggested Benjamin abandon medicine, and the schoolmaster, Timothy Walker, encouraged his cousin, another Rev. Timothy Walker, schoolmaster of Concord, New Hampshire (a bigger town higher up the Merrimack River from Bradford), to engage Benjamin as an apprentice teacher there. Benjamin arrived to take up his duties in the summer of 1772, six months after the French chemist Antoine Lavoisier wed Anne-Marie Paulze, who would one day be Benjamin's second wife.

At important junctures of his life, Benjamin was singled out as being brighter, smarter, taller, and politer. This striking pattern showed itself at his third and last teaching post, in New Hampshire. He was now in a position to socialize with, as it were, his betters, the Walker family, who had relatives in Woburn, being farming gentry. The Rev. Timothy Walker was no ordinary schoolmaster but a prominent person who had been sent to Britain three times on diplomatic business related especially to which province the town lay in, New Hampshire or Massachusetts, a crucial matter for whether people owned and could sell their land.

King George II and his council drew the New Hampshire–Massachusetts border in 1740, at which time the jurisdiction of Rumford was transferred to Governor Benning Wentworth. Wentworth took the occasion to turn Rumford from a town into a district; now it would have to renew its compact each year and pay an annual tax for the privilege. When Benjamin Rolfe, representative to the Massachusetts General Court, was sent to the provincial assembly in Portsmouth, the assembly refused to seat him in 1745 and barred him again in 1749. A controversy flared up in which the people of New Hampshire tried to get lands from the people of Massachusetts. Sponsored by his flock, the Reverend Walker, Sarah Walker Rolfe's father, went to London three times over this, and hired lawyers. The Massachusetts people ultimately prevailed to keep their lands and, in the resolution of this long argument, the British Crown changed Rumford's name to Concord.

Concord, New Hampshire, was a town—of about a thousand inhabitants—on the north banks of the upper Merrimack River. It was a log-cabin settlement named Pennycook when 26-year-old Timothy Walker was ordained at the log blockhouse. Each property owner had a house lot in town and also land for pasturage or cultivation at the fringe of town. The parsonage on 276 North Main Street, on the outskirts of the town, was built in 1733–1734 and is the oldest gambrel 2½-story house in New England between Massachusetts and Canada. Though an elegant house with 24 panes of glass inside of nine front windows, it was protected by a stockade, making the minister's property one of as many as ten garrisons in the village.

Next to the house was a horse block, an immense round piece of granite of the first Congregational Society, dating from 1751. People came on horseback or carriage and could step down onto the rock. Here the Council of New Hampshire would meet in the south parlor and make Concord the state capital. On the northwest corner of the big barn that once belonged to the Walkers and next to the Walker-Woodman House today is a huge stone etched with the following: "1st House-Lot of 1st Range, Pennycook May 1726." The barn was on the Underground Railroad, according to Timothy Woodman, the last direct descendant to own the property. He was aware of the anomaly of a family of abolitionists who had slaves themselves.[2]

A Massachusetts faction insisted on Rumford, after the hometown of the early English settlers, who were brewers, and for a while the town kept the name Rumford. On the other side were the people of Bow, named after a bow in the Merrimack, with their land grant. The Reverend Walker and Colonel Rolfe, the other bigwig in town, carried the dispute all the way to London, where after long arguments on both sides, King George II and his council drew the New Hampshire-Massachusetts boundary as it is now. Eventually the town took its current name of Concord, betokening harmony. However, this was understood by many in Rumford as a proprietal type of harmony, a name expressing "the entire unanimity in purpose and action which had characterized the inhabitants of Rumford during the period of their controversy with the proprietors of Bow, and, indeed from the first settlement of Penacook."

As for Colonel Rolfe, he had position, land, military prestige, a fine house and carriage, and a forceful, voluble personality. He decided at the age of 60 the time had come to have a wife and beget an heir, so he proposed to his friend the Reverend Walker's daughter, Sarah. The Seven Years' War began when she was 15 and ended when she was 24. This meant a considerable fraction of the young men were called into the New Hampshire militia and departed Concord for the various campaigns: it was a poor time to court, wed and set up house. Benjamin must have appeared especially dreamlike because he was 19 when Sarah laid eyes on him, just the age she had been when the rush to arms of colonials to fight for Britain against the French occurred in 1758. Not only did marriage to the colonel lift Sarah, age 30, out of the doldrums of spinsterhood, but also it raised her on the social ladder. As friends of the governor of New Hampshire, John Wentworth, the Rolfes had entrée into the colonial aristocratic milieu of Portsmouth.

Sarah Walker Rolfe Thompson's silver thimble, from circa 1750–1760 (New Hampshire Historical Society).

Sarah was the namesake of her mother and also for an older Sarah who had died as a small child. A plausible conjecture is that Sarah didn't have confidence-building upbringing from her widowed father. Her only extant letter, at the New Hampshire Historical Society, passes on her father's advice about a cart horse in a few words to her brother in Bradford, in 1757; it was written by someone who didn't use the pen or formal written grammar often. The lovely silver thimble she would pass on to her daughter indicates a lady who did fancy needlecrafts rather than utilitarian chores. The Reverend Walker appears to have had inner conflict when it came to love relations with women. At about age 52, Walker wrote a distinctly misogynistic dedication to a diary that he kept for some of 1757:

> The words of a Latin Poet—
> Trust to the Winds your Bark, but trust not Eve,
> For Woman's Faith is Falser than a Wave.

> No Woman good, but if some share that Grace,
> Tis strange how bad for good should change its place.

In this diary Walker mixed talk of weather and cows with snippets for sermons. One page after an entry noting that a bishop of Antioch was the first to call "3 Persons of the Godhead" the Trinity came "a Definition of Love,"[3] mortal love to divine love: "Love is defined to be that Passion of the Soul whereby we delight in anything and take Pleasure in all opportunities in the enjoyment of it, consequently feel ourselves very, uneasy if we are deprived of it." Kicking mortal love down the stairs as lust while aspiring to the promises of spiritual purity carried a message to the next generation of women, his daughter Sarah and his granddaughter Sally, both of whom dreamed of princes beyond the reach of their real lives. Sarah bore a child, Paul, and then Colonel Rolfe died.

In the meantime, teaching was not to be Thompson's vocation any more than farming. He noted that, typical of rural parts, going to school in Concord was a fairly casual affair. Of the 106 pupils, a third did not show up at class on any given day. Benjamin was well mannered, and tall, slender, and muscular (buff from chopping and hauling wood and horseback riding), with large blue eyes, reddish hair, and chiseled features. Sarah Walker Rolfe could see he would fit in at a governor's ball. In a short three months after they became acquainted, Benjamin asked the Reverend Walker for his daughter's hand in marriage. The engagement concluded Benjamin's job of schoolteacher. As Sarah's husband he was a man of considerable property. Furthermore, his esteemed father-in-law the Reverend Walker had been minister of the town for a half-century and could recall when attacks by Native Americans still periodically threatened the settlers.

Thompson fit neatly the mold of the young man who marries an older woman who bolsters his status and financially supports him. The year before, when he was 18, Thompson paid for a "Blue Hussar Cloak" by delivering 15½ cords of wood to Zebediah Wyman.[4] In the fall of 1772, Sarah and her betrothed traveled to Boston and sought out a tailor for clothes and a hairdresser for Benjamin's wig. Benjamin also bought a scarlet coat with fancy braid and buttons. (Sam Adams would dress in red to go to the first Continental Congress. The suit can be seen in J.S. Copley's depiction of Adams on March 5, 1770, telling the British to get out of Boston.) There were family connections for Sarah in Woburn, so it was all the more natural to stop by Benjamin's mother's house as the engaged pair traveled back to Concord. They arrived in a two-horse curricle (also called a chaise) that had been Colonel Rolfe's, a vehicle so remarkable that in all New Hampshire only the royal governor had another such carriage. When Ruth Pierce saw her son in the splendid outfit of imported wool, purchased in Boston, she is reported to have said, "Why, Ben! My son, how could you go and lay out all your winter's earnings in Finery?"[5] She thought at first (tradition has it) that his female companion was a trollop, so Sarah too must have been fabulously dressed.

Colonel Rolfe had died in midwinter. Eleven months later, on November 14, 1772, the wedding of Sarah and Benjamin took place. They attended a splashy military muster in Dover of the Second Provincial Regiment of New Hampshire. Thompson (henceforth called by his surname or title) arrived on horseback looking stunning, and Governor Wentworth asked him the next day to dinner in Portsmouth. In this time, clothes made the gentleman. A man had to have them tailored, and someone had to maintain them in tiptop condition, keeping the valuable buttons on, storing items when they weren't being worn, and protecting them from insects.

The phases of Thompson's career show dramatic changes with the aspect of positive lessons learned as well. The first signal encounter of his adult life was a colonial English gentleman—both were involved in what Longfellow would call "the forest primeval" of North America. You didn't have to be from the British Isles to be an English gentleman with ties to the land, a sense of obligation to the body politic, and interest in learning generally—witness George Washington. Governor John Wentworth represented the epitome of the gentleman Thompson aspired to be, and became, without the presumed advantage of birthright. The connection ran deep. Both men displayed enormous confidence in the ability of humans to understand and apply natural law; both accepted the transfer of power to the colonists with detachment; and both were progressives and caretakers.

Almost all New Hampshire towns had a militia unit. Every man from 16 to 60 was expected to drill, have a serviceable musket, powder and ball, and be ready for service. Musters were held on the town green, and all men were required to be there. Frequency of these musters was determined by the expected threat, varying from weekly to only occasionally. Young single men were to be ready at a moment's notice. This was the origin of the Minuteman of many tales.

Dover, which has now been broken up into six towns, was the second largest town at the eve of the American Revolution. Both towns were first settled in 1623, but Portsmouth was larger and was where the royal governor had his official residence. The grounds for the muster of the militia units may have been on the site of a former garrison. Favorites of the governor headed the units. For example, John Sullivan, who would become a major general in the Continental Army, was appointed by Governor Wentworth because of his local prominence. He had the best uniform, and like Benjamin Thompson he looked the part. A man like Sullivan could afford to supply his men and for Sullivan it was a way to move up socially. In contrast, John Stark, known as the man you wanted to follow into battle, kept quitting the military because he was not promoted due to his lack of social skills and connections.

The newlywed Thompsons were on a bridal tour and thus were making a series of visits. They would have stayed with kin and not in an inn. Douglas and Susan MacLennan live in the General John Sullivan House, built in 1717, in Durham, New Hampshire.

Thompson and Sarah were guests at Wentworth's table that day or the next for dinner. Benning Wentworth, uncle to John and previous governor of the colony of New Hampshire who had vast properties in the province and up to what is now Maine, had built the 40-room Governor's Mansion, now the Wentworth-Coolidge Mansion. Hospitality and largesse gave social credit and power to the landed gentry in America as it did to the British aristocracy and as it would continue to do into the mid–20th century in America. The 20-year-old newlywed impressed Wentworth so much that he commissioned Thompson with the rank of major. Conceivably the governor might have been putting him in the militia with the idea he would be an informer. In any event, getting the appointment from a personage whom Thompson admired sealed which side he would be on in the conflict to come. Thompson now ranked over many experienced officers who had fought in the regiment in the French and Indian Wars.

More than apparently any other interlocutor, Thompson would tell his life story to Professor M.A. Pictet, the Genevan scientist and journalist. To Pictet, as a middle-aged man Thompson summarized his personal picaresque:

> I was then launched at the right time upon a world which was almost strange to me, and I was obliged to form the habit of thinking and acting for myself and of depending on myself for a livelihood. My ideas were not yet fixed; one project succeeded another and perhaps I should have acquired a habit of indecision and inconstancy, perhaps I should have been poor and unhappy all my life, if a woman had not loved me—if she had not given me a subsistence; a home and an independent fortune. I married, or rather was married at the age of nineteen. I espoused the widow of a Colonel Rolfe, daughter of the Rev. Mr. Walker, a highly respectable minister and one of the first settlers in Rumford.[6]

Pictet quoted the phrase "I married, or rather was married at the age of 19"—"I didn't marry her, she married me"—as indicating that Sarah, 33, fell for the young schoolmaster and pressed for the marriage.[7] He was a virgin and she introduced him to sex. Thompson was of lower status, not to mention younger and new to Concord, which meant Sarah would have had to take the initiative. Decades later, Thompson encapsulated an explanation for the marriage when it had become a faded part of his life. Yet it may be that Pictet ran with a misunderstanding of what Thompson said, turning it into a put-down.

First of all, Thompson credited Sarah for getting him on the tracks to success and acknowledged her love before indicating that she was the initiator. Second, in French, *"on épouse"* is "one marries" plus a direct object. Therefore Thompson, if he began with the verb *"marier"* in mind, would not want to say *"j'ai épousé"* but would correct himself and say *"elle m'a épousé."* Usage of épouser and marier often trips up foreign speakers. The tie to Sarah and the baby wasn't enough to pull Thompson back to them, but the marriage wasn't a sham. Baby Sally was three months old and Thompson was refuged to Boston, still under British control, when he wrote his father-in-law, the Reverend Walker (January 11, 1775) in New Hampshire that he wanted his wife with him. Thompson said was missing Sarah and thought he would be less miserable with her. He may have needed the domestic help or been strapped of funds. In any event he saw himself as married. "And as Mrs. Thompsons Company is almost the only thing that can be any alleviation of my present troubles, and as my being absent from her is the greatest unhappiness of my present situation, I hope I shall be so happy as to obtain your consent for her leaving Concord."[8]

The above letter had the word "almost" before "the greatest unhappiness"; as he penned the words he was feeling sorry for himself for being pushed out of both hometowns (Woburn and Concord) and not being sure about his future, let alone his reception at home. After all, his first winter in Concord he had told his mother that all was peace and quiet in that part of the world and that if there was good sledding he was coming home to Woburn—not a care in the world at 21 years of age. Thus he whipped up some not wholly sincere enthusiasm for bringing Sarah and the baby to Boston, as Mrs. Clark, his landlady, "will let us have house room sufficient for our small family for a very trifle." If Sarah came to him, he concluded with a rather preposterous flourish, "it will be so far from embarrassing my affairs, that it would lessen my expenses."

What is essential is that Thompson spoke with respect of Sarah. Even when he didn't want her to know where he was in Munich lest she pursue him for money, he did not speak or write badly of her. Marriage to Sarah had constituted, he would say, good fortune. Thompson now settled down to manage her estates. He must have found his farming gene, as he took enough interest in farming to order seeds from England and ask Loammi to supply him with good seeds as well. He was now a squire with considerable property and a distaste for insurrection. He would state after the Revolution, "From principle I supported the king because I considered this to be the lawful attitude."[9] As he would write his father-in-law on the eve of leaving America, he was in favor of the rule of English law: "My reason has led me to come down on the side of a limited monarchy equally far removed from an Asiatic despotism and a dictatorship of the people."

By subterfuge, in a secret arrangement with the British authorities, Thompson tried to serve king and country. Some of his majesty's army were deserting due to the usual complaints like corporal punishment or because they didn't see the point of fighting against their brethren. Thompson devised a plan to catch a few of them. He would hire deserters and give them an incentive to go back to their military units, as he could guarantee no punishment if they did. Two soldiers, however, promised to return to the army duty but did not. Rumors that the patriotic Timothy Walker's son-in-law Benjamin Thompson was a Royalist simmered.

Thompson avoided the scourge of persecution for a time. When, in the summer of 1774, he was summoned before the patriotic Committee of Safety in Concord to reply to the charge of being "unfriendly to the cause of liberty"—corresponding with General Gage in Boston and returning to him four deserters—the Sons of Liberty couldn't pin the subterfuge on him. Thompson wrote sardonically, "I am to be solemnly Anathemised and consign'd over to the fury of the enraged Populace, to receive punishment equal to the blackness of my agravated Transgressions."[10] Despite the acquittal, suspicions played in the minds of his enemies. Concord was a very patriotic town, partially explained by its history, as when Benning Wentworth was provincial governor Rumford's self-government was called a "District" and its legal entity had to be renewed every year and taxed every year.

One fall night in 1774, while the First Continental Congress was winding up in Philadelphia, a group of Concord citizens performed a threatening charivari in front of the Rolfe mansion where the Thompsons lived. The populace surrounded the house and demanded Major Thompson. When the crowd hissed and hooted Sarah came out with her baby in her arms. She assured them that her husband was out of town and the crowd disbanded. Having notice of their intentions and knowing that he was liable to be tarred and feathered, Thompson had borrowed a horse and $20 from his brother-in-law Timothy Walker Jr. and made his escape a few hours before. From Charlestown, near Boston, he wrote his father-in-law that had he waited to take his "retreat" the next day it would have been cut off. He barely escaped with his neck. The danger he was in found expression in the polite language Thompson used in a letter on Christmas Eve to Timothy Walker: "I thought it absolutely necessary to abscond for a while, and seek a friendly Asylum in some distant part: I must humbly beg your kind care of my distressed Family."[11]

In winter he left Charlestown and was back in Woburn, where his wife and three-month-old Sally joined him for several months. But he was a lightning rod for the Sons of Liberty. There, in March 1775, the Minutemen marched in to his mother's house to arrest him. Baldwin, who had his barn near the Pierces' home, defended his friend and got the Minutemen tipsy on hard cider.

There is a parallel, whether typical of the time or an anomaly, between the Committees of Safety of Concord, New Hampshire, and Woburn, Massachusetts, in their mission to break off all dealings with suspected Royalists. Two years after Baldwin helped Thompson out of a fix, the same thing repeated itself in Concord. Timothy Walker Jr. had followed Colonel Rolfe as Concord's town clerk. Walker was on the Committee of Safety and proceeded within the law to establish the town's patriotic bona fides. Others in town wanted to take steps outside the law. One spring day he mounted his horse and saw a number of "West Parish men" hurrying to the tavern. A Mr. Bradley, whom he met, confirmed trouble brewing. The men were gathering to pull down the house of one Peter Green. Colonel Walker "detailed them from executing their purpose till near sundown. Then inviting them all into 'Mother Osgood's' tavern, they called for bowls of punch, and treated the company liberally. All being by this time in a better mood, Col. Walker made a brief speech which he closed by saying—'Every man to his tent, O Israel!' and they quietly dispersed without tearing down Esq. Green's house!"[12] Peter Green, like others arrested in New England at this time as Tories, had to take an oath of allegiance to the patriots as a condition of release.

Detained in Woburn, Thompson was released but never publicly exonerated, as too many thought him guilty. He retired to Charlestown. At one point he requested a public hearing in Woburn and began to write defenses. He was freed but not vindicated when hearings were held in the spring. After the arrest of Surgeon General Benjamin Church as a spy, Thompson made his escape and disappeared. "Taxation without representation" was the object of increased wrath and Thomas Hutchinson, governor of Massachusetts, despaired. He left in 1774 and was replaced by General Gage. On May 25, 1775, Hutchinson wrote, "I see my contemporaries dying away so fast, that I am more anxious than ever to hasten home, lest I should die here."[13] This is when it looked as though Cambridge might become a battlefield (before the battle of Bunker Hill), and when George Washington requisitioned Harvard's buildings as barracks, Thompson and Baldwin are said to have helped move out the library books to safety. While documentation which went from Samuel Curwen, Royalist, to Samuel Eliot Morison, is slender, Thompson would have enjoyed packing up the 5,000 books with Dr. Winthrop. Strongly suspected of being a Royalist that spring of 1775, Thompson was still in Woburn with his wife and child. Strong hands packed and moved the library to Lexington, and back again the next June when Harvard reoccupied its buildings.

When Baldwin was promoted to colonel on the rebel side and was on George Washington's staff, Thompson wrote congratulations. Thompson demonstrated his lively spirit of enterprise, if risible lack of political savvy, when he came up with a wartime moneymaking scheme. He planned to get local women in Boston to sew epaulets to sell to the Continental forces for noncommissioned and commissioned officers (every unit had slight variations and it was usual for insignias to be made locally as Thompson was offering to do in Massachusetts). Likely it distressed his sense of order and correctness that officers were wearing armbands to indicate their rank, and he saw a chance to further his fortune whereas he was complacent about which side of the conflict lay on the side of justice. On Thompson's behalf, Baldwin showed General Washington the samples.

In Boston, there would have been no possibility of having a wife and baby daughter along, as Thompson lived behind British lines and, additionally, had his clandestine movements to carry out for General Gage. On May 6, 1775, he wrote Gage a spy letter enclosed in a short letter in invisible ink (now located at the University of Michigan).[14] Thompson's father-in-law had written urging him to repent the stance he had taken, but Thompson refused, with assurances he had "the tenderest regard for my Wife and family," and spoke of his belief that he had "an equal return of Love and affection from them."[15] Samuel Williams bonded with the patriots. After a visit from Williams, Thompson wrote his shock of being treated with "distant formality"[16] by his admired teacher. He gave two globes to Williams (see Chapter 3), instructing Sarah to send them from Concord to Bradford.

2. The Young Schoolmaster (1770–1776)

Three-inch miniature table globes, one terrestrial, one celestial by James Ferguson, circa 1755 (Sotheby's Image Library). These were probably given to Benjamin by John Wentworth in about 1774.

On October 10, 1775, Thompson was rapidly settling his affairs with creditors and debtors. He even sold his share in the family pew in the new meetinghouse at Woburn, a share he had inherited at the death of this father. He kept untilled the parcel of land, then unsalable, in Maine he inherited from his father. On October 13 Josiah Pierce, Thompson's stepbrother, drove him in a country wagon to the shore of Narragansett Bay. They said good-bye and Pierce returned to Woburn. Thompson's purported voyage was to the West Indies, but in fact he was taken aboard the *Scarborough*, a British ship at Newport bound for Boston. General William Howe had replaced General Gage the previous month. At this point Thompson did actual espionage behind the American lines.[17]

Thompson is famous for many inventions and social ideas but what came to light almost two centuries after the fact is that he authored the letter in invisible ink, then called "sympathetic ink," to convey to British authorities details about the rebels. He had been playing with secret codes from the time he was a teenager, four years earlier concealing his private thoughts with a flowery code using a heart as a symbol.[18] The invisible ink, an old cipher discussed as early as 1480 by Jean Batista Porta, had as its chief ingredient nutgalls from the twigs of oak trees. Very Agatha Christie–like, Thompson complained openly of being "much troubled with Putrid Billious Disorders," the medication used to treat diarrhea being nutgall tea. (Thompson did have a digestive disorder all his life, but Sanborn Brown was of the opinion that the health complaint was masking the true purpose of his visits to the apothecary.) The invisible cipher could be developed by the mineral iron oxide. The script on the letter was Thompson's and the sealing wax was a type he used. An idiosyncratic spelling, "oppertunity," was his as well.

Thompson detached from the rebels' cause step by step. He did so in reaction to aggression from his neighbors and fellow Americans, like many not being political per se. Yet he was sincere from his perspective in his August 14, 1775, letter to his father-in-law, a hard letter with the news that he was quitting America, "determined to seek for that Peace & Protection in foreign Lands, & among Strangers, which is deny'd me in my native Country. I cannot any longer bear the insults that are daily offered me.... I have done nothing that can deserve this *Cruel usage*. I have done nothing with any design to injure my Countrymen, & cannot any longer bear to be treated in this barbarous maner by them."[19] For all his native intelligence, Thompson was naïve of the historic context and so took personally the anger at him, his *soi-disant* persecution. He missed the point of the rebellion because he himself did not feel the crushing weight of the yoke of being ruled by Britain.

Loammi Baldwin's son George told George Ellis that his father communicated with Thompson when the latter was in Boston but that his father did not know the exact date his friend left for England: "My father, I think, heard occasionally while in the Cambridge army that the Count was in Boston, and communicated the news to Woburn." George Baldwin added, "There was much curiosity at Cambridge and Woburn at the time he was suppoed to be in Boston, whether he was there or not—My father, I think, heard occasionally while in the Cambridge Army that the Count was in Boston, and communicated the news to Woburn."[20]

Mrs. Pierce told Loammi in January that she was eager to know where her son was, but the family had no information. The next October, Loammi Baldwin wrote that he still was trying "to find whether Major Thompson is with the enemy or not." In fact, being in touch with his family was out of the question, as Thompson had been passing information to General Howe. Staying loyal to the king and making his escape from New England would be the defining event in his life.

3

Thompson and the Wentworths (1772–1775)

> It is a public scandal that gives offence, and it is no sin
> to sin in secret.—Molière, *Tartuffe*, Act 5, Scene 4

Benjamin Thompson did not meet his first great lady when he was a lad. If he had been from high society and gone to Harvard he would have met belles at balls or in drawing rooms or when they descended from their carriages and gave him a coquettish glance before church. Had he been born to a mother of the upper levels of society she would have dressed in finery and that would not have awed him when he encountered it later. Young society women would have been told by their parents whether he was a catch and they would have played out the game accordingly, while sophisticated older women would have idly teased him. But the first elegant woman Thompson ever spoke to was Frances "Fanny" Wentworth, the pretty, flirty wife of New Hampshire's governor and one of the great beauties of the colonies. When Thompson met her he was making the sartorial statement of a spiffy officer with prepossessing looks, a stranger in their midst whom her husband praised. He was at least as good looking as the handsome young gentlemen she flirted with at Portsmouth's Earl of Halifax Hotel, and at 6'3" he was taller than they.

After Thompson's marriage to Sarah the die was cast, making a society woman like Fanny even farther out of reach than she would have been otherwise. She had been married four years and must have wished for a child and sought distraction. Thompson must have suffered the contrast of this self-confident beauty with his bride. Even Mrs. Wentworth's speech was exquisite, as she had received a lady's education in Boston, whereas Sarah's father had not bothered with her education and she likely spoke somewhat rudely if one can judge from a letter she wrote to Timothy Williams of Bradford telling him her father said of the colt, "when you ties him he eats." Also, Thompson now realized he could please a woman. This chapter takes in a broader swath of time in order to consider the influence of seeming paragons of an aristocratic couple, John and Frances Wentworth, on young Benjamin Thompson.

While there is no record of what "Fanny" and Thompson said to each other, it's clear that John Wentworth was key in Thompson's new life as a country squire. Among all the provincial governors, Wentworth stood out for fairness, possessing a nonsectarian attitude, and being a fifth-generation colonial. For Thompson the association with Wentworth was reaching and touching the heights of prestige and authority. It is hard to

Left: John Wentworth, an engraving by Henry W. Smith after the work of John Singleton Copley (The Miriam and Ira D. Wallach Division of Art, Prints and Photographs: Print Collection, The New York Public Library). *Right: Mrs. Theodore Atkinson, Jr.* (Francis Deering Wentworth), 1765 by John Singleton Copley (Sotheby's Image Library).

overestimate the excitement of the future inventor at Wentworth's offer to place his cabinet of scientific instruments at Thompson's disposal, excitement Thompson expressed to his friend Samuel Williams.

Wentworth liked to give gifts. He gave to Dartmouth's first president a silver monteith, or punch bowl, that normally chilled aristocrats' wine glasses. Today called the Wentworth Bowl, it marks the succession of presidents of the college. Wentworth's beneficence extended to young Major Thompson, to whom he gave two small globes, one celestial and one terrestrial. The maker of these globes, James Ferguson, like Thompson a prodigy of self-education, had written *Lectures on Select Subjects* (1761), which contained problems on mechanics and astronomy to solve. The globes were of great value and attested to Wentworth's high opinion of, and connection with, young Thompson. Concord was a different world from Portsmouth and Thompson must have made trips to the home of the governor and his wife subsequent to the first meeting on his bridal tour.

When Thompson met the Wentworths, John had been governor of New Hampshire as well as surveyor general of the King's Woods in America since 1767. His family oligarchy governed New Hampshire for most of the 18th century and Wentworth had been riding high. In his work John was his entire life a model of probity. This was partially in reaction to his uncle, Benning Wentworth, governor of New Hampshire for 25 years before him. Benning had become fabulously rich through misuse of his office, a situation Wentworth did his best to rectify when he became governor. Benning was a man who responded to bereavement for his two sons and wife by having a party, inviting the cream of Portsmouth society and shocking them by marrying his maid Martha Hilton at the dinner table. Henry Wadsworth Longfellow wrote it up in gossipy detail as

The Poet's Tale; Lady Wentworth, from which comes this couplet:

A creature men would worship and adore,/ Though now in mean habili-ments she bore/A pail of water, dripping, through the street/ And bathing, as she went, her naked feet.

Such behavior made the powers that be in London doubt Benning's sanity; rumors circulated that he "had Maried a Dirty Slute of a Maid." The picture conjured by Mrs. Mary Anne Williams, a niece of Benning, to her granddaughter is much gentler: "The bride, who had been his housekeeper for seven years, was then thirty-five, and attired in a calico dress and white apron."[1]

Fanny Wentworth played an important part in John's life. Their association seems to have been a result of manly, princely John—despite the interest in him of many other women—making a headstrong decision based on the same concept as the uncle he disassociated himself from: as governor he could do what he wished. After graduation from Harvard, John soon noticed his young cousin Fanny and she him. The budding romance did not keep him from exploring the woods and going to England on family business and mingling with society. Fanny gave up on John and married, at 16, Theodor Atkinson Jr. of Portsmouth, a wealthy young Harvard graduate who wooed her. The painting of Fanny by J.S. Copley was done of her at 19, for which she wore a pewter-colored, low-cut gown, this painting making a pair with a portrait of Theodor in 1757, gorgeous in his cinnamon suit over heavily embroidered long, silvery white vest.

Atkinson was unwell. When John Wentworth returned in 1769, now secure in his rank as governor of the province, Fanny's father was recently deceased and two of her brothers had died tragically, one drowning at sea and another having committed suicide along with his lover. Fanny looked at her sickly husband and desire and ambition for John reawakened in her heart. From John's home on Pleasant Street he had an unobstructed view of the Atkinson home. "Rumor had it that Frances informed John about her husband's declining health by hanging a handkerchief out her window."[2] Two years after John returned from England as governor of New Hampshire, Atkinson died (of tuberculosis, which John's brother died of that same year). Ten days after the funeral John and Fanny, now 23, were wed; had Fanny waited a year and a day to don a wedding gown that would have been seemly. John explained the haste to his horse racing friend and patron, the Marquis of Rockingham, as deriving from the pressure of his parents and uncle to get married (John was 32). It was a case of entitlement, as with Uncle Benning's marriage. When a child was born to John and Fanny six months later, it did not live long but was baptized "John." Relations between John and Fanny had occurred while she was still wed to the dying Atkinson: "The fact that he was given a name, John, and was baptized seems to belie Wentworth's attempt to mask the event as a miscarriage, Sustain'd from Mrs. Wentworth's being frighted by an attack of a large dog."

John took his official responsibilities seriously. He enforced the broad arrow laws, by which big, old trees were marked for the king, and inspected sawmills. He made long journeys into the interior, for instance seizing 500 illegally cut logs frozen in the Connecticut River. Despite such punitive measures, Wentworth was very popular. The law was the law and John Adams himself had prosecuted trespassers of the king's timber, in the Boston Court of Vice-Admiralty.

When the governor said he would join Thompson's projected surveying trip in the White Mountains, Thompson was ecstatic. But to be a young man on the fast track in the coterie around Wentworth was an uneasy fortune. Wentworth and Thompson had commonality in their love of horses and the out-of-doors and their keenness on science. Wentworth must have enjoyed good conversation, given he was a close friend of John Adams at Harvard and a lively correspondent with him for some time afterward. Thompson on his wedding day sat at the table with the great lady the governor's wife and must have remarked her grace and beauty and the governor's regard for her, as well as her love of adornment and charming attitude towards handsome officers.

Wentworth had already climbed Mt. Pleasant, which was the highest peak visible from the governor's mansion in Wolfeboro. Then, and even after leaving New Hampshire for good, he contributed many facts of natural history to the portion of a history of the province being written by his friend Jeremy Belknap. He also rode over the mountains to graduations at Dartmouth College, which he helped found. But the forces of revolution roiled the region and the White Mountain expedition did not occur. Yet Wentworth's favor would stamp Thompson as a Royalist in New England. The governor, by his peremptorily giving Thompson the rank of major, likely stunned his other officers. For Wentworth it was a display of his full prerogative to do as he wished. Moreover, giving young Thompson such a marked leg up repeated a serendipitous encounter in Wentworth's own history. His association, as a colonial in his twenties visiting England, with the august Marquis of Rockingham began with a meeting of the two at a horse race. Doubtless, to Thompson, the Wentworths were the greatest figures he had met when he was a young man of 20. When he needed a reference for a military promotion in London it was Wentworth he named.

This commission as an officer set Thompson on the military line of his variegated career. While an inventor and courtier/statesman in the main, he was a military officer three times over. First he was a major while the British still ruled America, in 1772; then he became a lieutenant colonel of the King's American Dragoons at the end of the Revolutionary War, serving on Long Island; last, promoted and retired when the war ended, he was off to the Continent, where he was made colonel and then general in the Bavarian army.

Fanny must have bedazzled him. She probably struck visitors not only with her beauty and fashionable attire but also with how blasé she was about having a husband who adored her yet continuing to flirt herself. That very quality of being unfazed by being attractive was a counterpoint to Thompson's own ambition. Fanny, by her position, would have seen herself as being entitled to flirt. The governor named two New Hampshire towns after her, Deering (her maiden name) and Francestown.

One of the causes of dissatisfaction with British rule was a commodity of more moment than black tea: timber. The British royal navy had urgent need of the majestic white pine and hardwood trees then a part of the Massachusetts Bay Colony (now a section of Maine and New Hampshire). When the colonists saw the biggest trees marked with the triangle of three slashes, indicating they were the property of the king, it was a provocation. Sometimes the colonists damaged the trees so they lost their value for masts, yards and bowsprits and could be taken for timber. Other times they risked felling the trees and selling them outright for commercial or foreign ships at enormous profit. While John Wentworth gained popularity for going to England and working successfully for the repeal of the Stamp Act, his authority in the woods was a tinderbox for colonists who made their livelihood there. As surveyor general of His Majesty's Woods in America he had the unpopular charge, like a grand gamekeeper, of the trees that were 24 inches and more in diameter.[3]

Meanwhile, Wentworth had political worries. Specifically, his uncle Benning Wentworth's highhanded land grant scheme involved skimming the cream of acreage from each transaction, thus ending up with vast acreage of personal property throughout New Hampshire. John tried to make it right, doing what colonials with big issues did, going to the seat of government in England. In the summer of 1773, the Lords of Trade found Benning guilty, but when all the facts got before the Privy Council he was cleared of wrongdoing. Part of his defense consisted of testimonies of his subjects, which he solicited, one of these being anonymously written by Benjamin Thompson and entitled "Address of the Inhabitants of Concord to Governor John Wentworth." Benjamin's typical prose, whether in essays or epistolary, was emphatic and had flourishes. Here he stated that whatever "aspersions your Excellency's Character may have injuriously met with in England, from prejudiced and designing Men, if the truth be known he would receive praise from King George and 'be applauded in New Hampshire province.'"[4] Wentworth acknowledged Thompson's help in New Hampshire in a letter written to the Earl of Dartmouth on November 15, 1774: "I have been successful in prevailing on soldiers deserted from the King's troops at Boston, to return to their duty, through the spirited and prudent activity of Major Thompson, a militia officer of New Hampshire, whose management the General [Gage] writes me, promises further success."[5]

Fanny gave birth on January 20, 1775, to their second child, Charles Mary, after the Christian names of his powerful godparents, Lord and Lady Rockingham (the Marquis of Rockingham as prime minister would push for American independence to end the Revolution eight years later). When the British forces were driven back to Boston, a Portsmouth mob dragged a cannon up the street to the governor's mansion and placed it ready to fire at the front door. The mob pounded on the house with clubs and demanded that Wentworth give up an unpopular member of the provincial assembly, Colonel John Fenton. It was declared that no one, including Fanny and the baby, would escape alive unless they got Fenton. The Wentworths fled in the night and Fenton bravely surrendered—eventually to be discharged from jail and allowed to go to Britain, by order of George Washington.[6] John, Fanny and baby Charles stayed in an earthen garrison called Fort William and Mary, or "Castle William," on an island three miles from Portsmouth on the Piscatuqua River. A frigate offshore protected them. Wentworth persuaded the frigate's captain not to shoot at Portsmouth when the rebels captured the coxswain. As late as May 1775 Wentworth tried to reconcile the Crown and the colonists by pleading with the provincial assembly for "an affectionate reconciliation of our mother country." In July 1775 he wrote a friend: "It would be poignant censure on a people I love and forgive—for truly I can say with the poet in his Lear, 'I am a man more sinned against than sinning.'"[7]

Unlike Boston and Charleston, South Carolina, Portsmouth had no tea party, because Wentworth persuaded the sea captain to reship the goods to Halifax. Yet in July 1774 the Committee of Correspondence in Portsmouth and other New Hampshire towns became actively restless and voted to send delegates to the Continental Congress in Philadelphia. Wentworth's control was failing. When General Gage sent out a request for carpenters, Wentworth advertised for them without revealing the jobs were for Gage's employ. Wentworth must have been very removed from the common people to imagine that the nature of the actual job could be concealed or the hiring wouldn't matter to the carpenters once they got the work.

Wentworth sailed into Halifax in the summer of 1783 as the surveyor general of the

King's Woods for British North America when Britain recognized American independence. Understandably disenchanted with life in the colonies, Fanny stayed in London, separated from her husband, when her son was a little boy recovering from scarlet fever. She got their son settled into London's Westminster School and then sailed for Halifax to join John and embark on life as the wife of Nova Scotia's first civil governor.

John had received the governorship of Nova Scotia he had angled for, making him the only Revolutionary-period royal governor to serve again as head of a North American colony. The Wentworth fortune was founded on the export of masts and timbers, and as a surveyor John personally inspected trees in the wilderness all over the province of Nova Scotia and eastern Canada. He had drafted the new policy himself of granting settlers land that was away from rivers and harbors and having smaller packets of land than had previously been the case for the Crown. Settlers were hired to cut the masts, thus reducing alienation and the purloining of big trees. He had explained this policy to Lord Germain on October 12, 1778, while still governor of New Hampshire. Doing his job in Canada, Wentworth became the preeminent authority on the woods of North America, with as much time in the forests as any other European.

Meanwhile, when Fanny arrived in Halifax the next spring her husband was not there. He was out for 14 months in the forests and returned only for Christmas. She worried about her son and was unhappy with the community of displaced Royalists. The governor's residence was a rundown wooden structure where she was alone while her husband was off in the woods. She found solace furnishing her home in great elegance (solid mahogany and the best glassware and china, rugs and mirrors). In context, this was a time when Nova Scotia's economy was distressed from the influx of Loyalists beginning the exodus from the colonies. About 13,000 Loyalists would migrate to Britain by the end of the Revolution, but 30,000 settled in the maritime provinces of Canada.[8] The Wentworths being perennially in debt, they could ill afford their expenditures. According to Brian Cuthbertson, "Women whom Frances knew to have been maids and cooks now drove around the town in their own carriages parading the new wealth of husbands who had been humble drivers of carts and drays only a short time before. It was intolerable that they should become rich by exploiting the sufferings of the Loyalists.... To Lady Fitzwilliam she wrote that she wished she could be content with her situation, but 'it's the first time in my life that even I was totally the reverse—I am unhappy to a degree in it.'"[9]

Still, Fanny shone at a round of balls and when in 1783 Prince William Henry—the third son of George III and the same prince who would as King William follow George IV and be known as the "Sailor King"—sailed into port he and Fanny became lovers. She was 41, sophisticated and gorgeously decked out (she favored splendidly colored feathers in her hair); the prince was, at 21, notorious for his wild ways; John was away in Cape Breton. Noted Canadian historian Brian Cuthbertson deemed it an affair of "mutual convenience." Fanny must have looked like a princess. She appeared at one ball "in a gown richly interwoven with gold and silver, and trimmed with Italian flowers and the finest silk lace; the gown's train was four yards long, and in her hair and on her wrists was a profusion of diamonds." How else to be seen dancing with the prince? Halifax society, however, was less than charmed and Fanny was ostracized for straying from her marriage bed.

Prince William visited another two times and stayed at the governor's house for a time. Wentworth's policy towards his wife's indiscretion was initially to overlook it and then, through his connections back in London, have the prince sent packing. The third time the prince showed up at Fanny's door she was entertaining a young officer and when she merely gave the prince a room of his own for the night he was piqued and their affair ended. Prince William had a penchant for sleeping with commoners—the reason George III sent him away on naval assignments—and his dalliance with Fanny was not a lasting amour. When she was later in England visiting her 16-year-old son she is said to have resumed the affair with William, by then the Duke of Clarence, who gave her a "Damasc Sopha" they lay upon. In the portrait of him by John Hoppner (1796) in the Royal Collection in Britain, of the Prince of Wales, he is decked out in opulent clothes including ribbons, pleats, and embroidery from head to toe.

Considering one detail of what men of rank were wearing, the buttons of the time were really beautiful. By 1790 they were solid metal: repoussé silver or gilt brass or sheet copper. A British soldier's coat had as many as 40 large buttons and his waistcoat and breeches (unless he wore trousers) had a dozen more each. Some were lacquered (japanned) or enameled to highlight the decorative device. During the Revolutionary War the enlisted men wore unmarked flat brass buttons. Washington's army got lots of their uniforms from salvage and sinking ships, according to Amanda Isaac, associate curator at the Historic Preservation Department of Mount Vernon. When captured regimental coats were over-dyed, the brilliant red coats became brown.

The whys and wherefores of Thompson's perspective on his having taken the Loyalist side and spied on the colonial forces might have been explicated in a sheaf of papers he left at his death. "Papers to be carefully preserved, as they may serve for my justification," he noted at the end of his life, which Sally wrote down "during her stay in my house at Auteuil."[10] The papers presumably stayed in Sally's possession and were lost or destroyed. John Wentworth and General Thomas Gage were both British officials connected with Thompson's spying. These documents would fill out the picture of why and how Thompson became such a faithful follower that he engaged in perilous activity in their service. But given how utterly bowled over Thompson was by the prospect of going into the White Mountains with Governor Wentworth, it seems apparent that both the Wentworths, John and Fanny, imprinted the newly minted squire as the embodiment of perfection.

When he borrowed instruments from the governor's scientific cabinet he also saw the vision of Fanny in its opulent gilded frame. How different she looked from his wife Sarah, whose misogynist father had not bothered to find her a husband in her twenties and she married the cantankerous Colonel Rolfe. Clothes again tell a story, as Thompson was glad to wear his wedding suit, but Sarah was pushing the matter of his transformation into what she needed, a fancy country squire, by going to Boston with him during their engagement for his new attire. She wanted to take over Thompson's being and add to his demeanor a grandeur which was a quality youth can hardly have—and a gangly athletic who did acrobatics to amuse his pupils certainly did not have. She was playing Pygmalion and she virtually handed him over to a sophisticated milieu.

The English country manor house that Wentworth built as his official residence, then a little way out of the town, is still used as the Governor's House today (open to the public on guided tours in July and August). A gem of Georgian-style architecture, it was constructed with stones, bricks, and other materials from across the province of Nova Scotia.

The Wentworths both liked to entertain and were an 18th century power couple.

They made their home together and cared about each other. But Fanny had an eye for the handsome officers and felt entitled to flirt with or sleep with them. John, when she was in England and he in Halifax, had a mistress of some duration. He arranged for the mistress, Bridget, to marry a Fergus Lowe, who after the marriage vanished from her life. She and John had a son, Edward, who was baptized on July 2, 1799, and brought up in the house of Wentworth's friend, a Loyalist minister, Theophilus Chamberlain.

Eventually the Wentworths returned to London but they could not keep up with the pace of their social circle due to debts. The government had a policy requiring that a governor had to account for all his expenses before being reimbursed. As governor of Nova Scotia Wentworth had given his personal bond for 1200 pounds to clothe the Royal Nova Scotia Regiment. He was at this point not flush and living on a pension. Fleeing his creditors under an assumed name, Wentworth went to Halifax to marshal his papers and sell property. In his absence Fanny died. John remained in Halifax until his death in 1820 at the age of 83. His time as governor has been called a "Golden Age." Summarizing his accomplishments, a biographer wrote, "While aiding the Indians, organizing and outfitting the militia, building roads, and founding the first life-saving station in North America, he set an important tone in a young and developing province."[11]

4

The Royalist and the Printer's Wife (1776–1779)

> Though women are angels, yet wed-lock's the devil.
> —Lord Byron, *To Eliza*, 1806

On the west coast of Nova Scotia is a strategic channel connecting the Bay of Fundy and the Annapolis Basin, called, as it is deep and narrow, the Digby Gut. From the prospect of steep cliffs overlooking the channel you can see a mile across to the other side. Near the lifesaving station, and down the hill from my aunt and uncle's place, a path led down a wooded embankment to the cliff's edge. Here lay a cannon buried in underbrush and trees. Children were not to go there. My brother and I were smart, so adults warned us only once or twice about the 30-foot tides on the Bay of Fundy's rocky shore, but my uncle forbade our hiking down to the cannon repeatedly and most severely. Attention to the cannon, he said, could bring marauding thieves whose ancestors had been on the rebel side of the American Revolution. Naturally it was a great game for my brother and me to skulk down to examine and sit on the cannon. What puzzled us was how our respected uncle believed that separatism from Britain had justice on two sides. Weren't Redcoats bad and the heroes on the winning side? Surely our uncle was deluded. It is necessary to remember when following Thompson's steps from young husband to spy to taking to his heels to leave his native land that he was being loyal to a country he had no reason to revile. If the rebels had lost, the activities of British spies like Thompson would have been remembered as heroism.

Thompson was separated from his wife and felt the disapproval of her family. He was writing letters to Sarah, which is known from the testimony later in this chapter of his lover, who first cavorted with him while he had been writing to his wife. Thompson thought of having Sarah and the baby live with him in Boston. He wrote this to Sarah's father but it was a pipe dream, as if he clung to his old life. Gradually, Thompson was developing the defeatist but realistic attitude of "you can't go home again." Once he made that interior break he did not seem to have second thoughts about it and never considered bringing Sarah over from America once he escaped. Thus spying, as in crime fiction, ended up a petri dish for sexual knavery. When the pretense of why he was doing what he was doing was lifted he knew he could also shed the persona he had taken on during that interlude.

Thompson had married Sarah Rolfe when he was 20 in 1772 and they lived together for about two years. After he was nearly tarred and feathered in Concord he zigzagged between Woburn and Boston, during which time he lived for 13 weeks on Hanover Street, close to Hopestill Capen's dress goods shop, At the Sign of the Cornfields, where he had apprenticed five years before. Around the corner on Union Street lived Isaiah Thomas, a salient figure in the annals of the Revolution as well as in the history of printing. Isaiah participated in clandestine meetings with other prominent leaders of the rebel cause, including Paul Revere, James Otis, John Hancock and Dr. Joseph Warren, and Major Thompson could not have lived closer.[1]

The togs Thompson wore signified he was a major in the British militia, even if he had no visible assignment. ("Could I have obtained a troop of horse or a company of foot," wrote John Adams at 82 to a friend, "I should infallibly have been a soldier.")[2] Thompson was shunned and hated by many compatriots, but soldiers had flare in the eyes of both young men and women. Being a major was now his best identity, one created by the august Governor Wentworth. Overall, Thompson would, like Wentworth, be a paradigm of accomplishment who emerged from the revolutionary period unscathed, and it was Wentworth who encouraged Thompson into secret activities.

In the Revolution, often neighbors had to strive to become enemies. The enemy was an artifice that the psyche built out of a political agenda. William Franklin, the illegitimate son of Benjamin Franklin and the last colonial governor of New Jersey, was close to his father but broke over the cause of the rebels and was imprisoned for Loyalist activities, and George Washington refused William's plea for parole when his wife was sick. According to Loammi Baldwin's son George, uncharacteristically Thompson and Baldwin stayed in touch while Thompson was a Tory in Boston. For his part, Baldwin put friendship over whatever suspicions he may have harbored when, to save Thompson, he invited Minutemen into his barn and plied them with food and drink. But Thompson could not ask more favors of his best friend and if he went back to Concord to see his wife and child he would endanger them.

The heart of Boston was a hotbed of rebellion. Here lived and worked Isaiah Thomas, who had lived in many places as a printer since leaving England. While working as a journeyman printer for two years in the Carolinas he met Mary Dill, daughter of Joseph and Ann Dill of Bermuda. The two married on Christmas Day 1769 in Charleston. For Mary, Isaiah's being from afar meant he did not know her past, and she did not reveal what he discovered only after the wedding, that she had borne a son out of wedlock and had been a prostitute. Isaiah wrote that he found out his wife had a bastard son "years before," and as she was probably around his age of 20 when she married Isaiah, her childhood had been cut short. She may have been ejected by her parents and had to sell her body.

Isaiah returned to Boston in 1770 and went into partnership with his old master, Zachariah Fowle. They had a markedly off-and-on association. When Isaiah was 16 he one morning left his indentureship. Penniless, he got a job and did well in printing in Halifax, Nova Scotia. Zachariah invited Isaiah to return. Because he liked nice clothes, and to appear more mature than his years, Isaiah drew his salary of two months in Halifax in the form of five yards and a half of "black serge." When he entered his old shop in Boston, seven months after quitting it, his master did not recognize him, just as Ruth Thompson did not recognize her son in his scarlet coat. The two men, Zachariah and Isaiah, quarreled again and Isaiah determined to work in the printing business in the southern colonies, and then go to England. According to biographer Clifford K. Shipton,

Isaiah at one time almost completed a contract to settle in the West Indies, but thinking the climate better for both his wife and himself he decided to return to Boston.

The printer Zachariah specialized in ballads and broadsides rather than news per se. He sold his interest in their newspaper to Isaiah, who moved the business to the south corner of Marshall Lane, into the left half of what would become the Union Oyster House. Here Isaiah published low- and high-quality materials and had a discerning eye for the New England market. He established one of the most important newspapers of the American Revolution, the *Massachusetts Spy*, and gradually began espousing radical politics. The paper had home delivery, which became the system of post riders of the Sons of Liberty. The arrival of a newspaper regulated the day or week and galvanized the interest of readers.[3] A poem called "In Promptu," written by Englishman Christopher Anstey, shows how in the late 18th century people were reading their newspaper avidly:

> In Promptu, written in 1779
> You say, my Friend, that every day
> Your company forsaking,
> In quest of news I haste away,
> The Morning Post to take in:
>
> But if not news nor sense it boast,
> Which all the world agree in,
> I don't take in the Morning Post,
> The Morning Post takes me in.[4]

Sexual interest caught fire between Benjamin Thompson and Mary Dill. They were attractive, brazen and lived practically next door to each other. He was lonely, bottled up, and at odds with old friends. She was the wife of a furious worker who many nights stayed out and drank with his political buddies. And, undoubtedly, she might convey something about her husband's buddies that would abet his undercover work. Meanwhile, Isaiah must have chosen to ignore the signs that another man excited his wife. He was busy with his lives of printing, politics, and feeding his family. He even played to the crowd by putting entertaining features in the *Spy*. For instance, he resuscitated a portion of an old Puritan sermon warning women to be modest, which possibly his wayward wife was not: "They who colour their locks with red and yellow begin to prognosticate what colour their hair shall be in hell. They who colour their faces otherwise than God hath created them, let them fear, lest when the Redeemer cometh he will not know them."[5] It can be inferred that Isaiah played the part in the breakup of his marriage to Mary of the neglectful husband. He spent long evenings with likeminded rebels who smoked tobacco and drank smuggled Madeira. Adultery, along with desertion, bigamy, and impotence, had been grounds for divorce since 1629, although after 1776 divorce was removed from the legislature to judiciary bodies, which were presumed more efficient. Divorce nevertheless remained rare.

With Mary flagrantly promiscuous Thomas had a strong case. The divorce proceedings went on for several months[6] due to the need for discovery of witnesses, who all lined up on the side of Isaiah Thomas. His petition for divorce, represented as "libel," was made on, ironically, Valentine's Day 1777 and ended when the Council of the State of Massachusetts Bay in England dissolved the marriage on May 27, 1777. The luridness of the case makes it a rare footnote to an American patriot, the printer Isaiah Thomas: "The proponent doth allege that since his marriage aforesaid at divers times in the month of February, Anno Domini, 1775, the said Mary hath been surpriz'd in such familiarities with one Major Thompson as give the strongest Reason to suspect that she was guilty of Adultery with the said Thompson." She was said to have told her husband that regarding the major "she would roast in Hell rather than give him up."

Circumstantial evidence declared that Major Thompson was Benjamin Thompson, from his confidence he could borrow a coach (even if he actually did not) to whisk away Mary Dill on their adulterous trip to Portsmouth down to her saying that her lover came to her bed from writing a letter to his wife. Sanborn Brown—the MIT physicist who for his book *Benjamin Thompson, Count Rumford* spent several decades researching documentation about Thompson's life—had a source that clinches that the British major in the libel case was in fact Benjamin Thompson. In an endnote Brown stated, "In the collection of Mrs. Edward N. Horn (whose maternal grandmother was a Thomas) there is a genealogy of Isaiah Thomas attached to which are scraps of notes for an autobiography of Isaiah which read, 'Discharge my Debts—domestic troubles—Count Rumford—Sue for divorce—obtain it—begin business in Worcester.'"[7]

As is today no longer a matter for surprise, the prominent men of 18th century America were no angels. They kept slaves and had children by them and had mistresses. Dr. Joseph Warren himself, a great Revolutionary hero, when he died on June 17, 1775, left a fiancée and a pregnant mistress (one of his patients).[8] In the proceedings before the council Isaiah made a case that the marriage was irreparable due to Mary's being impossible to live with as well as being unfaithful.

The proceedings referred to a law of 1692, part of the Massachusetts revised charter, as justification of Isaiah's plea for divorce, "for that she the said Mary hath had criminal conversation since her intermarriage with the said Isaiah with one Major Thompson and so hath committed Adultery." Thomas had petitioned the council on February 14, 1777. Mary was served with a citation and two men of the law, Theophilus Parsons and Nicholas Pike, esquires, were assigned to examine the witness and give Mary three days' notice of the time and place of her examination. The council (the major part, or 15 men, being present) determined that "nothing material having been advanced in behalf of the said Mary to the Contrary," the printer won his case. The decision elaborated:

> From which Time till the Present he has strictly observed on his Part the Marriage Contracts and during the Continuance of Conjugal Harmony he was blessed with three Children by her—but to his great Mortification he at last found that his said Wife was not only destitute of that Affection, and regard for him, which is necessary to render a State of Matrimony easy and happy, but that she had not even that Confidence in him, without which, by a mind not strictly virtuous, the Marriage Covenant could not be preserved inviolate: That petulance of Temper and unhappiness of Disposition which she daily exercised to the disturbance of domestic Peace added to the many Indecencies and unbecoming familiarity which it was usual for her to practice. The Proponent endeavor'd to reclaim her from [these] by mild, and dispassionate council: Soon after his marriage to his astonishment he found that his said Wife had had a bastard Child some years before and that she had been prostituted [sic] to the purpose of more than one; This the proponent, tho ignorant of at the time of his marriage, would most willingly have veiled in Oblivion forever, but such has been the Conduct of his said Wife of late that nothing but an Appeal to the Justice of this Honorable Court can repair the flagrant Injuries the proponent has suffer'd, or ease the disturbed State of his Mind.

Thomas offered a damning list against Mary, as follows:

- That Mary was surprised in familiarities with Major Thompson at various times in February 1775. This was precisely when Thompson had left his wife and child in Woburn and was acting as a secret agent for the British, based in Boston.

- That on February 23 Mary and the major set out on a journey together to Newbury Port. The printer tried to dissuade Mary from going on a trip for no apparent reason in the winter but she swore she would go "if it was to her eternal Ruin."
- In Charlestown Thompson was seen in Mary's bedchamber conversing with her while she lay in bed.
- At the house of a Mr. Newell in Lynn, Thompson and Mary were discovered in bed together, "constantly uttering such Expressions of Endearment and Affection to each other as plainly indicated the wickedness of their Hearts."
- At the inns of Mr. Greenleaf in Newbury Port, in Portsmouth, and at the inn of Mr. Williams in Greenland, New Hampshire, the major and Mary lodged shut up in a room together and in Greenland claimed to be man and wife.

According to the printer, sometime after Mary's return home rumors of her infidelity reached him. He questioned her, and Mary confessed that she had been guilty of "a criminal Conversation with the said Thompson at the House of Mr. Williams aforesaid. Ever since which the proponent has forbore to cohabit with her." The pain of Thomas over the straying Mary comes through in that final touch to the allegations. Isaiah was wounded as well as angry and certainly did not want another child; therefore he shamed his wife by not sharing her bed.

Presuming that the major and Mary did not want to be found out, they made a muddle of their adulterous trip together even if they were managing to keep a secret well enough in Boston. Why they registered at an inn as the Isaiah Thomases is almost incomprehensibly bumbling or naive, unless Thompson hoped rebels would divulge information to him while he had his lover's husband's false identity. It seems unlikely he was wearing his uniform if he was posing as a printer.

Nicholas Pike and Theophilus Parsons were busy getting depositions that repeated themselves and matched up with the allegations of Thomas. The public mistake that Thompson and Mary made of traveling to lodgings together isn't the kind of thing done in a settled society, not even by a Tom Jones character, without reprisal. Thompson knew he was on the way out of America, and Mary Dill, who doubtless saw very little of the work-obsessed printer, didn't care, at least for the moment when Boston was in a state of convulsion.

The articles of the libel reveal many things about the adultery between Mary Dill and Major Thompson. First, they didn't seem to care about pretending to be the Thomases, a married couple. Second, Major Thompson was arrogant in asking for a private room for them. He was also arrogant in showing displays of affection in the public area of an inn; both members of the couple were remarkably bold. Third, they seemed to know the area around the towns where they conducted their trysts. Fourth, in the libel case "Major Thompson" was presented as a shadowy figure, since he had disappeared into the ether, having left American shores for England after working as a spy for General Howe.

The nine depositions came from people employed by or owning taverns, as well as from a guest who was staying for several months in the Thomases' home and from the driver of a stagecoach Thompson and Mary traveled in. Several of the people who gave depositions said this concerned a period sometime before the Battle of Lexington on April 19, 1775. John Piedmont recollected that about two years before,

> A Gentleman & Lady came to my House (it being a Tavern in Danvers) & call'd a Room by themselves, & had one, & as I accidentally went into the Room where they were, I saw the said Gentleman's Hand in the Lady's Bosum, & she was leaning on his Breast. The Gentleman call'd for a Chamber, but as I suspected they were not married, & as their Conduct was too indecent for any unmarried Persons & too immodest even for married Persons in a Tavern, I did not grant his Request. I did not know either the Gentleman or Lady; But Mr. Lunt, who as I remember bro't them in the Stage said They were one Mr. Thompson & the Wife of Mr. Isaiah Thomas, printer of Boston, I knew that the aforesaid Gentleman was not Mr. Thomas as I was personally acquainted with him and further say not.

When the pair arrived at Samuel Greenleaf's tavern in Newbury Port, Major Thompson asked for a room with two beds but was refused. Like most towns around Boston, Newbury Port (later Newburyport) was anti-British. Anne Greenleaf, Samuel's wife, recalled that the first night Major Thompson slept in a front room with other male company while Mrs. Thompson had a back room with the maids and that except in the evening he was in her chamber. The couple stayed two nights. "I saw no indecency in Mrs. Thomas while she was at our house, and I saw her but seldom as I went into her chamber but once or twice feeling a reluctance to wait on her because of the Account which one Mrs. Bates gave me of her indecent conduct in the stage in her journey from Boston to Newbury; for Major Thompson and Mrs. Thomas came to our house."

They took a curricle on the road to Portsmouth and returned a few days later. (Two of Samuel Greenleaf's relatives were sent to the convention to frame a state constitution that year. Their colleague John Lowell suggested a clause that all men are created free and equal, which influenced the abolishment of slavery in the state of Massachusetts.)

The witness from Portsmouth said that the couple after dinner "called for one bed in one chamber" but the tavern keeper's son told his mother that the woman was the wife of Mr. Thomas the printer in Boston. When the tavern keeper learned this he marched upstairs to prevent their lodging together and "they were finally separated that night." The son recalled, "The next morning the Gentleman and Mrs. Thomas were early up and were together in one chamber which had a bed in it." Toward night they were gone in a curricle in bad weather. As in the other reports, the couple were wrapped in a cocoon of sex in tumultuous times.

Margaret Tufts was living in the home of a Mr. Newhall, who kept a tavern in Lynn. She recalled that one morning before breakfast a Mrs. Thomas arrived and with her an officer, with a cockade in his hat, who was not Mr. Thomas (she too knew Isaiah Thomas by sight). The officer said he had a headache and proceeded upstairs to his chambers, whereupon Mrs. Thomas went up too. When Margaret went up to call them down to breakfast she found the chamber door shut: "I looked thro' a large key hole and saw them on one bed with the bed clothes on them with the gentleman's leather leggings on the floor taken off; that I saw no motion of either of them; that I called them down to breakfast if they would come down and they came down in about ten minutes." (Mrs. Thomas asked Margaret to go upstairs to look for a sleeve button she had left upstairs). Curiously, at Mr. Newhall's tavern a person named Sarah who lived there and signed with her mark said that not Margaret but she herself called the couple down to breakfast sometime after the coach arrived in Lynn from Newbury Port and that she descended to tell Margaret, who went up to get the laggards downstairs.

John Williams, a tavern keeper in Greenland, New Hampshire, recalled in the same time period the arrival of a curricle from Portsmouth with a gentleman and a lady one evening during disagreeable weather:

They called for a Room by themselves where they had a Fire made and supped and desired nobody might disturb them and nobody did, the Door of the Room where they were was kept shut. After being some Time in the Room they called for a Pen and clock which Mrs. Williams carried them. About 10 o'Clock they called for a Bed. I asked them if they wanted two Beds or but one they looked at each other and smiled at which Time I took particular notice of the Ladie, and one of them answered (I think it was the Gentleman) "one to be sure" Accordingly they had but one Bed provided for them in a Chamber which had but one Bed in it and in that Chamber they were shut up together till morning and nobody with them. The next morning they staid for Breakfast and also tarried according to the best of my Remembrance great part of the forenoon keeping the Door of the Room they were in shut and then proceed on their Journey. They said they were going to Newbury Port.

On top of all the preceding testimonies concerning the spree of Thompson and Mary Dill to Portsmouth in the winter, a mother and daughter reported on a longer span of time back in Boston. Mary Fowle of Londonderry, New Hampshire, was visiting Boston to see friends, and Mr. and Mrs. Thomas invited her to "tarry" at their house. She stayed there "most of the time" from September 20, 1774, until April 16, 1775, and declared that three or four months after her arrival (thus around Christmas or January), "I observd Mrs. Thomas had commenced an acquaintance with one Major Thompson then a refugee in Boston who borded in a house opposite to where Mr. Thomas lived." Mary Dill was observed going over to the Major's four or five times a day. Mary Fowle presumed she was visiting people of the house and "I thought nothing Material of it" until one afternoon Mary Dill spent the whole afternoon at his lodgings. The major was drawing her picture and would complete it the next day, said Mary Dill. The following day Mary Thomas was off to the major's lodgings again: "She dressed herself, shifting her Linen, which I knew was not her custom on Saturdays." At the end of the day Mary Thomas came home with the picture she had been sitting for, "a small piece of parchment, on which a Lady's face was drawn with a black lead pencil, and asked me if I did not think it looked like her, and added that she thought it was a great likeness and, that the Major had taken much pains with it." Thompson remained captivated with drawing people's faces as he did while an apprentice. Also, he liked to be with Mary Dill for companionship, in his room or at her house; it wasn't a brief sexual encounter.

It was more apparent by the day that the printer's wife and the major had taken a shine to each other. The printer's wife, Mary Fowle said, continued that the major "did not like to set in the room where the people of the house were, and where others were coming in, and therefore he had a fire made in his bed-chamber, where they staid the whole afternoon and part of the evening." It seems as though Mary Fowle was at first looking the other way but soon parsed the extent of the flirtation. She did not have to pry, as Mary Dill was chirping like a bird in spring about her inamorato: "The high spirits she was in, and the fondness with which she spoke of the Major joined to the circumstances of her shifting her Linen made me conclude that they had agreed to be in private the day before, and I could not but think there was more intimacy between them than I before tho't of; however, I kept my opinions to myself, which daily observation more and more confirmed." The major was showing up at the Thomases' house often, especially when the master was absent: "I perceived them very fond of each other and used great liberties with one another such as kissing each other, laying in each others laps, speaking fondly of each without regarding me.... I really thought they seemed to live but in each other's company."

Thompson went out from his lodgings at dark and immediately Mary Dill would take her cloak and hat and follow in the same street. The lovers had the not atypical bravura, from willful indifference to being watched or even an ill-fated desire to be observed. Mary Fowle disapproved of the immoral liaison but her way of describing the couple of seeming to "live but in each other's company" has a touch of the wistful romantic. By this time, Isaiah had established his system of post riders. The distribution of his newspaper linked the committees of correspondence of many towns and villages. His face was so well known that it was all the more ludicrous for Thompson to pose as the printer.

The Thomases' household consisted of a servant or two, the visiting Mary Fowle, Isaiah and Mary Dill and the two children, Mary Ann, born on March 27, 1772, and little Isaiah, born September 5, 1773. If the lovebirds were not inclined to hide their amorous regard for each other, Isaiah's intense involvement with the Revolution is a partial explanation. One day Mary Fowle and a servant went to fetch the missus back home because Isaiah had arrived. They found that the game of cards was more or less a ruse, as Mary Dill and the major were "not playing cards but fondling and kissing each other, she often laying her head on the Major's shoulder, and their arms round each other."

The bewildered 26-year-old printer comes across in Mary Fowle's account. His thoughts were all on abuses of the British Crown; Thompson was to Isaiah just another young army officer. The divide between them was even more than that, as Thompson was interested in "natural philosophy," while Thomas wanted to sway public opinion to his politics. There could be few greater contrasts in focus than the printer fomenting revolution, as he had attempted with less success in Halifax, Nova Scotia, and Thompson, who collected secret information and got most exercised about things like the perpetual motion machine he had carried from Salem to show his friend Loammi Baldwin a few years before.

Isaiah Thomas had remonstrated about the impropriety of his wife's intention to go to Newbury in the winter, saying she had no reason to go. Accompanying the major in a curricle would have constituted both a free and classy way to go, rather than by coach; Thompson was trying to impress his ladylove with his clout. One can see the impudence in Mary Dill's reply that she "had a mind to go," as well as her swearing as the dispute escalated how she would go if it was to her eternal ruin. The true situation seems to have been obvious, but either a flagrant affair was just not done among Isaiah's peers or he was a little thick. Or it could perhaps have been that he didn't want to deal with problems at home.

Mary had done up her hair "in the greatest taste much powdered" for departure on the misadventure. As it turned out, the major did not have use of a curricle; they went by stage and returned a week later. Mary Fowle let on that she did not miss a trick and relished the lovers' downfall. She saw how on their return the sexual attraction did not waver, and they "kept their eyes almost continually upon each other in a very languishing manner." The major gave Mary Dill little presents, among them a "new dollar and an eighth of a Dollar," which she averred she would never part with. "Indeed they seemed to be more fond of each other, if possible, than before."

One day the printer and Mary Fowle went to church and when they returned little Mary Ann came to her father and showed off a "copper" the major had given her to go into the other room. The child said, "The major kissed her Mama and felt her bosom." Mary Dill said her child was a liar and, according to Mary Fowle, either whipped the little girl or threatened to whip her. Thompson did not yet fully recognize that children are little people with ears and eyes about their parents' conduct.

Love's madness is imprinted on the scandal. The young matron was deeply in love, and the major saw her as a wench who might pass on information about the rebels and in whose company on the trip to Portsmouth he could cover whatever his activities were.

The wronged husband could abide no more. He may have let his wife have the rope with which to hang herself. A showdown occurred and the adulteress confessed, which was witnessed by Mary Fowle's mother. Mary Thomas was made to tell on two occasions the story of how the affair commenced, which she swore was true: she was under the covers in bed, Major Thompson writing his wife a letter in the same room, when he lay down beside her.

Isaiah refused to lie with Mary Dill anymore and had a bed made up to sleep in alone. Pitifully she asked for things to be as they were and for Isaiah to write for the major to come for dinner, a curious codicil, as that makes it seem that Isaiah and the major were friendly though politically at odds. Mary Dill also tried a desperate bribe. The major would pay Isaiah one thousand pounds, which Isaiah thought ridiculous, but it is very unlikely that the major offered it. If Isaiah was burning with jealousy he did not appear to be; rather he had given up on the marriage and believed that with all the reports of Mary Dill's adultery from various sources he could extricate himself from the marriage. For her part, his wife tried one more ploy when she acted "light and gay" and pretended her confession was all made up.

Thompson must have known he was leaving American shores and thus would leave his lover behind. For Mary Dill the liaison had greater significance. While the affair was devolving after disclosure to Isaiah of the goings-on, one evening Mary Fowle, either maliciously or turning tail and feeling compassion for Mary Dill, went from her chamber to Mary Dill's just after the latter went to bed and called her to the window to see her lover at his window: "Major Thompson is at his window about undressing himself, she instantly jumped out of bed, and ran to one of my windows, where she continued till I was in bed, looking over the Major and said to me, I have often heard people talk of Love, but I never knew what it was till I knew him, pointing to the Major and staid at the window in her shift, altho it was a cold night, till she said he was gone to bed."

Infatuation dazed Mary Dill. Her lover was so near but so far from her. The old good times where he was welcome in the house as a visitor for supper were past. She had fallen for the officer hard. Standing and staring at the window long after Thompson's figure had disappeared, whatever he felt she was sure she felt the emotion of true love she had heard of. This might be something she heard from other women or from romance and true-confession-type stories such as those in the *Royal American Magazine* that her husband published for 15 months beginning January 1774. Isaiah also leavened that publication with a *Directory of Love* to which the lovelorn were invited to write.[9] Her words resonate, for which Vickery in her study gives a context: "The mid–eighteenth century saw the phenomenal success of the novels of sensibility, which glorified the supposedly female qualities of compassion, sympathy, intuition and 'natural' spontaneous feeling, while neglecting the cardinal virtues of reason, restraint and deference to established codes and institutions."[10]

Another aspect of the fling is that Mary Dill said the reason the major took her on his journey to Newburyport was as a cover, so he would not be recognized. This was the period when Thompson was a spy for General Gage. During the last week of April 1775 Isaiah left Boston. At Concord he met with John Hancock and other members of the Provincial Congress and on their advice dismantled his printing office on the night of

April 16. With the help of Joseph Warren and Timothy Bigelow he transported half of all his printing equipment, his press and type, on the ferry to Charlestown, from which the press went by wagon to Worcester. Isaiah Thomas stayed in or near Boston and on April 18 was one of those who rode with Paul Revere to warn the countryside of the impending British invasion. The morning of April 19 the printer was in Lexington when the Minutemen assembled. After the battle he went to Watertown to see his wife and children and then to Worcester, mostly walking the 40 miles.

For some time, Thompson went in and out of Boston, until April 15, when he left for his mother's house in Woburn and became stranded there when the fighting began on April 19. Around the same time, Isaiah Thomas relocated his printing press in Worcester to protect his contraband publishing. Thompson continued to see Mary Dill, who was left behind in Watertown with the Thomases' two children. Apparently Thompson was a frequent visitor there.

Isaiah Thomas, Esq., by Benson John Lossing (The Miriam and Ira D. Wallach Division of Art, Prints and Photographs: Print Collection, The New York Public Library).

In March 1776, when General Howe abandoned Boston, Thompson sailed to England as well. A letter from Thompson, unsealed because it was put in the hands of a British sentry, went to the Rev. Sam Parker of Trinity Church asking him to look after papers and clothes he left behind. Thompson thought the British would rule and he would be back for his belongings or that they could be sent after him. Clothes had the more detailed mention in the letter: "I have a very good Hussar cloak faced with scarlet shalloon with yellow mock-spangle metal buttons, and an old plaid red gown, lined with crimson shalloon, in Town, which I should be glad you would likewise take under your care."[11] He says "cloak" but this may have been a uniform jacket in the style established a hundred years before, originating in Hungary, for light cavalry units. Such a cloak, or cape, was thrown back over one shoulder and did not interfere with the arm that bore the sword.

Isaiah Thomas was living in New Hampshire when he instituted divorce proceedings in Massachusetts. He had moved to a 40-acre farm he had bought in Londonderry, New Hampshire, in February 1776. His brother Joshua lived on a neighboring farm. This was to be a temporary home for Mary and the children, as, according to Shipton, "Isaiah had in mind a quiet country town where there would be no tempting uniforms and where a reliable relative could keep an eye on affairs during his own absences."[12] It is as though Isaiah looked at Mary Dill as a straying animal that might wander from its place of keeping. He was a decent father, a leader in his field of printing and a brave patriot, but his passion was for radical politics and not Mary Dill. She responded to a lone wolf who was

4. The Royalist and the Printer's Wife (1776–1779)

Minerva Shielding a Sleeping Youth from the Arrow of Cupid and the Wiles of Venus (1797), watercolor on ivory. Signed Sully [Thomas or his brother Lawrence]. Doughty ambition can be sapped by sensual desire; the goddess, wearing plumed helmet and blue stole, uses her shield to deflect Cupid's arrows (Walters Art Museum).

sensual and spent long hours in her company. Apparently Thompson made the first move but both her background and the nature of her husband made it a foregone conclusion that she would betray Isaiah. The divorce was concluded May 27, 1777, while Thompson was in London, where Lord George Germain had appointed him the month before as "Secretary of the Province of Georgia." Now an outlier even if the Province of Georgia was no more, two years later he was promoted to the lucrative and highly responsible position of undersecretary of state. Mary Dill was surely filed away and closed in his personal book.

Later Mary Dill went south, perhaps to South Carolina, where she resided when she married Isaiah on Christmas Day 1769. In May 1779, two years after the divorce, Isaiah married another Mary Fowle—that is, not the prying houseguest who testified about the adulterous relations of Mary Dill and the major but Isaiah's own half-cousin and widow of Zachariah Fowle, the first employer to whom he had been apprenticed at seven years of age (this Mary now became Mary Thomas Fowle Thomas). It was not a marriage of passion like Isaiah's first but of trust: Mary Thomas Fowle Thomas was a "good manager" and Isaiah called his second wife his best friend.

The couple had a house in Worcester and a stately mansion at 52 Newbury Street in Boston, with orchards and gardens where Isaiah liked to work. They entertained throngs of relatives and friends, as many as twenty houseguests at a time. Isaiah wrote *A History of Printing in America* and became rich through his business properties. In Worcester he was the first person to own a coach, which he sometimes would rent out. This second Mary, Mary Fowle, died in November 1818. Isaiah married the next summer her cousin Rebecca Armstrong. Rebecca had been taking care of his house in Boston for him. Shipton wrote as follows:

> He immediately found that instead of simply making his housekeeper permanent, he had acquired a whole new bundle of unsuspected conflicts. She simply loved to go on long trips, and she apparently saw no reason to inform him of them in advance. He was a very social man, fond of having the house full of guests, but he did not care for her kind of entertaining, even when the company was of the best.... Tradition has it that the two and a half years that this marriage endured were stormy ones. His diary does not record such storms, but under the date of their separation, May 6, 1822, there is the entry: "very bad headache, and, I may add, heartache—these have attended me for the last two years."[13]

The first husband of Isaiah and Mary Dill's eldest child, Mary Anne Thomas, was a printer and publisher of the *Federal Spy* in Springfield, Massachusetts. That marriage ended in divorce and Mary Anne divorced two more times, whereupon she and her children (by the third husband, a Vermonter, Dr. Levi Simmons) returned to live with her father. By Mary Anne's first husband she had a son, Isaiah Thomas's grandson Isaiah, whom he sent to Harvard. When Isaiah made a will twenty years later he left $500 for Mary Dill at the discretion of his son.

Benjamin Thompson left his wife to be a spy, during which time he had a fling with Mary Dill Thomas, the printer's wife, and then fled Boston thinking the British would prevail. And if they did prevail did he suppose he could return to his wife or to Mary? It would seem obvious that property and status would have magnetized Thompson to Concord, and he tried not to burn his bridges with his father-in-law. Yet as persona non grata he would not have been able to reclaim what was his and would have been unwelcome personally. Might love and being a pariah have caused him to return to Mary Dill? Mary Dill loved him but likely did not expect him to jump over the hoops of their situation to be with her. It was wartime, he was a military officer, and the sexual relationship ended after a year, when the British evacuated Boston. Thompson loved less deeply than she, and he did not protect her or care about her feelings during the breakup with Isaiah. Being expelled from America was an overwhelming trauma for Thompson, which he handled by finishing with his past.

5

The Affair of the Letters and Dr. Jeffries' Wife (1776–1779)

> Love, love love is like a dizziness, Won't let a poor man go about his business.—Royall Tyler, *A Love Song* (1757–1826)

The affair with Mary Dill may have been a frolic of free spirits but it probably was about spying too. In choosing to make love to the wife of the pivotal revolutionary printer Isaiah Thomas, Benjamin Thompson likely had a hidden agenda. Either by assignment or on his own accord he took Mary out for a several-day whirl and gathered or passed information on behalf of General Howe, the temporary commander in Boston. As a guest at the Thomas home, he would hear incidentally about Mary's husband's coconspirators. The next known sexual escapade of Thompson again combined illicit sex with a married woman and careerism, only this time the husband seems to have been a willing cuckold.

Like Fanny Hill, the protagonist in John Cleland's *Memoirs of a Woman of Pleasure* (1748), Benjamin Thompson "soon came to a resolution of making this launch into a wide world, by repairing to London, in order to seek [his] fortune." Fanny noted that many adventurers of both sexes come to ruin. Thompson was lucky. He had confidence bred of the success he had so far experienced in the throes of the strife in America. He was an aspirant to high society and ambitious. He was determined to ascend in his position in life and did not identify with the American refugees who despaired of losing theirs. He had earned his first stripes in the closely woven nexus of patronage, as a spy, before coming to Britain. Thompson had something else in common with the plucky survivor. Like Fanny Hill he would not stop at using a sexual liaison when indicated by his future fortunes.

By 1776, every family and individual had made the choice in the contest to rule America. The rebels rejected all ties to Britain while the Royalists held onto them. In *Common Sense* (January 10, 1776) Thomas Paine wrote, "'Tis time to part." So the Royalists understood the time had come to leave for Britain or a British possession. Thompson was not an ordinary refugee and did not go to Canada as many refugees did. He bore to London dispatches that gave sorry news but exacting information to the British secretary of state for the colonies, Lord George Germain.

A page was turned. Thompson had made his explanation to his father-in-law the Reverend Walker and entrusted the preacher with his wife and child. In times of war, the cause came first. The Marquis de Lafayette wrote of his suffering to his wife, Adrienne, when he left her pregnant with Anastasie, their second child, but he left for America without being mired in guilt. The daughter Benjamin Thompson left behind with his wife was now in her second year, about the age he himself had been when his father died. Any letters he might have written home during the Revolutionary War, if indeed he dared write them, are not extant.

In London the young man of 23 became his own Booted Cat, with the references he brought from Wentworth and Gage accessorizing his prepossessing energy and mien. He had talents and he knew how, in a world of minute differentiation, to show deference. The combination worked immediate wonders. The letter from General Howe referred to the rebels' shabby treatment of Thompson and his usefulness in and outside Boston to the British government; he was "deserving of Protection & Favours."[1] Thompson's appearance, politesse, and energy, along with his knowledge of distant America, impressed Germain. England was a face-to-face society where pluck and tenacity had value and there was elasticity to the status quo. Thompson pulled strings to move up the ranks at a time when opportunism gained respectability.

The job of Germain's undersecretary given to Thompson made him the intermediary between the Loyalists from the colonies and the British government. He was the rare émigré who prospered, and generally the refugees felt they had been good citizens and wanted to be compensated beyond the small amount they received. Few loyalists would have been thrilled at how the undersecretary conducted the business of dealing with their demands. Besides that, Thompson was an upstart. For example, Judge Samuel Curwen, who sought Thompson's help, had known him when Thompson was a shop boy in Salem.

Lord George Germain was a figure to reckon with, a man in his late 50s known for being ruthless to his enemies and generous to his friends. He had made a tactical mistake at age 44 at the Battle of Minden, fought on August 1, 1759, when he didn't smash the French forces when they were routed. This shadowed him. His own belief was that England ought not to get involved in wars on the Continent, which could have influenced this decision. This one misstep became known as "the ghost of Minden."[2] It led to the court-martial of Lord Germain and his exclusion from the royal court for a decade. He regained power when George III became king, which is when Germain became someone not to oppose. Lord Germain actually had a private secret service force. Thompson became a favorite of his and socially a friend of his family. The break in letters and diary entries for almost four years when Thompson was working for Germain, according to Sanborn Brown, who researched British official papers, may signify Thompson was on some secret missions for his boss.

A story told by novelist and Whig politician Horace Walpole goes far toward explaining why Germain was pleased to employ Thompson, a young man technically savvy who was good at maps. Germain received news in December 1775 that the Continental Congress's rebel army was trying to take Canada. Major General Guy Carleton had fled Montreal disguised as a commoner and was in Quebec with a military force of only a few hundred. Germain quickly asked the Admiralty to send four ships with soldiers to relieve Carleton, provoking guffaws at the lord's ignorance of America, as the St. Lawrence River was frozen solid all winter.[3] This had happened a few months before Thompson's arrival and now Thompson had maps and detailed information and knowledge of New England that Germain required. Thompson had his midday meal with the general daily and visited his country home often. He was recommended to the king on December 15, 1776, to be secretary and register of records for the Province of Georgia (a rather meaningless position). George III concurred.

Sanborn Brown suggested Thompson might have been gay, although it is hard to concur with that conclusion given he had three children by three different women and preferred spending much of his leisure time overnight with aristocratic women friends. He having been torn from his family by the winds of war, his friends, beginning with Loammi Baldwin, became as important to him as any family. Friendships were a matter of strong feelings and passions. Also, as a courtier he revered the powerful Germain, who gave him livelihood, in England and later in Germany, and sided with him against foes. Brown did give an account of how Germain's enemies accused him of homosexuality, a typical swipe, even before the Battle of Minden, and how Thompson's name was associated with such gossip.[4] Thomas Hutchinson, as ex-governor of Massachusetts, says an acquaintance spoke of someone who lived at Germain's as "that Scoundrell."[5] Hutchinson wondered that Lord Germain "would give such cause for the world to insinuate such things of him. I was astonished at the freedom with which he spake of what it's shocking to think of." Brown gives indirect credence to there having been forbidden love between the general and Thompson: "A scurrilous pamphlet published by John Wilkes during the furor over Minden quite openly accused Germain of sodomy."[6] Yet, in letters, Thompson said that Germain was like a father to him. It seems that the spying operations Germain was conducting explain the closing of doors and meals à deux.

Fifteen years after the "ghost of Minden" injured Lord Germain's reputation he went along with the hawks, politicians determined to crush the American rebellion. In 1775, George III appointed him as secretary of state for the colonies, under Lord North, the first minister. Thompson was in a key position as a junior grade army officer and intermediary with the Royalists in London, and was in Lord Germain's employ for the next five years. Another refugee, Samuel Curwen, quipped that Thompson had his meals "breakfast, dinner and supper"[7] with Germain, "so great a favorite is he." Thompson's success must have thrown Curwen for a loop. An American Tory in London, Curwen had been deputy judge of admiralty and provincial impost officer in Salem when Thompson was an apprentice for Mr. Appleton.

Thompson continued to collect information as part of Germain's private secret service, cut a dashing figure and was remarked upon socially. Lord Glenbervie wrote in his diary many years later: "Lady Glenbervie remembers him going about with Lady George and her daughters to balls as a sort of humble dependent and dancing with the young ladies when they could get no other partner. At that time he was considered as the favourite, at once, of the father, mother and daughters, and the ill-fame of the father then, and the conduct of the daughters since, have served to keep the scandal alive with regards to them."[8]

The evidence weighs in on Thompson's adapting famously to his new life, yet a letter he wrote Germain on October 7, 1776, shows that while circumstance and ambition had taken him to Europe he cared about his family in America: "I have not yet heard one syllable directly from New Hampshire though I have made many attempts. I begin to be at a loss to guess the reason of this dead silence. They must know I am here." Whatever letters Thompson might have written home at this period, his daughter destroyed before her death.[9]

When not at the Colonial Office, Thompson spent his free time experimenting with guns and gunpowder at Germain's country seat in East Sussex, Stoneland Lodge, an ancestral estate open to the public today as Buckhurst Park. Artillery was the most sophisticated science of war and to Thompson military technology was both natural and prudent. In July 1778 he and a local rector experimented on firearms to get the optimal vent and measure the speed of bullets and recoil. They determined the muzzle velocity of bullets by shooting into a pendulum and measuring the swing. These were his first recorded scientific experiments, and his essay "Experiments in Gunpowder" says that he had been investigating the subject "for many years," which meant earlier in America. Thompson now came to the attention of Sir Joseph Banks, president of the Royal Society, and was elected a fellow in 1779 "as a gentleman well versed in natural knowledge and many branches of polite learning."[10]

The work on firearms was related to the physics of heat. He concluded that the heat was the result of a sudden expansion and contraction of the barrel, which would lead him to postulate heat as a mechanical action, not an inherent quality as was previously thought.

He advanced to be undersecretary for Britain's northern colonies, which gave him oversight of the recruitment, transport, equipment, and commissary matters for the British troops in America. He held this post from 1780 to 1781. As one science writer has commented, "Science was never to Thompson a mental divertissement, but was always intimately associated with his daily duties." The appointment was strategic for naval operations and lucrative for Thompson, and this must have been the source of his funds to back his own regiment in 1781. Just as with the inventions and experiments he did in his life, Thompson's personal interest in flowers, interior decorating, horses and clothes meshed with his career. In 1775 he had been planning to get local women in Massachusetts to supply epaulettes to the American forces; now he was in charge of the suits of clothing and other apparel going to America on transport ships; and later he would be redesigning and seeing to the manufacture of army uniforms in Bavaria.

Thompson was a cynosure for the many Tories who had fled from American shores. They had expected rewards from King and Crown but what they got was a 100-pound-per-year stipend that would barely cover their food, along with a general reproach that they had sat by and let the revolution flare up. As Lord Germain had given Thompson charge of the American Royalist community, many people beat a path to the door of junior officer Thompson with petitions and asking for favors. Dr. John Jeffries was one such Tory and the racy story of his making friends with Thompson at all cost, and Thompson's behavior, evidences Thompson's mindset at the time.

The refugee colonials in London went to Germain's undersecretary to seek help because this was an era when privilege and prestige counted for everything. Thompson helped some in the line of duty but they did not receive the hero's welcome they expected and he was not empowered to rectify their losses. The story of one loyalist reflects the desperate attitude of refugees in London. The intrigue it involves reveals that Thompson was the kind of civilized lover a husband could tolerate. Dr. John Jeffries had arrived in London with his wife, Sarah, called Susan, on April 2, 1779. He intended to return to Nova Scotia in British America. This aim differed from Thompson's and was unlike many of the Royalists who had left early in the rebellion, before the anger against them became vicious and combat broke out.

Formerly of Boston, Jeffries and Susan fled with General Howe's evacuation and had gone to Nova Scotia, where Jeffries, an ambitious man, was given the appointment of pharmacist and where, being ambitious, he became the head of three hospitals as well.

To make the job formal, so he could draw a salary, required a confirmation by the British government. Therefore he had applied to the commanding general in Halifax for a leave of absence. Day one he wrote in his diary, "Major Small brot me to Mr. Thompson (an American, the present Favorite of Lord Germain) and introduced him to me and Mrs. J.—& said he would inform him fully of me my past & present Situation etc."[11]

The initial interchange between Dr. Jeffries and Thompson was about Jeffries' appointments. The doctor that year began keeping a daily record of the weather (he was the first to do this so consistently) and his activities. The John Jeffries Papers at Houghton Library of Harvard include 20 volumes of Jeffries' diaries and journals from 1779 to 1819. The doctor's diary entry for April 28, 1779, records this: "Called upon Mr. Thompson, Pall Mall ... had long conversation with him upon Speculative Philosophy and Happiness, Good & Evil etc.—he talks well, fine ideas, but not easily attained to reduce to Practice." This is interesting because Thompson was at work on his experiments on cannons and gunpowder and had a political job but wanted to speculate about ideas. And so began a five-month pas de deux, where Jeffries used Thompson as a conduit to a commission, and generally to the doctor's advancement, and Thompson led him on and trifled with Susan.

Jeffries recorded in his diary several times that Thompson spent the night with his wife. In London, Thompson was popular with the ladies as an unattached male. He was ready to dance with wallflowers and please mothers. But his affair with Susan Jeffries was of a sexual order. Jeffries banked on the fact that Thompson could restore his fortunes and turned a blind eye. Thompson took Susan out on lengthy jaunts such as visiting Vauxhall Gardens, was continually at the Jeffries for tea, and paid visits exclusively to "Mrs. J." When Jeffries had to make a trip to America, Susan stayed in their London lodging with the children, in Thompson's charge.

At first the diary has notes about "Mr. Thompson (Lord German's)" as if Jeffries needed to justify to himself as to why he was soliciting a politician. Between April 22, 1779, the first time Jeffries presented his case, informally, to Thompson, and June 15, when Thompson departed from Portsmouth on his naval cruise, Jeffries went to see Thompson 13 times. Thompson in the same 54-day period went to the Jeffries' lodging 22 times. If Thompson showed up, usually Jeffries himself left the entertaining to his wife. The excuse for Thompson's calls was usually in the evening for tea. If Thompson and Susan went out together it was without the doctor. Jeffries appeared not to object to Susan's and Thompson's being on an overnight, yet, he kept track, and sometimes noted that they "returned." Twice he met them out somewhere when they were returning from an overnight. There is no mention of physical intimacy. Contrarily, Jeffries invariably presses the matter of his commission when Thompson sorties with Susan, while Thompson manages invariably to come up with some progress report that keeps Jeffries in a state of solicitation. This in turn allows Thompson and Susan to pursue their dalliance with the husband looking the other way. Coinciding with the inception of tête-à-têtes between his wife and Thompson at the Jeffries home, the doctor noted he gave Susan a portion of her money. Jeffries may well have been showing his approbation of what he construed as her cooperation in politicking for the family future.

Samples from the diary entries of Dr. Jeffries during the spring of 1779 are circumstantial suggestions of that dalliance:

> May 24—This Eve Mr. Thompson, Pall Mall, called on us 10 o'clock (I being in bed), and sat with Mrs. J. until past 2 o'clock Morn, left a card for me.

> May 30—Mr. T sat drank tea and spent eve with us. He would present to Germain this night at supper!
>
> June 2—Called on Mr. Thompson, left card. Mr. Thompson went to Vauxhall with Mrs. J. This day, gave Mrs. J. four more guineas of the money I have been keeping for her. Mr. Thompson arrived late with Mrs. J said Lord Germain had read my letter and wished to serve me—Mr. T. said he would do whatever he could for me.
>
> June 4—Mr. T. called on us, dined and sat till Evening.
>
> June 5—Mr. Thompson drank tea with us—walked out with Mrs. J.
>
> June 6—Mr. Thompson drank tea with us—in the even rode out with Mrs. J to Hampsted and returned.

On June 8, Thompson and Susan went to Vauxhall. Jeffries met Susan and Thompson by appointment June 9 at Sadler's Wells. Sadler's Wells was a good place to meet without one's comings and goings being remarked upon. Around the popular theater were entertainments including jugglers, acrobats, ropedancers, street singers, dancing dogs and automatons. That Jeffries met his wife and Thompson at Sadler's Wells suggests that the pair's tryst had extended overnight. They rode to the Jeffries' house together and Thompson dined with Susan. And so it went. Sometimes the amorous pair went to a destination, such as the "Furnace and Foundry near Black Friar Bridge," that was potentially more interesting to Thompson than to Susan. They also took in Westminster Abbey, St. Paul's Cathedral, Vauxhall and the Tower Armory.

An appointment for Jeffries at a hospital in New York was imminent, and soon after Thompson left on his naval cruise a letter came from Portsmouth to Susan "desiring they not leave until he returns from his cruise." The next week another letter, to Jeffries, "engages me all his Friendship and intent." When the fleet was back in Portsmouth, Thompson arrived exhausted and was not at his old lodgings when Jeffries came looking. Jeffries was told that Thompson "had gone to bed at Lord Germain's." However, at two o'clock a refreshed Thompson called and saw Susan, "[Jeffries] not at home." Clearly, from the diary (July 9) the night of his return was another night Susan and Thompson spent away from the Jeffries family in each other's arms—as Jeffries reconnoitered them the next day.

Susan seems a Bathsheba figure when, thanks to Thompson's lobbying with Lord Germain and others in government, Jeffries gets his wish of a commission and is off to New York on a ship that Thompson had assured him was "armoured." Susan accompanied her husband on a London diligence, a covered wagon with at least four horses, to a post near the naval base at Portsmouth. Jeffries had mentioned warmly the two Jeffries children but this is the first time in the diary for the period discussed where he says something sweet regarding Susan: "September 21—Took leave of dear Mrs., hand her to the diligence—God almighty, preserve and bless her and our little ones and of his great goodness permit us to meet together again."

A relevant sideline of this romance is the affair of the Benjamin Franklin letters. Jeffries had in his possession a collection of two sets of letters he had brought from America, which he was aware of as tempting fare, described in his diary as "on American political affairs from 1769–1774." King George III collected books and papers that could throw light on the colonies. This made the little packet of correspondence between Benjamin Franklin and Dr. Samuel Cooper, with a sprinkling of additional letters from Cooper to Thomas Pounall, Whig member of Parliament and former governor of Massachusetts Colony, marketable. Jeffries himself refers to them on June 14, 1779, in his diary as "the Political Letters & c. of Dr. Franklin, Gov. Pounall &c." While Jeffries was a Royalist his

5. The Affair of the Letters and Dr. Jeffries' Wife (1776–1779)

father was not. John Jeffries' father's friend the Reverend Cooper wrote a very detailed brand of letter, e.g., the deprivations in Boston during the British blockade of the city. Cooper, on the surface, was a quiet minister but he was entirely on the side of the insurgents and an influence on John Hancock. Cooper had entrusted the elder John Jeffries with the letters when Cooper left Boston during General Gage's occupation, whence John plucked them from his father, and Thompson, ambitious to impress George III, got them from John Jeffries' wife.

It is hard to get over bafflement today that George III would have had such a keen interest in the letters. The king was grappling with his fractious colonials and besides that had an amateur interest in the gossip of the players among his rebellious subjects. As the letters were old news by the time John Jeffries showed them to Benjamin Thompson in London, it has to be understood that their value to the king was almost as souvenirs of the conflict, riveting gossip with contents that did not signify a great deal.

Good lord, I did not offend you; he's my husband! [*Die de misericord/Je ne t'ai point offense; C'est mon époux!*] **The soldier's rival is but a husband (Napoleon Collection, Rare Books and Special Collections, McGill University).**

Thomas Hutchinson (1711–1780) was not only the governor of Massachusetts Bay in the years before the Revolution but also a historian over decades of the colony. He described in his diary a visit from Thompson in 1779 related to the letters. Hutchinson intimated that Dr. and Mrs. Jeffries wangled the letters from Dr. Jeffries' father back in America. Hutchinson moreover referred to a whiff of hearsay linking Mrs. Jeffries and Thompson in a sexual affair:

> Mr. Thompson (Lord George's) [Germain's] called, and among other things mentioned that he had a great curiosity to show me—but I was not to speak of it—all Gov. Pownall's and Doctor Franklin's correspondence with Dr. Cooper of Boston, and then related the particulars. I showed him the extract I had made from one of Franklin's letters, and mentioned another which he said he well remembered. He said he had copied them all over, and made a present of the originals to the King, who was vastly pleased with them. I thanked him, and said I should like to look them over, but had seen them, and taken a cursory view of them. One of Franklin's letters in 1770, in which he declares his opinion upon the constitutional Independence of the Colonies, and another, in which he gives an account of my Letters, I copied, and returned all the originals.
>
> I think Jeffries would have given them to me, if I had desired it, but as Dr. Cooper had left them with Jeffries' father for security, and they came into the son's hand by some accident, the father not

intending they should, I scrupled desiring the son to do a thing which I doubted whether he could justify, unless some important purposes for the public could be served by it. It is very extraordinary that he should afterwards give them to Thompson, if he did do it. I remember to have heard that Thompson was more intimately acquainted with Mrs. Jeffries than with the Doctor. This is a curious anecdote. Franklin will not care who sees his letters, but Governor Pownall will think himself ill used if he should ever hear that his private correspondence with Cooper for many years, has been given to the King.[12]

This was when, for three months beginning July 1779, Thompson had an unusual assignment: he went out as a gentleman observer on a cruise on the ship *Victory*. His appointed task was to experiment with firing guns, based on his expertise from the paper on the force of gunpowder that gained him entrance into the Royal Society of London. Another assignment was to report on the situation of the Channel Fleet, which was in turmoil as the commander in chief and one of his vice admirals had just been court-martialed. Focusing on technical details, as was his wont, Thompson reported incompetency to Germain in that the command had got their signals crossed so that instead of ordering the fleet into a "line of Battle" with a half blue and half white flag from the mizzen peak, Sir Charles Hardy instead announced with an all blue flag that it was payday. The signal flags came to interest Thompson, who came up with a system that he told Germain used ten flags and allowed a thousand different signals to be sent. While undocumented, the system was admired and Judge Curwen noted of the undersecretary, "It is said he is of an ingenious turn, and inventive imagination and, by being on a cruise in Channel Service with Sir Charles Hardy, has formed a more regular and better-digested system for signals than that heretofore used."[13]

Thompson studied naval architecture during his tour of duty and set about designing a swift copper-sheathed frigate carrying 40 guns. The admiralty did not take note but contemporaries praised the design for correcting the sagging that occurred on naval vessels at their bows and sterns when they carried heavy cannon. The published drawings of his frigate in *Naval Architecture* (by Stalkartt) show an innovative sharp "deadrise [the V-shape at the bottom of the hull, making it slice through the waves]." The polymath began his paper by saying that designing boats "has long been my favourite study."[14] He also drew a plan for a ship that would be superior to the one he sailed on. As he was not a naval engineer this was never built. While he was away he wrote to Susan Jeffries nearly every day.

John Jeffries' diary entries that mention Thompson's part in the little society of him and his family go from April through June 1779. When Thompson came ashore briefly, he rendezvoused with Susan. Dr. Jeffries wrote, "Mr. T. engages to protect and take care of Mrs. J. ... when I go to America." Jeffries did receive the commission from Germain that came from "waiting on Mr. Thompson" for days. He was turned down for the position of purveyor of hospitals, the job he had been doing, because he had left Halifax without official approval and was thus illegal in London. If he were to ask for this position his illegal status would be remarked, so much like deportation issues in the contemporary United States. Thompson arranged a meeting of Dr. Jeffries with Germain in which the doctor asked for a switch from Halifax to New York for his commission as apothecary. He got the position he sought, although he would not, it turned out, stay in America but rather set up a medical practice in London.

While Jeffries in the diary says he gave them to Thompson "for his Inspection," the letters did not come back. Thompson had them bound in gold-tooled red morocco and presented them to the king with the inscription, "Mr. Thompson ... now resumes [*sic*] most humbly to lay this ... at his Majesty's feet as a literary as well as a political curiosity."¹⁵ Regarding the packet of insurrectionist letters, Hutchinson provided history with a last word, implying that Susan Jeffries let Thompson keep the letters, Hutchinson's conscience didn't permit him to take documents the father had not given to the son, and, finally, as he so tactfully stated even in his own diary, "Thompson was more intimately acquainted with Mrs. Jeffries than with the Doctor."

After Thompson's cruise with the fleet, folded in with the prestige of his position as inspector of the colonial forces came the opportunity for financial aggrandizement. Responsible for supplies like uniforms, clothes, saddles, and swords to be sent to the colonies, true to form he gravitated towards a question of science: he tried to figure out the strength of silk fibers, as silk was used for clothes for the army. He noticed that it was difficult to measure the volume of the fibers because silk "possesses a power of attracting and imbibing water from the air."¹⁶ He realized that a merchant could make a profit from exporting bolts of silk if he bought them by weight in the driest state in London and sold them after a damp transatlantic voyage on the docks of the eastern seaboard of America.

Dr. Jeffries was sailing as far as the equator and then finally to New York in the spring. He wrote in his diary about life on shipboard, whales and flying fish, surgical operations, weeks of bilious disorder, hobnobbing in the Bahamas and South Carolina, and so on. He received a letter from "Mrs. J." dated in early November 1779 and otherwise did not record news of home or his thoughts. He was focused on duty and business. Then on April 26, 1780, a letter came from Thompson written in January "informing me of the Death of my dear dear wife." This was possibly the first time Jeffries opened up emotionally in his diary. His immediate thoughts were for his children's welfare:

> [M]y dear tender Orphans to visit not God, them for their fathers Transgressions—surely there is a something peculiar and foreboding in my misfortunes—I have been oppressed with extreme Anxiety from the Day my dear Wife left me at Portsmouth—all my Letters have announced it—I wished to give up my Commission and return to the Arms of my dear Family, from Ireland I certainly should have done it but for fear of dishonoring Lord Germain and Mr. Thompson and General Masy [?] who had patronized me—I have not had one joyous Hour since I left London, and now God only knows when I shall.... This melancholy Day, had I been endeavouring to comfort & amuse myself with handling and looking over Dear Mrs. J.s Letter to me when in Ireland and those I received from her when she was Miss Rhoads.

The entry written during his first shock ends with prayerful utterances in which those to whom he had entrusted his family are unusually prominent: "Thanks for the kind friends that have stood forth as guardians of my dear Children." When Jeffries was away from his family for almost six months without word from his wife he simply trusted those he had appointed to look after Susan and the children and it was not until hearing the tragic news that the floodgates of his emotional connection to her burst. Susan and John had been married only seven years when she died in January 1780; one child, Ann, survived her. Jeffries resigned his commission in America and returned to London. He would marry a second time in 1787, another widow, Hannah Hunt (1764–1835), who corresponded with Abigail Adams. Jeffries thereafter had a medical practice on Cavendish Square in London.

By the fall of 1780 Thompson was in command of a broad swath of the military operations, from Quebec to the West Indies. He still had some jurisdiction over the community of refugees, as he served formal notice to the government that the painter John Trumbull, not yet famous and a former aide to General Washington, was in London. Thompson might have worked for Trumbull to have diplomatic immunity but he had an exacting nature and saw only that Ben Franklin, enemy of Great Britain, had given Trumbull letters of introduction. Privately Trumbull had been given leave by the king to study with Benjamin West, but now it took the king's intervention to prevent the artist from being hanged. Trumbull was in prison until the following June and would accuse Thompson of preventing Germain from seeing friends' testimonies on his behalf.[17]

Meanwhile, Jeffries now had a thrilling escapade. In 1785 he was a wealthy physician able to sponsor balloonist Jean Pierre Blanchard on the first successful air flight over the English Channel. Blanchard was interested in adventure and Jeffries in the science of flight; they were in constant disagreement. Blanchard let him come along when Jeffries agreed that if the balloon was sinking he was willing to jump overboard. On the trial flight in 1784 Jeffries took atmospheric samples, recorded a mass of data and discovered the path of a hydrogen balloon as looping ascents and descents. They made the flight in January 1785. Just before departure Blanchard—either wanting to keep the weight light or not wanting to share in the glory—put on a belt rigged with lead weights in an attempt to trick his backer into foregoing the trip, but the canny doctor found out the ruse.[18]

The flight took about two hours and to stay aloft they first stripped the balloon of ballast and then they stripped themselves, until they were wearing only underwear and jackets made of cork in the freezing cold. Jeffries came up with the final tactic to reduce weight in the gondola: they pulled down the leather bladders that were hung in the rigging and urinated into them, thus reducing the weight of the two passengers. The balloon sank so close to the water that they had to tear off the decorations from the gondola and then the steering apparatus, arriving some miles inland in their underwear. The heroes were feted and Jeffries spent several evenings with Benjamin Franklin at Passy "discovering the future of flight, and the beauty and intelligence of French women."

Blanchard was a character and self-promoter who would eventually open a balloon school in London. He would also demonstrate balloon flight before George Washington in Philadelphia in 1793, while Jeffries is credited with having delivered the first airmail when he dropped a letter from the gondola on their flight from London to Kent in 1784.[19] After 15 years based in London, Jeffries returned to Boston and resumed private medical practice there (1789).

On the defeat of Cornwallis, Parliament censured Lord Germain's department. He resigned from government and was created Viscount Sackville but not before conferring on Thompson a commission as lieutenant colonel in the British army. Germain's resignation and rumors of Thompson's being part of a spy ring with a French agent named La Motte, who was executed, might have decided Thompson to leave the Colonial Office. He had amassed money and purchased a commission of lieutenant colonel, then became involved in forming a cavalry regiment. The officer class was not long-term professionals but aristocrats who looked to get booty from war and land and money upon retirement. Most British mounted forces in America were Loyalist militias. Thompson sent a Major Daniel Murray to America to recruit a regiment of Loyalists not currently in the armed service, to be financed entirely by Thompson. The lure to draw recruits was ten guineas for enlisting and five guineas for bringing someone in. The King's American Dragoons became a real operation in the summer of 1781. With Thompson now a lieutenant colonel he had to go over to America to carry out the job of raising the regiment to battle

5. The Affair of the Letters and Dr. Jeffries' Wife (1776–1779)

An exact representation of the departure of Monsr. Blanchard and Doctr. Jefferies from Dover Castle on Jany. 7th, 1785 (Lewis Walpole Library, Yale University).

strength—and as its leader reap the rewards. He sailed in October 1781. By the time Germain resigned, the hostilities involved the Continental powers of Europe. Thompson reached Charleston, where contrary winds had driven the ship he was on from its destination of New York.

The replacement he trained for Lord Germain's office was Governor Wentworth's brother-in-law, John Fisher, who had been a collector of customs in Salem when Thompson was an apprentice there for Mr. Appleton. The colonial war may have been going poorly for Britain but Thompson saw a moment to shine. Corps of Loyalists like the Queen's Rangers, which originally formed in the French and Indian Wars, had distinguished themselves in the war.

In Charleston he learned that the British were losing their grip on the colonists and that Cornwallis had surrendered to the Americans at Yorktown. The commander in chief, Sir Henry Clinton, was no friend of Germain's. They had, for instance, argued over Germain's directive that provincial officers be subordinate only to officers of their rank, not to British officers on active duty with them. Predictably, Clinton made things difficult for a lieutenant colonel under the patronage of his enemy. The day of arrival, Thompson had his baggage—including cannon, horses and a goat—taken to shore before being told that the *Rotterdam* was scheduled to depart the next day. He scrambled to get everything back on board only to be told by the harbormaster that this had been an error. Again his belongings came off but indeed the ship raised its sails and departed for New York, leaving him in Charleston for the winter. "I find I shall stand in need of all my prudence to steer clear of all the snares and lures that will surround me," he wrote Germain.[20]

Embracing his first active duty, Thompson reorganized what remained of the royal army, under General Leslie, raided American patrols and stole cattle and other animals. The Tory press hailed him for a cavalry raid against the forces of the "Swamp Fox," General Francis Marion. Thompson tried to cross the Ashley River and capture by surprise Nathaniel Green, the American commander in chief. Not realizing it was a tidal river even miles from its estuary, Thompson ordered the men to swim from the marshy banks. The tide rose, and his regiment's best swimmer and his horse could not ford the mud flats. The horse drowned and the sergeant had to be rescued. Details of Thompson's command are of interest, considering he was a British officer in New England and then South Carolina, and an officer again in Bavaria, but this was his only battle action. How did he fare? With cleverness, zeal, and imprudence in a whole ball of wax.

First of all, Thompson took cavalry and mounted militia and a cannon to attack Colonel Horry, whose colonial regiment was still being organized. Being sick, and thinking his position secure, Colonel Horry had taken leave of his brigade and gone to his own plantation. By the very spirited exertions of the troops and by mounting the infantry occasionally on the dragoons' horses, Colonel Thompson was enabled to carry on the whole corps thirty-six miles without halting, when falling in with a party of Horry's [Colonel Horry, under General Marion], an officer and six men, none of whom escaped to give intelligence, he pressed on with the cavalry and mounted militia, leaving the infantry posted at Drake's plantation.[21] The classic history of South Carolina from which this account comes has a mention that Thompson's adeptness at finding female informants gave him an advantage: "The Assembly did not, however, finish its business until the 26th, and in the meantime the enemy, doubtless through the women who were allowed to go to town against Marion's orders, were fully apprised of the disorganized condition of the forces on the Cooper River, and prepared to take advantage of them."[22]

Meanwhile, the new commander of the British in America, General Guy Carleton, was positive towards Thompson and let him raise his King's American Dragoons in Long Island. Despite incentives, the recruitment of soldiers was a stretch. Thompson bought smaller units that were undercapitalized, including several officers and 25 men from the Wentworth Volunteers, which he had incidentally briefly tried to help organize in America. Thompson lent money at interest to his commissioned officers and offered a bonus for recruits and the purchase of horses. Recruits could not be just anybody. The British government stipulated they had to be Tories who had suffered because of their allegiance to the Crown.

Thompson believed in pomp and fine clothes. He arranged for Prince William Henry, age 17, the third child and son of George III, who would reign as William IV (succeeding the prince who had the sexual affair with Governor Wentworth's wife, Fanny, in Halifax), to review the troops once the regiment had cohered. Thompson paid for Prince William and his retinue to come to the camp, three miles east of Flushing, in Long Island (August 1, 1782) for the presentation of the colors. Things were not looking good for the British but it was not too late to put on a good show. The 17-year-old prince and the top officers sat under a canopy. Trumpets sounded, music played "God Save the King," and the regiment formed a semicircle around the canopy. The chaplain gave an address and the prince presented the colors with his own hand to Lieutenant Colonel Thompson. Then everybody partook of an ox that had been roasting on a 12-foot hickory spit.

During his six months in Long Island, Thompson was involved in a skirmish to catch smugglers in whaleboats, with few casualties. He wrote proudly to Lord Germain that "what is very singular, since I first joined the Regiment there has not been a Desertion while I was actually Present."[23] That was splitting hairs given the frequency of desertion. Thompson also wrote in this letter of his good treatment of the troops and his popularity as a commander.

Meanwhile, it was war, and the populace of Long Island detested him. The infamy went down in the annals of history that he had built soldiers' barracks (called Fort Golgotha and built by local forced labor) from the timbers of a Presbyterian church and the chestnut rails of the fences of Huntington, and used over 100 tombstones from the hallowed ground of the graveyard for fireplaces, tables, barrack floors, and ovens. It was said that the bread baked for the soldiers was stamped with partial epitaphs of the tombstones in reverse and that Thompson forced town residents to provide labor.[24]

Several local historians of the 19th century concurred about Colonel Thompson's cruelty while in command in Huntington. A fourth historian, however, Henry Onderdonk, disputed all their invectives in his two letters (February 7 and March 22, 1870) to George Ellis, now at the Massachusetts Historical Society. When Onderdonk visited the site of the fort in 1842, there was no trace of it in the Huntingtom burial ground. It was typical, according to Onderdonk, to use church timbers to build structures in which to quarter soldiers; Thompson would have gone by the book and not unreservedly harassed local inhabitants; and the hill was studded with only a small number of grave markers. Onderdonk observed of those who damned Thompson for his actions in Long Island that one author "borrowed thunder" from the other. Onderdonk offers a perspective on Thompson's command at Huntington while a judgment of this period in Thompson's life is outside the purlieus of this book.

Colonel Thompson certainly did not suffer during his assignment in Long Island. He had two English servants and an African American groom, a stable of six horses, and a phaeton to ride in around the countryside. He sent Lord Germain, now Viscount Sackville, presents of a load of firewood, three American horses and a buck and doe that were "rather larger than your Deer and I think more beautiful."[25] It is interesting that Thompson judged firewood would have value to Germain.

Peace and the final disbanding of the British forces occurred in 1783. Four months after the Old First Church had been disassembled and the fort built, the British troops evacuated. Before he left New York on March 14, 1783, Thompson wrote General Carleton on behalf of the men in his regiment that these young men, "having no Profession, but the Profession of Arms ... will be unable to provide for themselves by their Industry in any other Calling"; and for their bravery and suffering as Loyalists they were "objects worthy of the countenance and Protection of Government."[26] He put forth his merits for promotion to full colonel, which included a boastful fib to Lord North that he might like to check with Sir John Wentworth how he, Thompson, had been promoted to colonel in New Hampshire and commanded a regiment of over a thousand men. Since Wentworth was in Nova Scotia as surveyor general of the king's woods this appears to have been a ploy.

King George saw no reason to promote Thompson from lieutenant colonel to full colonel, yet three weeks after he demurred, Thompson was promoted all the same. He reported to Carleton that the king had approved of his promotion four days before Lord North asked the king for his approval. Finding a place for the dragoons elsewhere in the British colonies proved futile. Thompson wrote Daniel Murray, who had settled on lands given him on the St. John River in New Brunswick, Canada, that he was off to the

Continent "and if there should be a War I shall engage in it, on one side or the other, I dont care a farthing which."[27]

With his new rank (and half-pay for the rest of his life), Thompson obtained permission to travel and find occupation for his talents on the Continent. Before he left in August or September 1783 he arranged to be painted by Thomas Gainsborough, in the scarlet uniform of a colonel. The portrait of Colonel Thompson sat in a plush box forgotten until a dentist unearthed it from his family stateroom in the 20th century and the work's artist was identified as Gainsborough.[28] Colonel Thompson has a penetrating gaze. The artist understandably wanted his works hung at eye level. As a result of the Royal Academy's refusal, some of Gainsborough's paintings were not exhibited there and the portrait was forgotten. It is now at the Fogg Museum of Harvard University.

6

Advice from General Burghausen's Wife (1784)

> Industry, knowledge and humanity, are linked together by an indissoluble chain.—David Hume, *Of Refinement in the Arts* (1752)

Thompson liked domesticity as much as anybody but was constantly on the move. Employers impelled him and so did his wanderlust and ambition. We can picture dust kicked up on his trail, horseback or in a coach. From age 30, he dashed for about the next 33 years like a post rider on a grand scale, to and from destinations in Germany, Austria, England and France. Not only was the travel strenuous and his need sometimes to get places rapidly but most of his journeys also faced impediments due to the Napoleonic Wars. The more significant trips will be covered in the rest of his story. He could meanwhile have brought his wife Sarah to Europe but there is no indication he tried to do this. He did not want her to know where he was once he was on the Continent, so perhaps he was actually avoiding her. Once the Treaty of Paris was signed he might have thought of an eventual return to America except that he was having a fine time and he had suffered a trauma in being chased out of his homeland. Thompson was settling his affairs in London. He wasn't needed in the British army, he had a pension, and he saw serving in some Continental European army, perhaps to fight the Turks, as the logical next career step. Lord Germain was going to be in charge of his effects in his absence; Thompson expected to remain on the Continent for a year or two.[1]

Charles Francis Adams, Sr., historian and son of John Quincy Adams, summed up the character of Thompson aptly in a letter to George Ellis on December 24, 1869, saying he was "half adventurer and half hero."[2] This is fair. Other commentators have judged him more harshly, as for example John Meurig Thomas, who wrote, "Rumford was something of a scoundrel and undoubtedly an incorrigible opportunist.... In Rumford's case there was more sinner than saint."[3] This obloquy is familiar in biographical works. Thompson was in a perennial state of tension and abstraction in his work. How few who achieved fame for good in this era—the stock character of the picaro notwithstanding—earned their living and decided a course of action by their own initiative.

Thompson set out with alacrity on his knight errancy, a combination job search and grand tour. On September 17, 1783, he traveled across the Channel on the same boat as Edward Gibbon, who would write his famous history on the Continent, and Henry Laurens, former head of the American Congress, who had recently been released from the

Wooden trunk, painted maroon and covered with vellum, its iron handles and brass plate engraved "Le Comte de Rumford/N: 6." "No 6" is also painted in black on each side (New Hampshire Historical Society).

Tower of London after a year of confinement as an exchange for General Burgoyne. High winds delayed the crossing several days, and Gibbon wrote from Dover, "What a cursed thing to live in an island." About his shipmate he remarked, "Mr. Secretary, Colonel, Admiral, Philosopher Thompson, attended by three horses, which are not the most agreeable fellow-passengers. If we survive, I will finish and seal my letter at Calais."[4]

Operating on the assumption that the military was his ticket to success, Thompson fashioned himself a soldier of fortune. In this he was both right and wrong. A peerless arriviste, he had a meteoric ascent but being an officer was the first step. His arrival in Strasbourg coincided with a review of the Royal Alsace Regiment. A large contingent of German and French troops had fought on the side of the rebels in the American Revolution. Prince Maximilian of Deux Points, then Field-Marshall of France, was on parade. Maximilian saw among the spectators the striking foreign officer on a fine mount and asked whom he served. It was an identical scenario to Wentworth's noting Thompson on his bridal tour ten years before. Being at least 6'2", Thompson stood out in his British colonel's uniform as George Washington had in his when he attended the First Continental Congress. Thompson showed Maximilian his usual civility and deference and said he came from the American war.

Maximilian was heir to the Duchy of Bavaria by one of those quirks of heredity in monarchies. His cousin Charles Theodore, Elector Palatine of the Rhine and Duke of Bavaria, had no surviving legitimate children, and Maximilian would become king of Bavaria in 1806, despite having been married to two Protestants. In the meantime he lived on tight funds. He probably could empathize with Thompson and he knew Bavaria was open to talent. Thompson accepted an invitation to visit the garrison and meet the French officers who had served in the same war as he but against him. Thompson produced a portfolio of plans of war and maps for them to examine, which he must have either carried since leaving America or kept from the time of his service to Lord Germain. After several days as the Prince Maximilian's guest, Thompson left with an introduction to Karl Theodor in Munich.

After that stop, Thompson went on to Vienna, where he spent the winter of 1781. The Austrians were not fighting the Ottoman Turks, as he had counted on, but he met Sir Robert Keith, the British ambassador, who discussed his being an undercover agent to report on whatever country in which Thompson found employment, be it Germany, Russia, Austria or Turkey. Thompson had spied for Generals Howe and Gage in Boston, but that was specifically on arms and maneuvers. While both Keith in Vienna and later the British envoys in Munich, as well as more casually the Elector when Thompson settled in Paris, wanted him to eavesdrop on a government; he upset them by relaying there was nothing to tell. Evidently (according to records in the British Foreign Office), when Keith asked him to spy, Thompson made only a desultory start.[5]

Vienna was a turning point in Thompson's thinking. The volte-face occurred at the home of an Austrian statesman who gave a party. Wenzel Anton Kaunitz (1711–1794) was the fifth and only surviving son of a count. He concluded a secret alliance between Austria and France, two formerly hostile powers, during his stay in Paris as ambassador from 1750 to 1752 and was created prince of the empire. He was the trusted chancellor to Empress Maria Theresa and had an active role in carrying out reforms under her and her son Joseph II.[6]

Thompson met, at the Prince of Kaunitz's, General and Mrs. Burghausen. Heinrich Otto von Burghausen saw active duty on the Austrian side during the Seven Years' War two decades earlier. He had led two battalions and two companies of grenadiers against the Prussians. Mrs. Burghausen often entertained Emperor Joseph II as her visitor and "conceived a warm friendship for Thompson. She, as a biographer wrote in 1820, "gave him wise advice, and imparted to his ideas a new turn, by presenting to him in perspective another species of glory than that of conquering in battles." Why did he devote himself to armaments when he could work on peaceful advances?[7] "For the cure of this martial madness, he was indebted to a lady whom he met accidentally at the Prince de Kaunitz's ... wife of General de Burghausen who often entertained Emperor Joseph II as her visitor. For Mr. Thompson she conceived a warm friendship, gave him wise advice, and imparted to his ideas a new turn, by presenting to him in perspective another species of glory than that of conquering in battles."[8] In a version of the same quoted by Professor Pictet: "'I owe it,' said he to me, one day, 'to a beneficent Deity, that I was cured in season of this martial folly. I met, at the house of the Prince de Kaunitz, a lady, aged seventy years, of infinite spirit and full of information.... This excellent person conceived a regard for me; she gave me the wisest advice, made my ideas take a new direction, and opened my eyes to other kinds of glory than that of victory in battle."[9] This epiphany occurred while the idea of glory on the battlefield still had wide currency, which it would not have after Napoleon's wars.

Thompson's writings on science gave lip service to a divine creator but he was deaf to religion, a qualified freethinker. He certainly did not believe in Revelation, thus the subtle evocation of Mrs. Burghausen herself as a transformative influence, a "beneficent Deity" whom he gratefully recalled. Ever a maverick, Thompson would have especially related to the nonsectarian openness of the world of Mrs. Burghausen. He had probably already considered, for instance, the matter of patenting his ideas and would on principle never do it. Moreover, one can guess that while Europe was simmering with republicanism, Mrs. Burghausen, born at the beginning of the 18th century and wife of a general, was a monarchist. Burghausen saw active duty on the Austrian side during the Seven Years' War.[10] Two decades before, he had led two battalions and two companies of grenadiers with 400 horses against the Prussians during the Seven Years' War. Thompson, of course had been anti-revolution since his teenage years. Sharing the combination of conservative politics and progressive values with Mrs. Burghausen would have made it easy for Thompson to consider her vision of cooperation and toleration among countries.

Could a single conversation with a chance acquaintance have changed the young military officer's path? Biographers discount the possibility, saying that Thompson was inclined to dress up his past. But there is no reason to doubt that, adrift in Europe after being retired from the army, he was forming new beliefs that would direct future actions. He says that someone he looked at with regard influenced him and he retained what emerged in conversation with her. The assertion of a historian of this period, Eric Nelson, about the relation between beliefs and actions of "historical actors" suggests an answer. Nelson writes, "The claim that we lack psychological access to the true source of our preferences is very different from the claim that we are disingenuously engaged in 'legitimation.'" He points out that no more than for us as individuals are elaborate moral or political constructions designed only to mask other agendas of historical figures: "We might instead adopt the supposition that historical agents generally mean what they say.… Those drawn to this approach need not deny that agents sometimes deploy arguments disingenuously in order to advance their interests. Certainly they do. The view in question simply suggests that we should begin by trying to take seriously the account that agents give of the content of their own beliefs and of the relation between those beliefs and their actions."[11] Thus we take at his word Thompson's attributing to an Austrian general's wife an impetus to become engaged in making humankind happier.

The encounter with the general's wife was pivotal for a second reason. She had spirit and she offered him friendship. Thompson in his twenties was a gallant towards women. That period was over. Having dealt with the real world of war and politics he hungered for affectionate reciprocal relationships, and his eyes were opened to the potentiality of having these kinds of balanced exchanges with women. Such exchanges would not be the fulcrum of his emotional life. The line between friendship and romantic love would not again be as clear as with the general's wife, who extended her friendship selflessly.

Kaunitz had not only been a diplomat and founder of the Austrian navy when the empire had Trieste and the Slovanian and Croatian coasts, but he also was a refined person who was a patron of the arts. Kaunitz must have been stirred by the Enlightenment because he believed in education for common people. It was natural that he would socialize with others with progressive ideas. Thompson had been heading back to Munich, on the frontier of Bavaria coming from Austria, when he introduced himself to the Prince of Kaunitz. Bavaria, seen by the rest of Europe as backward,[12] its army in shambles, was a fine place for Thompson to exercise his organizational abilities and make a name for himself, which he literally did. That no one who wasn't Catholic was allowed to stay in the country for a prolonged time until Maximilian became the ruler didn't seem to have thwarted Thompson if he was aware of Bavaria's xenophobia.

Karl Theodor, Elector and Duke of Bavaria, welcomed the officer who had impressed his cousin Maximilian and invited Thompson to enter his service in a civil and military capacity. Karl Theodor gravitated to anything foreign because he was a stranger to Bavaria and considered the country uncomfortable. He preferred the other lands he had ruled over for 35 years, the Palatinate, which bordered France. The duke had a quantity of staff beyond the ordinary. He told Thompson his function would be as tutor to an illegitimate son, while he would have the rank of colonel in the Bavarian army and be aide-de-camp at court. In February Thompson made his decision to stay. He wrote Keith on December 20, 1783: "I made a bold stroke and it has succeeded. I offered my Service here and it has been accepted, and accepted in the most flattering manner."[13]

Permission had to be obtained from George III for Thompson to be a general and privy councilor for a German prince, so Thompson traveled to London. England's king so much approved of the appointment of a British officer to be aide-de-camp to the ruler of Bavaria that on February 23, 1784, he conferred knighthood on Thompson, who was now Sir Benjamin. Sarah, Thompson's wife in America, living in Concord surrounded by an extended family as she always had been, was now the de facto Lady Thompson; but for her Thompson had shrunk to a small silhouette somewhere in her large house. The order for knighthood shows the fictitious island of his ancestors in Boston harbor, which could have been a family myth but seems more likely a mischievous note of Sir Benjamin: "that an Island which belonged to his Ancestors, at the Entrance of Boston Harbor, near where the first New England Settlement was made still bears his Name."[14]

Edward Winslow, a friend of Thompson's who had a similar charge of settling Loyalists (in Nova Scotia as opposed to in London), was in the process of creating the Canadian province of New Brunswick. Winslow marveled to his friend Ward Chipman in London: "Well done Sir Benjamin! The next news we hear will probably be that he has mounted a Baloon—taken his flight from Bavaria—and is Chief Engineer to an Aerial Queen."[15]

Thompson thrived in the employment by the Elector Palatine, Duke of Bavaria, Karl Theodor, which lasted until about 1798, 13 years, and marked the apex of Thompson's career. His rank would rise from Colonel of Cavalry and Court Chamberlain to Minister of War and Minister of the Interior. For the first four years he studied the possibilities of army and social reform, and the German language. The bon vivant duke gave his new courtier time he used well. Thompson experimented and invented and carried out social reform. Most of all, he wanted to know the causes of things. Being employed by the Duke of Bavaria gave him the leisure to learn, experiment, and apply his ideas. By 1788 Thompson was made major general of cavalry, privy councilor of state, and head of the War Department, with instructions to carry out any ideas he developed to reform the army and to solve the duke's problem of Munich's beggars and indigent persons, viewed by the aristocrats as a potential tinderbox.

Karl Theodor gave Thompson a lot to do and plenty of time to do it. The assignments could have been rope to hang him but inventors rally to problems. Analogous to a mythic hero, Thompson accomplished all his tasks. The prince's first directive was with regard to shaping up the Bavarian army, and the newcomer's ideas were eventually submitted in a memorandum in French. Later Thompson would write in German. This plan covered providing food, clothing and adequate pay to soldiers. The topic of army reform numbered in Thompson's first volume of writings, of which there would be 18 essays in all.

The first order of business was to rid the army of graft. For instance, in one swindle the officers sold uniforms on credit to the recruits. The soldiers' allowance for food and clothing was not enough, resulting in their getting deeper in debt each year. The begging and stealing and child abuse resulting from these practices were the other social problems Thompson was determined to solve. He seemed to agree with Edmund Burke that greedy people would pursue self-interest at the destruction of the rest of the population, so he built into the social reforms a very considered framework. The welfare facilities he set up, sometimes called workhouses but more accurately houses for the poor, were within a few years a model for many in Europe. In Switzerland, for example, a commission was set up in 1799 and tickets were distributed with Rumford's face in a drawing so people would associate the famous man with the nourishing rations; 600 people were fed daily from two "fourneaux à la Rumford" in Geneva. "We must make benevolence more fashionable," Thompson would write. He actually reformed how people performed acts of charity so that it would improve conditions and not be just palliative. To support his house for the poor in Munich he circulated the lists of contributions, letting people know that the lists would be published. Mostly the house for the poor in Munich was set up to make clothing for the army and for sale. Everyone learned some part of the manufacture, including the children, who did light spinning and attended school in the same building as the work was done. Every loaf of bread and skein of yard was accounted for.

Learning a language by immersion is an intense way of entering a culture. Having studied German for, and researched and cogitated about, Bavarian society, Thompson aimed to transform it across the board—the military, charitable institutions, hospitals, prisons, and trade schools—just not the political structure, as he believed in a benevolent monarch and would let sleeping dogs lie. But his first reform was of the military from top to bottom.[16] Interestingly, he carried this out a decade before Thomas Jefferson's parallel first project on becoming president in 1801, to reduce the size of the American peacetime army by half. The American officer corps, like the Bavarian, had swelled. Mostly Federalists filled its ranks, but Jefferson instructed his secretary, Meriwether Lewis, to be guided by military qualities before politics (which would have brought in more Republicans). "The army is undergoing a chaste reformation,"[17] Jefferson observed, the very phrasing Thompson would have chosen in trying not to stir widespread opposition while making sweeping changes.

Karl Theodor, who preferred music and art to governing and Mannheim and its French ways to Bavaria and its rural character, gave Thompson an ambitious Enlightenment person's dream opportunity. Thompson initiated in Munich most of the scientific experiments that made him famous in his time. While his approach to questions was to devise solutions based on experimentation, this does not mean he came to them philosophically as a blank slate. He was a Mason. When he came to Bavaria he was involved in reorganizing the Bavarian Academy of Science, some of whose members were also members of the Illuminati, a Bavarian Masonic order founded in 1776 by Adam Weishaupt, an ex–Jesuit who had republican sympathies, was a rationalist and had connections with various Masonic lodges.

By the time Thompson arrived in Munich, the Illuminati had over 3,000 members. A few months later, having heard rumors that the Illuminati were organizing to overthrow the government, Karl Theodor issued edicts to dissolve them, which he repeated the next year. It was no longer safe to be associated with them, yet the Illuminati circle had powerful and liberal people. "Mitgleider des Illuminatenorders," a roster of the order's members of this era, lists the artist Johann Georg von Dillis, whom Thompson patronized,

Joseph Karl Baumgarten, the husband of a famed beauty at court who would take Thompson as a lover, and several members of two families whose members were his friends, the Lerchenfeld and Turn and Taxis families. Evidently these were a liberal group of Freemasons who were coopted by the associations for science more acceptable and not hermetic in the early years Thompson served the Bavarian prince.

7

Honors and Enterprises (1784–1790s)

> I believe I forgot to tell you I was made a Duke.—Duke of Wellington, postscript in a letter to his nephew (1814)

On June 5, 1784, the versatile émigré took his oath, in French, as a Bavarian officer. Thompson's ties loosened with Britain as he found expression for his talents, ambition, and love in his new home in Munich. He was a forward thinker with an affinity for the ancien régime and he had found his niche. True to his Freemasonry, he did not see himself as belonging to any political entity. He viewed violence as stupid and wasteful. A citizen of the world, he was a high-level mercenary and canny courtier; naturally he would admire Talleyrand when he met him in 1801 in Paris. A most telling remark about Thompson was in a letter, a decade later, from Lady Palmerston to her husband the Viscount: When one made plans one could not count on someone "in service" like Thompson, who didn't have aristocratic leisure and was employed. So many of those noted in history were elite-born that to encounter a political figure, before the modern era, who was primarily a wage earner was an anomaly.

The next piece in the puzzle of why Thompson was such a neat fit at Karl Theodor's court derives from Thompson's philosophy. Reforms were in high fashion in Europe and Thompson believed that a monarchy could best solve problems of society. He admired China as a strong, not tyrannical but effective state. He viewed the American Revolution as an unlawful action and was hostile to the French Revolution. He had a passion for order and organization and a top-down approach to bettering the world. His view could be compared to Goethe's. When Goethe and Beethoven walked on a street at a spa resort, they passed through a group of German royalty. Beethoven, hands in his pockets, passed right through the dukes and their cortège and told Goethe to keep walking.[1] Goethe reacted differently: taking off his hat, he stepped aside. Thompson too would have taken off his hat. He enjoyed being "His Excellency" after the duke made him a count in 1792. He was a firebrand about improving social conditions and practical comfort for all but was a political conservative.

For European aristocrats of the absolute mold, a hired hand from England with Enlightenment ideas but monarchical values had particular attraction since Britain's kingship was stable. At the very time when Karl Theodor saw Thompson as the answer to many of his problems—the army, the indigent and how to please his populace—Queen

Maria Carolina was giving John Acton more and more power over Naples, first as head of the navy and eventually as prime minister. Like Thompson, Acton was connected with Freemasonry, and, curiously, he too began as an untitled person and became "6th Baronet" only when a cousin died and he inherited his title and estate. In the *New Yorker* Adam Kirsch wrote about Goethe that he "belonged to the courtly past, when artists were the clients of princes, while Beethoven represented the Romantic future, when princes would clamor to associate with artists."[2] And so Thompson profoundly, as inventor and social reformer, found his productive niche in being the client of a prince.

A palatial villa in Schwabinger Gasse in Munich, near the duke's winter palace, in a neighborhood of diplomats was Thompson's abode, which, at least initially, he shared with the Russian ambassador. It was during this juncture of stability in his life that 33-year-old Thompson's thoughts turned to family in America, bringing his daughter Sally from Concord and sending his mother in Woburn a gift. Probably especially for a son from the artisan class, it was signally important to provide for a mother. He often expressed a wish to see her again—a contrast to his indifference to or avoidance of his wife Sarah.

Similar to Thompson's caring for his mother was the continuing love of the revolutionary Thomas Paine while across the ocean from his mother in her English village. The free thinker to whom John Adams ascribed the American Revolution was in England trying to raise funds for a bridge of his design. He visited his mother in Thetford. He had not seen her for at least 15 years and did not know his father (a corset-maker to whom he had been apprenticed as a boy) had died. Just as Thompson's mother was proud of her own son, Mrs. Paine, now 90, was proud of Thomas and said she fasted each July 4 in honor of his contributions to American independence. Paine arranged an allowance for her before he got drawn into the French Revolution.[3] Beginning in the 1790s Thompson expressed in correspondence a wish to see his mother again. He made nebulous plans, but the son who had made good provided only financial support for his mother. He ultimately set up a trust fund for her in U.S. government bonds, but he did not return to America to visit her.[4]

Thompson came back in contact in the late 1780s with his two closest friends in America, Loammi Baldwin and Samuel Williams, after a 13-year silence. The last he had seen of Baldwin was when they were doing espionage around the Boston area gathering information for opposite sides of the conflict, sometimes, curiously, in company. Baldwin, who had been a patriot and officer under George Washington in the Revolution, had become a politician and engineer. He represented Woburn in the Massachusetts General Court from 1778 until 1784 and would be a candidate to the U.S. House of Representatives in 1794, by which time he and his older sons were leading the work on the Middlesex Canal.

Samuel Williams last saw Thompson in the fall of 1775 when he went to visit him in Woburn and they had a heated dispute, as Williams disinclined to separate politics from personal friendship as Baldwin did. All the same, when dispersing his belongings before fleeing in the spring, Thompson sent a letter averring his continued friendship and giving Williams his most valuable possessions, the two globes, which he hoped would be accepted, with a typically jocular faux confessional remark: "Believe me Sir, they are of no use at all to me for I am so heartily Sick of this World that I cannot even bear the sight of it in miniature with any patience."[5] Williams had continued on his successful path of minister and astronomer. His Bradford congregation had dismissed him so he could accept the distinguished position of Hollis Professor at Harvard, following John Winthrop, where Williams was making significant observations about solar and lunar eclipses, partnering with a meteorological study involving international weather stations and directed from the academy of science in Mannheim, Germany, which was under the aegis of Karl Theodor. Williams was asked to be a member of their society but the invitation was lost in the post. Thompson, whose bailiwick included Mannheim, at first supposed that Williams, who had rebuffed him just before he fled America, still was inimical towards him. That resolved, a second invitation went out. Thompson requested that Williams do him a service and deliver to his mother the first installment of an annuity. Williams answered warmly and Thompson set parameters of privacy and stressed to Williams to enjoin his mother she "must neither mention the present, or even the circumstance of her having heard from me to *any person whatever*."[6]

Williams said he would go to the Baldwins' home in Woburn and ask to see Ruth Thompson but say only he wanted to inquire about a relative. The mission, in other words, was being kept secret from Baldwin, too, because he knew the whole family might say something that got to Sarah, and Thompson did not want to be entangled, namely financially, with his estranged wife. Williams reported when he had done this and gave the kind of details he supposed would be appreciated, relaying how Ruth loved and missed her distant son and tearfully received the money. When Baldwin heard of the truth of this episode, he passed on an earful about Williams to the count, claiming the professor had pocketed most of the 70 pounds sterling that ought to have gone to Ruth: Thompson should know about the scandal because it backed up Williams' malfeasance in this instance as well. "The Revd & Learned Doct. Williams Profes. of Nat. Phylosophy &x at Harvard College is now in disgrace having in the course of the year pass'd been charged with several Forgeries & Frauds, has in consequence thereof lost his place in the University, all his property seized and he has faild in sums to a very considerable amount, and I hear was Indicted by the grand inquest for the County of Middlesex last October term, he has absconded."[7]

Not only did Baldwin report that Williams had embezzled college funds but also that he had miscalculated a total lunar eclipse so thoroughly that when his group set up their instruments at Islesboro (the island now in Maine), they saw no eclipse at all. Baldwin stated, "Mrs. Ruth Pierce is very Suspicious that he has done injustice to her, in withholding part of the donation of her son who is in affluence in a foreign country, you know who I mean. She has never received more than thirty dollars." Likely if Ruth's suspicions were raised it was by Baldwin himself.

This murky matter was a recent scandal that had caused Williams to resign from Harvard. The Massachusetts General Court had indicted him on December 1, 1788, for having tampered with two promissory notes, for six pounds to a tavern owner who supplied refreshments at Williams' inauguration eight years before and 12 pounds to a young Harvard graduate, Joshua Paine, meanwhile deceased. Despite the trivial amounts and the unexplained question of why Williams would have forged a date change on them, Williams went from supposing he would weather the scandal (he wrote Ezra Stiles offering to teach science at Yale) to fearing the most severe sentence.

That Williams would steal from his old friend seems far-fetched, all the more so because he would be so readily found out, as he arranged to meet Ruth Pierce at the Baldwins' home. Could Baldwin, caught up by the case at the court where he had previously been an official, been lining up against Williams? It may have made Baldwin jealous that his old companion Thompson, now an official in a royal court and an inventor, did not ask him to do this favor. When Thompson was thirteen and he and Loammi were best friends they had gone fishing off the craggy rocks of Nahant. Dr. Hays of Woburn was in their party. After they had caught the fish and had their lunch, they saddled up and somehow Loammi got left with all the fish to clean and bring home. Benjamin wrote him a long letter begging forgiveness, even though he could have walked over to the Baldwins' in a trice to apologize. That was in the summer of 1770 and in the fall Benjamin was angling to be an apprentice to Dr. Hays for medical training. Pleasing the doctor may well have been more on his mind than sharing responsibility for bringing home the fish. Loammi was furious and a rupture had briefly occurred.

Vermont was not yet a state but a frontier area. It was not under the jurisdiction of the Massachusetts court and Williams disappeared to Vermont and was later joined by his family. His life there would be active and bright. After six years as a minister in Rutland he helped found the state university (writing an enlightened charter saying religious affiliation would not be a factor in admission), founded the *Rutland Herald* and Vermont's first periodical, and wrote a scholarly two-volume *Natural and Civil History of Vermont*.

As for the annuity to Ruth, Thompson broke off contact with Williams. Later, in 1797, he had Baldwin look into his mother's welfare and a legacy to his daughter and set up a charitable donation for a dozen poor boys in Concord. He reminded Baldwin of the presumed false friend: "a man in—America—whose name I cannot pronounce without indignation."

According to what Thompson told Gouverneur Morris when he visited Munich, Karl Theodor was shy and would duck officials of his realm and let Thompson deal with them. Karl Theodor loved culture, parties, and pretty women, had a huge entourage, and wanted to be enlightened, but he ruled by whim.[8] Thompson too liked to hunt and dance and he solved problems on his own, thus he was on unceasingly good terms with his prince. And Thompson was not modest about either his influence with the prince or his accomplishments in Bavaria. Then again, if he did not talk proudly of his accomplishments to Morris when he visited in 1789, who else would? In Munich Thompson comes across as a modern urbanite without elite forbears, a gentleman scholar but also a government official and precursor to a rising class of bureaucrats in terms of how he made a living.

Twice the prince made moves to return to Mannheim and make it his capital. He preferred staying close to the French border and French culture. It was said by Louis XVI's minister of foreign affairs that Karl Theodor was ruled by his father confessor, Ignaz Frank, and "his soul is filled with the amusements of the hunt and music, and by secret liaisons." At Mannheim, Karl Theodor was a patron of the arts, an enlightened despot who corresponded for 10 years with Voltaire, founded a museum of antiquities admired by Goethe, and brought Lessing and Wieland to his court theater. As a counterpoint, he inflicted heavy taxes and sold titles not only to Germans but also other nationalities including Hungarians and Swedes. Munich, however, was the capital of Bavaria and where Karl Theodor was obliged to live in his palace. Bavaria was not pulsating with ideas of the Enlightenment but, rather, the Roman Catholic Church governed the politics and the society. It has been estimated that when Karl Theodor died, one in 50 people in Munich was clergy. At mass the churchgoer was given a ticket as proof of having gone to confession, and the handful of Jews in any town were obliged to stay inside and close their windows at Easter.

Analogous to Karl Theodor's decision to bring in a foreigner to modernize his state, in Denmark 20 years earlier the king had done much the same thing. But Thompson was innately conservative and wanted reforms without giving power to the people.[9]

Thompson had a passion for natural philosophy in common with other Enlightenment gentlemen and an ambition to rise in worldly rank by satisfying political patrons. With no notable person does he seem to overlap so much as with the Danish physician and politico Dr. Struensee. They are paralleled here as a brief study in a difference between persons of genius, ideas and ideals—the doctor who underestimated the Danish king, his patron, and the American-born Thompson who worked his way up in Britain and later suffered from Bavarian court intrigues but did not lose his footing and therefore could pursue his scientific and philosophical work to the last days of his life.

Karl Theodor by **Moritz Kellerhoven (New Hampshire Historical Society).**

Benjamin Thompson had a near contemporary and analog in Johann Friedrich Struensee (1737–1772). The parallels of the ambitions of the two men prove that each was a participant in the Enlightenment zeitgeist. Just as Karl Theodor brought in a foreigner to modernize his state, in Denmark 20 years before the king had a German minister who addressed social problems (when a foreigner became inconvenient he could be disposed of). Struensee made brilliant changes in Denmark just as Thompson did in Bavaria but fell dramatically out of favor and was executed at age 40. Struensee was a German doctor who became the court physician and personal friend to King Christian VII, whose antics caused him to be judged mad. The authority of the absolute state was crumbling and King Christian dismissed the old-guard council and appointed Struensee as council minister.

Struensee had Enlightenment ideas and with him a coterie of libertarians came into action in Denmark. In partnership with the king, he put into practice theories of the Enlightenment, enacting 1,069 laws between 1769 and 1772. The very day after gaining power he instituted freedom of the press, causing Voltaire to write to congratulate him. Struensee thereafter limited the power of the nobility, instituted labor laws to protect the peasants, and followed some of the most idealistic of Enlightenment thought.

Legitimate and illegitimate child alike was given equal status—there was no bar to bastardy. "Free Love" was no crime. Foundling hospitals were established, and a chapel was converted into a clinic for the treatment of venereal diseases. The project was praiseworthy, the choice of building unfortunate. Brothels were thrown open to all and were no longer for the privileged classes under police supervision. The gardens of Rosenborg were made public and used for dancing and concerts, but unfortunately they were kept open on Sundays and masquerades of a doubtful character were not. Streusel also became the lover of the queen, Caroline Mathilda, the younger beloved sister of George III of England. Caroline and Struensee had a child but the queen was exiled and died at 24, while the king's stepmother, banded with the disenfranchised aristocrats, had Struensee arrested and tried for lèse majesté. He was executed after giving a stirring speech in his own defense.

Thompson in Bavaria echoed the feelings Struensee had for the poor, his establishment of public gardens, and his galloping ahead into many areas of public life. Both were men of science who alienated the aristocrats and both were nervy about who they slept with. Neither made lasting changes and today only the gardens they established remain to show the power they wielded. But both cracked the ice of a crumbling state and dazzled the populace with revolutionary thought that did not involve warfare. Their political careers were both comets. Each had that spirit of knowing better than everyone else and sheer inventiveness. Both were sexual libertarians. The salient difference between these two reforming courtiers was that Thompson was innately conservative about society, and wanted reforms without giving power to the people.

Karl Theodor had his eye on an exchange of parts of Bavaria east of the Black Forest for several western provinces, which would extend the Rhine-Palatinate to include Brussels and Antwerp. Sir Robert Keith, in Austria, knew that Thompson had been introduced to Bavaria under the patronage of the House of Deux-Ponts and heard that Thompson had become sexually intimate (not necessarily an enduring affair) with the prince's "favorite," a former mistress, Countess Baumgarten, and was sure that Thompson would have insider information. He wrote Thompson with appeals for information, to which Thompson replied, "With regards to the *'Secrets'* you mention, supposed to have been in agitation at Munich; I declare upon my honor I know nothing of them."[10]

After acclimating to Bavaria and studying the society, Thompson was brimming with ideas and set out to change the face of the state. The prince was so pleased with the early results (military reform) that he arranged for Thompson to receive the Royal Order of St. Stanislaus in 1785. As Thompson was a nominal Protestant, he could not be presented with honors in the Catholic country. The prince went around this obstacle by having the king of Poland, Stanislaus II Augustus, issue the award. Thompson welcomed official recognitions in his adventurer's life. He wrote Germain: "I can say with truth that I hardly know what there is left for me to wish for. Rank, Titles, Decorations, Litterary distinctions, with some degree of literacy, and some small degree of military fame I have zacquired, (through your availing Protection), and the road is open to me for the rest. No man supports a better moral Character than I do, and no man is better satisfied with himself.... Look back for a moment my dearest friend upon the work of your hands.— *Je suis de votre ouvrage* [I am your handiwork]. Does it not afford you a very sensible pleasure to find that your Child has answered your Expectations?"[11] Thompson had a series of elder statesmen in his life that he looked to as fathers and to whom he was a good obedient son. A self-invented person, he recognized those who mentored him. As Sanborn Brown notes, the letter did not reach Germain. When Thompson wrote it, Germain lay dying at Stoneland Lodge and did not live to read it.

At that time the Bavarian army was discredited, largely because of the corrupt officers. For instance, the status of a soldier was so low that criminals were customarily sent to the army as punishment. Moreover, the soldiers had to buy food and fuel from the officers; having done so, they accrued debts that required them to remain in the army indefinitely to avoid debtor's prison. The prince promoted Thompson from colonel to general to make his job easier, and Thompson carried his appointed task of reorganizing the Bavarian army to lengths that stretch credulity. For one, he reduced the size of the officers' corps by 800.

The plan Thompson spent four years working out was comprehensive. The soldiers could work in home industries and off-duty jobs on roads and repairing riverbanks and draining marshes. Regimental bands played music to lighten the work. Leisure-time games, sports and amusements were organized. Children had to work and if they were too young they were put into the workrooms so they would see the older children working and wish to imitate them. Soldiers could go home on leave for months to help with sowing and harvesting.

Soldiers were stationed in garrisons when there was no war instead of being moved around. They were stationed where they could get home for home leave; in fact the idea was to spend the great part of the soldier's life at home. They could marry. Most dramatic of Thompson's innovations was giving each soldier a garden of 365 square feet, a gardening outfit, manure and tools and seeds (especially potatoes, which Thompson made popular in Bavaria). Each company was given a hothouse for raising early plants. Gravel alleys ran through the gardens for pleasant strolls. Upper officers could not appropriate what the soldiers raised or even receive the produce as gifts, but the soldiers could sell it.

Thompson changed the very landscape of the city of Munich. It had beautiful churches and grand buildings and conspicuous consumption by aristocrats who lived to spend, contrasting with desperate conditions and beggars organized in thieving bands. Moreover, the existence of the paupers was a public misery. Poverty was no natural state of affairs, Thompson maintained; it was a correctable breakdown of the social order. Therefore he collected from all over the country truly needy indigents and had them put to work in his poorhouses (also called workhouses), where they made accouterments for the army. The first was in Munich and occupied an abandoned factory. It became a model of its type, universally praised. By June 1792 this workforce amounted to approximately 10,000 people. The poorhouses taught trades. Men, women and children from the age of five were assigned tasks according to their ability. Schooling was provided for the children, and conditions were good—clean, well-ventilated and heated surroundings and nourishing if sparse food. Feeding the large group of boarders in the poorhouse spurred Thompson to innovation. This is where he brought in a kitchen range with its enclosed fire directed to the saucepans. Bavarian housewives were still cooking on open fires and the minister of war advised them to install ranges of this type in their own kitchens. He came up with many recipes, the most famous of which became known as Rumford soup.

Thompson's enthusiasm to put the world right, his organizational ability and his personal charisma all were brought to bear in solving problems. His methods of eliminating the mobs of beggars and drifters in Munich and getting the army in shape were related by his program, which he wrote up as his experiments in science and technology to share the results. The introduction to *An Account of an Establishment for the poor at Munich* says his goal was "in all my operations to unite the interest of the soldier with the interest of civil society, and to render the military force, even in time of peace, subservient to *the public good*."[12]

Reflecting on the city of Paris, Voltaire contrasted "appalling luxury" with "hideous

Alms (1790) by Johann-Jakob Dorner (Münchner Stadtmuseum, Sammlung Graphik/Plakat/Gemalde).

misery." The hideous misery in Munich took a particular form, as the beggars were organized into gangs. Thompson engineered social reforms in Bavaria by appealing to people's generous feelings and also by addressing the fear among the "haves" of unrest among the "have-nots" that could lead to mob violence. Feed them, keep them occupied, and give adults and children education, and the drain on society and the shame of the cities would be eliminated. Having the paupers work and learn was revolutionary. It was during Thompson's time in the duke's employ that he made a success of the "Houses of Industry." His sway extended throughout Bavaria as he had an inventory made of the poor all over the country so that steps could be taken to assist them. His forte was addressing every aspect from how accounts were kept to how rooms were lit. Yet his very detail, including what became known in Europe as "Rumford Soup," left his endeavors open to derision. His social experiments, although a triumph in Bavaria, would not transplant to England. He believed in law and order and a strong ruler but he expressed his enlightenment philosophy in his belief that people should be comfortable, well fed and content before they were pushed to achieve in their work. In the poorhouses where the former beggars were employed 14 hours a day making army uniforms and clothing they had every comfort he could arrange. Why Thompson's socioeconomic solutions have been considered sophisticated and liberal despite their top-down nature is that he reversed the process usually prescribed in the 18th century of making people virtuous and then entertaining their happiness. Social reformers after his time have often quoted the following basic tenet of his philosophy, first published in his *Essays, Political, Economical, and Philosophical* (1796). "To make vicious and abandoned people happy, it has generally been supposed necessary, first, to make them virtuous. But why not reverse this order! Why not make them first happy, and then virtuous! If happiness and virtue be inseparable, the end will be as certainly obtained by the one method as by the other; and it is most undoubtedly much easier to contribute to the happiness and comfort of persons in a state of poverty and misery than by admonitions and punishments to reform their morals."[13]

Cultivate your garden, the wisdom that concluded Voltaire's *Candide*, had an important application in the Bavarian army reform. Thompson's vision of what an army could be in peacetime was one of his most innovative ideas. He placed garrisons at the borders of Bavaria and attached to them military gardens, where the soldiers grew their own food and vegetables. He estimated that the food from the military gardens at Mannheim amounted to 10 percent of the cost of provisions for the entire army. He set up schools to teach the soldiers farming and to experiment with new methods. For example, breeding mares were given to peasant farmers and each spring a commissioner brought around a stallion. The peasant farmer could keep the foals except in times of war, when the army could claim them. The soldiers were to be encouraged to be merry on their time off with sports and dancing, and some of their labors on civic projects would be carried out as military bands played. When Thompson persuaded the prince to give Munich the world's best park, labor was provided by the Bavarian army.

As opposed to just legislating change, Thompson conducted experiments to see what change was best. He carried out studies to determine whether to invest in candles (beeswax or tallow) or lamps (two types burning olive, rape, or linseed oil) and then what kind of lamps were suitable for the poorhouses. He settled on the Argand lamp, invented by the Swiss Ami Argand, and rape oil, for maximum light and economy.

The prince had the commission examine Thompson's plan. It reported back favorably, at which point the prince dissolved the commission and put 35-year-old Thompson totally in charge of the reform of the army. For the next five years he implemented his plan. He would apply what he learned from reforming the army, for example, introducing the potato and the steam engine to Germany.

The priests and courtiers who dominated the prince's Bavarian court would never like Thompson and he despaired of this to Lady Palmerston. Nevertheless, he could and did achieve popularity with the people of Munich. He shone the light of his ideas in many areas. One idea was to establish a fund from the state treasury to reimburse those who lost their homes through fire, and if Gouverneur Morris is to be believed Thompson had a house built for aristocratic mistresses to live privately and arranged for their children to be educated (providing an elite for a military academy). His most spectacular contribution, however, remaining to the present day in Munich, was independent of his work reforming institutions. This was the magnificent 600-acre park named the Englischer Garten.

In my childhood, those of us lucky enough to go to Europe had little idea what we would see until we arrived. Before we went to Bavaria, I dreamed of Neuschwanstein Castle and my brother campaigned to go to the salt mines of Berchtesgaden. We collected pins as we traveled for the felt hats we wore. After college I studied German and my teacher read the essays of Schiller with me. But when I got to Bavaria to continue study and work as an au pair, I could hardly say hello in German. My job was to tutor two boys. The idea was that before their school day they would get up and each have a half hour of English with me. But they were very sportive and rarely had time. The mother and father communicated politely with me by note—"Tomorrow at 7 not 6:30" or "Please not the green umbrella, use any other." We rarely saw one another in their very large house, although I sometimes ran across the father in the indoor pool. One day one of the parents drove the boys and me to the Englischer Garten for the day. We were left there shortly after an early breakfast and were to be picked up at the same spot at four or five o'clock. Did I have spare money? I would be reimbursed. "Yes, yes," I said from the backseat. In fact, I had not brought a penny or known that the Englischer Garten was immense, larger than New York's Central Park, acres and acres and many things to do, some of which required money. But the entrance was free, and the boys and I drank from a water fountain. We passed a pleasant day in that heavenly park, although we were very hungry when we were picked up.

The Englischer Garten was landscaped to look almost like a wilderness. It incarnated the contemporary ideal of the picturesque. The former swampy terrain was now streams and bridges and gardens. It also had several Chinese features, including a pagoda (as did Kew Gardens in England). This was not only due to Thompson's high regard for the traditions of China and the status of their intelligentsia. He must have seen objects from the Asian trade in Salem and thus chose a Chinese-motif lining for his trunk and Asian household objects (at Brompton Row). The pagoda was a preeminent symbol of the lure of China. A 1795 watercolor of the City of Lin Tsin, Shantung, by William Alexander, for example, has a wondrously tall eight-story pagoda. Thus Thompson insisted on the Chinese Tower, with its pink roofs and wooden bells hanging from its gables, which the royal landscape designer, Friedrich Ludwig Sckell thought very garish.

Thompson persuaded the prince to give up the Hirschanger, his hunting sanctuary, and Arcadia, for his courtiers, for this public park, named Theodor Park. A dike had to be built on a river, swamps were drained, and lowlands were filled in. The landscape gardener, Friedrich Ludwig Sckell, had studied in Paris and London and had already laid out Thompson's military gardens at Mannheim. Sckell created meadows, fields of wheat and clover, a stand of a thousand birches, bridges, roads, dams, and inns. Theodor Park had summerhouses, taverns and dance halls. The prince was so pleased with all this that he made Thompson his privy councilor in March 1790, before the park was open to the public, and ordered a lifetime retroactive pension. Just as in a folktale, additional honors followed. The lovely stone monument in the Englischer Garten, erected by public subscription in 1795 to honor Thompson's contribution, remains there today.

Thompson became chief of Karl Theodor's general staff, and when, for five months, the prince was interregnum monarch of the Holy Roman Empire, he elevated Thompson to the nobility, on May 9, 1792. Thompson chose his own title: Count Rumford. The professional soldier and fellow of the Royal Society of England now was a titled minister of the state of Bavaria. Rumford was the former name of Concord, New Hampshire, and had an archaic English sound. Romsey Abbey was near Broadlands, where Thompson often stayed with the Palmerstons. At Broadlands in 1800 he put in a public kitchen in the nearby village, with its ancient name being a cognate with Rumford, either Romsey or Rumsey. He had certainly visited the village earlier and thus the name Rumford may have been a tribute to both the New England town and his friend Mary Mee. The name was also practical, as it was easy for Germans to pronounce. Thompson liked a jest and must have seen the humor in rising to nobility. He was like the cat in Charles Perrault's tale that proclaims the peasant boy the Marquis de Carabas to get the attention of the king.

IMPERIAL TITLES MATTERED
by Peter H. Wilson, Chichele Professor
of the History of War at the University of Oxford

Karl Theodor was the elector of Palatine and as such, along with the elector of Saxony, held the function of imperial vicar and was entitled to use imperial prerogatives during an interregnum. It was common for the Saxon and especially the Palatine electors to use their powers to promote clients, and Karl Theodor did this in Thompson's case in the interregnum between the death of Emperor Leopold II and the election of Francis II. Only emperors or the two vicars during interregna could confer full nobility, i.e., noble titles, with validity anywhere in the empire. The rank of count was senior, outranking baron (*Freiherr*) and knight (Ritter), so Thompson would have used it in preference to his English knighthood. The Duke of Marlborough also changed his coat of arms to reflect his status as imperial prince (1705–22). Imperial titles mattered. Victorious at the Battle of Blenheim, which allowed Emperor Joseph to have the principality of Mindelheim, the duke became Prince of Mindelheim (prince trumping duke).

There was a long tradition of foreigners entering the ranks of the imperial nobility, especially for military service. This was a lot less common by the late 18th century than during the early 17th. As an American, Rumford would also have stood out. He needed his status to assert his authority during his period as senior general of the Palatine-Bavarian army. This was not a happy period for him, as many of his reforms were unpopular and met with resistance from other senior officers.

Contemporaries distinguished between "personal" and "territorial" titles in the Holy Roman Empire. Aristocratic and princely titles linked to constitutional rights (such as representation in imperial institutions like the Reichstag) were tied to specific territories (i.e., the legally distinct pieces of land making up the Holy Roman Empire). Thus, whoever legally inherited or ruled a particular territory received its associated title and rights. Personal titles developed through the award of comital or princely status to individuals without any associated territory. Sometimes they possessed territory (like a fief of an imperial knight) that might be simultaneously "upgraded" to match their new status, but this became much harder to achieve after constitutional changes in 1653. Nonetheless, acquisition of a personal title was still the first step towards joining the ranks of the full imperial aristocracy. Recipients would try to buy a suitable territory and then get it formally associated with their new rank. Their name would change in line with the most prestigious territory they possessed, even if they had a family name usually deriving from an (often subsequently lost) ancestral home. For example, the Habsburgs derived their name from the Habichtsburg castle in Switzerland but were known as Archdukes of Austria, Kings of Bohemia, etc., after their more prestigious possessions.

All this is a preamble to saying that those receiving new personal titles often lacked territories to associate them with. They were sometimes given made up names, like Philipp Fabricius, who was one of the three Habsburg officials thrown out of the window in the Defenestration of Prague (1618) and was subsequently ennobled as "von Hohenfall" (of the High Fall). Various Irish and Scottish officers serving the Habsburgs during the Thirty Years War were ennobled with (sometimes spurious) names from estates they claimed to possess in their homelands. Thus Thompson was following a long tradition.

The idea of "nations" defined linguistically emerged only in the fifteenth century, so earlier notions of "foreigner" do not match those of our own era. The Holy Roman Empire was never a German nation state, and even in the eighteenth century, Czech and Slovenian were recognized as "national" languages in "Germany." The tradition that Rumford was a part of really got going in the early seventeenth century when the Habsburgs used their position as emperor to reward the various officers from Italy, Britain and elsewhere by ennobling them.

Usually the person was addressed by the most prestigious rank, although conventions differed in England, where contemporaries often had only a shaky grasp of foreign ranks and titles. Privileges varied depending on whether the title was personal only or also territorial. The real value of the personal title was the aristocratic status it conferred. Aristocrats were personally "free" and "noble," able to command deference from their inferiors, including taking precedence when entering and leaving buildings. They were also exempt from punishments considered degrading (unless degradation was specified for them by a court determined to punish particularly heinous behavior). For example, nobles were normally beheaded, whereas commoners were hung.

Once one became a count of the Holy Roman Empire, it was a hop, skip and jump to be ennobled by George III, despite the fact that the king had balked at making Thompson a full colonel for his services in America. One sympathizes with the king, who thought the conclusion of the war left him with enough colonels.

That Thompson never fell out of favor with the Bavarian regents is a remarkable leitmotif of his story. He certainly complained of enemies at the court, but several reasons for his staying power emerge. First, Bavaria was, after Prussia, the most powerful German state whose ruler had diplomatic issues but was not racked by war. Second, having a courtier who darted from England to Italy to France to England had advantages in terms of prestige and information gathering. Third, Karl and his cousin and successor Maximilian were personally fond of Thompson.

Thompson contrary to Struensee believed in enlightened despotism. Even the castaway hero of *Robinson Crusoe* (1719) could only imagine himself into that form of government on his island, i.e., being a king with "no rebels among my subjects." Baron Cuvier, Thompson's eulogist, would say Thompson regarded the government of China as coming "nearest to perfection" by "giving over the people to the absolute control of their only intelligent men."

SINOPHILIA
by Jedidiah Kroncke, professor of law, FGV São Paulo

During the late 18th century, Americans were among the world's leading Sinophiles. Europeans of the era, especially the English, still sought luxury goods from China, and they had also begun to reject China as a social exemplar as they attempted to grow in confidence as imperial powers. Americans explored Chinese commerce for material goods and gain but were initially committed to an anti-imperial stance. This was represented, in part, by the iconic Boston Tea Party, where it was Chinese tea that was dumped into Boston Harbor in defiance of the English ban on direct American trade as a colonial possession.

Part of this more amenable stance toward China included a strong persistence of the original Jesuit infatuation with Chinese governance that had inspired Enlightenment figures such as Leibniz and Voltaire to argue for European emulation of China. Founding-era intellectuals commonly possessed artistic and scientific interests in China ranging from architecture to agriculture but also actively sought out treatises on Chinese law and administration. Thomas Jefferson and Benjamin Franklin were the leading American Sinophiles of this age, attracted to China's claims to meritocratic civil service and the ideals of secular rationality. While such texts were in rare supply, other Founders lobbied Jefferson to help provide them information on Chinese practices, and Franklin's interest was deep enough to inspire him to write columns for the *Pennsylvania Gazette* as if he were Confucius. While some of this dynamism would erode over the course of the 19th century as China's international status came under continued assault, the curiosity and interest of late 18th century Americans in China was a sign of their general commitment to a cosmopolitan world view that energized the foundations of the new republic.

Thompson ascribed to the popular economic philosophy of his time, "physiocratie," whereby a ruler's wealth derived not from accumulated gold or domination of world trade but from productive agricultural labor. The theory was developed in France, inspired by the agricultural society of China (laissez-faire is a translation from Chinese *wu wei*), and became familiar to Karl Theodor through his French education.

Count Rumford gestated inventions. To say he invented something in Paris, London or Munich doesn't take account of his approach: see a problem, solve it, generalize and publish on it. And being tenacious, if he addressed cooking pots he considered the source of heat, the fuel, their appearance, how to clean them, and variations for domestic use or large groups. It is accurate, though, that much of his science was carried out during the Munich years of 1784–1795 and broadcast by the publication of his essays in, initially, England. Then he returned to England for the purpose of publishing his essays on heat and public institutions for the poor. Many of his manuscripts were taken when his trunk was stolen from his carriage in St. Paul's Churchyard, a blow from which he recovered after pouring his misery out in letters to Lady Palmerston. He soon went to Dublin and made improvements in hospitals and other institutions there, and then outfitted the kitchen of the Foundling Hospital in London. While he continued to work for the Prince and was only leaving on an extended leave of absence, he was seen as a dove in violent times and he had few cards to play in Munich. Only a crisis of appeasing the big powers of Prussia and France, who were ready to swallow Munich, would bring him briefly back into political power in Bavaria, coincidentally when he brought his American daughter to Munich.

He wrote at this time that he "had not had less than 500 smoking chimneys under his hands."[14] He helped establish soup kitchens and poorhouses in England and Ireland, and steam cooking in institutions. Models of his fireplaces, stoves and cooking utensils were put on display, as he refused to take out patents for his inventions.[15] Since as a scientist it was characteristic of Thompson to turn his mind from studying a natural law to its applications in daily life, his published papers usually begin with the telling of a trivial incident or accident that made him see the lacunae of information on the subject, then they describe his experiments and end with deductions and applications. From the study of heat he proceeds to cooking apparatuses and his pea and barley (later adding potatoes) "Rumford" soup.

8

The Highborn Sisters (Mid–1780s)

> I had just as much love as you had virtue.—Choderios de Laclos, *Les Liaisons Dangereuses* (1782)

The amorous adventures of Benjamin Thompson picked up speed in Germany and Italy. Now a mature and solo person Thompson became a sophisticated dessert for elite women whose main course was a life with their affluent and distinguished husbands. Several of these women cared for Thompson with steadfast affection. Their husbands were away or not giving them attention and Thompson's sexual conduct managed to escape troubling scrutiny. Influenced by his projects for the betterment of society and advancing applied technology, the several noblewomen gained more attention from him and more purpose in life, e.g., by working on a hospital or charitable establishment of his design or by encouraging publication of his essays.

The pattern for Thompson's love life was that women looked to him for sexual and intellectual divertissement and gave back favors such as access to power, help seeing his works got wide publication (and translation), and, last but not least, holidays in their castles. He had extraordinary success in *les affaires de coeur*. He was alluringly different. He had energetic physicality without debauchery and loved to recreate in the out of doors all his life. He discussed weighty issues with men and women indiscriminately. His genius made him attractively elusive, as his greatest quest was not Eros but to understand physical phenomena.

Thompson was a courtier but he related to his world, and talked, like a scientist. He was said to be a little boring when he went on about physics and technology, yet the women who loved him were glad to have him share more with them than wit and woodland rambles. Due to their education and curiosity they could bridge the distance with him. The inventor-courtier represented an attractive package—handsome, intelligent, and presentable—and he treated women well. These ladies tended to be in a position to have liaisons without repercussions. That several came to love him deeply and became melancholic over the partialness of these affairs did not mean he was a knave. Rather, partialness was doubly built in because of his wife in America and the archetype of singlehood in the officers' corps of the armies of Europe. He was their object not vice versa. Thompson was susceptible to sophisticated elite women and acceptable in their milieu. The seesaw of relationship became unbalanced when a mistress's feelings intensified, yet he continued to make himself, if irregularly, available. The ladies were, after all, married, and that had to diminish the scope yet increase the spice of the liaisons, adding an element of tension and irresolution. Yet for all that these women were safely secure in position and finances and aware that the friendship with Thompson was worthwhile. For a man who had to be on front stage in the elite circle around the Bavarian court but who had a private and retiring nature, the solution was liaisons with the aristocratic women who did not ask too much and gave of themselves privately.

At court Thompson was new and American had a baton of power. Thus he also had enemies. As a stranger in a new land often will, he must have quickly established a special rapport with one family, the Lerchenfelds, and their two daughters. The Lerchenfeld family's influence extended from northern Italy to Austria. Josepha, her sister, Maddelena (Mary), and their parents moved between properties in Italy and Germany, their home in Munich being a social center for the cultural elite. Josepha was a married woman, Maria Josepha Lerchenfeld, Countess of Baumgarten, sometimes spelled Paumgarten (1762–1816) when she began an affair with Thompson. Her husband was Hermann Joseph Paumgarten. He was 54 and she 17 when they wed. As he was a count and gentleman in waiting to the prince, and her father was but a Freiherr (baron) the marriage elevated her. The same year they married she had her first child, Karl Theodor Joseph (1779–1852). The child's first names came from the prince and her husband, and the child may well have been the prince's; however, to name one's son after the sovereign was also common.

Countess Baumgarten (circa 1790), attributed to Moritz Kellerhoven (New Hampshire Historical Society).

The Lerchenfelds' house off the Schwabingergasse was only a few houses away from the palace of the Baumgartens, which became one of the leading addresses in Munich's cultural life after Josepha and Hermann Joseph's marriage. Right next door to the Lerchenfelds is where Thompson moved in when he first arrived in Munich. It took letters of introduction to approach people of status, but as Thompson's first appointment was as tutor of the illegitimate son of the prince, he was aware of his boss's affairs and had a back (as well as front) entrance to the court.

Once he had formally met Josepha it would have been a simple matter for Thompson to see her. He knew he could benefit from her salon and she knew that he was special and had a prepossessing future. Through Josepha, Thompson, who was not outstandingly skilled in court etiquette, had access to other privileged families. Every day was made easier because Josepha was his dainty slipper in the door. That he was a welcome guest, perhaps a fixture, at the Lerchenfelds is attested by the fact that he designed for their house a new kitchen he later published as a prototype for his new cooking methods.

Josepha's younger sister, Maddelena Lerchenfeld (1770–1810), was, when Benjamin met the Lerchenfelds, fourteen years of age. He called her familiarly "Mary" and whether or not he became the lover of the younger sister he was close to her and valued her as a critical reader of his work because she spoke English "uncommonly well."

Josepha was a butterfly. She was already entertaining diplomats and important figures at court when she met Thompson. She was conscious, as a young adolescent, of the fact that having visits from the glamorous genius, as well as from Wolfgang Mozart, added to her cachet; also, she found the conversation of foreign gentlemen more entertaining than of local ones (her beauty had impressed several ambassadors.) Mozart would actually state that the Lerchenfelds' was the most useful house to him as he ingratiated himself at Munich. Thompson must have breathed with relief when he realized that he had an Ariadne to help him through the maze of social conventions of a foreign court.

Josepha had Thompson's child, Sophia, whom he called "Sophie," on August 17, 1788, within the purlieus of light friendship with him. Sophia was accepted as a Baumgarten. This was Josepha's sixth child. Josepha's younger sister, Maddalena, soon became a countess too when she married Dinadano Nogarola (1753–1827), who belonged to a noble family tracing to 1410 and was in the service of the prince of Bavaria.

At court the beautiful, vibrant Josepha had achieved the post of mistress to Karl Theodor while, during her liaison with him, having five children. That Thompson slept with and impregnated the prince's mistress did not damage his career in Munich, but it could have swung the other way. The continuing favor bestowed by both Karl Theodor and his successor on Thompson derived from the latter's primary identity: he lay outside the club and demonstrated industry and effectiveness, and even if he had an affair with the prince's favorite lady he was never a threat.

Bavaria's haut monde was dazzling. Though a very earnest person, Thompson liked to be surrounded by gaiety. Munich's high society felt right to Thompson from the first moment. Contemporaneous travelers to Bavaria observed a party mood, free and easy relations between the sexes of high rank, and many illegitimate births. The court of the duke was a realm of intrigues and affairs (typically, the child Thompson himself fathered would never take his name).[1] Munich offered music, recreational riding, fine clothes, and sumptuous balls, and Thompson loved it. He must have been separated out for no interest in wine or lavish food, however. He responded to feminine kindness and seemed to have an instinct for friendship with women. He talked to them as intelligent people. A woman in Italy complained of his going on about science but Lady Palmerston would correspond with him on practical matters about his inventions. Baroness de Kalb helped agent the publication of his essays, and Countess Nogarola translated his work into Italian, as well as helped him with French and German writings. Thompson received the almost universal approval of women of the haut monde. In Munich Josepha and Mary remained friends with him for a long time, and he was friendly with their husbands as well.

Early in his time in Munich, Thompson was diplomatically persuading members of the avant-garde Bavarian secret society, the Illuminati, to operate as an Enlightenment influence in the public domain and under and Karl Theodor's benign authority.[2] Thompson and the prince did not accept the idea of a state in a state. Thompson was, as it were, a card-carrying Mason who came to control these clubs, making their potential effective for the state. Count Baumgarten was his friend and a fellow member. Thompson may have met Josepha's husband at court, at his in-laws, through a common interest in the Illuminati, or riding and hunting. With the sisters, Thompson went on excursions rowing on a lake or hiking, and he made extended visits to their homes. Whether or not the Countess Nogarola slept with him, the two sisters seem to have tossed him like a ball where he did not too heavily cloud their emotional lives and was a *compagnon* who knew how to be retiring and not disturb one's husband.

Portraits of both countesses are in the New Hampshire Historical Society in Concord, New Hampshire, which also has a portrait of Thompson's mistress in Mannheim, the Baroness de Kalb, discussed in Chapter 11. Johann Georg von Dillis, a priest and Thompson's protégé, a leading portraitist and landscape painter of the day, also painted Countess Baumgarten and Thompson together. The watercolor, which was exhibited at the Frick Museum and is in a private collection in Germany, depicts them from the back as they enjoy a climbing outing in picturesque surroundings. It is in the spirit of Asher B. Durand's famous *Kindred Spirits* of a half century later. It may have been discretion not to show their faces, or this may have been an artist's way of focusing the eye on the woodland scene. A third figure in the painting is suspected to be Countess Nogarola. Over many years, Dillis was woven into the friendship set comprising the countess sisters, Thompson and Lord and Lady Palmerston, friends Thompson had made on his holiday in Europe (see Chapter 9). Thompson was a patron of Dillis's and introduced the painter's work to the noted art collector Palmerston.

It is telling that all the three *compagnons* of Thompson from his 30s until his 50s whose paintings belonged to him or his daughter Sally were painted as glamorous, vivid ladies and individuals. Lady Palmerston, curiously because her husband was such an avid collector, was painted modestly, even dowdily, dressed with her hair covered. The elegant lady in Lord Palmerston's dining room was Lady Hamilton.

It is interesting that in his careful, scholarly account, *Rumford: Rezepte für ein besseres Bayern*, Thomas Weidner calls Josepha, Mary and the count a ménage à trois. Even more important is Weidner's affirmation of how unusually secretive, when court gossip was rampant, Thompson's relations with the sisters were. Weidner actually calls it a "conspiracy of silence" and found no answers to why Josepha's husband, Joseph Karl Baumgarten, drowned in the prime of life on October 26, 1790. Was he an inconvenience to the prince or another lover of Josepha's? According to Weidner, Josepha even before this time was leading the life of a *strohwitwe*, or grass widow. In this era people of high society, like those of lowest rank, sometimes disappeared without any investigation. This is the only available explanation for Count Baumgarten's death.

Sarah Rolfe Thompson died on January 29, 1792, after years of being unwell. "A correspondent" to the *Concord Herald* eulogized her: "She was possessed of a noble and strong mind—her liberal hand was ever open to the poor and needy; being possessed of a fortune sufficient, she never neglected to show her benevolence to every class of the human race. She has left a son and daughter—the former now at the University of Cambridge—the latter an amiable young lady, worthy the attention of any gentleman. Tread lightly on her ashes, ye fair sex, for she was your kinswoman weed her grave clean, ye females of Genius, for she was your sister."[3] Now Benjamin Thompson was a widower after 16 years of marital separation. When he came to London in 1795 he wrote Sally to meet him there. Sally, 22, arrived in late winter 1796, staying in London for under a year and Bavaria for more than two. She recounted her life story when she was in her sixties, focusing on this period in her early twenties in Europe, in an unpublished manuscript called "Memoirs of a Lady, written by herself."[4] She drew the account from her diaries for Loammi Baldwin's second wife, Margery, in the years 1842–1845, as well as reminiscing in many letters, especially to the wife of George Baldwin.

It was a threat to the Bavarian regime that forced Thompson to return to Munich at Karl Theodor's precipitous call. The prince had left the city for Saxony in August 1796 in advance of a possible Austrian attack. Sally went with her father and the trip ended in celebration, as Thompson saved the city by diplomacy, engaging first the Austrian general and then the rival French generals, so neither side entered the city. True to form, Thompson took the occasion of so many soldiers being in Munich to carry out experiments in cooking on a large scale. On the return of the duke, Sally was made a countess with a lifetime income of one-half her father's pension. She became the first American-born countess, a mixed blessing, as no one would know what to make of her status in New England or she of herself.

The affairs of the count were not publicized and when Sally came to Munich she must have initially seen that her father had only women friends. Eventually of course she would hear rumors about Josepha and her father and see that when her father brought a female guest to the palace, e.g., Laura de Kalb, he disappeared into his rooms without inviting either Sally or the Countess Nogarola (who was present as often) to come to his rooms for chocolate. In fact, the countess was so much a part of the count and Sally's daily life that when Sally in the sunset of life gave a "farewell" gift to a friend of a knife, fork and spoon that once belonged to her father, her accompanying note said, "I hope it will not make it less valuable from my having partaken of meals with him with these said articles, as likewise the Countess of Nogarola."[5]

Countess Baumgarten was a talented and ardent soprano. At 18 and recently married she became the intermediary between Karl Theodor's commission to Mozart to compose *Idomeneo*. She was at that time considered the mistress of the prince and was a celebrated beauty. All known sources agree that the countess helped with Thompson's rise. She had influence with the prince when, and if, she was no longer his court mistress. Because Charles Theodor retained feelings for her, she might have wielded power like a Madame de Pompadour or Madame de Maintenon at Versailles, except that reports are that she was frivolous, carefree, just liked to sing and did not keep her svelte figure. Moritz Kellerhoven's portrait of her against a landscape—dating from 1787 and presumably painted for Thompson—and the Dillis watercolor on the cover of this book suggest the countess loved the outdoors. As noted earlier, the love affair of Josepha and the count led to the birth of a daughter, Sophie (Sophia Baumgarten, 1788–1828).

Either previously or (less likely but some biographers believe) concurrently, the celebrated beauty was the mistress of the prince and remained in his good graces.

Wolfgang Mozart composed the aria of *Idomeneo* for her to perform in 1780. He wrote his father, Leopold Mozart, on November 13 in code (the initial letters of each noun forming the ciphered word) that he was conscious of the sexual liaison between the celebrated beauty Countess Baumgarten and the Duke of Bavaria. The bon vivant duke had a sad core. His only son died within hours of a forceps delivery and his wife was cautioned against further pregnancies, but Karl Theodor, a Catholic regent, stayed married. Nevertheless he had many mistresses and many children. His wife died in 1794 and as he had no legitimate heir he quickly married a teenage second wife, a marriage that did not produce offspring.

The affair of the Countess Baumgarten and Thompson began in Thompson's first years in Munich, sometime after 1784. Their daughter, Sophie, was raised as a Baumgarten child, with Thompson looking on in the self-regarding 18th century male way. When Count Baumgarten died in October 1790 the love affair would not necessarily have been more open, as a widow had to wear widow's weeds. It is thought, according to Thomas Weidner, senior curator of the Munich City Museum and a Rumford scholar, that the affair went on for a number of years. How could it be so acceptable for the prince's mistress to have the child of his courtier? According to Dr. Weidner in a personal communication on June 22, 2016, "due to living in a court during the ancient regime, it was delicate, of course, but not unusual."

Typical of the times, Sophie was betwixt and between. An out-of-wedlock child normally would not have the same last name as the legitimate children, not to mention a noble rank. Thompson was fond of Sophie. He told Lady Palmerston that six-year-old little Sophie was perfectly well and as beautiful as an angel. Sometimes, as he did in August of that year, he referred to Sophie as "your little friend" to Lady Palmerston, implying she had met Sophie in Munich.[6] Having the child with Josepha was an ambivalent experience. He felt affection for Sophie but was chary lest the relationship with Josepha bind him in fetters. "What a beast!" he proclaimed to Lady Palmerston,[7] reflecting on his foible of sex with the countess.

It can affect a man mortally to have a child by a woman in an affair that he envisioned as a passing fling. As he began to see Sophie as an individual, the count wanted to relate to her and influence her upbringing. He must have enlisted Josepha's sister, Mary, in the idea of having Sophie live with her instead of with the arty mother. The father who absents himself on purpose often becomes curious and thus wants to be involved over time. Thompson's interest became trained on the child as his memory of the relationship and hassles with the mother faded. Thus he told Lady Palmerston he regretted his fling with Josepha but he cared for Sophie, who "often came to dine," and concocted some sort of initiative for Sophie, when she was no longer a tot but a sentient child, to live in the placid household of Mary Nogarola: "I do not see her as often as perhaps I should do—were she not quite so—(the word is composed of nine letters)—As an old acquaintance I cannot quite neglect her, but she sometimes makes *me* blush."[8]

This comment is telling about each of the three—Thompson and the two Marys. It emphasizes his gentlemanly character, as well as hints that he was generally dignified in his sexual affairs, which were along the same lines as his relation with her (Lady Palmerston). At the same time, Countess Baumgarten was, his reference to blushing suggests, racy and indelicate. She was his first mistress after coming to work for the Elector, popular, vivid, and likely willful or aggressive in choosing her lovers. Meanwhile, Mary (Countess Nogarola) did watch over Sophie, who also visited Verona. Tension between the wild and flamboyant singer sister and the quiet *comme il faut* sister is exhibited in two letters Mary in Verona would write Sally Thompson when Sophie was ten and showing more personality.

> March 22, 1798—I did your errand with my parents and Sophie. They all send you their affectionate regards. I wish I could say something pleasant of the latter, but she is more frivolous than ever and I confess I feel my interest in her growing less, though, on the other hand I realize she has improved greatly in form and superficial charm.[9]

On April 15, 1798, Mary alluded to an unnamed plan Thompson had for his daughter, doubtless related to her education given his pleasure over an earlier present to her of a clavichord:

I received one letter from my sister, but simply compliments and excuses for her silence, but she doesn't make the slightest mention of the plans that your father communicated to me touching on Sophie; which makes me fear that she [my sister] only relented for the moment to his entreaty ["à ses instances"], and that she is no more disposed than formerly.[10]

Mary Nogarola and Benjamin Thompson were confidants and dear, fast friends. The intimacy of their friendship trumped the amorous liaison that Countess Baumgarten had with Thompson. Mary was ready to point out her sister's faults and Josepha did not fall in with Thompson's plan, from a critical distance, for Sophie.

Sally may have dryly called Sophie "the beautiful illegitimate" but she also played with her at court when Sophie was nine or ten and was determined to be sisterly to her no matter her jealously. Perhaps Sally's primary concern was lest her father remarry, which caused her to keep an eye on whether his servant Aichner wore a white cockade in his hat (a sign the employer was engaged). Discerning but also judgmental, Sally wrote that Sophie suffered from possessing the same trifling character as her mother. After her marriage, Sophie's surname became Miletz. In a note Emma Burgum wrote we find the following: "She marries a nobleman by the [name] of Milteese, but who proved so unfeeling … first to destroy her health then her mind … dying in a mad-house at Geneva in Switzerland."[11] Much later, Thompson remarked to Sally on Sophie's being sick when he made a trip to Munich in around 1810.

Having carried out a diplomatic maneuver to prevent the warring Austrians and French from entering and destroying Munich, Thompson was back on track at wanting to beautify the city, an ongoing enterprise for which he had Karl Theodor's imprimatur. Embarking on a new project at Lake Starnberg for the prince, Thompson wrote Lady Palmerston zestily: "As to myself, I am to be ranger for life with the unlimited powers to plant, build, and beautify. What do you think of this scheme."[12]

Thompson thought his daughter was becoming a fine lady and was enjoying herself. It was not until March 1797, at the 44th birthday party Sally gave for her father, that a shadow fell. Sally became aware of a quiet scandal involving her father. Countess Baumgarten was absent at the party. Her sister, Countess Nogarola, said gently to Sally that this was why little Sophie's father was paying attention to her. Sally knew now for the first time she had a half-sister.

Both Josepha and Mary were musical. Josepha sang and collected music, while Mary, suiting her personality, played the harpsichord and was more of an accompanist. Josepha and Mary's daughter were immortalized by having a piece of music by a great composer dedicated to them. In Munich the director of theater and opera, Count Seeau (1713–1799), brought in new, lighter genres and energized the scene of opera and theater, but his part in taxation made him unpopular with the people; also, he was Viennese and had come originally to the court in Munich on the lam. Sunday, November 12, 1780, Seeau presented W.A. Mozart to Duke Karl Theodor as he was coming out of mass in the court chapel. The same day, the orchestra leader took Mozart to lunch at the home of Countess Baumgarten. There must have been shop talk, as the stage manager, ballet master and Seeau were present.

Mozart reported to his father, Leopold: "This is the best and most useful family for me. I owe them my good fortune here and, God willing, things will continue in this way. She is the lady with a Foxtail sticking out of her Ass, and she has V-shape chains dangling On her ears, and a beautiful Ring. I saw It myself, even if death should Take me, I, unfortunate man, without a Nose." Mozart imbedded code in the nonsense, the initial, capitalized letters spelling out "favoriten," an allusion to Countess Baumgarten's being Charles Theodor's mistress.[13]

The countess must have made special contact with Mozart. The Greek Electra, daughter of Agamemnon, in the opera sang the aria he dedicated to Countess Baumgarten. Mozart took the opera type but gave more dramatic realism, which is why discussion with the theater production people was of importance to him. Writes a music historian, "After the performances of the opera were over, Mozart wrote for her the aria, 'misera, dove son,' K. 369.... If Mozart was right, hers was the final weight that tipped the balance with the Duke and decided him to commission Mozart." Notably, Mozart dedicated six violin sonatas, KV 301–306, to the Duke's wife as well. Karl Theodor commissioned 24-year-old Mozart to write an opera for the "court carnival" after Seeau introduced him. *Idomeneo*, an opera serial, carnival in the sense it was mythological and for a court occasion, was first performed on January 29, 1781.[14]

Thompson's relationship with Countess Nogarola had the traction of intellectual exchange and offering sisterly support. Mary showed herself very sincere in her letters, and one's impression is that her intimacy with Thompson might have lasted longer than her sister's. For fourteen years, until her death, Mary was Thompson's friend and then his daughter's. Writing Lady Palmerston in 1794, Thompson said that the mother of these two women might suppose he would have sex again with the mother of his child, but the sister, Countess Nogarola, was his intimate friend and love interest—as evidenced by his long stays with her, his wish to travel with her, and her devotion to his daughter (for which her motives were never revealed). As one does of a lover, she recalled (1798) the following: "It was five years yesterday since he first came to this country." Her son died as a teenager but her daughter Thérèse would be the toast of Paris and immortalized in a piece of music by Chopin. Born in Munich, Mary Nogarola described herself in a letter to Sally as a German woman. But the family estate where Thompson spent much time was in Verona, Italy. He joined her and her children in July 1793, traveling from Milan to Verona. It is from Sally that a description of the Countess Nogarola and her close friendship to Sally's father can be gleaned. Thompson wrote from Munich, on a short stay before returning to Paris, that Countess Nogarola sent Sally "100 compliments."

By spring 1794 Thompson had left Naples and traveled forth; he stayed three or four months with Countess Nogarola in Verona. He would have been no fun if he had been forced to live as a bored aristocrat and while there he worked on the kitchens in two local hospitals. The countess had died when Thompson visited Munich in about 1810.

Silvia Curtoni Versa wrote a tribute to the Countess Nogarola, extolling her beauty, good character and skillfulness and pointing out that when her son died she educated her daughter to a superior level. Curtoni Versa was penning a type of poetry that also pointed out character weaknesses, but with regard to the countess she gave only praise.[15] Some of the passages of Curtoni Versa that describe the countess are as follows, translated by Marco Girardi of the Biblioteca Civica of Verona into modern English:

> *Attiva negli affari domestici*
> [She deals with domestic and family chores];
> *E amorosamente sollecita al letto, non sol de' parenti ammalati, ma pur delle am:*
> *celle, che assiste con ispirito di religiosa carita fino agli estremi della vita*
> [She takes care of ill people, not only relatives, but also staff people, until their death];
> *Nessuma donnesca passione signoreggia la sua anima*
> [Her spirit is free from feminine passions];

Non desiderio di galante corteggio
[She is not attracted by flirts];
Non volubilita di umore
[Her mood is not unstable];
Comparisce al pubblico elegante nel vestito senza avvedersene
[She is naturally elegant when in public];
Cortese nelle maniere, e d'un nobile riservato contegno
[Her attitude is polite and honest];
Nulla per se esige, et tutto merita
[She doesn't ask anything for herself, while she achieves everything].

When the poet complimented the countess's "translation of a public institution work from English to Italian" she was referring to Thompson's first essay on public establishments for the poor in Bavaria (1798). Silvia Curtoni Versa also dedicated some pages to "Maddalena Lerchenfeld" (Maddalena was Mary's birth name and Lerchenfeld her maiden name) in her *Ritratti*: "It is a flood of praise. She is delicate, blond, with dark eyes, noble bearing and dress. Every gesture is graceful. She is educated, multilingual, translates from English. She has a generous spirit. She plays the piano forte with a style original and inimitable. Saddened by the death of her only son she transferred her efforts to the education of her daughter."

Luisa Ricaldone of the University of Torino has described the brief character sketch, or portrait, that was fashionable for literary women in Verona in 1800. The genre was "linked to private sentiment, belonging thus to a conceptual and linguistic code considered feminine, dealing with matters of the heart, of individual feelings and affections." These portraits, or "ritratti," "turn on a parallel drawn between physical appearance and character, moving from physiognomy to intellectual inclination." A sketch of this genre of eulogy might list a failing, but Silvia wrote ones that piled on the compliments in total praise. Silvia, according to Professor Ricaldone, depicts noblewomen who are part of the Enlightened Catholic culture and who favor social reform and charity. Silvia denounces the destruction, suffering, and disease brought by the Napoleonic campaigns.[16]

That the poet especially noted that men did not turn the countess's head as they did many women is baffling. Why did she accentuate this? It serves as a hint that Thompson and the Countess Nogarola may have had closeness without sexual intimacy. On the other hand is Thompson's remark to Lady Palmerston that he was not interested in renewing the affair with the sister, seeming to imply that Countess Nogarola had replaced her.

Von Dillis's painting shows Thompson and his mistress in walking outfits, hiking. This period witnessed the beginning of the popularity of hikes, which men and women could enjoy together rambling, as well as the beginning of seeing the landscape of the Alps as a pretty view instead of one inspiring terror. Dillis was a forerunner of the Impressionists; besides doing portraits, he liked to paint in open air. Josepha Baumgarten is the figure wearing black, as she was in mourning for her husband, who died the year before. A note on the back of the watercolor attests to the identity of Thompson and Josepha. The third figure is likely to be her sister, Countess Nogarola. She has a look as though she is attending the movements of the pair. Thompson is tall and thin and carries the only walking stick.

Thompson would have been acquainted with Mary Nogarola's only surviving child when he was in Paris at the start of the 18th century, referring to her, "Teresa," as the daughter of his friend. Sally knew her too and called Thérèse charming when she was six, in 1796. Mary Nogarola's daughter, "la divine Thérèse," must have been as enchanting as her aunt. Chopin dedicated to Thérèse his Nocturnes opus 27 numbers one and two, composed in 1837.

Lady Palmerston (1800) by George Engleheart (Christie's, 2002). The next Viscount Palmerston became British Prime Minister. While he was Foreign Secretary, Sally wrote the Baldwins, "I have a very pretty miniature of his mother which she gave me. My Father was very intimate with the present Lord Palmerston's Father and Mother." August 21, 1840, AAAS.

Mary Nogarola's daughter married the Count Apponyi, an Austrian diplomat who had different posts from a young age and served as minister to Florence in 1814, ambassador to Rome in 1819 and then ambassador to Paris, where Teresa (Thérèse) was a popular figure in the latter. In 1823 Jean-August-Dominique Ingres did a pencil drawing on paper of her as a mature woman. She and her husband entertained a great deal, continuing to give balls in 1816. She had children and died at a young age, like her mother, when the children were not yet grown. The second wife of the Count Apponyi, a friend of Teresa's who was also from Italy, raised the children and earned their affection.

Teresa's eldest child, Rudolf, went into diplomacy like his father and became attaché from Austria-Hungary to Paris. The ties to Central Europe were strong. The family had an ancestral manor in a valley of the Carpathian Mountains. Perhaps Teresa was drawn more in another direction, south to her family in Italy, at the time she and Thompson visited her in Verona, but Rudolf was born in the Apponyi Castle in 1802.[17]

Karl Theodor was on an ice flow due to Napoleon's conquests (Belgium by the end of 1792). Yet the prince did not waver in his support for his American minister. In March 1793 he granted Thompson permission to travel to Italy to convalesce. Thompson would eventually send back via Sir Charles a message to the prince that he was still sick, because he was enjoying Italy too much.

9

An Italian Idyll on Which He Met Lady Palmerston (1793–1794)

> A man who has not been in Italy is always conscious of an inferiority from his not having seen what it is expected a man should see.
> —Samuel Johnson, in Boswell, *The Life of Samuel Johnson* (1791)

It was after Thompson had recovered from an illness (perhaps a relapse of typhoid fever, which had caused prior malaise) that the prince elector gave him leave to travel on an extended tour of Italy, the itinerary during the protracted, 16-month Italian idyll from March 1793 through June 1794 being as follows: Munich-Milan-Pavia-Verona-Florence-Pisa-Rome-Naples-Verona-Munich. The illness had been grave enough to be thought life threatening. The count was, like Benjamin Franklin, famous on the Continent for being a benefactor of the common people. Peasants all over Bavaria lit candles and said prayers for him in churches. They prayed for him again when it was reported he was ill in Naples.

Thompson's travels throughout his life gave him contact with dynamic and eminent individuals, from the English who participated in founding the Royal Institution in London to the members of the French Institute in Paris. But the vacation in Italy turned out to be a sheer idyll lasting a year and four months. He journeyed in two carriages, the second one for servants, followed by two baggage carts. Along his journey, due to his leisure, lady friends became manifestly more central. In Italy he seemed to enjoy his relations with women more openly and freely, to the point that he extended his trip and urged a visitor passing through to tell the prince back in Bavaria he was working hard.

After being forced out of his native land in his early twenties, Thompson never saw his mother, family and best friends of his youth again and was estranged from his wife; really he had no choice but to self-invent. He was, moreover, hungry for love. He didn't think about this all the time. He was a scientist and adventurer. People were emotionally a backdrop even though it looked as if they were central because he was "on stage" in prevailing establishments. He lived at the time when democracy, Jean-Jacques Rousseau, the education of some women, and the quest of Mary Wollstonecraft for women's equality with men were topical. He had men as mentors but women as more intimate friends; he attracted the kind of women who liked the reflected light of extraordinary men. From the time he had made a success of his position in the Bavarian court, everything pointed to friendships with women being the fulcrum of his emotional life. He traveled with women friends, enjoyed music and dancing with them, went on hikes and rode horseback with them.

He had enlightened friendships: he did not trivialize his liaisons or denigrate the women and even when the sexual closeness was paused the relationships endured. Surely in Italy as in Munich his relationships had a physical dimension—the enjoyment of horseback riding, rowing, walking, hiking and dancing. The importance to him of these women emerged when he had interludes of leisure, this being so especially when, with the Prince of Bavaria's blessings, he visited Italy for the first time.

Eight years before Thompson's trip, Goethe went to Italy for two years beginning in 1786. He had at this time a sexual liaison with a widow in Rome, which is said to have matured him and altered his work: "This newly liberated erotic spirit trailed him back to Weimar."[1] Thompson's own complicated love affairs in Italy seemed to make him very happy. The young Royalist had come to London during the American Revolution and then worked and lived on the Continent most of his life. According to the general drift of Enlightenment thinking, so long as women conducted themselves by the rules of polite society they could express in conversation independent thought and ideas. Stylish thinkers on the radical fringe, people like William Godwin, were even questioning the institution of marriage as an outdated element of the ancien régime.

When people are traveling they often meet lasting friends from back home. The foreign context seems to bring out valued as well as familiar characteristics, while people are more carefree about whom they associate with and how they spend their hours (a leveling influence). The conditions for the meeting of Count Rumford and Lord and Lady Palmerston (Henry Temple and Mary Mee)—the second Viscount and Viscountess Palmerston—were ideal. Lord Palmerston wasn't able to buy all the art he wanted but he could indulge his love of touring and share sightseeing with his wife and children, or sometimes just his wife. Both were curious and open about new people and Mary Mee would enthuse over Rumford and weave him into the rest of her social life.

Many instances in Thompson's life while he was attached to the Bavarian court verify that he enjoyed opposite-sex friendships. He said during an absence from Lady Palmerston that he felt he was in love with her, yet he traveled with her husband (and children) in Italy and Germany, as he would accompany them when they took their son, the future prime minister (Henry John Temple, Third Viscount Palmerston), off to school in Edinburgh, with Lady Palmerston weeping the entire journey home. This was no ménage à trois like Lord and Lady Hamilton (whom they all knew) and Lord Nelson. Rather, the Palmerstons were outstandingly gregarious. If sexual intimacy did light the match of Lady Palmerston's and Thompson's attachment, it embodied the Enlightenment ideal of free-floating alliances, friendship being, according to Jean-Jacques Rousseau, the most sacred of all social contracts.

With a friend, one could indulge in personal reverie and confession. In December, from Pisa, Thompson wrote Lady Palmerston, in Florence, that he was lonesome and melancholy without her company, "an exile doomed to roam in the wide world, without a home and without a friend." Thompson could also tell Mary Mee when he had a letter from Laura de Kalb and joke with her that if she saw "anything advertised [about a prospective wife] that you think would suit me you will be so good as to inform me of it." His nicest compliment was one day in the winter of 1795 when he was, he grumbled, obliged as a courtier to dine at Karl Theodor's court and "the sight of your handwriting … enlightened my countenance."

With his friends of the opposite sex, Thompson achieved a balancing act: enjoying intimacy without disturbing the woman's identity as a wife. Compounding the error of previous biographical writings that present Thompson's intimates as mistresses is the spicy but groundless claim that the Countess Baumgarten was concurrently Thompson's and Karl Theodor's mistress. That is simply not known. Neither can it be known with certainty that the aristocratic women Thompson met and loved—and who loved him— in Continental Europe ended up having sex with him. I shall make my guesses but what is paramount, as it was then, is discretion.

Early American history scholar Andrew Cayton proposed this theory: "Many of Wollstonecraft's contemporaries were imagining the possibilities of reconfiguring relations within families and states through commerce, moving from an axis of kinship based on consanguineal ties or blood lineage to an axis based on conjugal and affinal ties, of the married couple." Cayton identified a shift that occurred in the late 18th century Anglo-American world: from defining family as a group of people who resided together in a multitude of forms to defining it as a nuclear unit of parents and children. "Suddenly, the term 'friends' meant strictly people with whom there was no connection of blood."[2]

In her rich and thoughtful study, *Founding Friendships*, Cassandra A. Good calls friendships between men and women—"affectionate, reciprocal relationships that the historical actors themselves cast in terms of a friendship"—a "national phenomenon" in the 18th century. It was no less so in Europe, where similarly the friendships were maintained "through exchanges of letters, gifts, and services, establishing a dynamic of reciprocity that erased gender differences and built on the strengths of each friend." Nonetheless, she notes, there was not a word for friendship between a man and a woman in this era: "Although the term 'platonic' existed and was sometimes used to describe friendships between men and women its meaning at the time was most often associated with unconsummated romance. Even the word 'friend' was problematic because of its multiple meanings.… For men and women who became friends, the fact that the term could apply to lovers and spouses complicated their efforts to define the relationships as something apart from conjugal love."[3]

In Milan on June 18 Thompson met Sir Charles Blagden, secretary of the Royal Society, with whom were traveling Lord and Lady Palmerston and their four children. Sir Charles was a close friend of Joseph Banks, a former army physician and explorer to Labrador, as well as the Society's president. Sir Charles was the sort of person everybody knew, and Thompson was traveling in style with many servants and trunks of books and clothes. Lady Palmerston welcomed Sir Thompson as "a great acquisition to our Society."[4] She wrote her brother Benjamin about it:

> This morning, Comte de Rumford, Lord P., Miss C [an employed companion] and I set off at nine and had a pleasant drive to Como.… After we had dined we took a boat and rowed to the opposite shore.… Count Rumford is particularly agreeable and a wonderful pleasant addition to our Society. He draws well, takes sketches as we are on the lake and has a thousand resources. His history is a very extraordinary one and not the least surprising part that as a stranger he should have governed the Electorate of Bavaria for five years, reformed numberless abuses in the state and put the army on a most respectable footing, founded manufactures and almost new modeled the system of government, with the whole kingdom against him and no-one to support him but the Elector who stood by him with the strictest sincerity and gave him the most unbounded confidence.[5]

The Second Viscount Palmerston (1739–1802) was a Whig aristocrat and active member of the House of Commons for most of the long reign of George III. Palmerston first held the position of commissioner of the Board of the Trade and Plantations for colonial territories, while Thompson was apprenticing in Salem. Palmerston cast a vote on the side to give up the dispute in America, which won by a narrow margin. The viscount was a connoisseur, bon vivant, and avid traveler. According to the entry about him in *The Dictionary of National Biography*, he liked to sing popular catches and rounds, he stuttered, and he became friends with Sir Joseph Banks as well as the painter Joshua Reynolds, the actor David Garrick, and the history writer Edward Gibbon.[6] Palmerston had an astonishing social life, detailed in diaries and travel journals from 1765 to 1792, which give an account of who he saw and where he dined every day. Travel helped him get over the loss of his first wife, who died in childbirth. A salonist in Paris gave him an introduction to Voltaire, who asked him to lengthen his stay at Ferney. He bought antiquities more than once from Lord Hamilton in Naples and guided Lord Hamilton and Emma around Paris during their honeymoon.

Revamping the Palmerston country estate Broadlands into a Palladian mansion (the exterior went from Gothic to Georgian, as did Highclere Castle) was a 13-year project done by famous architect and landscape designer "Capability" Brown. It put a cramp on Lord Palmerston's art buying when Brown presented the bill in 1779. Some of Palmerston's love notes had homey bits—he told his fiancé (Frances) that he was getting all the fleas out of Broadlands before her visit. Palmerston also brought in an artist for Captain Cook's second voyage and dined with him on the *Resolution* before Cook set off on his last expedition.

After his first marriage, Palmerston had a mistress named Madame Gallina—the wife of a surgeon in Milan and the daughter of an Italian officer of dragoons—who came to London and met Palmerston in 1778. Palmerston installed her in a house in Great Marlborough Street, but within two years he had tired of her and found her a post as governess with a family she left when the husband made improper advances. Palmerston was then deluged with begging letters from her, and in the end he arranged through a Monsieur le Turc to have her fare paid back to Geneva, where her husband met her, "fortuitously." Palmerston had ascertained that the man wanted his wife back and instructed le Turc to advise Signor Gallina of her movements.

In the fall of 1782 Lord Palmerston noted in his diary a mishap. He was driving two ladies in his phaeton when it "overturned near Stoneham. Miss Mee's elbow dislocated; set very soon by Mr. Mears."[7] As seems to happen in all romance novels about damsels in distress turning their ankles, a romance was kindled. Palmerston soon sent Mary Mee a piece of cloth for a riding habit, in gorge de pigeon, which he assured her was the most fashionable color in Paris that winter, followed by a muff because he had remarked that the color of her muff was not fast and had run onto her skin. Another story is that Palmerston was injured and she nursed him to health, but since the reverse is what Lord Palmerston wrote, his account is more likely the truth. Mary Mee became Henry Temple's second wife. She was the daughter of a London merchant and sister of a director of the Bank of England (but she was not an heiress).

The second Lady Palmerston, Thompson's friend, Mary Mee, was as extroverted as her husband and their hospitality became famous. Thompson could not have become more part of the in-crowd by any friends than the Palmerstons.

As so often happens, travel throws together people of different backgrounds. Lord Palmerston decided to return to Como and then to Switzerland because he had heard about the scenery of the Gotthard Pass. Settling the children at Bern, he and Lady Palmerston made "our rambles from thence." She was "quite sorry that Comte de Rumford will not go with us, but means to return to Verona."[8] Lady Palmerston soon was writing her husband back in England that Thompson "reserves to himself the full privilege, which I hope he will not fail to use, of coming over to England every year. But I fear if he gets deeply engaged and interested in plans to be carried on in Bavaria he will feel less disposed than he now thinks to make such frequent absences." Thompson could take leave from the Bavarian court each year, but he was someone who when focused on a project might not want to detach from it.

It was prescient of Lady Palmerston to put her finger on the difference between her and her husband, grounded in lands and established position, and a brilliant comet like Thompson. He was something new, born of republican America, and what Thomas Jefferson would talk about as the "natural aristoi."[9] But to Lady Palmerston, this wonderful friend was not lesser but rather a bit out of reach because of being self-made and having a job. When she wrote in her diary she was sorry the count would not alter his plans to mesh with those of the Palmerstons to go to Switzerland, she noted that the count "is a Serving Man and those are never to be depended upon,"[10] an uncanny reflection of class differences.

When, at 43, Lord Palmerston married Mary Mee, he was keen on introducing her to his favorite European destinations. The count traveled some in their coach in Italy and would have traveled with them more if he had been free from his obligations back in Munich. Thompson, who had as a schoolteacher done tricks and acrobatics and vaulting, was more likely a lively companion to the Palmerston traveling party than he was a sighing paramour of the mother. From his trip to Italy until the turn of the century, Lady Palmerston became over the next years Thompson's beloved friend and booster and his affectionate correspondent. The rapport she and Thompson had exemplifies the complexity of the line between a friendship and a romance. A curious connection is that on October 16, 1784, the balloonist Blanchard, who had gone up with Thompson's mistress's husband (Dr. Jeffries), came down on a farm that formed part of the Broadlands estate.

To call Lady Palmerston the mistress of Benjamin Thompson is to jump over a huge temporal bridge to that conclusion.[11] Lady Palmerston loved her husband, who was a very popular Whig aristocrat, art collector, social leader, and so forth who spent much of his money making their homes in London and the country beautiful and entertaining all their fascinating friends in arty, scientific and literary circles. One son was the future prime minister and a famous Victorian, and Thompson was there at the tender moment the Palmerstons left the boy, the 3rd Viscount Palmerston, at his school.

Thompson was often a Palmerston houseguest, especially in Italy, where his tour included Verona, Milan, Pavia and Naples. Part of the confusion over whom he slept with during his wifeless interregnum arises from underestimating the custom of the houseguest. The customs around having houseguests favored the lively and undemanding guest who fit in to a situation. The more servants one had and the more civil the relations of husband and wife were, the more a houseguest felt welcome. For a male houseguest to sleep with the lady of the house was a custom often invoked, but it would have to have been exceedingly confidential. Lady Chatterley, for instance, had clandestine sex with a member of her husband's intellectual circle who visited their estate (before she fell in love with the gamekeeper). Then again, Mrs. Ramsay, in *To the Lighthouse*, needed her "core of darkness " to deal with the idiosyncrasies of Mr. Ramsey, her children and her houseguest; and the richer Charles Dickens became, the more his house at Gad's Hill teemed with houseguests. Perhaps the most apt description of the houseguest tradition comes from the Russian novelist Turgenev. In Faust, a distant, well-to-do cousin having a large family and "always a crowd of people" arriving at his palatial country house" invites the narrator to visit: "The days were spent in noisy entertainments, there was no chance of being by oneself. Everything was done in common, every one tried to be entertaining, to invent some amusement, and at the end of the day every one was fearfully exhausted."[12]

Count Rumford—handsome, brilliant, multilingual, and adaptable—became a regular guest at the home of a number of women who were in arranged marriages (the Palmerstons being the only love match among the couples where he was intimate with the wife). To be unsettled was familiar to him. During his visits to and with his lady friends in Italy is when he might, in particular, have borrowed the Latin motto that Sir William Hamilton had on his bedroom wall in the Palazzo Sessa, the British embassy to the Kingdom of Naples: *Ubi bene, ibi patria*—Where I am at ease, there is my homeland.

The month before, on May 8, 154, Thompson's fellow scientist Antoine Lavoisier had been guillotined in Paris. The scenes of terror gave aristocrats all over Europe nightmares. How to appease the masses became a more acute concern as the cry of "*Changer ou mourir*" jangled in their ears. Thompson's success in keeping the indigent fed, clothed and busy in Bavaria made a great impression on the Palmerstons as a palliative to republicanism, Whigs though they were.

An entry in Lord Palmerston's diary, now in the Broadlands Archive of the University of Southampton, illuminates the enthusiasm of Palmerston's travels of discovery (effectively a Grand Tour many times over). Thompson, with his scientific curiosity and desire to appear intrepid, was a lively participant on one trip to Mount Vesuvius (note that Thompson had by now been ennobled as Count Rumford for over a year).

Lord Palmerson on Vesuvius, January 1794

At this time we saw to our surprize Count Rumford who had separated from us early in the ascent with one guide standing on the very edge of the crater during the very moment of an explosion with the stones flying round and over him. We saw him soon after retreating and in his way down we saw him overtaken by another explosion which from the quantity of stones we observed rolling by him alarmed us much. However he came down without material hurt and the account he gave was this. Instead of quitting the lavas when we did and directing his course directly upwards he continued along the edge of them which went upwards in an oblique direction to a point much nearer the summit and where there was much less way to climb up the loose ashes in order to reach it. This was just over the point where the preceding year we used to see the running lava issuing to appearance out of a mouth and first becoming visible. Here he took the resolution of pushing upwards to the edge of the crater which he imagined he could have done in less time than he found it required. During the ascent there were four explosions during which he was obliged to stop to watch and avoid the stones. He arrived at the top edge of the crater which he found very thin just as the smoak of one of the explosions was clearing away. He could then see the sides and the whole circumference tolerably distinct thro' a light thin smoak which was constantly rising. He guesses the diameter at the mouth to be from 120 to 150 feet ... to an opening at the bottom of about 12 or 15 feet from which arose constantly a thick vapour which prevented him from seeing down it. The sides were marked with very bright colours red yellow and green and in one part was a great projection like a shelf. After having waited a very short time he heard the approach of an explosion by a violent noise which seemed to be at a great depth below and which increased as it rose up till at length the head of it issued out of the opening at the bottom of the crater in immense masses of black smoak mixed with great stones which by hitting against each other and against the sides of the passage as they came up and by their shrill noise in passing thro' the air owing to their velocity and the raggedness of their form produced an effect and an appearance thoroughly tremendous. There was very little wind. The greater part of the stones fell into the crater & / those which went beyond the edges fell indifferently in all directions. The large ones passed over C Rumford's head and fell lower down in the side of the cone. A small one fell on his shoulder as he was stooping down and gave him a smart blow which left a bruise but not of any consequence. As soon as the effect of the explosion was over he began to descend as quick as he could in hopes of getting to the place from whence he came which was beyond the range of the stones and out of the direction of their course before another explosion should come on. But in this he was disappointed for there happened one before he had got down which was more violent & threw a greater number of stones than any of the preceding ones. This was what we had seen and to us who were at some distance the stones appeared so thick that we thought it impossible to avoid escape [from] them. However by dexterity and good fortune he contrived to avoid all the large ones many of which passed close to him on each side whistling as they went by like cannon shot and if they had struck him might probably have proved fatal. As to the small ones it was impossible for him to attend to them and many of them hit him but without any material damage. After this we turned back to the Hermitage where we dined and walked down to Portici in the evening.[13]

Lady Palmerston's and Thompson's paths crossed several times that year. He showed Lord Palmerston experiments on cooking and fuel consumption, shadows and the harmony of colors, mostly when they were in Florence. The latter was like a parlor game but of scientific significance all the same, as he showed that when two lights of different colors cast shadows, the shadows were of the complementary color, one real and the other one an illusion. So often solitary, he needed a discerning response to his ideas.

Likely when his Bavarian employer made him a count Thompson chose the name Rumford to commemorate the previous name of Concord, New Hampshire. He had become a country squire in Concord upon his marriage to Sarah Williams Rolfe. It's also possible, as Thompson spent happy times with the Palmerstons at Broadlands near the village of Romford on the Test River, that he called himself Count Rumford after that. Romford Abbey had owned the manor of Broadlands before the Norman Conquest. After the Suppression of the Monasteries by Henry VIII in 1547 it was sold to an aristocrat.

A painting of Emma Hamilton hung in the dining room at Broadlands, the estate Thompson often visited. Possessing a portrait of a woman was a kind of possession of her person. Emma Hamilton's series of lovers and her husband argued over and vied for paintings by famous artists she had posed for. Lord Palmerston commissioned Thomas Lawrence to alter a painting by Joshua Reynolds in order to put Emma at the center. This seems to have been like hanging an Andy Warhol of Marilyn Monroe rather than implying an affair of the viscount with Emma, as Sanborn Brown postulated. The Palmerstons gave evidence of being deeply in love. Lord Palmerston, a Whig in the House of Commons for 40 years, was a bon vivant who loved science and art more than politics. But since he often traveled to Europe to shop for artworks, it was natural for him to carry from his political colleagues some papers to the revolutionaries in July 1789. In September, he was still in Paris when the Hamilton newlyweds came through, and he acted as their cicerone. Palmerston wrote Mary impressions he knew would interest her, that Emma was charming, the marriage seemed devoted, and he hoped to see her perform her celebrated tableaux, the Attitudes, which he did four years later on his Italian tour with his family.

Lady Palmerston did not condescend to Thompson but rather sought his company and later would welcome his daughter into her family circle. A sense of Lady Palmerston comes from what her guests said of her. It is known she entertained actors and artists as well as patricians. When Joshua Reynolds and the actor David Garrick died, Lord Palmerston was a pallbearer at their funerals. Dr. Johnson and Gibbon were other friends. It was remarked that other than posh women were invited to her parties: according to Lord

Glenbervie, she invited "women of equivocal character." At the beginning of the French Revolution, the Palmerstons considered the French revolutionaries enlightened, although their attitude stiffened when violence broke out. Even so, Lady Palmerston evinced egalitarian thoughts.

Relevant to the nature of the friendship of Thompson with Lady Palmerston is the importance of motherhood to her (the same is known of Thompson's other longest female intimate, Mary Nogarola). Mary Mee had five children in a little over five years, beginning with Harry, who would become the 3rd viscount in October 1784. He was followed by Fanny in February 1786, William in January 1788, Mary in January 1789 and Elizabeth in March 1790. Mary died subsequent to inoculation from smallpox but the other children lived to adulthood. Lady Palmerston and Thompson met just after she emerged from an intense period of childbearing and she and Lord Palmerston traveled with children. They made a two-year Continental visit, predominately to Italy and Switzerland. During their exodus, when Lord Palmerston sold his London house in Park Street and purchased a larger one on Hanover Square in August 1792, they were in Paris paying court to the Bourbon royal family in the Tuileries less than two weeks before the revolutionaries stormed it, and little Harry, the future third viscount, played with the ill-fated dauphin. In August 1793 they parked the children in a house on the outskirts of Berne with their tutor and servants and traveled as a couple for a month, shopping for art and playing faro with each other for small stakes. From Paris the Palmerstons went to Italy for the winter, stopping over in Lausanne to see Lord Palmerston's friend Edward Gibbon, who was busy writing the *History of the Decline and Fall of the Roman Empire*. It was fashionable for English aristocrats to pass judgment on Emma Hamilton's attractions and the Attitudes, or classical poses, she took. Lady Palmerston was among the charitable and was favorable in her appraisal.

The trips of British aristocrats on the Continent were done at a leisurely pace and were lengthy. Parties left each other, rejoined by design, and ran into each other by chance. Each encounter, if the people wished, could be the occasion of deepening the friendship. The Palmerstons and Thompson's friendship became fast (while Emma Hamilton was more of a sightseeing monument). Not only would they see one another at various points of Thompson's sabbatical but Mary Mee would visit him in Munich soon afterward.

In early July a Lady Elizabeth Webster was visiting in Milan. Lady Webster's husband, by whom she had five children, was dissipated and violent and gambled recklessly. A way to mitigate the hardship of such an aristocratic mismatch was to spend some time abroad. Italy, particularly after the French Revolution, became a playground of the British, as Napoleon had taken Paris temporarily off the holiday map. Lady Webster gave birth to a son and six months later was traveling in Italy. Here she would become acquainted with her second husband, Lord Holland. In Milan, Lady Palmerston was sympathetic about her female friend's bad marriage. On a day that was unbearably hot and also humid (reminding Lady Webster of extreme heat in England), Sir Benjamin came to call. She was barely recovered from pregnancy (and would become pregnant again in September) and suffering from the heat. Her marriage was in shambles and she would shortly take up with Lord Holland (the next trip to London she would stay briefly with Lord Webster but then move in with Lord Holland and have Lord Holland's child in November 1796). Lady Webster noted the following in her diary: "Saturday, 6th [1793] – The heat unbearable; close suffocating feel, like a hot day in England. Miss Carter [the Palmerstons' companion] and Sir Benjamin dined with me. After dinner, instead of the custom of the country to take the siesta, I took a long-winded discourse from Sir Benjamin upon politics, happiness, mortality, etc."[14] Incidentally, Lady Webster's first husband, to whom she was married then, nearly dueled with her second husband. The score to be settled was not for her but for a portrait of her, a reminder of the importance of a painted portrait in this era.

In Pisa, Thompson made friends with a Lady Bolingbroke, whom he "visited at her own lodgings." He reflected, "Luckily I leave Pisa soon, or I do not know what I might have been tempted to do to cheat away her tedious lingering hours."[15] South of Milan, he and sir Charles visited with Count Alessandro Volta, who showed them his experiments on "metallic electricity" (in contrast to his friend Luigi Galvani's experiments on frog tissue). At the end of July 1793 Rumford wrote Sir Charles and asked him to show them to the prince back in Munich, adding "Don't forget, I beseech you, when you are at Munich that it is for the recovery of my health that I have the Electors permission to travel.—You must therefore take care to make me sick enough, particularly if the Elector should ask after me."[16]

Thompson went next to Verona, where the Countess Nogarola was residing with her children. Her husband was overseeing the fortifications of Mannheim for Karl Theodor. Thompson spent August and September moving around northern Italy, together with the countess at Desenzana on Lake Garda and by himself to Turin and Genoa. He wanted her to come with him south on his journey to Rome and Naples, but someone, perhaps her husband, frustrated the idea. He told Lady Palmerston that "those who thought it in their interest to prevent the journey, tho' they feigned to approve of it, have found means, in an underhanded way, to prevent it."[17]

In October, he left the countess in Verona for Florence and met up with the Palmerstons, perhaps by design. Their feelings for each other were amorous but there isn't proof of what Brown postulated, that their sentiments turned into "a full-fledged love affair" in Florence. Despite the strong emotional pull Mary Mee felt for Thompson and he for her, the considerable archive of letters written by both the Palmerstons seems to indicate that theirs was an ideal, devoted and monogamous marriage. Not only was the marriage a love match, but Mary Mee also had every reason to thank her stars for Henry Temple. He liked sex, gave her thoughtful gifts, took care of her relatives financially and looked after the career of her dear brother Ben, and took her on his travels. When apart they exchanged hundreds of caring letters. After the marriage he spent far more time home and was a good father to their four children.

Josephine probably wouldn't have cheated on Napoleon if she hadn't been worried about her fading looks and infertility; and Mary Mee had no apparent cause to seek a sexual relationship outside her marriage. Friendship was a different matter. Even the day their son (the future prime minister and 3rd viscount) was born, Lord Palmerston preceded its mention by noting the five dinner guests; and from their very first travel adventure the couple, finding their adventures livelier with friends, took a popular bachelor, Henry Englefield, along. At this point, early in the friendship and parted from Lady Palmerston, Thompson expressed sentiments that were about friendship, good company and nostalgia, not romantic yearning: "I have been so long used to your agreeable company that I really feel quite awkward when I am deprived of it."[18]

In Florence for two months, Thompson studied the properties of various gasses with Professor Felice Fontana, who had a well-equipped lab. Fontana had published an important text on viper venom in 1781 and was the most important chemist in 18th century Italy. Also, the Palmerstons came to town. Interested in the harmony of colors affecting the choice of furnishings and clothes, the count did color experiments with the Palmerstons as observers.

Thompson continued his journey south through Pisa, Livorno and Rome, writing Lady Palmerston at length about what fascinated him. Even riding a carriage piqued his curiosity and he wondered whether it would be less tiring for the horses to travel the whole day at a walk or to go faster for four or five hours a day and rest longer in the stable. He noted to Lady Palmerston that he "made some experiments to settle this question; and I found, in fact, that my horses were in much better condition after travelling fifteen days, going eight or ten leagues a day at a trot, than ... going over the same distance at a walk." He arrived in Naples in January (1794), at which point he wrote his old friend Loammi that he wished to be acquainted with his daughter and "to lay a solid foundation for her future happiness." He stayed for the spring and eventually became seriously ill. In France this was the time of the Reign of Terror and in May the father and husband of Thompson's future wife, Madame Lavoisier, were executed.

In September 1793 Emma Hamilton had met Lord Nelson in Naples. Two years earlier Lord Palmerston had given Sir William and Lady Emma a guided tour of Paris. The scenario Brown believed had two pairings, Emma Hamilton and Lord Palmerston, and Benjamin Thompson and Lady Palmerston. Brown wrote, "We know that one of Lord Palmerston's favorite mistresses, Emma Lady Hamilton, frequently joined the Palmerston party during their Italian tour and traveled with them ... just as Rumford did in order to be with the viscount's wife."[19] If Emma Hamilton was riding in the coach with the Palmerstons and Thompson it must have been jovial, but it is fictitious that these four were indulging in sexual follies through the Italian countryside.

In Italy Thompson fastened his attention on various projects that seem inspired by the beauty of the landscape. First he was examining the nature of color and color shadows, going over some of the same turf as Joseph Priestley had in his book on light in 1772 and playing with the color illusions of shadows, the Palmerstons his audience. When he arrived in Naples he puzzled over why the sand on the seashore of the hot baths of Baiae was burning hot yet the water only two or three inches away was cold.

The "Serving Man" had to get back to his employer eventually. When he traveled north he lingered for three or four months with the Countess Nogarola in Verona. There he set out to build new kitchens in a hospital. He proposed to the directors of the hospital that the House of Industry in Munich manufacture clothing for the hospital's use. This would supply "the poor of Bavaria with income and the poor of Verona with clothing." In Verona he also furthered his achievements for kitchen design, replacing the open grate with enclosed insulated fires. In Professor Fontana's laboratory he had proved to his satisfaction that the flame had to be in contact with the cooking pot to maximize the heat exchange from the fire to the pot, and his design had separate fires for each element of the stovetop, a revolutionary change. He applied his concept to improving the kitchens of private families and several convents. He wrote Lady Palmerston that he had no more excuses to offer Karl Theodor and he needed to return to Munich: "People here will hardly believe I have been ill, I look so much better (they say), than I did when I was here last year. How the air of Bavaria will agree with me I dont know, But I own I am much afraid of the experiment, which however I must soon try."[20]

On November 3, 1794, Thompson wrote Lady Palmerston describing an experiment with heat and asking the price of coal in England. He thought his heating improvements would clear the skies of London. This type of letter is hardly in the passionate tone one would expect of lovers. Lady Palmerston was happy with her family and her husband, kind and fair to people of all rank, and sincerely liked Thompson, including him and later his daughter in her closest circle. She also was likely a little reserved. When people met Lady Hamilton they had opinions—judging her looks, her lifestyle, and her attitudes, which revealed insights about themselves as much as about the notorious Emma. Lady Palmerston thought Emma had a

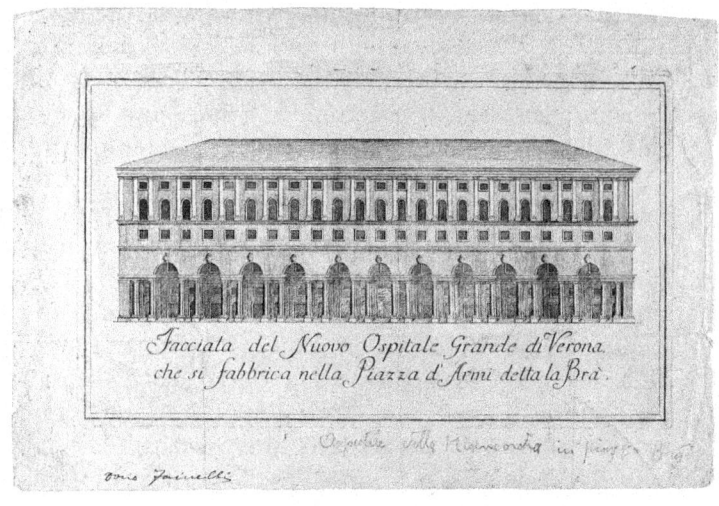

Hospital of Mercy, Verona, the kitchens of which were by Count Rumford. It was built in Piazza Bra from 1788 to 1793, where previously there were houses next to the arena. Thompson rebuilt its kitchens and arranged for the Munich poorhouse to make its clothing. The hospital was demolished in 1820 (Biblioteca Civica di Verona).

vulgar voice and she and Sir William were "rather too fond."[21] At a dinner Emma hosted for the Palmerstons (and 50 others), Lady Palmerston said of Sir William that she did "not wonder he is proud of so magnificent marble" but observed critically, "Now and then to be sure a little vulgarness pops out."[22]

The friendship with Lady Palmerston opened a happy current in Thompson's life. As he wrote her, he had feelings of love for her but she was his friend: "I cannot describe the impatience I feel to see you. Nothing, surely, could afford me so much delight. You may perhaps have found out that I am in love with you, for that is what could not be hid. But neither you nor anybody else beside myself can form an adequate idea of the affect, regard I feel for you, or of the heartfelt pleasure it affords me to reflect upon your kindness to me and to know that you are really and truly my sincere and affectionate friend. It comes to the share of few to have such a friend, and if I do not deserve it, I am at last grateful for my good fortune."[23]

This is an "I love you but" letter. The count was no Casanova. As soon as he says "in love" he switches to words of "regard," "kindness" and "good fortune," all socially acceptable feelings. Perhaps he did this to try to bring her feelings to the level of his feelings, as he surely did not want complications with Lord Palmerston. Some compact had been reached of being "really and truly" each other's friend, possibly beginning with sex, but the count does "not deserve" such a friend because he is calling a halt to the progress from friendship to committed love. In his letters Thompson often is reassuring Lady Palmerston that he is not gallivanting but staying in and working. When he at times chided her for being "spoiled" it might have been in response to her, a landed and married aristocrat, having expectations of him that he could not manage.

Lady Palmerston was more of a sophisticated friend, whether or not she ever had sex with Thompson. As such, they could gossip, which true lovers stay away from lest it trivialize their own relationship. For example, she had queried Thompson in a letter as to whether he had slept with Karl Theodor's new wife (about a half-century younger than the prince), the count wrote back: "Tho' I have not, it is more than probable that somebody else has. It is confidently said—and believed—that it is so."[24] He could, to please his friend, be funny and he did not seem in life to show levity about affairs; he was too lonely for that. But in his correspondence with a trusted female friend he could enter into levity about an amorous affair of his patron. With gliding buoyancy his riposte turns the question around as though he were leading in a waltz, a dance newly fashionable at the Bavarian court.

The expression between Thompson and Lady Palmerston is tender, evidence of an abiding friendship based on respect, regard, and helping each other. He modernized heating and kitchen appliances for her; she befriended his daughter. In the years before her own death and in mourning for Lord Palmerston, she would copy Thompson's account of his first visit to Paris—just because. The abiding friendship had a covenant in which Thompson put himself in the position of a knight to his lady. The viscount was outside this type friendship, although he was also Thompson's friend. Now the count had someone dispassionately interested in his ideas who was nonjudgmental about his melancholic broodings and brought him into her family life.

Countess Nogarola (circa 1790) by Moritz Kellerhoven. Inscribed by Sally in 1852 on a label: "This is a likeness taken by the celebrated painter Kellerhoph of Munich, of the Countess of Nogarola of the same place, Munich, a friend of 18 years of Count Rumford, a most excellent one of his Daughter, She, as we say, a perfect woman" (New Hampshire Historical Society).

Mary Mee expressed jealousy in her letters because Thompson answered it in his. This may well have reflected her entitlement as an aristocrat and her intense friendship for him, not the emotion of a lover. If there was some frolicking it may have sealed the friendship, been their secret; the friendship did not pivot on sex. The Palmerston marriage gave no indication of being an open marriage, an opinion on which I have the agreement of the staff of the Broadlands archives at the University of Southampton. It was a marriage of love. "How much I think of her and long for her society," Lord Palmerston wrote once and thus would always feel.

It was with Lady Palmerston that Thompson wanted to share how beautiful the English Garden looked when he returned to it after Italy and that he had constructed an amphitheater there and was having concerts in his apartments:

My Concerts are the most magnificent Assemblies you ever saw. I have literally all the World at them. At my last I had near 100 Ladies. I have fitted up my great apartment in the front of the House, which as you remember, consists of a very Grand Hall, and three handsome Rooms adjoining to it, in an elegant manner. The Hall and all the rooms are bordered by Turkish Sopha's which completely surround them on every side. My Concerts are given in *two Acts*, and between the Acts the Company retires to another handsome Appartment consisting of three large Rooms, on the opposite side of the Court, where they find tables spread, for Tea, Punch, and other refreshments. I wish you were here to see in what style your friend does the honors of Munich.[25]

Asking Lady Palmerston about the price of coal certainly squares with a friendship rather than a romance, whether or not they ever slipped into physical relations. All in all, for the Palmerstons, Thompson was like a stag useful at a party. Her affection for the count notwithstanding, Lady Palmerston wrote her husband that their friend could not be counted on, as he was sometimes irritatingly unavailable. As for Countess Nogarola, Thompson was a light of the viscountess's life.

Infused with the reception in Italy of his ideas, Thompson wrote up his essays and in September 1795 got a leave of absence from the Elector to go to England to oversee their publication and to meet his daughter, who was coming from America.

10

Educating Sally (1794–1796)

> Work banishes those three great evils, boredom,
> vice, and poverty.—Voltaire, *Candide*

When Thompson returned from Italy, the swirling power plays at the Bavarian court frustrated him. Being out of the inner circle seems to have given him the time he used to further work out and write up his ideas related to kitchen stoves and kitchen equipment (he designed his "roaster," or convection oven), nutrition (he developed recipes for using Indian corn, macaroni, potatoes, barley and rye), cooking wholesome food for large groups at minimal cost ("Rumford soup"), and enlarging the English Gardens. He wrote accounts of his workhouses for the poor and fuel. Whether the topic was highly technical or basic he pursued it to minute detail. For instance, he invented croutons, soup with floating, hard, dry bread that would take a long time to chew and so make the meal more satisfying. A beautiful statement about his attempts to rectify the lot of indigent people appears in an essay he wrote after his trip to Italy:

> I have lived much in the world, and have studied mankind attentively.... When I see, in the capital of a great country, in the midst of summer, a coachman sitting on a coach-box dressed in a thick, heavy great-coat with sixteen capes, I am not surprised to find the coach door surrounded by a group of naked beggars. We should tremble at such appearances, did not the shortness for life and the extreme infirmity of the human character render us insensible to dangers while at any distance, however great and impending and inevitable they may be.[1]

In the summer of 1794 Lady Palmerston was in Munich as well. After she left to return to England, she and Thompson kept in touch. This was an intense point in their friendship. Work on her fireplaces in England was a year ahead. After Lady Palmerston left, Countess Nogarola came to Munich: "The Countess will probably leave me in a fortnight or three weeks at farthest to return to Verona with her caro sposo." He mentions his daughter by Countess Baumgarten but never, in his letters, Josepha herself: "The little Sophia was perfectly well, and as beautiful as an angel."[2] The next year he wrote, "The little dear Sophie ... is as charming as ever, and often comes and dines with me. But the Prophecy of her Mothers Mother that her father and her Aunts Lover would renew an old conection [sic] with her younger Daughters elder Sister, is not likely to be verified."[3]

Perhaps Thompson felt the relationship was too hot to handle or too complicated or one of the sisters called a halt, and he was not going to have further sex with Sophie's mother, Countess Baumgarten, the older of the two sisters. He was certainly at ease with the situation, to the point that he could make a joke. He was also friends with the Countess

Lerchenfeld, the sisters' mother, who clearly knew of her daughter's affair with the count, which resulted in a child. She also knew her daughter was not having sexual relations with the count, because she wonders if it will resume, supposing that proximity or affection due to the shared child might be a factor drawing the count and the countess together.

A chain of biographical writings describe Thompson as a womanizer—he thought only of himself, was cold, treated women as doormats, and so on. This imputation seems based on his having had two illegitimate children and a pair of aristocrats as lovers. If he had been truly a cad, some diary of a contemporary would likely have picked up on and broadcast it. Instead, there is no indication that any woman, including either sister, was discontent with Thompson's place in her life, and Countess Lerchenfeld was friendly to him as well.

It was less than a year after the wife of Karl Theodor died that the prince married a 19-year-old Austrian princess. That the court was rife with amorous entanglements is indicated by Thompson's tattle about her already entering into the sport of liaisons. Yet the Bavarian court had no orgies, only rather a level of discretion. This adhered to the French model and Thompson observed its custom. The tongue-in-cheek remark to Lady Palmerston about his sexual relations with Countess Baumgarten—i.e., that he was not recommencing it—was as unguarded a comment as Thompson ever wrote about a mistress. Even that one is a denial, not an affirmation.

Once Thompson had been back in Munich for over a year he was eager to go to England to carry out publication of his papers. Karl Theodor gave him permission in September 1795 for the six-months/six-months mythic sort of arrangement that worked for the prince and his courtier. The count was also going to meet his daughter Sally, who in the half-dozen years since her mother's death had been living with the Baldwins and writing with more frequency to her father. Sally was now 19, the same age Thompson had been when he had married her mother.

Thompson the cosmopolitan did not love any one country. He suspected that his political enemies in England had executed the theft of his trunk containing records of experiments and philosophical disquisitions.[4] Moreover, he offered a reward of ten guineas for the return of his papers and some were returned. He also found himself shunned by the Crown because of being employed by the state of Bavaria, which was at the time not aligned with British policies on the Continent. He wrote Lady Palmerston bleakly: "I hate mankind with a most perfect hatred, and so deeply rooted is my aversion to them, that if I were to see a brute animal stand up on his hind legs I should run away from him. God grant me patience to finish the period allotted for my sufferings here, and quiet rest

Sarah Thompson [at 22] (1797) by Moritz Kellerhoven (New Hampshire Historical Society).

hereafter. Amen."[5] He now looked up Lord Sheffield, who had helped him get his rank of colonel years before and was also the person who had helped arrange publication for Edward Gibbon. Thereafter his essays on heat and poorhouses, among his most important, were published to acclaim.

Over and over those who have told Thompson's life story have called him an unfeeling egotist, e.g., he worked for the betterment of the poor without having love for them.[6] Yet there is no evidence of Thompson's ever treating a person whose status was beneath him unfairly or condescendingly. To the contrary, there is good reason to take his repeated statements at face value: that his purpose was to increase the enjoyment and comforts of life, especially in the lower classes. His personal affection for his manservant and that servant's family, the Aichners (discussed later) also comes through vividly in his correspondence.

Another slur repeated against Benjamin Thompson in 20th-century biographical writing is that he was deceitful and amoral.[7] It is perplexing that even Sanborn Brown, who knew Thompson's achievements inside and out, called him "a physicist who violates the standards of men about him" and therefore "cuts himself off from rewards which might have been his if he showed a normal respect for human values." This started with his spying for the British on the American rebels, and likely for Lord Germain against his enemies in London. But at this time, spying was an unpleasant job and not a character trait. In his time, his having been a Royalist would have been swept under the rug had he returned but he would not have regained his lost land. Nevertheless, by the time Sir Robert Keith in Vienna asked him to inform on the Bavarian political machinations, Thompson wanted to avoid spying altogether and did this by refusing to possess secret knowledge. It was disappointing to Keith and upsetting to Walpole when he was the British ambassador in Munich that Thompson failed to pass on secret information. Viewed from another vantage point, Thompson was a spy when there was something real to spy about, the gathering colonial forces under General Washington, but he wasn't going to fabricate information or dishonor his employment by Karl Theodor. When Thompson came back to London on this trip for the purpose of seeing his essays published, his character caused him to put work first. Thus he wrote Lady Palmerston: "If I find a moment of leisure I will dedicate it to you and Broadlands. I must however get two more of the Chapters off my hands before I stir from Town, or I shall have no peace of mind any where, and shall be good for nothing if I come to you."[8]

An astounding fact of his science emerges from Thompson's life: given his obligations to aristocratic employers and his continuing travels, even when at the Bavarian court back and forth from Munich to Mannheim, he fit his investigations in at all. His scientific endeavors were what he inveterately was moving towards while he led his active life as a courtier. For example, he wished to study heat when he had to do his duty as head of the Bavarian Army. His letter to Professor Pictet from Munich in October 1796 refers to these conflicting obligations while also indicating a perennial fact about his science—that he gave his conclusions freely. It also demonstrates his flowery writing style (even for the period), signifying his trained effort to please:

> I am to acknowledge the receipt of your letter of the 18th of August and of the Books which accompanied it, which came to my hands the day before yesterday.
>
> I might justly be taxed with want of feeling were I insensible to the distinguished honor which you and your Colleagues the Editors of the Bibliteque [sic] Britannique have done me. The approbation of so respectable a Society is highly flattering to me, and will be a powerful inducement to continue those exertions which you so kindly encourage me to hope may be of some use to Mankind....

> Inclosed I send you a Volume of Essays which was published (as a Volume) in the Month of July last, a few days before I left London. Should you find in it anything new that you think would interest the readers of your Journal, you will be pleased to consider every thing it contains, as well as every thing else I have published, or may hereafter publish, as being intirely at the Service of your Society.
>
> It would have given me pleasure to have been able to send you an account of the continuation of my experiments on heat, as I think the result of them would interest you, but these details are not yet ready for publication. I expected to have been able to send them to the Press by the end of this Month, but by being called upon, a few days after my arrival at Munich (on the 13th of August) to take the Command of the Bavarian Army, I have since been so much employed in the line of my Profession that I have not found a moments leisure to pursue my favorite Studies. I will however resume them as soon as possible, and hope to be able before Winter to finish two or three Essays I have in hand, and which are in considerable forwardness.[9]

With Thompson it was always work, not human relations, first—a lifestyle and not a reflection of denigrating others or subordinating women. By now he might have sunned himself and enjoyed the luxury of his aristocratic friends but he was usually busy solving problems of thermodynamics, outfitting hospitals or retrofitting chimneys.

On this trip to England he spent May and June with Lord Sheffield in Ireland, pleased to be staying in an apartment in Dublin Castle and consulting on improvements for poorhouses, hospitals and orphanages. At heart Thompson was a man of action. Thus, staying in London in the colder months of the year, and often visiting the Palmerstons' town house in Hanover Square, he determined to help Mary Mee when she complained that her fireplaces smoked. She didn't want to redecorate or get new furniture because the smoke would only ruin it. Not only Lady Palmerston but also her husband wanted to have Thompson improve their fireplaces, as Palmerston had complained to her about the operation of a fireplace: "The chimney in the inner drawing room smokes when the fire is first lighted, which is very provoking and must not be suffered as it will spoil everything. The proper grate is now brought home.... If this does not answer we must either try Count Rumford's plan entirely or have a close stove."[10]

The count began modifying chimneys by placing a masonry shelf, narrowing the throat, and making the fireplace, which burned wood or coal, shallower, with angled sides. This gallantry has its equivalent in the person of Aaron Burr, who in 1810 remodeled for a lady in Paris her smoky chimney and fireplace (mentioning what he learned from Ben Franklin and Count Rumford). The count's essay replies to the issues addressed by Benjamin Franklin in his "Observations on the Causes and Cures of Smokey Chimneys." Word traveled via the upper crust of society and his paper and he traveled in England, Scotland, and Ireland building and reconfiguring kitchens, stoves and fireplaces and advising local governments how to care for the poor and needy.

In 1795, he went on to remodel the fireplaces at Broadlands for Lady Palmerston. Thompson's Rumford stove was noted three years later by Jane Austen, writing *Northanger Abbey*, in which Catherine Morland is the Tilneys' guest at their great house, which she expects to be as creepy and Gothic as she had encountered in the pages of *Castle of Udolpho*. Instead she finds it updated: "An abbey! Yes, it was delightful to be really in an abbey! But she doubted, as she looked round the room, whether anything within her observation would have given her the consciousness. The furniture was in all the profession and elegance of modern taste. The fireplace, where she had expected the ample width and ponderous carving of former times, was contracted to a Rumford, with slabs of plain though handsome marble, and ornaments over it of the prettiest English china."[11]

The count's essay "Chimney Fireplaces, with Proposals for Improving Them to Save

Fuel; to Render Dwelling-houses More Comfortable and Salubrious and Effectually to Prevent Chimneys from Smoking" came out in 1796 in the *Bibliothèque Britannique* in Geneva, and in volume one of his *Essays, Political, Economical and Philosophical*, in London. Hundreds of fireplaces in London alone were built in the course of a few months. The American edition of his essays was published in 1799. Thomas Jefferson remodeled on the Rumford model six fireplaces at Monticello and installed two more. The plans Alexander Hamilton approved in 1802 and 1803 for chimneys at the Grange, his country house, were based on Rumford's type as well (not surprisingly, both Founding Fathers slightly altered the designs).[12]

At this time Thompson had full confidence he would someday return to America, to visit or, if he was welcome and found an outlet for his skills, to live. Loammi Baldwin was a primary link to home. At this juncture Thompson was asking Baldwin about the prospects of returning to America: How would he be received? The next year he wrote Baldwin that he was tired of state service but his time in Italy restored him. After Sarah Rolfe Thompson died in Woburn, the way was clear, without raising their marriage from the ashes, for Thompson to see his daughter Sally. He was 40, free and his heart went out to have her visit. He wrote Baldwin on March 18, 1793, saying he would like to be reconciled with her and he began to send her money regularly. When her mother had become ill, Sarah, age four, had gone to live with an aunt.

Sally did a drawing that George Ellis copied into his book *Memoir* of Sarah, her mother, as an invalid in bed. Being removed from her mother caused the child to seek affection from someone new. This would not be the paternal aunt to whom she went when she was four but a female slave in the household named Dinah, who became Sally's surrogate mother, spoken of with lifelong affection, and who had fairly exclusive care for her. Thus a slave nurtured the child and also smoothed over things for her. All her life, being sensitive, Sally had the need to go to someone to perform this same function and give the emotional support the enslaved black woman had provided. By the time Sally had the wistful family portrait painting, in which her mother and father were placed in the foreground and Dinah held her infant self,[13] the American South was sentimentalizing slavery, which fed into Sally's nostalgia and the artist's stereotypical plantation mammy depiction so at odds with the parents, who look like cutouts of New Englanders.

The family portraits of George Washington depict enslaved African Americans in livery or uniforms but Benjamin Thompson's family of yeomen had no slave culture or interaction with it. No other province had as few African Americans as New Hampshire when Sally was born: 1 percent, or about 600 (whereas, for example, persons designated as slaves made up 3 percent of Connecticut's population). The richer people obviously were more likely to have the extra domestic help and the prestige garnered from slaveholding. Sally's father, the Reverend Walker, owned three slaves, a man and two women freed when the New Hampshire State Constitution was adopted in 1783. The enslaved man "Prince," the story is told, left Walker's household, went to Andover, lived with a Dr. Kittredge, married, and at one point came back to Concord dressed in a red coat saying he rode with the troops. Sally's husband Colonel Rolfe left at his death as part of his property a slave, his estimated price at sale 55 pounds.[14]

The mark on Sally of the one-sided giving relationship of someone in bondage to her showed up in various crises of her later life as a craving or expectation to be taken care of, which she resolved by hiring people and adopting a servant's child, Emma, who

Benjamin Thompson's Farewell (1850) by Daniel G. Lamont. Sally commissioned this imagined family scene. Her note on the reverse: "This, of my father taking leave of my Mother, leaving me an infant in the arms of a favorite slave" (New Hampshire Historical Society).

was expected to submit to her discipline and was distrusted as soon as she went from a state of gratitude to wanting autonomy.

Likely because of the difficulties crossing the ocean in a period of war, it was four years between Thompson's invitation and the time Sally made the trip. She spent this interim at Mrs. Snow's boarding school in Boston and with her grandmother Ruth. The Baldwins also looked after Sally and were supportive all her life. The prestigious unofficial overseer, Dr. Joseph Willard, president of Harvard College, also helped. Thompson wrote and asked Sally to join him in London, and she went straightway, arriving in March 1796.

She would spend 3 1/2 years in Europe—three months in England, over two years in Bavaria, and England again in September 1798 for a year, returning to America in October 1799.

Much of the information about Sally's life in London and Munich with her father comes from a sort of fanciful diary she kept. She called it "Memoirs of a Lady, written by herself." On it she wrote a note: "The History of my Life, begun at Paris in possibly, 1842, and ended in May, 1845." She addressed it to Mrs. Baldwin, Loammi's wife, and called herself Serafina. The moniker goes with her self-image, being an angel of the highest order and burning constantly but ungrounded, like seraphim. An inevitable connection can be made with the fact she felt that a slave, her most intimate friend as a child, raised her. Sally expected people she loved to do her favors and services. Asking sweetly came naturally to her, so, for instance, when considering purchasing horses she threw up her hands and said she lacked the talent of some other people to manage a groom and a maid.

George Ellis copied part of the manuscript and even redrew some of her cartoon-like drawings in his biography. It is in this diary that Sally noted her crushes: the first when she was five or six when her mother and her playmate's mother thought the children might pair up when they grew up, and the second a shipboard flirtation when the young captain fell in love with her. Meanwhile, she was plucky and risk-taking as usual and won considerable money at gambling but her father, when he met the ship, made her give it back.

Before meeting Sally, her father had written her a long and formally affectionate letter, a period piece of fatherly advice. He started out by assuring her that he was not wealthy and so not to expect a change in her fortunes. He then went on to tell her how to behave, how to dress, and how to wear her hair. He ended by telling her to arrange to sit for a portrait, which she should send to him, and also said, "Send me in your next Letter a Lock of your hair, that I may have something that I can say has belonged to you."[15]

Sally had sailed from Boston at the end of January and after six weeks (March 1796) arrived in London bringing a letter from Loammi Baldwin about what a delight she was. Her father found her " better looking than he had expected ... a distinctly country girl." He was living in a large rental apartment in Pall Mall with Aichner, his Bavarian valet, and arranged for Sally to stay at a boarding house nearby, along with a German maid, Anymeetle, whom he had hired in Munich. Upon Sally's arrival, her father extolled her to Lady Palmerston: "No language can describe the events of yesterday. I have found a being who, I am persuaded is destined by Heaven to reward me for all I have suffered in the Storms to which I have been exposed during my whole life.... I have seen my Daughter—Good Heavens,—what an expression! when applied to a young Woman of twenty!... Notwithstanding all my fears of being blinded by paternal affection I cannot help thinking my Girl a charming Creature."[16]

For her part, Sally had expected a different-looking father. A silhouette in profile that was her mother's only portrait of Benjamin had formed Sally's mental picture. Her mother had said his hair was "carotty" and Sally described it as "a very pretty color":

"Indeed, so different from what I had thought were his looks, that I could hardly fancy him the person I sought after, would willingly have run from him, and ended in a violent fit of crying, which he did not consider as a compliment, asking me afterwards what I meant by it.... My opinion of him was naturally romantic.... I had heard him spoken of as an officer. I had attached to this an idea of the warrior, with the martial look, possibly a sword, if not the gun, by his side ... dark in complexion, possibly sunburnt; in short, in stature, size, and looks the perfect warrior."[17] The only criticism she recorded of his character, something she encountered right away, was his tendency to correct others and monopolize a conversation with his own interests

Thompson wrote Baldwin (March 26, 1796), "You will not expect that I should attempt to describe the pleasure I felt at seeing my dear girl after an absence of twenty years!" Years later, Sally elaborated her first impressions of her father, which were like a cameo: "The playfulness of his character (at times) secured love to my father. Witness the laughter, quite from the heart, nothing made up about it. The expression of his mouth, ornamented with the most finished pearls, was sweetness itself. But to see him accidentally, he did not strike one as handsome, or very agreeable, though not exactly to the contrary. At the time I met him having been ill he was very thin and pale." The author of *Leading American Men of Science* filled out a sketch of the hitherto unseen father that Sally now lived with:

> In early life he practiced music and he sketched his own inventions, but had no taste for painting, sculpture or poetry. He took pleasure in landscape gardening, but knew nothing of botany. His favorite games were billiards and chess, but he rarely played the latter because his feet became like ice. He was very abstemious in eating, partly from theory, partly on account of his poor health. He never drank anything but water.
>
> In spite of a tendency toward display and a liking for elegance in housing and habit, he was very careful in his expenditures and strict in his accounts. He never allowed any object to remain out of place after he had used it, and he was never late for an appointment.[18]

How Thompson related to his daughter was conventional for the time. He was strict, authoritarian, and not always diplomatic, but he was also caring, looking out for her best interests as he saw them. When Sally didn't have the clothes for London her father sent her to buy clothes, and she came back with lacy gowns. He suggested sturdy shoes and she bought six dressy pairs. The adjustment to London smart society was bumpy for Sally. She disparaged a performance at the opera until her father corrected her and said she should keep her comments to herself as he did. She observed to Lady Palmerston that the old buildings of London were dirty and ugly, and Thompson told Sally her opinions were "characteristic of savages."[19]

Sally wrote Mrs. Margaret Baldwin from Brompton Row that "those gentlemen of business seem odd things to us" and "I have found a very good father, but who is likewise prodigiously occupied in public affairs." She was ever her whole life comparing her nature to her father's and in so doing both finding him superior and poking sly fun at him. In the same letter she continues in this vein: "Had I acquired half his fortune and half his renown (for between you and I, let me tell you that neither Col. Baldwin nor my Father are enemies to a little well deserved renown) I should think myself as happy as tilly [and] should go and settle down in some little corner of the world and endeavor to enjoy the fruits of my labour."[20] That sentiment is paradigmatic of how she presented herself to the world: smart, willful, romantically impetuous, and, in sum, contrary to her serious father. Whereas most female readers of Jane Austen's *Pride and Prejudice* identify with Elizabeth or Jane, the thoughtful elder sisters, Sally in her early twenties in Europe seems modeled on Lydia Bennet—liable to run off with Wickham if someone doesn't prevent her.

After Sally had been in London a month, her father sent her to a fashionable girls' finishing school outside London. She was 23 years old and imbibing the etiquette of high society of a new land. She stayed at the school three months in the company of a dozen young ladies. Meanwhile, Thompson went to Dublin on a scientific trip. When he returned he deemed Sally "more appreciative of the refined enjoyments of cosmopolitan life." Now she wrote Mrs. Baldwin: "I enjoy very good health and am very happy. I should think it very strange if I was not to be. I am indulged in everything that I wish, and I am under the protection of a parent that I have not only reason to love, but to be proud of. On his account I receive every polite attention I could wish, and had I his merit, I should feel that I deserved it."[21]

Lady Palmerston, a steadfast friend to Sally as she was to Sally's father, eased Sally into London society. The gaffes she recounts evoke Eliza in *My Fair Lady*. She had gone with her father to visit a highborn lady, and the housekeeper received them. Sally had not been used to such a personage while she was in America, where "women of high rank and fashion were more inclined to do things for themselves." Sally laughed at herself and must have recounted the following faux pas often to others:

> Not finding her at home, my father inquires for the housekeeper, having a message to leave. Whether it was that I did not rightly comprehend the word housekeeper, we having few people of that description in the New England States—people of first fortune and family performing that office for themselves—or whether, from inattention, I did not hear the word, I cannot say; but on entering, disengaging my arm from that of my father, I placed my feet in position, and drawing back to allow myself a comfortable sweep, I made one of my very best, lowest courtesies. And this to a housekeeper! It was most cutting to my father's feelings. Poor man!

When Sally curtseyed to a maid in an aristocratic house, it was a breach in etiquette, even though the French Sun King doffed his hat to all women on his path, including chambermaids. Thompson instructed Sally on curtsying but also enrolled her for several months in a school kept by the Marquis and Marquise de Chabanne, French émigrés. He had learned the customs of the English elite and she needed to as well.

How could a single or divorced male parent treat a daughter as she was growing up to help her fulfill her potential as a woman? The possibilities of the relationship are rather stark when she is an only child. The caring, communicative and close father was liable to be accused of being too close (one of the reasons Aaron Burr dueled with Alexander Hamilton was slander that Burr, a superlative father, had an incestuous relationship with his daughter Theodosia). Or a father who elected to be more remote and a disciplinarian (like another single father, Thomas Jefferson) was criticized, too, just as Abigail Adams faulted Jefferson for not coming to England to pick up his daughter but having her delivered to Paris by a person who was a stranger to her. At a time when daughters were in general taught to be obsequious, it was an exceptional father who was supportive, protective, and progressive. A man with a career in the public eye would be especially likely to expect to rule, repress his sensitivity, and not be able to step off the stage of the world to be at ease with his daughter.

That Thompson was a star in the cast of the Bavarian court show made it possible for him to stay "on stage." He mentioned once being pushed off stage, in line with 20th-century sociologist Irving Goffman's "dramaturgical model of social life." A person is one self in what Goffman called the front stage and another self in the back stage. Thompson had honed his life stage performance. He knew his social cues and when he was meant to be playing a character and why. Being consummately aware of his own performances, he changed, shifted and adapted as he moved through different social spaces. In the back stage he was someone else, a reclusive individualist.

He saw to it that Sally had the remedial education—whether in skills like art, music and languages, or moeurs—to act on social cues and indicators for herself. All his interventions in her life in Europe were to train her to act on stage. He worried if she was unhappy. He might take her outdoors or on a trip or find her a friend. He did not see her as his equal. Father and daughter were remarkably close considering they did not see each other between her babyhood and age 22, yet they lacked the kind of rapport that would have made Sally more secure and less lonely. She rebelled by being intractable at lessons or performing poorly (she said she thumped on the piano), and haplessly flirting with men who were associated with her father.

Thompson himself was a master of backstage and front stage. Backstage he had people he was close to, of whom there were a number—fast friends and lovers dear to him who accepted him and with whom he could express himself and be himself. He needed to be in the front stage so much of the time in society. There was tension and he escaped to his lab (or became sick with exhaustion, and possibly the recurrence of typhoid fever). He had toleration to a point for society but his mind was on his work. He knew he was a performer. He did acrobatics as a schoolteacher and could summon up just the right demeanor on a horse. He was a major before any soldiering and exaggerated his military qualifications to rise in rank. When, towards the end of the Revolutionary War he involved the future King William in presenting the military colors in Huntington, Long Island (at the end of the American Revolution), he was evidencing a sense of spectacle and performance.

Thus he required his daughter Sally to learn the etiquette of society. He specifically taught her social cues and wanted her to act as an aristocrat's daughter, just as Sir Grenville required of Emma (later Emma Hamilton). Sometimes dealing with refugees in London, Thompson broke down in performance and was curt or indifferent in manner, but he did manage that job, which was all about demonstrating that Britain cared about the refugee Royalists. He had learned so much and did his utmost in London, and later Bavaria, to impart this knowledge of society to the country-bred lass, his daughter Sally.

For her part, Sally was all ears and eyes about her brilliant father. According to her he was "a great favorite with the ladies, though some of them sharply censured him." She noted in her diary after his death four aspersions, evidently heard firsthand, from ladies against him: he lived so short a time with each of his wives, he took sides against his country, he left his daughter in America when he lived in Paris, and he chose to live out his days in France instead of England or America. She added that several "female critics" put forth that as a young man he was "enticed" from his service to his native country because the British officers had handsome uniforms and the latest rifles, while the American volunteers were uncouth, "possibly with tattered garments, giving a shot, and then running behind a tree."

The most intelligent strategy of Thompson trying, and he clearly did try, to be a good father to Sally was to bring into her life his women friends Lady Palmerston and the Countess Nogarola. Both these women treated Sally with marked kindness. They could soften the regimen Thompson tended to create for Sally and have feminine talks with her about dancing, gallants, and feelings, including her conflicting emotions toward her typically autocratic father, of whom she had great expectations of closeness once reunited with him.

Sally preserved tokens of performing as a countess like her fan and Empire yellow ball gown and after 1794 would use the initials SR for her monogram.

11

With Sally in Munich (1796–1798)

> That which you love most in him may be clearer in his absence.
> —Kahlil Gibran, *The Prophet* (1923)

In midsummer 1796 Thompson had to return to his post in Munich. France and Austria were at war and approaching Munich, and Karl Theodor put the count in command of the Bavarian troops. Possibly Thompson's enemies encouraged the prince to give him an impossible job.

The count burst into Sally's room one day and told her to pack. A courier from Karl Theodor had arrived asking his state councillor (and former minister of war) to return immediately and deal with an emergency. Bonaparte was fighting the Austrians in Italy and a neutral Bavaria was at risk of being destroyed by the warring armies. Thompson leased two carriages. At short notice he had to take one discarded by a duke that still had the ducal armory, so he was told at every post stop that he needed eight horses, not the five prescribed for a count. This proved an irritation and expense.

The trip back from London was through Hamburg, the same detour that the violent progress of Napoleon's expanding empire had caused them to take coming in 1796. The count judged the inns along their journey to be unsafe, and Sally, the servants and he often slept in their carriages. (Sally later recalled how, on a bridge without a parapet, the horses backed up and almost threw them off a cliff. While the count leaned out to warn the coachman, Sally jumped out on the other side, an incident she said her father often described to his friends to prove that she knew how to take care of herself.) As the exchange rate would have made the Bavarian currency of low value in London, the count carried on the trip a bag of coins so heavy that it took several persons to lift it. Since there were robbers on all sides this was a source of constant worry day and night, whether the bag was in the carriage or taken into a room at an inn. Despite the seriousness of the mission, Sally saw sights during the journey and liked the Leipzig Fair and shopping.

Along the way they spent a night in Mannheim. Thompson was visiting, as presumably he had done before, with Baroness de Kalb, who lived there and in the family castle in Kalbsrieth. The Baroness Friderike Eleonore de Kalb was "Lore," whom Thompson identified in his private papers as "Laura" or "L." Lore (1764–1831) was the sister of Charlotte de Kalb (1761–1843). To some extent the sisters' lives paralleled one another. They married brothers of the Kalb family, whom neither liked. Lore married Johann August

Alexander von Kalb (1747–1814) in 1782. He became a wastrel and addict and ran through the family fortunes. By the time his brother—Heinrich Julius Alexander von Kalb (1752–1806), a major who served in the Royal Deux-Ponts Regiment in the American War of Independence and then fought in the French Revolution—returned to Thuringia there was no inheritance for him and no wife, as he and Charlotte had separated early in their marriage. Heinrich raised a family with a commoner and might have been happy except for having been bankrupted by his brother's excesses. He shot himself in an inn in Munich.[1]

The Baroness de Kalb undoubtedly had a sexual relationship with Thompson. She lived in Mannheim for several years in the 1780s. According to Mannheim historian Harald Stockert there are no documents indicating that she lived in Mannheim in 1800, and she was not mentioned in the civil registration lists of 1807, which shows her primary residence was elsewhere. In the 1780s various Kalb family members lived in Mannheim and were distantly related to General Kalb (1721–1780), who came to America with the Marquis de Lafayette and died at age 59 in Camden, South Carolina.

In this time of turbulence for the region due to the warring states of France and Prussia, a respite with the baroness must have been a little bliss. Stockert observed that, overall, the 18th century has been called Mannheim's golden age. Until 1720, according to Stockert, Mannheim was a rather new town with focus on military and business, in the shadow of Heidelburg. In 1720 prince Karl Philipp decided to move his residence and also the court from Heidelberg to Mannheim, where he had enough space to build up a great modern castle. From 1720 on, Manheim was the city of the prince's residence and therefore the city expanded and a lot of people moved there. Karl Theodor was the successor of Karl Philipp as he developed his court to a center of culture and science.

The cut came in 1778 when Karl Theodor inherited Bavaria and moved to Munich. Mannheim lost a great part of the court and many people left the city. However, in the following decades without a prince in town, the Mannheim atmosphere was rather free. There were intellectual circles, many newspapers, and the national theater. In 1782 Schiller's play about rival brothers, *Die Räuber*, had its world premiere in Mannheim.

Therefore at the time Rumford was passing through or visiting Mannheim the mood of the town was between dolor about the (especially economically relevant) loss of the court to Munich and more free possibilities. By the 1790s Mannheim was in the midst of the revolutionary wars; several times it was conquered and in 1795 it was destroyed. In his position as minister of war in the late 1780s and early 1790s, Rumford introduced several reforms for the military and also for the relief of the poor, which extended to the city of Mannheim.

The few times Thompson put pen to paper with mention of Laura there is banked passion. In one letter he stopped himself talking about her and himself to Lady Palmerston because it was not decent. Yet he looked at her as "innocent." Wishing to communicate to Lady Palmerston what Laura de Kalb meant to him, Thompson strung out the details of one visit because of its significance to him. He hadn't been to her house in Saxony before and arrived all expectation in the little village where she had told him to meet her. The chateau had barns and outbuildings and to reach it there was a bridge with fine trees on the banks of a stream. The stone double staircase announced someone of high rank lived there and Thompson approached. A woman came out and he gawked because it wasn't Laura, as other people in transit were staying there.

Laura and he had their romantic rendezvous at an inn another night. But for

Thompson to make a long story in a letter was unusual. He wrote like an engineer, matter-of-factly. He wanted to linger on the subject of Laura and conjure up the dream of their times together. To do so in a letter to Lady Palmerston came naturally to him because he didn't understand that ladies have a low tolerance for hearing about rivals past or present. Even the sophisticated Mary Mee, happy with her husband and family, was susceptible to a gallant stranger and relished Thompson's assurances that she was foremost in his affections.

The baroness's portrait, which she probably gave to Thompson, shows an intelligent and handsome person with large limpid eyes, high cheekbones, swanlike neck, and noble posture. In her paper label accompanying the pastel (anonymous, circa 1795, at the New Hampshire Historical Society) Sally would write, "This lady is the Baroness of Kalbe of Leipsic, a very particular friend of Count Rumford's—she being besides very good and beautiful, as of great celebrity." The words "particular friend" are an innuendo that Laura was Thompson's mistress, supported by his underlining her name twice (and exceptionally) in his diary of his first visit to Paris, after she had showed him his portrait in her favorite room of a new home and wept profusely over the few moments, as the count put it, that their love had constituted. It irritated Sir Charles Blagden, in the course of a travel conversation, when Thompson claimed he almost took advantage of her body when he saw her naked (the old "all men are pigs" line) but restrained himself. Sir Charles made no clever retort to what was apparently what psychologists called a deception clue.

George III had hung a full-length portrait of his new Hanoverian mistress Madam Wallmoden by his bed in the 1730s. It was unusual, though, for a woman to hang her lover's portrait and could only be excused by his fame. When Laura made a point to Thompson that she wasn't going to leave the home where she last met him, she was implying that her husband was not of importance in her future picture.

Life in Munich was not all *fêtes champêtres*. When Thompson returned to Munich after a year in England the French and the Austrians were approaching a neutral Bavaria like two black shadows on the map. Karl Theodor had fled to Saxony and the count served as deputized statesman of the sovereign. The Bavarian cavalry treated the Austrian general La Tour like their prisoner, making him go around the city of Munich when he wished to barrel straight through. La Tour threatened to burn the city down as soon as the French arrived. Thompson, Count Rumford, took command of the Bavarian army. He made a public apology to La Tour, assuring him that, if necessary, Munich would defend itself against the French. When General Moreau arrived with the French army, Thompson also kept them out of the city by promising supplies and the withdrawal of the Bavarian army. In two weeks, the main French army withdrew from Bavaria, and the Austrians left as well. The crisis was past and Thompson was the champion of the day, champion of a diplomatic coup. Now battened down with 12,000 troops, he had a chance to try out his portable kitchens. While Munich was under siege during September 1796, Bavarian troops crowded into the city and camped in public places. Thompson introduced for the soldiers portable stoves made of sheet copper and brick and experimented with his ideas about how to feed large groups of people. He also rationed firewood and fuel for the people of Munich.

The count's career had soared to its highest point. The prince rewarded him with the post of commander of police and for the next two years the count worked on the Englisher Garten and the poor houses, and lived a lavish life. When Gouveneur Morris, recently the minister of the United States to France, came to see for himself the heralded reforms in Bavaria, he wrote in his diary a unique and dispassionate account of the count's methods, achievement, and character. If Morris did not furnish a whole picture, he recorded salient details in vivid reportage.

The count's Munich apartments occupied the second floor of a palace originally built for a royal favorite. This is the base where Sally spent most of her first 3½-year visit with her father in Europe. The walls were inlaid with mirrors and the marble staircases so wide, she said, that six people could walk abreast. She could lie on her chaise-longue and drink chocolate, a kind of heaven. Sally's letters give a picture of her adjustment from New England country life to court society. Thompson wrote his friend Baldwin on February 13, 1797, that Sally was the comfort of his life, and she looked forward to visiting Baldwin and his Lady in his company:

> She is a very good Girl and is much loved here by everybody who knows her.
> The Elector has lately made me very happy by permitting me to resign to her one half of a Pension I enjoyed.... Two Thousand Florins a year (equal to about two hundred pounds sterling) are secured during her life to my Daughter (who has been received at Court as a Countess of the Empire). And this grant is accompanied by a circumstance which renders it peculiarly agreeable to her and to me, which is that she may enjoy her Pension in any country in which she may choose to reside.
> She is now above want, and her happiness in her life will depend on herself. The best advice I can give her she will not fail to receive.
> I was happy to learn that you are so busily employed in schemes of public utility. Our juvenile pursuits and our amusements were always the same, and we have neither of us any reason to complain of the frowns of fortune.
> I am, my Dear Sir, with unalterable Esteem,
> Yours Affectionately,
> RUMFORD[2]

Sally was lively and her feminine presence distracted her father pleasantly from his racing thoughts and constant work. Their rapport must have provided a bridge between his old and new lives. Meanwhile, Sally reveled at the round of balls and parties that to her father, who would rather be out riding, hiking and boating, were just part of his job. Wryly Sally noted that she would daydream under the arched painted ceiling of full-sized "heathen gods and goddesses instructive as well as amusing."[3] She found the society easier and more jovial than that of London, the court ladies sincere and accomplished and the gentlemen upright and unpretentious, everybody high bred: "The German Ladies, in general, are accomplished and charming, vying with parisieners, yet less celebrated; possessing the more substantial qualities of the English, those of sincerity. The German gentlemen are profound in knowledge, strict in probity, with not a shadow of conceit or foppery, with perfect high-breeding."[4]

To be a celebrity's child puts into the spotlight the artifice of a person's second self. Sally had to generate a second self in London quickly and as a young adult. She underwent a continued makeover in Bavaria, insisted on, but not unkindly, by her father. She continuously tried to please him for the rest of her life and in the immediate circumstances reach his standards for female education and manners. Meanwhile, understandably but unfortunately, her friends were not her own but in a sense borrowed from her father, and she was as much an outsider as Henry James's Daisy Miller. When Countess Nogarola wrote Sally warmly, for instance, she made rather a large point of a favor she bid Sally to do: buy a set of batiste handkerchiefs with the exact borders her father liked. A note of Joseph B. Walker on the provenance of the portrait of Countess Nogarola passes on that the countess was "a devoted friend" to Thompson and his daughter and "confidential advisor to the latter upon her appearance in Society."[5] It was sent to Sally on her way to America in 1799. Overall, with regard to the women who befriended Sally, the daughter was a conduit to the father. The countess could pass on other information about herself indirectly via Sally to Thompson, such as her aside in most letters that she had no interest anymore in goings-on at the Bavarian court, preferring to remain home alone. The Countess Nogarola and Thompson remained intimate friends and she translated his works into Italian, published in 1819, and helped him with his French and German writing.

It was a heady and unforgettable experience to be from Concord, New Hampshire, and spend several years in Europe. dance at balls, horse ride for pleasure, and go on excursions with her father. Sally was not very beautiful and often felt sorry for herself. Her gift was for analysis of the foibles of herself and others, not for flirtation, social climbing, or thinking of her own future. William Makepeace Thackeray drew the characters in *Vanity Fair* about this era, and Sally had facets of personality similar to Amelia Sedley, not Becky Sharp. Taking the role of a niece-daughter, Sally fit in with both her father's two closest female friends, Lady Palmerston and the Countess Nogarola, who made a place for her in their lives, gushing affection and giving the help Thompson requested of them as doyennes.

In London, Thompson needed Lady Palmerston and Lady Banks, the wife of the president of the Royal Society, to include Sally in select social functions and family events. In Munich, a woman friend to smooth his daughter's feathers, spend time with her, and keep her in the middle of the road was required. All of these needs the Countess Nogarola filled. Her being someone unusually prone to sentiment, even for the epistolary conventions of the time, speaks against her having bedded down with her sister's lover. She was too sensitive to have risked responding like a moth to the flame. Not only did she wreath her letters to Sally with assurances of love and requests for reciprocal assurances, but Mary also acknowledged sentimentality to a fault, e.g., "You know that I am to given to imagining to torment myself when friendship is concerned, and that it is probably that I always love my friends more than they can love me." [Vous savez que je ne suis que trop ingénieuse à me tourmenter quand il s'agit de l'amitié, et qu'il est probably que j'aime toujours plus mes amis qu'ils ne peuvents m'aimer].[6] Thompson was Mary's friend who could not (interestingly, not "did not") love her back with the same fervor.

Sally liked to analyze people in her diary and communications with friends back home. She summed up the sisters as follows: "It would be difficult to find two characters less resembling each other than these two sisters, the Countess of Nogarola, with a first-rate understanding, a model of virtue, not plain but not handsome, the other, a few years before, a celebrated beauty. She was so much admired and celebrated in the world that even crowned heads confessed her charms. All gentlemen were in love with her. Alas, poor lady! she ended in not sufficiently respecting herself."[7] Sally also mused that her father would have been "a happier and better man" if he could have had a legal union with "the excellent and lovely Countess Nogarola ... instead of an illegal relation with her sister."[8] The way Sally draws a parallel may suggest that Countess Baumgarten was the very secret mistress of Thompson for a long time. It also implies that Sally saw Mary Nogarola as steadfast in all things and not a woman to have been a mistress.

Mary Wollstonecraft's *Vindication of the Rights of Women* had come out in 1792 and was the intellectual talk of Europe. Sally's father's expectations did not reflect the more advanced ideas of womanhood of the age. He wanted Sally to adapt and be in a cheerful mood. That she proved a philosophical "Eliza Doolittle" comes across in her "Serafina" memoir. Sally never married, unusual for a young woman prone to crushes and possessed of a dowry in that era. She had suitors who came and went. She was well off and could navigate her life of being single as the only American-born countess in New England. She once wrote Colonel Baldwin that all she wanted to do was have fun and play billiards all day.

By her own account, she did not know how to soften her father's control. She didn't wheedle favors from him or quiver with helpless tears as a genteel girl might be expected to. She wrote in her diary that an indulgent mother (for years an invalid) had raised her, and she remained all her life in awe of her father. It wasn't in their rapport for her to charm him and it was too late for her to learn to cajole, the ability a daughter needed from a quasi-autocrat. Amanda Vickery explicated such an attitude in *The Gentleman's Daughter*: "However antipathetic to modern sensibilities, female pleading (to entreat, to mould, to determine, to prevail) was seen as legitimate policy in a society habituated to hierarchical relationships. In fact it was the exhibition of abject weakness which was the key to a successful petition."[9] This is not to say that Sally was placid. She recounted the following:

> My father observing one day, to friends present, that I was extremely docile and obedient to him, I burst into a laugh, saying, he was not to imagine it was all free-will and pleasure. My father was fond of having his own way, even, as I fancied, to despite me; but, as an excuse for him, he had led the life of a bachelor ever after twenty.
>
> It is well known to be a disadvantage, in many respects, for males and females to have little or no control. His wish for implicit obedience from me, and my early indulgence, as I may say, from a mother, made us at times not get on so well, at all events rendering me extremely unhappy.[10]

The social sins Sally committed stemmed from her insecurity and were the occasional outbursts of a young woman trying too hard. As Amanda Vicery has written, "to be mistress of oneself was paramount." Genteel ladies aimed to be self-possessed. In external manners, Sally exhibited more self-control, more of an ability to behave like others of high social status. When she liked and admired someone she could trim her sails. Underneath, however, she had sensitive emotions. When mildly provoked she became resentful and hypercritical. When her father saw her being moody he would try to do something to make her happy but it didn't count for her compared with her residue of bitter feeling. Yet for all that, the three years she spent in Europe were a continual round of elegant parties, lake trips, balls, horseback riding, music, pleasant private lessons in drawing, music and Italian, and visiting the castles of her father's friends.

While Sally would live in the shadow of her famous father from the time she came to England until his death, whether they were together or apart, this did not make her an object of pity at a time men were supreme. Yet he gravitated to women and spent lengthy time with them during his quarter-century of bachelorhood and he respected their intelligence, whether he was explaining his inventions to them, asking help to translate one of his essays, or relaxing in their company. He treated women with warmth and respect. His daughter elicited a different set of emotions—protectiveness, improving lectures, and upset if she was very upset, which he tended to solve by taking her on a trip.

Sally wished for her father to spend more time with her and be more demonstrative, as though she wanted him to make up for lost years, and commented to Countess Nogarola on the distance between herself and her father. The count rarely invited Sally to breakfast with him, hived himself away during bouts of ill health, and generally was distracted and aloof, while also liking to laugh and looking after Sally's happiness and wanting her to have a good time going places with him. She clung to her father and when he got into his carriage for a ten-day trip with the Princess L—, a stranger to Sally, without saying good-bye, her feelings were hurt. The count's friend Countess Nogarola had to comfort her that the Princess L. was a married woman. This takes one aback, i.e., wouldn't it be an element of danger if his paramour had a husband? But the Countess knew that Sally would be concerned that her father might have a new wife supplanting her place. In her father's absence she had a good time, sketching out of doors with the Countess and singing at the piano with her and her two children. When he returned she had accepted the tutors. However, her father was accompanied by "Princess L" (likely Lore de Kalb). It irritated Sally that he and the Princess L. were sequestered and that he did not greet either the Countess Nogarola or Sally right away:

> Twenty-four hours had elapsed before either the Countess or myself were informed of the arrival of my father. His traveling companions making a little stop to pay him a visit, we were not sought after. The system of the great world seeming to be "not to let the right hand know what the left hand doeth," perhaps that was the reason. In the less cultivated climes of America, in case of visits of the great and respectable the whole neighborhood even would have been summoned to help out in making things agreeable. The Countess and I were, however, invited on the evening of the second day to partake of the usual supper of chocolate. We were both thankful and glad to see my father again,—the Countess, from an angelic temper of forgiveness; and I, from the natural love of a child to a parent.[11]

Thompson knew his daughter was stubborn and didn't want more lessons. He therefore got her a pet. He had a small, white shaggy dog with black eyes, ears and nose delivered to her bedroom. It was a schlosshund, a lap or palace dog. Interestingly, he had chosen a fashionable breed. Brynn White, archivist of the American Kennel Club Library, explains that it very likely would be a member of the German spitz family, "which could include predecessors and variants on what we know as the Pomeranian, Keeshond, and American Eskimo dog. White Pomeranians were brought to England by Queen Charlotte in 1767, and became a pet frequently depicted in portraits of the late 18th and early 19th century. And the 1785 travel journal of Baron Riesbeck noted that little black or white Pomeranian or spitchen were very fashionable and could be purchased in the dog market of Vienna for ten or 15 ducats." This kind of dainty dog suited a lady. An anonymous painting of Goethe conversing with his platonic (in the sense she wanted more than he gave) friend Charlotte von Stein has the same type of small white dog, with a long brush of a tail, slender neck and dark eyes, nose and ears.

In about 1850, Sally commissioned an artist, Daniel G. Lamont, to create an imaginary double portrait in oil of her and her father, based on the portraits done in Bavaria by Moritz Kellerhoven. The result was like sentimental Victorian hair jewelry. In the pose, her father bestows undivided attention on her and she is a young woman. She wears a subdued gray dress while the figure of her father is in a dressy blue coat and wears his decoration from the Holy Roman Empire. Sally holds the shaggy dog, Cora, her father's gift to her in her arms. (Years later Sally was visiting the Cambridge home of Joseph Willard, president of Harvard, when she decided that Cora would be unhappy if left among strangers and carried her in a muff to church).

One day Sally was petting her puppy when three people entered, a woman and two men. The woman announced she was to teach Sally in French and music, curtseyed and then stepped back and let the others speak. One was a Catholic priest and professor of drawing. The other was Italian, unattractive and with a harsh voice that made Sally especially resistant, although she acknowledge he was good, kind and a fine teacher. She dis-

Double portrait of Sally Thompson and Benjamin Thompson, pastel (1799) by William Lane. Sally's note: "Being highly favorable to characteristic likeness in general" (New Hampshire Historical Society).

missed them all. Mary, Countess Nogarola persuaded Sally to be tutored by the woman and the priest and the count returned from a trip to hear this good news. It was the afternoon and the count, the Countess Nogarola and Sally were sipping chocolate. Thinking about Sally's lessons, the count turned to the Countess Nogarola and asked how little Sophie was doing. "Not so well," replied the Countess, "owing to the peculiarly light, trifling character of her mother." Sally took this personally as a *moralité* to study with her teachers. When Sally progressed in foreign languages, a feminine arena, her father expressed his satisfaction within the content of newsy letters in 1797 to Lady Palmerston; whether he knew how to praise Sally herself without correcting and asking for more industry is doubtful.

As Thompson was soon to turn 44, Karl Theodor had given him a mandate to create a large park at Berg on the shores of Lake Starnberg. Thompson owned a chateau there, and a frequent visitor to the lake was the Princess of Taxis, whose sister also owned a castle on the lake. Rumford was often in the company of "my Princess," as he liked to call her, and she had been one of his main reasons for purchasing a castle in the first place. Now, laying plans for leaving Bavaria definitely, the count persuaded the Elector to buy the Rumford castle and "to purchase the two Chateaux on the right and left of it and to make of the whole one immense Park stocked with fallow Deer, and laid out in riding, pleasure ground etc. it will, with no very great expense make one of the very finest Places that ever was seen."

It was in the spring of 1795 that Thompson told Lady Palmerston the news of a visitor of interest he had met: "the young Princess of Taxis, Niece to our Queen. She is very pleasing, and really seemed to be much pleased with our attention to her, and with what she saw here. I had the honor or showing her the garden and the Poors House. Her husband was with her, *cela s'entend*."[12] In so many words, the flirtation was hampered in practical terms by the presence of a husband, even if that may have fanned the desire. That the count felt he could confide in Lady Palmerston speaks for the depth of their connection but does not impinge one way or the other on whether Mary Mee and he were lovers.

The Princess's portrait is in the family residence of her descendants, the residence known either as St. Emeram's Palace or the Palace of Thurn and Taxis. It was once St. Emmeran's Abbey, a Benedictine monastery converted in 1812 to a palace in Regensburg. Thérèse in the painting leans on a parapet in a garden, wearing an empire dress and looking rather knowing. After going on tour with Sally in July 1797, Thompson "spent eight days in Berchtesgaden and Salzburg with Princess Taxis in August, at the end of which he tried to persuade Lady Palmerston to come to live with him for the winter of 1798 in Vienna."[13]

Princess Taxis is also referred to by the title Duchess Thérèse of Mecklenburg-Strelitz. She was married to Karl Alexander and was the aunt of Empress Alexandra Feodorovna, the wife of Tsar Nicholas II. She was indeed young, 16, when she married Karl Alexander in 1789. A reminder that European royalty was like a big (if dysfunctional) family is that Princess Taxis's paternal aunt Charlotte was George III's queen. Queen Charlotte brokered Princess Taxis's marriage to insure she would keep her Protestant faith. Count Taxis (only a very distant relative of Princess Taxis), Rumford's aide-de-camp, was the gallant who most inspired romantic sentiment in Sally. Thompson left for a tour of inspection in the provinces and Sally stayed with the Countess, Mary Nogarola. Count Taxis accompanied the two women on their excursions, and a romance was kindled when Count Taxis picked up Sally's whip during a ride in the Englischer Garten. He was apparently interested in practicing his English and only reactively flirted with the American girl.

The apogee of the brief romance occurred at a riding party at the Englischer Garten. Thompson had brought two sidesaddles from England because he wanted to introduce that style of riding to the ladies of Munich, and he wanted to enjoy the garden on an outing with Mary, Countess Nogarola, who was about 26, and Sally, who was about 22. The ladies, on either side, descended the grand staircase from his apartments in the chateau to the first floor (the Russian ambassador's ornate quarters). They wore ermine-trimmed scarlet coats and plumed hats, and Thompson wore his decorations, star and garter. He chose horses for each of them, a gentle horse called Lambkin for the countess, who did not ride much, a steady mount for Sally, and an impressive horse called Fawn for himself. The park was Thompson's creation, so naturally he wanted to impress. But the countess had trouble mounting and Sally struck off ahead. She hid to the side of the porte-cochère to tease her father, and when her father and the countess reached her she galloped off on the by-roads and paths of the garden.[14]

The next evening at court, Taxis turned away from Sally instead of sweeping her into his arms for a waltz. After he had inquired about her health he began a conversation with Mary Nogarola. She would have promoted the marriage but someone, possibly Thompson but as likely someone else in the honeycomb of court, had nixed the match. The gallant officer may have suffered pinpricks, or, contrarily, have felt he dodged matrimony without a scratch. Sally, who was infatuated and inexperienced, suffered more.

Sally and the Countess Nogarola planned the count's gala 44th birthday party for three weeks. Children from the poorhouse performed, and the countess's children sang songs. Sally made a speech in Italian because her father had encouraged her to study it. All the ladies wore white. Sally felt let down after the party and ambivalent about the day. Her father's expression of gratitude struck her as inadequate, and she realized for the first time the full complexity of the relations with the countesses and that she had a stepsister:

> The little Miss Sophy Baumgarten ... had a more dignified part to act than any of us, being signalized out by my father (while the Countess, her children, and myself were barely noticed) as the object of great attention. So pointed was it as to attract the notice of all present. At all events, so undoubtedly was the intent; for if it was to cross the room this child was led by the hand, and, if seated, placed by his side.
>
> Contemplating some time this singular sight, I applied to the Countess to know what it meant. She, not giving me a positive answer, smiling, said I was to take notice that her sister, the Countess of Baumgarten, was not present; which, in the crowd, I had not observed before. This adding still to the mystery in which before the matter was enveloped, I returned with eagerness to my business of watching, and in consequence of it the truth was revealed to me.... The striking resemblance that existed between my father and the said Sophy put it beyond a doubt that I was no longer to consider myself an only child.[15]

Having a rival for her father's affections stung; the fact that the child was conceived by an extramarital affair was not upsetting, but how cute Sophie was and her resemblance to the count rubbed salt in Sally's wound. She considered revenge but was pleased overall with herself that she engaged playfully with the child when she met her at court.

That Thompson took delight in having this child was clear as he praised her to others. When she was about 12, he said to Lady Palmerston, "The little friend you saw on the lake promises to be a charming creature. She is very clever and very accomplished."[16] How well Sophie played the harpsichord he had given her for her fourteenth birthday would have been a natural thing to say but it inadvertently hurt Sally. Beneath the surface of a high society where extramarital liaisons were the norm, there had to have been a sensibility that with cousins marrying cousins there should be no watch set to keep out newcomers from the breeding stock. A brilliant father might have a brilliant child or at least contribute to the breeding stock. Nevertheless, a man who did not give an offspring his name or rule the house in which the child lived, even if, like Thompson, he was positively disposed to do so, was irrelevant. When the child was a young woman, the distance required of any adult male from her applied to the natural father. As Sophie's stepfather died in 1790, Josepha (the Countess Baumgarten) and Sophie were under the protection of the Lerchenfelds and Josepha likely had a lover or lovers, and Thompson's presence in Sophie's life would now add an undesirable complexity. In parallel fashion and as an example of the times, William Wordsworth returned to London at age 23 in late 1792, leaving behind his lover, Annette Vallon, and their illegitimate daughter, Anne Caroline, neither of whom he saw again during the tumultuous decade. Dorothy Wordsworth, the poet's sister, in an October 14, 1814, letter to her good friend Mrs. Clarkson, wrote that she had learned that Anne Caroline "resembles her father most strikingly, and her letters give a picture of a feeling and ingenuous mind."[17] There was no censure of the man who sired the child and left it to others to raise, nor was there condescension towards the child whom the poet legally acknowledged.

Timing was not the count's strong suit. The day after the birthday party he invited Sally to breakfast with him, an honor, and told her he disapproved of her "conduct" toward Count Taxis: "I received my admonition in silence, without making a reply.... I did not say, as I could have done ... if he expected me to be so perfect in my conduct towards Count Taxis, why was he not more so in that with his beautiful illegitimate?"[18]

After her father took her to visit the island lake monastery of Herrenchiemsee as a distraction, back in Munich Sally met Count Taxis by chance dining at the house of the Countess Lerchenfeld, Mary Nogarola's mother. Sally's father supposed it was a ploy, "some female conspiracy," and accused her: "I feeling myself innocent, as I was (being as much a surprise to me as to my father that the invitation to the dinner was to meet Count Taxis, that being the subject of the difficulty), I at first only stared. After which, on knowing what he meant, like many young people who laugh when there is nothing to laugh at, an irresistible inclination seized me to laugh; which I having for some time suppressed only burst forth with the greater violence, and it ended in my father's boxing my ears."[19] As Sally recalled the matter, Countess Nogarola was a go-between. "The negotiation with your father has not succeeded," Mary reported a few days later when she called on Sally. "To end further importunities, the Captain Count Taxis and his regiment quit Munich this morning, to have their residence in the country. And I only am left to tell you." Sally went to bed with the ague the next night.

In the end, her prince would not fight for her. He was killed in the Napoleonic Wars. Countess Nogarola had fanned the flames initially when she told Sally the captain had just turned down a match made by his family. When Taxis came to practice English, the group was Sally, Mary, and himself. With the Countess Nogarola as duenna the flirtation might have after all resulted in a proposal of marriage. However, according to Sally's diary, as Mary and she were speaking about Taxis a messenger from Count Nogarola called Mary home to pack her things for Italy, as they were going to set out that very night.

Thompson's physician, Dr. Haubenel, eventually recommended a journey to cure Sally's depression over the loss of her dream man. Countess Nogarola came along and Sally indeed dried her tears. They set out towards one of the Prince Elector's palaces, stopping two successive nights in castles that were all-male establishments, some type of monastery or enclave of Illuminati. Then they hiked on foot through fields and up a mountain. The Countess Nogarola stayed behind in a pasture while Sally and her father climbed to the top. Mary's stockings were wet so she took them off. Sally liked to recount moments she was the person close to her father and noted the amusement that a cow ran away with one of Mary's stockings and chewed it to pieces. She also liked to see her father weak and noted her amusement when "the Count himself, who had made the ascent before, did not escape without a fall and a roll over the rocks."[20] Another trip to divert Sally was more extensive: by raft on the Isar from Tolz to the Danube, a coach excursion to Salzburg to see the salt mines, and on the return a visit to the toy factory in Berchtesgaden. She recalled being silent, tearless and listless. The romance with the aide was the most thrilling and disappointing of her life.

To show Sally that he really did appreciate the birthday party, Thompson wrote

Loammi Baldwin that the eight boys and girls Sarah had invited from the "House of Industry" to entertain at his party were such a success he wanted to commemorate in perpetuity Sally's gesture. Therefore he would give two thousand dollars to the town of Concord in U.S. government bonds so that on Sarah's birthday 12 poor children could be furnished with new sets of clothing. Furthermore, the clothes would be identical to the uniforms in which Sally had outfitted the Bavarian children for the party. Baldwin passed along the offer and the councilmen of Concord accepted the money for educational use, saying delicately that educational supplies would be more lasting in value than the "temporary comfort" derived from clothing.[21]

Thompson had two aides, a valet, a groom, and servants for the house. He was addressed as "Excellency" and had a box at the opera. A hairdresser came each day and the count was required to attend a formal court function once a week. Looking good was salient and he wanted his daughter to ride in the English style, sidesaddle, which he perceived as more elegant. But she could not master it, or claimed she could not master it. While Sally perceived a fairy tale realm, her father would desperately write his confidante Lady Palmerston that everyone hated him and political maneuvers were constant.

Karl Theodor's teenage bride loved to dance and he indulged her with court gaiety. Sally was swept up in this and wrote, "Balls succeeded balls; drawing-rooms, concerts, the same. The splendid palace of Nymphenbourg, the summer court residence, became the scene of hilarity, fashion and elegance. The young Electrice figured at the head of it, singing agreeably, often performing in public and dancing well, although a little lame. It was amusing to bystanders to be witnesses to the conjugal struggles; the Elector looking steadfastly to the door, impatient for the moment to arrive to retire, and she, in the supplicating, artful manner of youth, saying, 'One dance more! Once dance more!'"[22]

Keenly aware of the musical beds at court, Mary Nogarola was less charitable. Describing the prince's wife, the Electrice, after a broken love affair as speaking of suicide and telling random peasants and servants that she was thinking of killing herself, Mary said no one ever made less use of her liberty, and she feared the Electrice would end up institutionalized as an insane person.[23] On one excursion, Mary Nogarola was sketching a view and asked Sally to try too: "It's easy."[24] When they returned home, Dillis helped finish Sally's sketch and became her art teacher, as he had tutored children at the court, a sideline to appointments like head of the royal art collection.

When Sally had been in Munich 18 months, before Countess Nogarola was obliged to leave for Italy because her husband "thought of taking his family with him," Thompson, Sally, and Mary went on a pleasure trip a day's drive away to the Ammerland See. They stayed in a residence of Karl Theodor, where they had sumptuous dinners, sailed in a boat manned by rowers, and enjoyed excursions with a guide to a monastery and hiking and fishing. Thompson encouraged the ladies to tie up their dresses into trousers when they had trouble hiking up a mountain. In the evening, attended by a maid, Sally and the countess bathed in the lake.

From Verona, and wracked for her son's poor health (he would die while still a boy, whereas her daughter became a diplomat's wife and the toast of Paris), Countess Nogarola wrote Sally fond letters. Yet between the lines it was Thompson who was on her mind: translating for him, getting a good dictionary to aid her translation, having Sally give an enclosed sheet to him "with mille amitiés de ma part," and asking Sally in the closing for assurances of continuing affection and declaring, "Give my best love to him in the mean time—and believe me I am unalterably yours."[25] She might go on for several pages before asking Sally to buy for her father six batiste pocket handkerchiefs of the same quality and size as he always used, leaving it to Sally to choose the border.

The letters that Countess Nogarola addressed to Sally from Verona, which are now at the New Hampshire Historical Society, exhibit a pattern: avowal of the tie between the two women, personal news, current events, a leavening of reportage about people they both knew (or if no gossip, an apology for the letter's being lacking) and, always, a wispy sort of kiss blown to Sally's father, whom the countess never mentions by name in any letter. A few times Mary's daughter wrote at her mother's bidding. This was "little Terese," the future Countess Apponyi, who married and was the belle of Paris. For instance, Terese added the following to her (not to her mother's) March 11, 1798, letter: "My dear Sally, I think of you, and I hope that I shall be able to speak English with you when I shall come back to Munich. Meanwhile accept the duty of your obliged little Thérèse."[26]

Gouverneur Morris's trip from Paris to Germany began with his being so charmed by the circle of the Princess of Taxis that he lingered several weeks in Ratisbon before going on to his destination of Munich for a briefer visit. As soon as he called on Count Rumford (December 30, 1797), the count told him the history of Bavarian farming, nobility, forests, and then spoke of his own role, how he had gained the confidence of the prince "by holding out that history never fails to do justice to sovereigns.... According to the Count, it is from the love of honest fame that the Elector [Karl Theodor] has been stimulated to the amelioration and embellishment of his country [and] led into the labor and vexation of reform."

One evening during his nine-day stay in Munich, Morris dined with the prince and tried to direct the course of conversation to encourage the prince "in the pursuit of laudable objects." Thompson relayed what he had done that day and went into "abstruse" ideas about the science of human blood. Morris heard from a third party at the dinner that Rumford was "a man with much genius and information, and the zeal and activity of a projector [sic]; is apt to neglect a business when once he has brought it to its point of maturity. Moreover, as of a man extremely vain, who is the hero of his own panegyric."[27] Morris did not doubt the effectiveness of the multivalent projects he saw that were under the count's initiative and praised to the skies the military reforms, the poor houses, hospitals, and the Englischer Garten. The purported vanity of the count seems to amount to not hiding his accomplishments and preoccupations under a basket.

In addition to the major projects Morris saw there were two interesting minor ones. The count, according to the much-impressed Morris, had invented a gun from which he could shoot an arrow three miles and which could go through a dozen inch-thick boards, but the count would not "communicate to the world," this "being too dangerous." Morris also wrote of going to an establishment under Count Rumford's direction, not yet completed, for poor children. As Morris was the notorious Lothario of the Founding Fathers, he must have been riveted and described it as follows: "This house was built by the States for ladies to live in privately, and is the most superb building in Munich. The idea is the most extraordinary that I ever remember to have met with. It was further intended for the education of those young scions of nobility which had been furtively taken from the noble stock. In England this would be called a strong legislative declaration of unchasteness."[28] Thompson called this combination lying-in hospital and boarding school for boys a "nursery for genius" and as usual with his projects invited the gentry to inspect it.

It was General Werneck, a Bavarian officer with whom Morris had discussions, who

Portrait of Countess Antoine Apponyi (1823), by Jean-Auguste-Dominique Ingres (Harvard Art Museums/Fogg Museum, bequest of Grenville L. Winthrop).

judged Benjamin Thompson "vain." Explaining to an intelligent and renowned person from his own country his activities, projects, scientific questions, and whatever he was wrestling with must have elated the count. He took credit where credit was due and was single-minded, fired up, and intent on his reforms. The accusation of "vanity" would rain down from detractors who did not know him personally. To his contemporaries, his was a case not of superciliousness but of someone with poor conversational skills who preferred a conversation with serious content to one with witty repartee. He carried himself well on a horse or at court but he lacked the suavity, valued in an 18th century elite man, born of reticence that said the man didn't have to impress anyone. But of course Thompson did have to impress people he worked for and other intellectuals who ran the scientific establishments of the time. If it was more tasteful to demonstrate restraint in causerie, his mistresses, it seems, enjoyed his enthusiasm generally, as they never complained of hearing about his inventions and his social reforms.

In 1798 the Duke of Bavaria, Karl Joseph, dispatched the count from Munich to London as minister of Bavaria. This single time in his life charm and intelligence did not get him the position. Despite Bavaria's being an ally, the British government did not go along with the Prince Elector's highhanded ways. The government would not receive as minister from another country someone who was a former member of their State Department and still on the payroll of the British army. Quo vadis?

12

The Stories Portraiture Tells (1800s)

> The picture of an absent relation, or friend, helps to keep up those sentiments which frequently languish by absence.—Jonathan Richardson, *An Essay on the Theory of Painting* (1715)

In 1797 Thompson was commissioned by the prince to create a park at Berg on the shore of Lake Starnberg, the large lake near Munich where the Bavarian court went for recreation. Apparently Thompson had a castle here and the Princess of Taxis came to Berg, where her sister Louise, Queen of Prussia, had a castle as well. Rumford was often in the company of "my Princess," as he liked to call her, and, according to Sanborn Brown "she had been one of his main reasons for purchasing a castle in the first place." Now, he was laying plans for leaving and persuaded Karl Theodor to buy the Rumford estate and "to purchase the two Chateaux on the right and left of it and to make of the whole one immense Park stocked with fallow Deer, and laid out in riding, pleasure."[1]

Designing the fabulous park occasioned Thompson's visit of several months to Lake Starnberg. As mentioned, the presence of the Princess of Taxis, Thérèse of Mecklenburg-Strelitz (1773–1839), had caused him to buy his dwelling in the first place. Thompson was fortyish and Thérèse 20 when he persuaded the Karl Theodor to buy the house he had bought and the two sisters' houses to the left and right and create the park, stocked with deer and landscaped for various amusements, rather more rustic than the English Garden. Both sisters failed in their negotiations with Napoleon Bonaparte but during the Congress of Vienna Thérèse succeeded in defending the postal interests of the Thurn and Taxis family.

The Tasso family had made their fame as post riders in the north of medieval Italy, having escaped from feuding Guelfs and Ghibellines to a village in the area of Bergamo. Their name derives from "tasso" (badger) in Bergamesque, an obscure romance language once spoken in eastern Lombardy. Early on, the Tassos's "pony express" linked Milan with Rome, Venice and Vienna. By 1506 the *Bergamashi* had become the public postal service for the Hapsburgs, linking the Low Countries to the Spanish court. For 200 years, until Napoleon dismantled the Holy Roman Empire, their couriers carried mail on a route through France or, during hostilities, across the Alps to Genoa. The family title of Thurn und Taxis involved a German rendering of the French "de Tassis" and from 1615 the post of postmaster general became hereditary and German.

Daughter of a grand duke of the Holy Roman Empire, and niece of Queen Charlotte of England, Princess Taxis was dynamic and independent-minded. Born in Hanover,

Thérèse was 15 when she wed 17-year-old Karl Alexander, Fifth Prince of Thurn and Taxis. The couple's first residence would be in Frankfurt and they also lived in Regensburg and Bavaria. Thérèse's mother had ten children and died giving birth to the tenth. She and Karl Alexander had seven children between 1790 and 1805. Approximately 15 months after the birth of their youngest, Thérèse had a child out of wedlock by her true love, a Bavarian diplomat named Maximilian, Count of Lerchenfeld (1772–1809). The pair had two children: Georg, born in 1806, and Amalie, born in 1808, both of whom lived to adulthood and had issue.

There is no evidence that Thérèse's extramarital life offended her husband, who spent much time in Paris and died, still married to her, in 1827. Thérèse's second son by her husband succeeded as the 6th Prince of Thurn and Taxis. Her daughter Amalie had a very romantic life with a happy ending when she was able to marry her lover by whom she had an illegitimate child, therefore legitimizing the child.

Thérèse was the power in the couple and politically a force. She became involved in princely matters including house and lands and the administration of the postal service that was the family's fortune. After her father-in-law resigned as postmaster general and Karl Alexander succeeded him, she negotiated with Napoleon in person regarding the traditional family postal rights. On the other hand, the British regents nipped in the bud the rumors that her husband was being considered for the new throne of the Austrian Netherlands. When Napoleon eliminated the hereditary postmaster general because the principality was no longer independent Thérèse oversaw it as a private entity and was instrumental in maintaining the private company (the Thurn-und-Taxis-Post) until it was nationalized by Bavaria.

An oval portrait (1800) by Carlo Restallino depicts the princess, famed for her beauty, as having soft eyes, a rosebud mouth, and a bright, humorous gaze. In the painting she has fashionable curls, wears an empire-style gown, corona, and diamond chokers, and is grace incarnate. Leaders and literati came to her receptions and she appreciated the arts. One painting shows her holding a lyre. At the Congress of Vienna in 1814, Talleyrand, Tsar Alexander I, and Metternich negotiated in her salon, and the Princely House of Thurn and Taxis was compensated for some of the revenue cost them by Napoleon's rule.

Thompson wrote with warmth of the Princess of Thurn and Taxis. Given that he was vulnerable to periodic sicknesses, whether from the aftermath of typhoid or anomie and depression, this friendship offered another occasion for a respite when his health dipped. But his sexual liaisons did not satisfy him, because he was powerless, a toy. The periods when he was with the aristocratic ladies for a month or longer he tended not to do physics. Naturally, he didn't have equipment, and he would work on outfitting hospital kitchens or doing healthy things like horseback riding and boating. In this way all the sexual liaisons were extrinsic to his most intense interest, which was inventing and exploring natural principles. Being a houseguest of women was no proof of sleeping with them, although it did go with affection on Thompson's part. And if he was intimate without sexual relations, that is always possible although these were attracted, pampered young women and Thompson was a man of experience.

Thompson says he wanted Princess Taxis to travel with him but "someone" would not like it. That is unusual, as he speaks of the women he visits more properly in general. It does suggest they were sexual partners and that clandestine was better than going on a trip together. Her husband seemed to have kept her pregnant and given parties with her in Paris. He was an ambassador from Austria for some years and had been indifferent to her indiscretions.

After the two countesses, the third aristocrat lady who seemed to offer her friendships with no demands was the Baroness de Kalb, "Laura." Laura Kalb, who lived in Mannheim, may be the "Princess L—" that he had two weeks with and brought back to his chateau when Sally and the Countess Nogarola were there. In mid–October 1801 he left Munich in the company of Prince George of Mecklenburg-Strelitz, brother to the Queen of Prussia, and visited the Princess of Taxis in Dillingen for several days, during which there was a masked ball of princes and princesses. Then Prince George and the count went on to Mannheim for another brief visit. This time they stayed with the Baroness de Kalb. There was not a day's interlude between visiting the two aristocratic ladies. Thompson wrote his daughter: "I found Laura (the Baronesse of Kalbe) in perfect health, and as enchanting as ever. She sends you a thousand compliments."[2] Twice when in London he mentioned in correspondence with Lady Palmerston the event of a letter from Laura to him at the Royal Hotel, Pall Mall as noteworthy in a letter of October 28, 1795, in which he underscored her name. In the fall 1801 diary by the count that Lady Palmerston copied, after his brief encounter with the baroness on his way to Paris, the name of Laura is likewise twice underlined. It must have been an extrapolation from his own personal needs that the count in an essay remarked with sensitivity on the feelings of the poor: "Whoever has taken the pains to investigate the nature of the human mind, and examine attentively those circumstances upon which human happiness depends, must know how necessary it is to happiness that the mind should have some object upon which to place its more tender affections—something to love, to cherish, to esteem, to respect, and to venerate; and these resources are never so necessary as in the hour of adversity and discouragement, where no ray of hope is left to cheer the prospect, and stimulate to fresh exertion."[3]

In the spring and summer of 1797 Thompson had time to write about his experiments for publication, as well as time for extended leisure. The count and Sally went touring during July and spent eight days in Berchtesgaden and Salzburg with Princess Taxis in August. Meanwhile, he asked Lady Palmerston to come to live with him for the winter of 1797 in Vienna. It was imperative to the count to continue to have employment rather than be a freelance intellectual. Thus when his appointment as Bavaria's minister to the Court of St. James was rejected in 1798 Thompson wrote Lady Palmerston about how he wished to disappear and hide from those who were "shy of a Courtier apparently in Disgrace."

Naturally, on his sojourn to Britain Thompson got to work on many projects. Sally was encouraging him to return to America and the prospect began to take form in his mind. He wrote Loammi Baldwin to reconnoiter what kind of welcome he would receive: "Are the remains of Party spirit and political persecutions done away with? Would it be necessary to ask leave of the State?"[4] Thompson's old friend of course reassured him that the slate was wiped virtually clean. The expatriate's vision was of a pacific retreat near the libraries and university in Cambridge:

> I have ... a scheme of forming for myself a little quiet retreat in the Country, to which I can retire at some future period, and spend the evening of life. Perhaps you may be so good as to assist me in carrying this plan into execution. As I am not wealthy and prefer comfort to splendor, I shall not want anything magnificent. From 40 to 100 acres of good land, with Wood, and Water belonging to it if possible, in a retired situation, from 1 to 4 miles from Cambridge, with, or without a neat comfortable

House upon it would satisfy all my wishes.... I should want nothing from the land but pleasure grounds, and grass for my Cows and Horses, and an extensive Kitchen Garden and fruit Garden.[5]

As the job search went on, Rufus King, the American minister in London, wrote the secretary of state, Timothy Pickering, that Thompson was the very person to upgrade American artillery. After making resumé-type remarks, King anticipated protest about the former Tory traitor and noted that Thompson "assured me that he wishes nothing more than to be useful to our country.... It is possible that attempts may be made to misrepresent his political opinions: from the enquiry that I have made on this head, I am convinced that his political sentiments are correct."[6]

Manpower with military expertise needed reinforcement from outside U.S. borders, the powers in the American government concurred. King suggested to the U.S. secretary of war that Count Rumford had founded a military academy in Bavaria and could do the same in America. The essays of the count were in the hands of George Washington, who had thanked him personally,[7] and Alexander Hamilton had even commended to his military staff the count's essay on feeding armies.[8] President Adams told Rufus King to encourage Thompson to come to America. Meanwhile, the count sent King his new model field piece,[9] a design he had developed for Bavaria that could be set up and fired rapidly.

Around 1798 Thompson began to center his activities in London, at 45 Brompton Row, Knightsbridge, a fine house he leased that was later designated 168 Brompton Road. He outfitted it with his preferences of ventilation and heating, décor (especially harmonious colors) and modern conveniences. It had double walls and windows, and the space between glass partitions was filled with plants. He arranged the decorations according to Newton's theory of complementary colors, installed folding beds and tables, and built-in wardrobes and drawers for bedding beneath the beds to economize space. Instead of being a separate room, the dining room was part of the kitchen. The staff lived in the basement. The property included a stable, coach-house and laboratory, which he had connected to the house by a centrally heated corridor. His friend Sir Charles had a house nearby.

For two years Thompson worked to found the Royal Institution, "a public institution for diffusing the knowledge and facilitating the general introduction of useful mechanical inventions and improvements, and for teaching, by courses of philosophical lectures and experiments, the application of science to the common purposes of life."[10] The concept had elite support, including Lord Palmerston's, and Thompson was a major private donor. The Royal Institution received royal approval in 1800. A key innovation of his project was to welcome all classes into the Royal Institution. Room and board was to be provided for 20 young men to study mechanics, and apprentices were to be admitted freely into the lecture room. The building would have a museum of models and inventions, a chemical laboratory, library, conversation room, experimental kitchen, a printing plant for publishing a journal, and workshops. But the Royal Institution departed from Thompson's original intentions of being a sort of technological school and laboratory.[11] When Rumford left England the instruction in mechanics was dropped because it was thought teaching science to the lower classes had a dangerous political tendency. The models were put away and the staircase to the mechanics' gallery torn down, but the Royal Institution prospered and many scientists carried on their research or had positions there or both. The count had chosen Humphry Davy, 23, as assistant lecturer in chemistry, for $500 a year and coals, candles and a folding bed for his accommodation. It was here that Davy decomposed compounds using an electric current, and discovered sodium and potassium.

After these intense two years, Thompson was ready for a change. He received offers from America, and Maximilian, his old friend and the new ruler of Bavaria, increased his pension. The count went to Paris instead in May 1802 and stayed until August, when he revisited Bavaria and stayed there until returning to Paris and making it his permanent home the following year.

Meanwhile, Thompson had become a celebrity in the British Isles as he had been in Germany. An incident suggests that he was used to being the focal point of female interest. One day when he was out, Lady Melbourne, whose sex partners included George, Prince of Wales, and Lord Byron, had come into his house and looked around. Aichner was much surprised.

When the first volume of his collected essays came out, Thompson, now in his forties, sent copies to grandees and heads of state. He was paving the way to move on in his peripatetic career. The king and queen of England, George Washington, President John Adams, Catherine of Russia, and the kings of Austria and Prussia all eventually received copies. Marc August Pictet, the scientist who reported from conversations about Thompson's life in the *Bibliothèque Britannique*, oversaw a French edition in Geneva, and the Baron Johann August von Kalb, the husband of Thompson's mistress Laura (see preceding chapter), made contact with a German translator that resulted in a German edition. To his publishers Thompson sent copies of his portrait by a painter at the Bavarian court and reproductions of the monument that was erected in his honor in the English Garden.

His time of greatness as a courtier was over and there would never be cause for him to make Munich his home as before. The relations between Thompson and the Lerchenfeld sisters had been characterized above all by a wall of silence. Did Thompson hide his ongoing affair with Josepha despite joking to Lady Palmerston that he would not start up with the older sister again? Did that mean the younger sister, Mary, was his mistress? The person who has spent a great deal of effort investigating Thompson's career in Munich is Thomas Weidner. Weidner was very careful to qualify all guesses about Thompson and he based what he wrote on looking at a large quantity of original material available to him. Weidner's opinion is that the withdrawal of Josepha Baumgarten to her castle in southern Bavaria, Ering, on the Inn River, was consequental of the departure of her lover from Munich in 1798 (correspondence, spring 2016). The two portraits of the countess sisters, Weidner has stated, reminded Count Rumford of his most productive period of life. Both portraits were painted in 1798, when he was already in the process of departing.

Thompson delayed going to America as he worked on not only the design of the Royal Institution but also creating the space for it. He worked out, with some difficulty, an innovative steam heating plant. He was disappointed when a feature was added of isolated seating for common people attending the lectures, a small gallery reached by a separate staircase that led directly to the street. Thompson believed in the equality of thinkers. To make space for a superintendent, he gave up his lodgings at the Albermarle property of the Royal Institution and put features and inventions in his own Brompton Row house for the public to view. The Royal Institution had political factions early on and strayed from his concepts, although today it is diverse and serves both the needs of scientists and the general populace.

While caught up with the Royal Institution, Thompson fell into ill health. To ward off a crisis like that of "five or six years before" he went to Harrogate in Yorkshire. Over and again Sally conceptualized how different she was from her father. She has been described as a shy country girl but she was also determined like her father. One day she would, in fact, get the last word by commissioning double portraits, where her father stared at her! Thompson was, in her opinion, used to his bachelor ways and she was used to being indulged by her mother. They crossed swords and Sally registered those differences of opinion in her diary. Placidity never suited her restless nature, and her subsequent life was a continual progress from one relative and home to another. It is also interesting that in her note to Mrs. Baldwin, speaking with humorous indulgence about her father's liking "a well deserved renown,"[12] she compared him to Mrs. Baldwin's husband, Loammi, and therefore did not consider it a personality trait that was out of bounds.

Sally was 25 when she returned to America in the summer of 1799. She wrote an incident that was likely fictitious, the gist of which was that Cora the dog was dropped overboard on the passage. "Serafine" told the sad tale in a poem with the peculiar name *Leisure Hours*, from which this is one quatrain:

> Captain! Captain! One cries,
> See ye that speck? That mote?
> Longer five minutes it dies,
> A Boat! A Boat! A Kingdom for a boat!

In the story, three dinghies went out, as the captain was disturbed to see the disconsolate owner of the dog. The dog supposedly was in view for five minutes and then went under the sea.[13] Sally liked to have things done for her and was prone to exaggeration and put these proclivities to work in her writings.

The Baldwins decided to give a ball in her honor. She was now a countess by reason of the connection with her famous father. The occasion chosen was New Year's Eve, the turn of centuries, when there were many parties, such as the one given by President and Mrs. Adams in the newly constructed White House. Sally wore an elegant blue satin gown she had brought from Europe.[14] She would recount her years abroad in retrospect like a fantasy—and what could symbolize her glamorous past better than a court dress with a lengthy train?

Sally would remain in America for the next twelve years. She took with her a letter from her father to Loammi Baldwin, who said that when he looked back "into that dark cloud that covers the early period of life, I can remember no person distinctly longer than yourself, except it be my mother."[15] Thompson said his earlier trip was frustrated but he thought it likely he would pay his old friend a visit the next spring. Thompson declined the offers pending of being inspector of artillery for the U.S. and Rufus King's to take charge of forming the military academy at West Point.

Since Napoleon's wars had tattered the lives of the aristocrats outside France—all over the Continent—the Countess Nogarola wrote Sally from Munich in May 1799 that she could have visited her friend in America before the war but now she would have to find a "buried treasure" to pay for such a voyage. Not lingering on the negative, Mary passed on court gossip of a family putting on airs at court and the Electrice, Karl Theodor's young wife, ending a love affair and consoling herself by learning to play the violin and being "as giddy [*étourdi*] as ever" and spending a fortune. Next Mary mentioned a drawing she had given Sally, apparently by Johann Georg von Dillis, a friend to their whole circle of aristocrats who had visited her and was off on a three-day excursion. "I flatter myself you will not part with it," Mary said of the drawing. In her last line of the letter—doubly shocking because Mary was chary of even asking for the gift of a packet of needles and was a devout, charitable person—she requested a slave: "A propos don't forget your promise to send me from America a pretty little Negress. Adieu my dear friend—my attachment to you will always exceed that of your americans. God Bless you! Your affectionate Mary." On the same letter, turned around, Mary found a small space at the margin to write in English, as if more intimate and set off from the letter to Sally, "My best love for your father."[16]

Countess Nogarola and Sally corresponded frequently when the Countess was in Verona or Munich and Sally was in Munich or America, years after Thompson had his Italian idyll in 1793 and 1794. When Mary interposed to give "my best love for your father," it seems as if mentioning his name would be too intimate and conjure up too intense a feeling. In the extant correspondence beginning in the late 1790s the ties of these people became clearer. Thompson was an outsider at the Bavarian court. The countesses were from Italy and therefore from elsewhere too, as was the Elector himself. Mary seems to have found Thompson the Aichner family of servants, and, watching closely, she believed that sometimes "Aichner" managed to keep the count from being ill. Mary kept an eye on her unspoken niece, Thompson's natural child, Sophie. Mary had the role of a steadying influence on Sally, and between the lines of her letters Mary longed for Thompson but had tucked her love into a locket in her heart. He received via his daughter almost tearful little indirect messages of that love, e.g., "You and I have no secrets from him."[17] In the touching letters that exist, either translated from French and transcribed by Sally or in the original (Mary and Sally probably wrote in French), just one single item sticks out like a sore thumb: the idiotic fact that towards the end of Mary's usual genre of letter mixing news and affection she said, "A propos don't forget your promise to send me a pretty little negress from America."

As has been discussed, it is known that as a child Sally had an enslaved black woman for a caretaker. Sally's mother was ailing, bedridden, from a picture Sally drew, and Sally's grandfather the Reverend Walker owned a number of black slaves. Sally had affection for this enslaved woman. Baron Cuvier, speaking of Thompson's social philosophy, said that Thompson did not trust people en masse to know what was best for them and "his views of slavery were the same as those of a plantation-owner."[18] But taking an antidemocratic position in argument, as it appears Thompson did, doesn't equate with being a proponent of slavery. Mary Nogarola's request would have likely astonished him. Thompson married into a family of slave owners. Did he brag about this to show off in front of his aristocratic friends? This seems preposterous. For Thompson his two years focused on being a country squire in Concord did not particularly imprint him and the fact his father-in-law had several slaves does not prove that Sarah Rolfe transplanted slave culture into her marriage. Dinah may have been the aunt's slave. Slavery tainted the wealth of these high citizens of Concord but was outside the radar of Thompson's short life with them. Cuvier's remark was made when European intelligentsia decried slavery and viewed it as an American sin whereas a New Englander would feel it endemic to their common cause with the South. If Thompson said slavery was part of a functioning society he probably was referring to the government of China, about which he knew next to nothing. It would have been like a socialist in the 1930s hailing Stalin from sheer ignorance. The form of government Thompson advocated was oligarchy and he did not theorize beyond the most general remarks about it and did not in print comment on the politics of the new nation, the United States.

Is the Countess Nogarola asking for a mere souvenir, a "romantic" painting of a black female, along the lines of the art and story about Americans that were popular in Europe at that time? Or is she asking Sally to send to her Verona estate a slave from New Hampshire? Slavery tends to be hidden from records. The slave was neither seen nor heard in New Hampshire until the slave petitioners of revolutionary Portsmouth (see Chapter 2) and the legislation of gradual emancipation statutes typical of the northern states in the early 19th century. The situation in northern Italy in the eighteenth century was parallel. Professor Paul Kaplan posited that the iconography of a black attendant to a white European began in the mid–15th century, in the late Renaissance, in the artwork of Andrea Mantegna. Showing Africans in a religious painting, whether in images of the Magi or other figures in the detail, also suggested that Christianity dominated the world. In the 18th century, slavery was largely gone from the Italian peninsula, but there was left an aura of social prestige around it, so it is not inconceivable that Mary imagined a slave from America as a sort of fashion accessory (although one hopes not).

Sally is likely to have wanted to impress her European friends when she had, and her father told her she had, so much catching up to do in terms of language and fashion to achieve their standard of cultivation. After all, her father too had stooped to feign that his forebears owned an island in Boston Harbor! During walks in the Englischer Garten or drinking hot chocolate with the aristocratic courtiers in Munich, she would have talked about "Dinah" the slave. She would have on the one hand been speaking of a person back home or from her childhood for whom she felt affection; on the other hand, Sally had wavering self-esteem, and to cover poor self-esteem by affectation was a coping mechanism. But it still seems incredible that the serious, modest and sensitive sister (versus the frivolous and carefree Countess Baumgarten) would want to accessorize herself with a slave. Certainly in Verona there were blacks free and enslaved as well as other slaves. Possessing a slave accrued to one's prestige in the Renaissance but this was the Enlightenment and slavery was anathema to progressive ideals.

As mentioned in correspondence, Mary and Sally gave each other small tokens of affection. Mary, however, discouraged Sally from sending something that would have high shipping costs: what would have happened legally if Sally had put a slave on a ship bound for Verona? The gift of a slave seems both disproportionate and preposterously complex when otherwise the two women at the outer limit gave each other a length of cloth or packet of needles. Mary's "a propos" comes after relaying that the artist von Dillis had visited her for a few days. Perhaps the Countess really did want a picture of a black person for her gallery. She had a quiet temperament and liked quiet family life better than balls and was in dread of court attendance. A portrait of an absent loved one meant something to her. Just as Mary wanted pictures of her friends, the fact that she used the word "pretty" and "little" might imply she wanted a representation in art of a feature of her friend's life in America. Whether the gift was made is unknown because no more correspondence on the matter than the single mention has surfaced. As for the request, which strikes a modern reader like a cannonball in the chest, explanation comes from Paul Kaplan, professor of art history at SUNY, Purchase.

Mary's Bizarre Request

The countess was surely asking for a human being, not a painting of one. There were portraits of slaves and free people of color made by European artists in the 18th century, but not in North America (except as pages or servants to white masters).

European aristocrats eagerly sought black African servants for their household as early as the 13th century, and several probably passed through Verona around 1240 in the entourage of the Holy Roman Emperor Frederick II of Hohenstaufen. There is a surviving wall painting in Verona from that era that is probably based on them, and quite a few other images in the city across the centuries. In the 18th century, German courts like the one where the Countess's husband worked were especially eager for black servants, who were typically obtained as slaves but usually manumitted at some point. This was generally true of European slavery (whether of black Africans or other groups)—slaves were often freed at the death of their owner, or as a result of conversion to Christianity. Most enslaved black Africans in Italy in the 1700s arrived via a trade that began in Northern Nigeria and stretched across the Sahara to what is now Libya, though others came from the West African coast. A certain number also came from the New World.

In seeking such court servants, European aristocrats were not always able to obtain them as slaves. In 1491 Isabella d'Este, the wife of the marquis of Mantua, told her agent in Venice to find her a little girl, not older than four years, and as "black as possible"; but such a slave was not readily available and Isabella's mother (the Duchess of Ferrara) scooped her by hiring the whole family of a free black gondolier in Venice, which included such a child. In the late 1600s and throughout most of the 1700s many such child pages to European aristocrats were evidently obliged to wear "slave collars," pieces of metal around their necks that denoted their slave status.

By 1799 the situation would have been a little different. The French Revolutionary government had abolished slavery in its dominions in the early 1790s, though this was eventually reversed by Napoleon. Nevertheless, given the tenor of the times, European slavery was much diminished in this period. By the 1820s slavery was generally illegal in much of Western Europe, and Americans who brought enslaved servants with them on a European tour risked having them simply walk away from bondage. For example, the Venetian guide who took Mark Twain to see the artistic sights of the city in 1867 was actually the son of an African American slave who had left his white American owner in this way several decades before. It may have been immaterial to the Countess whether the girl she sought was enslaved or free.

The more difficult question is whether the Countess was seriously or lightly making this request. She undoubtedly would have been happy to have such a servant, but it sounds unlikely that a young girl (slave or free) could easily have been shipped from America to Verona in this turbulent period. By 1799 slavery was pretty much over in New Hampshire, though there had been plenty of African American slaves there before the war. It was, however, still legal to engage in the slave trade in the U.S., and Portsmouth had several slave traders. I tend to think that the request was a kind of banter. Much later, during the Civil War, the English art critic John Ruskin tried to goad an American friend of his who he thought was naively enthusiastic about the Emancipation Proclamation by asking him, in a postscript to a letter, to send him "something American, a slave perhaps." Not that the Countess was trying to taunt her correspondent.

After living in Europe for many years, the count requested that his mother's picture be drawn by the best limner in Boston. Perhaps he realized he would never return to America and thus would not see her. Thompson said good-bye to Sally and she boarded her ship in October 1799. He described her "like a bird let out of a cage" and wrote her immediately after reassuring they would be together again soon: "I dare say you will be glad to see me when I join you in America next year, as I hope to do. Or if I come not there you will return here."[19] Sally and her half-brother Paul Rolfe had Loammi send a present to Thompson of a "cask of fruit" containing "half a dozen apples of the growth of my farm, wrapped up in papers, with the name of Baldwin's apples written upon them.... It is (I believe) a spontaneous production of this country; that is, it was not originally engrafted fruit."[20] Thompson never broke loose from his projects to visit or live again in his native land.

Sally must have been betwixt and between. Upon her return from Europe she went to live first with her old schoolmistress Mrs. Snow, who continued her elite establishment with high fees and few pupils. She also visited the Baldwins in Woburn and her relatives in Concord. Around Christmas 1799 she went to the theater with Colonel Baldwin. It seemed that her friendship ties were fixed for life with two generations of Baldwins; after Loammi died she would rely on his son, James, another distinguished engineer. She felt as dislocated in America as she had in Europe. She described her return as falling from heaven to earth, the virtual end to her life. As depressing as that sounds, her sentiment may be understood as a somewhat formulaic Victorian expression of deep regret for the passing of youthful adventures. She certainly had not lost the tie to her father. During the next eleven years before Sally rejoined her father, she counted 104 letters from him.

Before Sally's return to the United States, her grandmother Ruth had moved to Maine with Mr. Pierce, and when Sally got back home she visited friends and acquaintances in Portland, Brunswick, and Flintstown, renamed Baldwin after Loammi Baldwin in 1802. The year after she returned to America was when high officials had broached appointing Thompson head of what would be West Point. That coincided with the invitation of General Henry Knox, a major general in the Revolution, close friend to George Washington, and the first U.S. Minister of War to spend the summer with him and his wife at their estate, Montpelier, in Thomaston (now Maine). Mrs. Knox, who had married down for love (the general had started as a lowly bookseller), placed a high value on social status; Talleyrand and the future French king Louis-Philippe had visited in recent years and to have a countess as a guest must have registered positively. The extravagant tall windows extending all the way to the floor opened to a porch from which Sally could paint scenes of the St. George River.[21] Her father was very pleased to hear from General Knox that she was making progress in her watercolors. Sally continued to feel she was too idle to please her father and did her best to embroider him a fancy vest.

Having a burning mind that never stopped creating rendered his life exhilarating but it was also an affliction. Thompson was aware of the strain of his genius and wrote to Professor Pictet in Geneva: "The waters have certainly been of much service to me, though I do not think it likely that they will radically cure my complaint. Idleness and amusement would be the most efficacious remedy; but I cannot be idle, nor can I amuse myself with moderation. The ardour of my mind is so ungovernable that every object that interests me engages my whole attention, and is pursued with a degree of indefatigable zeal which approaches to madness. It is no wonder that my health should be impaired by such continual excesses."[22] Thompson took curative baths and, true to form, wrote an essay in an attempt to popularize their benefit.

13

Leaving London and Paris Opens Its Arms (1801–1802)

>Science seldom renders me amiable; women, never.
>—Edmone-Pierre Chanvot Beauchène (1748-1824)

Next stop would be Paris, "his dear Paris," as Sally would say, expressing her father's experience during the months of his first visit. Karl Theodor had charged him with delivering dispatches to the Bavarian minister, but for Thompson this first trip to Paris was like being one of Odysseus's crew eating the lotuses—not that Thompson partied in the fashion of many elite men of his era. He didn't whore or gamble; he would just as soon forego wine, drank sometimes beer, and didn't mount up debts. What thrilled him was coming upon what he had long heard about in Bavaria: Paris's concerts, plays, architecture, and glamor. What's more, he was off the leash, roaming without a wife. He arrived in the fall of 1801 and would stretch his visit to seven weeks and come back soon again, in time to be one of the 240 guests at Napoleon's sit-down dinner party on Bastille Day in the Tuileries. He wrote Lady Palmerston (November 1, 1801): "I find it quite impossible to leave Paris so soon as I intended.—there are a thousand things to see that are highly worthy of being seen, and as I am here I think it would be quite foolish not to take time enough to satisfy my curiosity." In the same letter he wrote, "It is quite impossible to be more civil than every body is to me in this place." There was also this: "Tho I have been at only one play since I arrived here, but I mean to make a tour of the theatres and other places of amusement. The whole business of the Parisians is to amuse themselves. If you were here you would amuse yourself too, I am quite sure of it."[1]

The intellectual coterie he entered easily might have been a Parnassus—given the enthusiasm of the intelligentsia and the first consul for science—but for the timing. The Napoleonic era seethed with suspicion of foreigners and intensified general chauvinism: "For fifteen years, France and Europe were to be at the mercy of a gambler to whom fate and his own genius gave for a time all the aces."[2] Thompson's great patron dead and his ties with Bavaria weakening, he had a mind to settle in London, but would instead soon settle in France. He was nevertheless present in Munich quite a lot during this period, meeting his requirement of living and working six months each year there. Notwithstanding these movements, he had not given up on returning to his homeland.

Keeping the safe distance of an ocean from entanglement with his estranged wife was no longer a factor and the Revolutionary War was beginning to look like a family

Drawing of a carriage on wooden springs, for one horse, by Count Rumford, Brompton September 11, 1801. "Intended for Hackney Carriage for London. To carry one, or two Persons. The Coachman to stand behind the Carriage" (Houghton Library, Harvard University).

feud. Gourveneur Morris, when he came to Europe for official and unofficial reasons, visited his brother who was a general in the British army. So Thompson, although cautious about his reception in America, would have sailed in on his laurels from Europe. The nascent Royal Institution, however, which Sir Charles described as Thompson's "favorite child," claimed consuming attention. From the Royal Institution he wrote Baldwin to do what he could to make his mother and daughter comfortable and contented—and that his daughter had his leave to marry if she wished and with whomever she wished.

Rufus King encouraged the count to revisit America, saying he was authorized to offer him the position of head of the new military academy being planned at West Point, specifically as Inspector General of Artillery (September 8, 1799). Instead the appointment went in 1801 to Jonathan Williams, a Harvard graduate and grandnephew of Benjamin Franklin. If the offer to an ex–Tory seems a leap, Williams himself spent the American Revolution mostly in England and was there when Thompson made his rise. Then again, having the completely new name of Rumford may have made it easier for the American officials to deal with the former Royalist.

Williams's forte was science and he had no military experience, whereas Thompson was a world-class artillery expert. Then again, Henry Knox, Washington's minister of war, learned about cannon from a British manual. (By contrast, with her jolly husband, Mrs. Knox aimed to have prestigious, in Sally's case titled, guests).

By the fall of 1801, the Royal Institution had been in possession of its charter for a year. Thompson's dream of a technological and scientific center was a qualified reality. It had a firm foundation and an impressive building, as well as Thompson's protégé Humphry Davy as head of the laboratory. Thompson wanted an institute open to people from all walks of life. Here they would learn state-of-the-art applied technology. This concept wasn't elevated enough for those who would run the institution as it evolved.

Looking back at Thompson's vision, Dr. H. Bence Jones, the institution's secretary in the 1860s, appraised Thompson's original vision: "His idea of a laboratory was a kitchen and a chemist."[3]

Sally was in America and not figuring in Thompson's comings and goings. Used to imperiously ruling his projects, he could not have this role regarding his brainchild, a public arena of applied science. Thus he could pry himself away from London. On Thompson's reasons for leaving Britain and never coming back, Neil Chambers, editor of the letters of Sir Joseph Banks, observes, "I think it is clear that he had lost interest in the Royal Institution and during the period that he finally departed was somewhat under a cloud in London society. His, as it turned out, unhappy marriage to Lavosier's widow and probably also age finally meant that he remained in France, where he died. The political climate in Europe at this time can't have been especially conducive to free travel of the kind that, in his youthful years, had typified Rumford's existence. So, I would imagine that his permanent departure was due to a combination of factors rather than just to one."[4]

In contrast to Lord Nelson, who acceded to his mistress Emma's flooding their house with his image, Thompson had only one portrait of himself in view and another in the attic. The art on his walls is known from his memoranda. Being conscious of rank, he identified Sally's portrait as "Countess Sarah Rumford," discreetly did not name the ladies in his pictures. At 45 Brompton Row he also had miniatures of Professor Pictet and Frederick William II; engravings of Bavaria, and in the back attic, framed in gilt, two ladies' portraits, one an oval miniature.

On October 18, the count visited the Princess of Taxis in her home in Dischingen, then part of the Duchy of Palatinate-Neuberg, now Bavaria. He was, in available correspondence, mysterious about this paramour, who comes across as a prize he captivated for a lesser time period than his other intimate women. His underlining the name by which he called her in the diary he kept briefly relating to his first Paris trip hints that the Princess was his lover. The underlining comes from his personal writing (a diary he kept for several months), as opposed to his correspondence.[5]

On the name day of the Princess, or Taxis, Thérèse spent the forenoon in her apartment after having breakfasted there at half an hour past 9 o'clock, with her select "Society" a distant family cousin. That night they enjoyed a "masked Ball in the Evening which was opened by a charming Ballet." The Princess danced with her brother the Prince of Mecklenburg "the principal parts in it and danced with infinite grace." Thompson recorded that he went to bed at one in the morning. What makes Thompson's dalliances with Princess Taxis distinct in his sexual and intimate history is that they were escapades. They had no undertow of a woman's longing. Thérèse would fall in love later, not with Thompson but a man who became her second husband. Also, worldly affairs of business preoccupied the princess, as she held the reins of the Thurm & Taxis postal service, quite a balancing act with unprecedented centralized control of highways by Napoleon.

Leaving the princess, Thompson put his toe down in Munich, staying less than two weeks. Karl Theodor died before the century turned, in 1799. Thompson looked toward his future. Was his unusual position secure now that Maximilian had succeeded his cousin? If not, there were options. The count had the credentials to have a high post in Russia or America. However, he found a welcome. Bavaria had concluded a treaty with France and Maximilian reassured the count of his future association with Bavaria.

Nearing 50, the count reminisced in his journal about the passage of time. He was staying in the same tavern where he had long before. He could not visit, he wrote, without seeing Aichner, his faithful servant, who had settled in Munich as an innkeeper with his wife and the younger of his six children. One daughter, Sarah Mary, named after Sally and the Countess Mary Nogarola, would be placed as a milliner in Paris by Thompson's second wife, Madame Lavoisier. The count was affected by their proofs of their attachment. The father was in the count's employ in London and Paris as well as Munich.

Thompson visited the Englischer Garten in the splendor of early fall, with his daughter Sophie Baumgarten, who "promises to be a charming creature. She is very clever and very accomplished for a child of her age. She is grown very much since I saw her last."[6] When she was 14 he gave her a clavecin and praised her for being sweet, modest, and playing well for someone her age. Sally Thompson had the portrait of Sophie, whom she had not seen since she was eight or so, in the room where she died. It was a sentimental age! It speaks for the morality of the times among the elite in a country where girls married very young and divorce was not an option that an out-of-wedlock child could not inherit a title or even sometimes the legitimate children's surname, but that child was not a matter of shame. Sophie was a child who had family and love and as far as her parentage she was an indiscretion.

When the count left Munich, Maximilian charged him to take part in potential negotiations with Napoleon. This was based on how the count diffused by diplomacy violence when Auspertria and France were on the city's outskirts in 1800. Now the way was clear in terms of the count's career and British-French relations for him to visit Paris for the first time. He traveled from Constanz to Mannheim on two successive nights, and in Mannheim at six o'clock he went to the "Cour Palatine." The next day he showed the Elector his plans for the court garden and then "dined with Laura and remained with her the Evening.... Found Laura the same good affectionate creature. She was very happy to see me."[7] He had allowed himself to commit to paper a matter of the heart—his ineluctable affection for the Baroness de Kalb—when he called her Laura, a telltale sign of their intimacy.[8]

Baroness Friederike Eleonore Sophie von Kalb, pastel on paper by unknown artist (circa 1795). Labeled in ink on reverse: "This lady is the Baroness of Kalbe/of Leipsic, a very particular friend of/Count Rumford's—she being besides/ very good and beautiful, as of great celebrity" (New Hampshire Historical Society).

The de Kalb completes the quintet, the Countesses Baumgarten and Nogarola, Lady Palmerston, and the Princess of Taxis beautiful, young, aristocratic women who found Thompson so intriguing they became intimate friends with him and possibly slept with him—were certainly physically warm with him, despite their marital status. Laura had literary interests and spirit like her sister Charlotte, memorialized by an anecdote that links her with Friedrich Schiller. Schiller read aloud to Charlotte his play, on which

Verdi based his opera *Don Carlo*. Charlotte, "after in vain endeavoring to restrain her humor at the extremely ridiculous pathos of the reader, burst out into a loud laugh. 'This is too much!' cried Schiller, throwing the manuscript on the floor, and leaving the room in the same instant." But a third person picked it up and read it aloud and "soon moved the fair critic to tears."[9]

Women don't like to hear much about their present or past rivals. Because Thompson felt close to Lady Palmerston he overlooked this fact and gave her the long version (not usually his style) of going to the chateau of "the aimiable Laura" in Saxony and not finding her at home. He described barns and a bridge crossing over a river to the big white house with a stone double staircase like one in a fairy tale. This was intended to amuse Lady Palmerston. If it did so, the account of how, soon after, Thompson and Laura de Kalb did manage to meet would have galled her. Laura, he said, took him into her bedroom and showed him "a single Picture ... placed to great advantage" on the wall of a certain someone:

> She says she never feels herself to be alone when she is in that room. She is a most interesting creature, and it is perfectly impossible not to love her with the most tender affection. She is innocence, candour, and sweetness personified. Her joy at seeing her beloved friend once more is not to be described. I thought the tears would never cease flowing down her lovely cheeks. Ah! My dear Lady Palmerston you were right!—I ought never to have suffered this angel to be torn from me.—Her whole happiness is at this instant concentrated in the recollection of a few moments of enjoyment, and so far from repining at her fate, she says she thanks God every day with the warmest gratitude for having given her a friend "who is dearer to her than the whole world, and who is equally worthy of her love, and her admiration."
>
> Pardon me, my dear Lady P.—it is a great consolation, when ones heart overflows, to give a loose [sic] ones sentiments. Heaven knows how far I am from feeling the smallest degree of vanity. On the contrary I am deeply sensible of my own inferiority.—but I must proceed no farther.—the subject is not proper for an epistolatory correspondence.[10]

Worship combined with romantic sentiments created Laura's intense love. Laura assured Thompson that her husband was away and came seldom and that she now (in 1801) meant to spend the rest of her life in her Mannheim house. She was essentially proposing to Thompson her sexual exclusivity, an offer bathed in affecting tears. She did not have the stable mutual respect in her marriage that would have toned down their intimacy to what Thompson had with other aristocratic women. Recounting the emotional scene, Thompson told Lady Palmerston, he too was affected. As he and the Baroness de Kalb looked at his portrait in her favorite room of the house, their underlying sadness derived from the passage of time and sex that didn't quite alchemize to a form that could bring either person lasting happiness.

Laura's place in Thompson's life can be compared to the other women in the quintet. Mary Nogarola gently yearned for Thompson, and after he moved from Munich recalled him and bathed her romantic feelings in as much solitude as she could (relayed by indirection to Sally). The countess was a Madonna figure, concerned for his health, smoothing relations with Sally during her time in Munich, and later having Sophie visit and being a stabilizing influence in her upbringing. Lady Palmerston wanted to be the most important woman in Thompson's life without his being the most important person in hers, as that place was taken by Lord Palmerston. Thompson, when she was ill, said she might like to go to his "little box" in London even in his absence, so she may have been accustomed to meeting him there. Because of her admiration of Thompson, Mary Mee set up a soup kitchen and school of industry near Broadlands. Mostly she and Thompson had a stimulating friendship that was a comfort to each. All the same, she did seem at times to slip into a net that entangled her with greater emotional intensity. Mary Mee was, Thompson chided her, "spoiled" because she had never experienced pain and suffering caused by a man. Nevertheless, a happily married woman does not feel passion for a man not her husband and if Mary had done so that would have disabled the friendship.

Then there was Laura, who saw Thompson's bright blue eyes and was lost to reality. She opened the windows of her heart to him. Every love relationship feels unique to those in it but Laura was unique among Thompson's *compagnons*, who was happy to share a time and place with her, but this did not answer her passion. A strong physical, emotional and intellectual connection could not exist between them, much less thrive, with his dropping in on her only now and then. Her bedroom became a shrine, a place for her to grieve. Scar tissue formed but wistful hope was ever-present in her heart. (What her husband made of her having her lover's portrait in her bedroom the baroness did not disclose).

Despite the attraction for him of Laura in Mannheim, the count's destination was Paris. He was keen to mingle with other scientists and had long been in a satellite to Parisian culture, that of Munich. The truce that would be finalized the next year as the Treaty of Amiens was being discussed, making the count's projected visit more feasible and less tense. To satisfy his employer he was also to get as close as possible to Napoleon himself. Many British were taking the opportunity of an ease in relations to see the sights of Paris. Thompson often was shepherded by the Bavarian ambassador.

Maximilian, the successor to Karl Theodor, had charged the count with delivering some dispatches, but for him this brief first trip to Paris was like being one of Odysseus's crew eating the lotuses. Not that he partied in the fashion of many elite men of his era; his constitution didn't allow it and he was completely against wasting time. What thrilled him was coming upon what he had long heard about from francophiles: Paris's concerts, plays, architecture and luminaries. Going from Munich to Paris was going to a Parnassus whose features the count already knew from the Bavarian court. He wasn't inclined to assert the moral superiority of his forebears or dwell on any inconveniences or miseries, or scars from the French Revolution. He was an openminded and enthusiastic visitor, as nine years later, likewise coming from the direction of Germany (Hamburg), former U.S. vice-president Aaron Burr had been. Applying for a passport Burr told Joseph Fouché, the minister of police, that the purpose of his visit to Paris was purely touristic—"The undersigned, desiring to visit Paris for motives of curiosity and amusement only." Both men's secondary political agendas dissolved in the fairgrounds of the French capital.[11] The count reveled in the energy of the cultural capital of Europe and the high place science had in it. For seven weeks he kept a journal, which he sent to Lady Palmerston and she would copy the next year while mourning the viscount. In the diary were recorded social engagements, the beauty of the society women, sights he saw, and the charitable institutions he visited.

Meeting members of high society was virtually the count's job, and he recounted it in the sole adult diary in his life as if that were also a job. Affability, manners, directness and naturalness are what he signaled time and again. Thus he saw Madame de Staël several times (she had wanted to meet him). His first impression was that she did not smile. At another meeting he observed that she wanted to talk politics and he led her away from the topic by telling her that she would find his opinions decidedly different from hers.[12]

How accepted the count was derives from a comparison with American businessmen and diplomats who visited around that time. Napoleon Bonaparte invited the count, when they met at the institute, to supper, where Thompson was the only stranger among the guests. Napoleon had not yet hardened into a machine of destruction or suffered an assassination attempt. He was not yet at war with England and he was focused on improving roads, water supply, laws and the system of measures. The count not only had conversations with the First Consul but also frequent interchanges with, and was the guest of, Talleyrand and his mistress. At the French Institute, the count was almost immediately brought into the Section of Political Economy and would be moved to a higher echelon of First Class in 1803 in recognition of his physics.

Yet, there was a gap between the American physicist and inventor and the French. It came down to both French-British hostility and how science was done (Paris was arguably the capital of scientific endeavor in Europe at the time). First of all, Thompson was looked at more as an inventor than as a physicist. To the French, a hands-on approach to science was inferior to mathematical calculations. In contrast, in England technological innovation came from the craftsmen class, like Josiah Wedgwood, curates with leisure time like William Lee, inventor of the knitting machine, or aristocratic hobbyists. Thompson's inductive research methods and his detailed approach were consonant with the Enlightenment advance in science but abraded the leading scientists of the day in Paris. The French savants respected theory and mathematics, while the count started with a concrete problem and as he worked with it figured out a principle that could apply to wider applications.

Rivalry was to be expected among the members of the French Institute and towards foreigners, given the top-down source of all privileges in the Napoleonic era. Yet Thompson was welcomed in the highest echelons on his initial visit to Paris. He had expected to stay two weeks and that stretched to almost two months. His activities were marked in a kind of extended memorandum. When Henry Temple, Lord Palmerston, died in April 1802 Lady Palmerston assuaged her grief by copying the diary Thompson kept of his social life in Paris from the end of 1801 through the beginning of 1802. Doing so brought her closer to the man who had been part of the happy times of her marriage, who had been way more than a pen pal for long years.

It was at the party of the minister of the interior, Jean-Antoine Chaptal, in early November that the count met the mathematician Pierre Simon de Laplace, who became his close friend. Laplace straddled science and politics successfully, so he was a valuable ally. He even teased Napoleon with a bold affirmation of empirical science. When Napoleon asked why God was not mentioned in his book, Laplace, an avowed atheist, replied, "Citizen First Consul, I have no need of that hypothesis."[13]

The second November (1801) morning in Paris, Thompson met Talleyrand. In one of the count's more piquant entries in his journal he observed, "I never saw a face more better calculated to impose silence on prattling fools than his." He also looked up Joseph Louis Lagrange, the engineer of the metric system. Alessandro Volta demonstrated, before Napoleon at the institute, the generation of electrical current through his battery. Thompson sat near the First Consul at the meeting. After Napoleon praised Volta, he acknowledged Thompson, complimenting him for his inventions, such as a roaster from Germany then being displayed in Paris, and invited him to dine. In France under Napoleon every gesture of the dictator was interpreted and signified, so that this "royal treatment" had a ripple effect and reinforced Thompson's glamor in Paris. The institute elected him and President Thomas Jefferson members at the same session in 1801, Thompson for his science and Jefferson for being president of the parallel American society.

Day after day Thompson visited Parisian highborn ladies, took them to the opera, and was invited in the daytime into their boudoirs, as was the convention for idle upper-class ladies of the time. When Voltaire and Emilie du Châtelet, the aristocrat and scientist who was Voltaire's *compagnon*, redesigned his chateau, she got a new tub and bathing room.[14] Here she installed sofas near the tub for visitors to sit and converse on, say, Isaac Newton's *Principia Mathematica*. Entertained by Madame Laplace in her bedroom, Thompson and Monsieur Laplace chatted all morning about galvanism, gunpowder and cannons while Madame Laplace really could not leave her bed. On leaving, Thompson apologized but she said "she was much obliged to me for having given her so much of the morning" and she invited him to dinner en famille. Madame Laplace is named in several biographical writings on Thompson as one of his mistresses, based on her entertaining him in the bedroom. At that time, having one's bedroom designed by architect Charles Percier in the very latest Neo-Classical opulence was the height of poshness. The woman who had an Empire-style bedroom wanted to show it off to guests.

The count met Anne-Marie Paulz Lavoisier about a week after the Bavarian minister took him to a party given by Jean-Antoine Chaptal, the chemist who was then Napoleon's minister of the interior. Making an impression at Chaptal's put the count on the loftiest guest lists of the intelligentsia. Anne Lavoisier's husband had been the great chemist Antoine Lavoisier, who shared his experiments with other scientists and whose wife's salon in the Arsenal had before the Revolution magnetized the international scientific community. On November 19, 1801, Thompson attended one of her salons and was impressed by her and the ambience. In her role of veteran salonist she had become attuned to the interests and ego needs of the scientific man. What Claude-Anne Lopez in *Mon Cher Papa: Franklin and the Ladies of Paris* wrote insightfully about the gentlewomen of 20 years earlier—"reared by governesses, convent-bred, trained from infancy for the role she would be called on to perform in society"—applied equally to Madame Lavoisier reemerged from the shadows. Describing the earlier salonist, Lopez noted, "Best of all, she knew how to make her salon a center for the diffusion of lights, those *lumières* so dear to the philosophic heart; and when she had captured such a gem as Franklin, she spared no effort to keep him entertained."[15] Madame Lavoisier saw Count Rumford as a gem also. She had suitors but the count represented the whole package—not tainted by participation in the French Revolution, having the esteem of fellow philosophes, and with the sheen of his aristocratic title.

Madame Lavoisier had been widowed seven years and was 43. Benjamin Thompson had been widowed nine years and was 48. When she received him, practically a stranger, in her husband's former laboratory at the Arsenal, Thompson showed delicacy in not asking about Antoine. Perhaps Thompson conceived of paying her court upon meeting her. Seven years is often a time in a marriage or out of one when a person thinks of a change, and by now the count had been widowed about that length of time. Thompson noted in his diary two days after meeting Mme. Lavoisier the somewhat awkward visit to her home: "I made several visits in the Morning Found Mad Lavoisier at home and alone. Sat with her an hour, and found her very lively witty, and pleasing in conversation. She received me in an elegant room which had every appearance of being a Cabinet de Physique. It was quite filled, and even crowded with Philosophical and chemical apparatus. The various instruments are constructed on the largest scale and finished with the greatest care and accuracy. It was evident that they were the apparatus employed by the late unfortunate Mr. de Lavoisier but I did not ask the question."[16] It must have made him pleased with himself to pass the test of politesse with the salonist, although the meeting does sound a bit awkward, as though Antoine might be hovering in his *cabinet*. Thompson saw her again on November 25, and on December 2 wrote, "Mad. Lavoisier is a very cheerful friendly good natured Woman and she is rich and independent." He further described her as "one of the cleverest woman I ever knew and ... uncommonly well informed." He called on her every other day, and on the Sunday of December 13, 1801, when he left for England, he breakfasted with her at nine and took a post chaise at eleven.

She was warm, friendly and agreeable, rich and independent, and liked to travel. If this sounds like a personal ad, this is how the pair matched up, not in temperament, lifestyle or aspirations. He saw that when he spoke of his research and publications he planned to do, observing that "nothing pleased her as much as experiments and she wanted the whole description. She said, '*Venez vous etablir ici et je vais être votre Secretaire—vous travaillerez et moi jécrira*' [Come live with me and I will be your secretary; you will work and I will write]. 'That would be charming indeed' was my answer." This extraordinary offer shows her self-confidence, her wanting to revive the kind of relationship she had with Antoine, and also that she was daydreaming remarriage.

Three distinguished men besides the count took a personal interest in the widow. Pierre du Pont, a liberal economist and trusted friend of Thomas Jefferson, eventually left for America with his son who was the founder of DuPont corporation (with headquarters still today in Delaware). Madame Lavoisier was always sighing over him and calling him back to her side, where his affection for her seems to have been the more passionate. Du Pont was the older lover, intimate with Anne in the 1780s while her husband was engrossed in scientific farming and who wanted to marry her after Antoine Lavoisier was guillotined. He also owed money to her husband's estate.

Sir Charles Blagden, scientist and secretary of the Royal Society, appears in this book frequently beginning with Thompson's idyll in Italy. Sir Charles was a connector and a bachelor ready to pick up and travel with Thompson and was also caught up with establishing relations between English and French scientific communities as well as possibly doing some spying in France. A marriage with Anne would have been convenient. He paid her many visits, but he was not in love with her, any more than he was with Sally Thompson, whose hand he had also sought from her father.

The Swiss science journalist Marc-Auguste Pictet often visited Anne and was, even if he did not propose to her, a single man buzzing around an available and appropriate widow. Pictet founded an important intellectual journal and represented Protestant interests from Geneva to Napoleon's regime. His interest in Madame Lavoisier was tied to her

Madame Tallien from an engraving by W. Bond from a painting by J.J. Masquerier (Napoleon Collection, Rare Books and Special Libraries Collection, McGill University).

stature in the scientists' social circle. When his son-in-law lost his job, Pictet asked her help. Moreover, Pictet sighed for Julie Charles, the tubercular wife of a medical colleague and chemist who was at one time Pictet's physician. In 1815 Madame Charles had a brief living-together arrangement with the poet Alphonse de Lamartine, whom she had met at a spa at Aix-les-Bains. She died from tuberculosis at 33 a year later. Lamartine became famous for his writing about her and being inspired by her. *Méditations Poétiques* (1820) was considered to be the first work of the Romantic period in France. Pictet appears to have been a faithful husband, much attached to his wife and family, although he was smitten with Julie and wrote her of his love while still married (his wife died in 1811 when he in his early sixties). As for Dr. Charles, he was at one point ready to move his office out of the Charles home so that Pictet could move in and cheer up Julie, who was high-strung as well as ill. Dr. Jacques Charles is remembered as the inventor of the hydrogen balloon.

Pictet was so passionate that he overspent on tokens. The first time he met Julie he sent her a box of pastilles genevoises, known to soothe a cough. "If each time you take one, a little memory is associated with it, I would have invented a happy stratagem to not be completely forgotten and the box would be almost a Pandora's because when you arrived at the bottom I would have the hope to see you again."[17] Pictet gave the young Madame Charles a fancy shawl when they were the rage in Paris and so many other gifts that his son chastised him. On a "séjour alpin" Julie visited Geneva, and afterwards poor Pictet felt remorse he hadn't anticipated her wishes well enough. Pictet recalled Julie as having a fiery soul that consumed the frail envelope of her being *("une âme de feu a consomé sa frêle envelope")*.[18]

The earlier salons before the French Revolution had put an accent on the arts and philosophy. Then politics became more salient, but science, known as natural philosophy, became very à la mode as well. Napoleon aimed to transform France into a modern, centralized state. Since the regime was new, ambitious people had to keep up to figure out who had power and who was out of power, a dizzying revolving door, no less among men of science than the new nobility, which during the imperial period took in many of the old nobility that had survived the French Revolution. Thus Pictet drove himself to exhaustion on his trips from Geneva, trying to go to salons and make the rounds of government officials and straddle science and politics. He had a high reputation and was a great friend and admirer of Thompson, and like him was an idealist, though from the base of devout Protestantism as opposed to the count's Enlightenment and personal fervor.

Paris was where scientists flocked. Women fit into the lively scene not only as salonists (only a few opened their houses to entertain regularly) but also as part of the discussions and the jockeying for position. Du Pont, Bladen and Pictet, like many other gentlemen of enterprise in the tumult of Paris during Napoleon's regime, ran around paying calls and attending receptions and having interactions with society women. Pictet, for example, had a close friend in Madame Gautier-Dellesert, whose husband was a Swiss banker.

Count Rumford was not a good candidate for running around Napoleon's Paris trying to get a leg up to greater prestige. First of all, he didn't gamble and didn't incur debts. Second, he labored on technologies that did not blow people away—not like electricity or the aerial balloon. Third, he was always liable to fall seriously ill when he was run down physically and emotionally. In general he suffered from but did not succumb to his ailments. A marriage with Anne promised some leisure to do his work, a steady female companion, and an advantageous closeness to the scientific powerhouses of Paris—he thought.

The count passed on to Lord Palmerston that Talleyrand had told him he would not be allowed to leave Paris because the French were determined to keep him there. Indeed the count decided to make Paris his home. Anticipating that he was not returning to his 45 Brompton Row house, on his last seasons in England before returning to Paris Thompson made an inventory at the beginning of May 1802. The inventory reveals his lifestyle and precision and shows him to be a minimalist as well as a detail person. The bedrooms have folding beds and folding chair cushions ("squabs"). He liked imported furnishings, Chinese and Japanese china and teapots, and Turkish settees. The ground floor of the five-story house had a parlor and dining room (he had guests over but never bothered to have dinner parties). The third-floor workroom next to his bedroom was lighted by big double-glazed windows forming an arch, with window boxes on the sills. He kept in the attic guns of different types and a sword. He liked gilt chairs and frames, satin upholstery fabric, silk curtains, and the colors green blue and buff. The whole second floor, including the "passage," was covered with a leopard skin carpet, which one can hope forlornly was faux. He lists everything from hearth broom and chamber pot to pillowcases and shaving clothes. Should any proof be required of his meticulous mind, there is the entry after the clotheshorse of "one Rat trap."[19]

Along with fine furnishings, he meticulously noted a "Rat trap." Page from Thompson's Memorandum book, George E. Ellis papers. Ms N-1172, Box 21 (Massachusetts Historical Society).

14

Pursuing Madame Lavoisier (November 1801)

> We must take the current when it serves,
> Or lose our ventures.—Shakespeare, *Julius Caesar*,
> Act IV, Scene 3

After his first short visit to Paris, the count returned to London, from around Christmas 1802 through early May. Then he focused on the Royal Institution, preparing all the while for an imminent departure. There are no records of his seeing Lady Palmerston during this last sojourn in Great Britain. It has been suggested by Sanborn Brown that Mary Mee felt marginalized by other women in Thompson's life. In fact, Lord Palmerston was ill and a visit to Broadlands would have been unmannerly. Art-loving Henry Temple died that April. Mary Mee became ill and died of cancer three years later.

Maximilian (Karl Theodor's cousin), the new ruler of Bavaria, wrote a curious "very friendly letter" to the count advising him while in Paris to "cultivate the acquaintance of a certain lady there who was said to have, among other attractions, great wealth."[1] Possibly Maximilian, like so many others, was groping for a network of connections to Napoleon and wanted his courtier to sleep his way into the corridors of power. This would have been an incentive for the count to pursue the high-toned and rich, as it was said Madame Lavoisier inherited three million francs, a fortune, when her illustrious father and husband went to the guillotine.

The 50-year-old count's epistolary pursuit of Anne Lavoisier began when he reached London, when he wrote a letter that ended, "Adieu amiable lady, be assured of my regret that I cannot enjoy your charming society." Soon he raised the stakes and said that all he had done since leaving her was to think of her: "Be certain that I love you with all my heart." He called her his "ami" and his "amant." She was less flooded with feelings. She told him there was nothing as sweet as admiring (as he did) what one loves, without reciprocating his level of sentiment. She retrenched to an attitude of offended dignity from his talk of physicality, so he assured her (I translate from the French, which he used to write her): "Your three last letters have really frightened me, dearest. I thought your mind was made up. I'll try to behave myself, let's not speak this way again."[2]

The count called her "cherissime amie" and daydreamed about their reunion, then paid her homage and spent a few weeks in Paris before going on the road again with Sir Charles. Along the way they discussed women. After meeting the Baroness de Kalb for

14. Pursuing Madame Lavoisier (November 1801)

Jacques-Louis David, *Antoine Laurent Lavoisier and His Wife* (Metropolitan Museum of Art/Art Resource, New York).

the first time, Sir Charles wrote in his diary entry of August 17, 1802: "Mad. De Kalb desired me to engage Count Rumford not to meddle much in affairs at Munich; they are all afraid of the present Elector's character and that Count Rumford would come to ill with him. Took affectionate leave of her.... I am the more struck with Count R's conduct in not having introduced me to her before. When in the carriage an accession of vanity led him to tell me her history; married to a man she disliked, remains a virgin; loved much a brother who died—then placed affections on Count R who had been with her in all situations, seen her naked but out of principle and at her earnest desire would not enjoy her."[3]

It was out of character for the count to reveal himself in that way. Perhaps it was titillating. And why did Thompson tell the anecdote? Was he being sly about his relationship with Laura, Baroness de Kalb? He may have at one juncture taken leave of her before their progressing to sexual relations or might have implicitly been boasting that he was the first man to lie with her. He was likely talking about how he didn't touch Laura on account of an inner struggle to reveal without revealing; a man who kept secrets certainly had his own and could have found this awkward way of confiding to his friend that Laura was special and he was close to her.

The death of the Countess Nogarola's only son, killed in battle serving Napoleon, and her subsequent death of a broken heart were the pieces of terrible news Thompson received in Munich. He must have felt friendless as, when he needed to pour out his heart, neither Mary, Countess Nogarola, nor Lady Palmerston was there for him.

He and Anne Lavoisier exemplified the couple who get along better when traveling far from home. They met in Mannheim and in June 1802 they toured Switzerland, pending a decision of the French government whether to give him a permit to reside in Paris. Reverent close encounters with nature are associated with the Romantic Era. John Ruskin was a forerunner in seeing aesthetic beauty as opposed to threat in the jagged awe-inspiring mountains.[4] Yet Chamonix's Mer de Glace transported Anne to rapture while Thompson was prone to be absorbed in issues of heat, cold, and glacial ice. When Anne wrote to du Pont, she said that Switzerland claimed her for more than a short time. She described her long days—getting up at 5:00 a.m. and going on strenuous hikes—although she said not a word about her traveling companion. Soon she was back in Paris.

Thompson too had found the trip stimulating. While in Switzerland he wrote a paper on glaciers and the transmission of heat through solids, which he submitted to the (British) Royal Society. Even this travel was touch-and-go, as Napoleon's expansion hampered movement out of France as well as into it. The agreement between the count and the Bavarian ruler was that he was on duty in Bavaria six months a year. Thompson would remain in Bavaria the summer, and autumn of 1802 through the winter of 1803. This would be his last prolonged stay. In November he wrote Sally from Mannheim that he was very busy but "would rather be in Paris and the certain lady would rather have me there." Sally annotated this letter with "meaning the widow Lavoisier. Oh! In Paris were centered all charms."[5]

Apparently sometime in 1802 Thompson proposed to Anne. Politics lengthened the engagement. French authorities scrutinized the count. He was a foreign courtier, a scientist who worked on military technology and a soldier of fortune; besides, Napoleon's policy was to keep everybody guessing where they could go when. It was a peculiar situation: Thompson retained his half-pay as an English army officer as well as being in Maximilian's employ. But countries were piling honors on him. He was now a member

Lavoisier Arrested in His Laboratory by the Revolutionary Committee, by Charles Levachez. The gesturing seated figure is Madame Lavoisier (Napoleon Collection, Rare Books and Special Libraries Collection, McGill University).

of the royal societies of both Gottingen and Copenhagen, and when the French Institute was reorganized to drop the political thinkers Napoleon mistrusted, Thompson was elected to the first class of mathematical and physical sciences, to which Napoleon himself belonged.

Thompson was in Mannheim until January 1803, when he returned to Munich and Madame Lavoisier joined him. Thompson needed clearance to live in Paris and Anne set to work to make this happen. Her fiancé was, she persuaded officialdom, harmless. The stipulation was that he must not participate in military experiments in France. Thompson followed her to Paris in May 1803 and began living at 356, rue de Clichy. Napoleon let him keep his Bavarian pension. French authorities demanded a birth certificate from Woburn, which Sally and Loammi Baldwin helped supply, and the proof of the death of his first wife—further delays.

Anne was also selling some of Antoine's farmland and they were house hunting together. Eventually they bought a house in a fashionable area close to the Champs-Elysées and the Tuileries, rue d'Anjou Saint-Honoré, behind the Madeleine. From London, Sir Charles, expelled from France after seven months because of suspicions he was a spy, wrote Sally Thompson in America, on August 8, 1803: "I am still as much at a loss as I was in June, to answer your question whether your father be going to marry. He is now, as I told you in that letter, making the tour of Switzerland with a very amiable French lady. But I have no reason to think that they have any idea of a matrimonial connection. When the Count comes to England, she is to return to Paris; at least, so he writes me word."[6] Sir Charles kept Sally up to date on the romantic developments. What for a long time Sally could gather was that her father was seeing a lot of Madame Lavoisier. "All I can tell you about your father is this: he continued travelling with the French lady till about the middle of September, when she left him at Mannheim, and returned to Paris.... He continues very intimate with the lady, but whether it will end in a marriage, I cannot say. My own opinion is rather inclined to the negative, yet I have no good foundation for it.... Since this was written I have received a letter from your father, dated at Paris, November 11th. By this it is evident that he expects to marry the French lady, though nothing is yet finally determined."[7]

The count wrote both Lady Palmerston and his daughter when the marriage was imminent. To Sally, on January 22, 1804, he used properly flat tones, since, while he was getting a wife, she was getting a stepmother, and romance would normally have been more in the purlieus of her generation than his:

> I shall withhold this information from you no longer. I really do think of marrying, though I am not yet absolutely determined on matrimony. I made the acquaintance of this very amiable woman in Paris, who, I believe, would have no objection in having me for a husband, and who in all respects would be a proper match for me. She is a widow, without children, never having had any; is about my own age, enjoys good health, is very pleasant in society, has a handsome fortune at her own disposal, enjoys a most respectable reputation, keeps a good house, which is frequented by all the first Philosophers and men of eminence in the science and literature of the age, or rather of Paris. And what is more than all the rest, is goodness itself.... She is very clever (according to the English significance of the word); in short, she is another Lady Palmerston. She has been very handsome in her day, and even now, at forty-six or forty-eight, is not bad-looking; of a middling size, but rather *"en bon point"* than thin. She has a great deal of vivacity, and writes incomparably well.[8]

The French language seems to have influenced his choice of several English words as he reflected on the lady—"not bad-looking," from *pas mal*, and "a great deal of vivacity," borrowing from *beaucoup de vivacité*, which sounds rather as though this was a description of Anne he had heard from others. What is clear is not the ardor he felt for the widow but that he anticipated a partnership marriage, along the lines of the well-known synergy between her and Antoine Lavoisier. Ironically, this ill-fated couple had several years to get to know each other, due to the slow motion of getting permission for the count's residency in France and the marriage. When the count enlisted Sally to get copies of his birth certificate and Sarah Thompson's death certificate he sent a duplicate request to his bankers and himself, temporarily at the rue de Clichy: for a while the act of getting married was a Gordian knot. Science evolves but Anne wanted her dear departed's theorizing, that heat was a fluid, to rule. This factor may have made her skittish about marrying the count. However, overall, and beyond the mere convention of the man in pursuit, the count's love letters were the more passionate.

The salons were the purlieus of amateurs. In the 17th century it was theorized that heat was a movement, caused by vibration; Francis Bacon, Boyle, Hooke, and John Locke had held this view. In the 18th century those studying natural philosophy (a precursor to modern science) inclined to the caloric theory, by which heat was a fluid. By the time of his last year in Munich, Thompson had done experiments involving cannon, which proved to him that heat came from movement. He published a paper, seminal in the history of physics, explicating his findings. In 1795 Humphry Davy, then a 17-year-old lad in Bristol, did an experiment with clockwork and ice at 29 degrees that showed that the only source of heat was energy, in contradiction to the caloric theory. This attracted Thompson's attention and the two became friends. Eventually the caloric theory would give up the ghost. Meanwhile, Lavoisier, who had discovered that things burned in oxygen, thought heat was a weightless, invisible substance and espoused the caloric theory.

Regarding Thompson's inductively proven conclusions about thermodynamics, the scientists in Paris turned a deaf ear. In Paris, when Thompson published his paper, the scientists were keener on measuring heat than reexamining whether it was a fluid or energy. Although Thompson did not specifically refute Lavoisier, his publically discounting the caloric theory must have needled and offended the widow. Dr. Sparrow described Thompson as scientifically "more of an amateur than most men of science in an age of amateurs."[9]

Meanwhile, central to Thompson's being welcome in Paris was the friendship of

Pierre-Simon Laplace (1749–1827). Laplace, the son of well-to-do apple farmers in Calvados, Normandy, was an astronomer and mathematician who was called the Isaac Newton of France. He was briefly minister of the interior for Napoleon, who could not bear his slow methodical ways. When a professor at the University of Caen noted Laplace's mathematical acumen he sent him to Paris to the great self-taught mathematician Jean d'Alembert. D'Alembert handed the 19-year-old a book and told him to read it and come back when he understood all of it. According to tradition, that took Laplace about a day. A genius in both celestial mechanics and probability, Laplace was made a peer by Napoleon and continued to have power and prestige during the Restoration of the Bourbons. He had to play some politics and lend support to Napoleon's new calendar, whose design he knew was flawed, in order to have a central involvement preparing the metric system. He collaborated with Lavoisier on the physics of heat from 1780 to 1784. When Thompson went to the institute he noticed that after the presentation Napoleon had most of his conversation with Laplace.

Laplace established his career first and then married, in May 1788, Marie-Charlotte Courty de Romange (or Romanges) from Besançon, in the east of France. She was 19, twenty years younger than he. According to historian of science Roger Hahn, "the match was a good one, since both parties were among these rising in the social hierarchy."[10] Her family had mining interests and Parisian real estate. The couple lived not extravagantly, but she was, writes Hahn, "stylish" and "devout." Hahn remarked a "veiled reference" in Antoine Lavoisier's papers to involvement by Madame Lavoisier for an arranged marriage in 1783, when Marie-Charlotte was a girl the age Madame Lavoisier was when she married.

Laplace bought a house in Arcueil next to his close friend eminent scientist Berthollet, who accompanied Napoleon's expedition to Egypt. Their gardens connected. Madame Laplace figured in later years in the informal gathering place of mathematicians and scientists known as the Société d'Arcueil: "Madame de Laplace, still young and beautiful, treated them like a mother who could have been a sister."[11]

The classy French ladies were adventurous but the count was physically of a nervous nature, hardly priapic or priding himself regarding sexual conquests. Paris has long had a reputation for sexual liberality and when Madame Jollien showed her bosom or a hostess gave him a private kiss she may have intended a provocation, but overall the custom was flirtation and these women were not inclined to such light romance as to take the physicist instantly to their beds. Such a mistake of several biographers, which a contemporary of the count's would not have made, was one visit he made to the Laplace's home. It was two in the afternoon, yet he found her in bed. Her daughter of eight or nine was also present. Madame Laplace received him without embarrassment and they conversed for an hour and a half. The count described her as a woman of taste and pretty looks: "Her bed-dress and night-cap were recherchés and everything about her displayed the charms of refined luxury."[12]

He was treated to a song (her own composition) by Madame Prony, who after singing "surprised me not a little by giving me an Affectionate Kiss. She was sitting very near me and I was assisting her in holding the Musick. Luckily I was not absolutely put out of countenance but had presence of mind enough left to return the compliment without hesitation—The Parisian Ladies are most exceedingly kind and obliging."[13] This was the soul of flirtation, not a directed seduction. An upper-class Parisienne had a fashionably Neo-Classical boudoir. If the lady of the house could afford it and had the connections, this was the work of Charles Percier and Pierre Fontaine. It was the height of sophistication to receive visitors casually on one's divan, a sensual but not a sexual overture, the same custom Aaron Burr noted in his diary for the year 1810 when he consulted on his friend Mme. Robertson's dresses in her boudoir.

Thompson was making brilliant acquaintances in France and if sometimes they disagreed with or even mocked his theories, and he naturally would like imperial approval, the rule of a patron no longer governed him. Supposing Madame Laplace had the foreign scientist to her bedroom as a sexual provocation is yet another example of the biographer overlooking the fact the women he met had intellects and a man and woman can relate to each other privately with restraint. At the Laplaces, Thompson felt he overstayed by hours and had some qualms after the fact about her being in a state of undress, talking shop, but she assured him it was a privilege. Contemporaries would never have made the mistake, found in some biographical writings on Count Rumford, of latching onto Marie-Charlotte Laplace as his mistress based on this polite visit.

15

Engaged (Circa February 1804)

> The problem with using sex to make the Founders relatable is that sex is not transhistorical.—Thomas A. Foster, *Sex and the Founding Fathers: The American Quest for a Relatable Past* (2014)

Eighteenth century women who presided over the salons of literati, scientists, and conjurers of revolution received the brilliant with little regard for their status. By so doing a woman like William Herschel's sister Caroline or Antoine Lavoisier's wife Anne shared a public life with the men. Who was the woman to whom the Thompson was engaged? Anne came from a prominent family. Her father was a *juriste parlementaire*, director of the French East India Company (set up to rival the Dutch and English trade blocs), and a director general of the Ferme Générale, a powerful private concern that collected the indirect taxes on salt (the gabelle), tobacco, and alcohol, and imposed duties on certain foodstuffs.

Anne's maternal uncle was Joseph-Marie Terray, a formidable royal minister with, in 1771, command of state finances. An anecdote involving Anne reveals the general loathing for those who collected taxes on the grand scale. Having acquired property near Ferney, where Voltaire lived, Anne wanted to meet the philosopher. She asked through a third party for this privilege and the intermediary told Voltaire that she was a niece of the famous Abbé Terray. Hearing that name, Voltaire shook with fury. He said that if he had only one tooth left in his head he would guard it from the Abbé's clutches.[1]

Anne Paulze became a hostess at a tender age. When she was 12, her widowed father, Jacques Paulze, swooped her up from a convent in Montbrison and took her to Paris. He had ascended in his administrative career and now directed the Ferme Générale's commission of tobacco. Paulze expected his daughter to govern his household and preside over his entertainments. The competency she demonstrated was admirable, and she would rely on its strength in her marriage to a most esteemed man of science. Yet, such a precocious girlhood also seemed to have made her bossy, the kind of person who has to rule.

Abbé Terray pressured Paulze into a marriage for Anne to an unattractive, dissolute, and financially ruined 50-year-old count in poor health. The abbé threatened that otherwise the father would lose his key position in the Ferme Générale. To protect his daughter from the match, Paulze married Anne, then 13, quickly to his young assistant and colleague, Antoine-Laurent Lavoisier, an up-and-coming young man aged 28 who often visited the house. Antoine was trustworthy, serious and had no vices. He approached economics like chemistry, matching Paulze's own exactitude.[2] An expression of his bears witness to his modern and impressive drive for true science: "In nature nothing is lost, nothing comes out of nothing, everything is transformed" (*Rien ne se perd, rien de se crée, tout se transforme*). As an inspector for the same tax collection system that gave Paulze his wealth, Antoine insisted on exact facts and figures and carried that over from and to his scientific experiments. He had played music with Anne and discussed geology, chemistry and astronomy with her. They married on December 16, 1771, Anne wearing a dress of black silk with lace. The most powerful echelon of the bourgeoisie attended the wedding. By this time Lavoisier had received a gold medal from the Academy of Sciences for his work on public lighting and had purchased a half-share of the Ferme Générale. Yet he was known for holding progressive views and spoke out for the liberalization of the economy, tempered by state control, as a means to national prosperity.

Anne was petite and pretty, with blue eyes, a small mouth, a turned-up nose, clear complexion and auburn hair. She was feminine and vivacious, and voluntarily learned languages to assist her husband. She epitomized the Enlightenment ideal of a feminine helpmeet to a celebrated man. "Yet something had changed in them [such women] beside the style of their dress, the pattern of their dance or the shape of their illusions. The women themselves had somehow changed. We find that those whom we meet in the latter part of the century project more authentically as individuals ... [and] in Diderot's *D'Alembert's Dream* in 1769 ... [we meet] a woman who grasps quickly and discusses the most challenging concepts fearlessly and soberly without affectation or flirtatious self-effacement."[3]

Gouverneur Morris once slipped late into Anne's loge at the opera and then had tea with her at the Arsenal (he noted it was while waiting for the return of her husband). Morris teased Anne for being a "paresseuse" (September 25, 1789) for not having children, "but she declares it is only a misfortune."[4] It has been surmised that the couple's not having children contributed to their close tie. The two of them formed a seamless unit. They got up at five in the morning and worked in the laboratory from six to nine and again from seven to ten at night. In the afternoon, Antoine did administrative duties. A friend described Anne in verse as both "muse and secretary."[5] Her signed scientific drawings to illustrate Antoine's *Traité Elementaire de Chimie* were of high quality and she did the engravings herself. Jacques-Louis David, who had arrived in Paris from Rome in 1781, became Anne's teacher. David was commissioned to paint the Lavoisiers' double portrait, completed in 1788, the year before the French Revolution. Stating that the painting, now in the Metropolitan Museum, attests to Anne's active part in Antoine's career, historian Patricia Fara observed, "David has bequeathed an ambiguous version of Paulze Lavoisier. Lavoisier seems to be beseeching her for guidance, and yet, draped decoratively on his shoulder, she could well be a devoted yet ordinary wife totally ignorant of chemistry.... It is hard to tell whether Lavoisier is awestruck by his wife's aura or by the subject he studies. On the other hand, she appears distracted, even irritated."[6]

Famous men became her serviteurs, given that the structure of the French salon was founded in or descended from the rules and conventions of courtly love (gracious intimacy without sexual touch). Twice a week Anne had her salon, receiving luminaries including Benjamin Franklin and Gouverneur Morris. She did a portrait of Franklin that he acknowledged with a letter from Philadelphia October 23, 1785, in French: *"Ceux qui l'ont vu declarent que la peinture a un grand mérite, mais surtout ce qui me le rend cher, c'est la main qui l'a fait*" [Those who saw it declare that the portrait that she had the goodness to give him has great merit, but above all what makes him cherish it is the hand that painted it].[7]

Lavoisier considered food the key social issue facing his country. Therefore, he bought a great deal of land and made it productive. Arthur Young was an English writer on agricultural subjects who championed the rights of farmers and came to Anne's receptions. He described her in glowing terms: "Madam Lavoisier, a lively, sensible, scientific lady, had prepared a dejeuner Anglois of tea and coffee; but her conversation on Mr. Kirwan's Essay on Phlogiston, which she is translating from the English, and on other subjects, which a woman of understanding, who works with her husband in his laboratory, knows how to adorn, was the best repast."[8]

That Paulze and Antoine were prominent tax collectors made them as evil as any nobles when revolution came. Both Antoine and his father-in-law were beheaded on the same day, May 8, 1794. Anne was given a meeting with a Jacobin who had the authority to save Antoine Lavoisier, but from the moment she entered his office she raged against those who put them in prison. It is believed that if she had shown some ladylike softness, her husband would have been spared. She was maladroit at a crucial moment when the chemist's life was in the balance and her blunder cost his life. Anne was arrested a month later. She spent 65 days in the Maison d'Arrêt (on the rue Neuve de Capucines) during the summer of 1794. Released, she cleared Antoine's name and wrote a "Denonciation" attacking the member of the Convention who had played a large part in sending her father and husband to the guillotine. She recuperated her husband's furniture, papers, books and lab equipment and returned to her role as society hostess.

When in 1774 Louis XVI had ascended the throne of France, Abbé Terray's day was over and A.R.J Turgot succeeded him. Turgot brought in the brilliant son of a watchmaker by the name of Dupont, not yet written with the space after "Du" that would elevate his status. Du Pont wrote a seminal work, *Physiocratie,* on laissez faire capitalism, which influenced Lavoisier to develop agriculture on his lands. It was also thus that Lavoisier, both economist and chemist, became head of the country's gunpowder commission and was billeted in the huge space near the Bastille called the Petit Arsenal, perfect for his scientific endeavors. The Arsenal was where he and Anne had both their laboratory and home from 1775; it attracted scientifically minded visitors from all of Europe.

Life had imitated literature and art twice over in Anne's love life. First was the influence of her art teacher, no less than the great Jacques-Louis David. David taught hundreds of European painters including the great artists Ingres and Gérard, but also many paying students like the talented draughts person Madame Lavoisier. David illustrated in works such as his *Intervention of the Sabine Women* (1799) love giving woman courage, when she puts family above herself. Anne was such a patriot and loyal wife and daughter, and when Antoine was about to be guillotined she stood up to his enemy ferociously (if, as we've seen, ineffectively).

Julie, ou la nouvelle Heloise, an epistolary novel by Jean-Jacques Rousseau, held readers spellbound during this era. The French elite debated its views of passion, marriage and emotions. Julia, daughter of a baron, has a passionate love for her tutor, but when her father forbids the match and her tutor goes on a long voyage she marries a staunch and steady man she respects but who doesn't enflame her passion. Rousseau raised questions about whether passion belongs in marriage and suggested that a stable attachment needs some fire at the core. Anne expected a great deal of marriage. She seems to have had both love from Antoine and passion from du Pont; her demands on marriage were, and would remain, considerable.

Pierre du Pont de Nemours, almost 20 years older than Anne, was a close friend of Antoine's. According to J.J. Peumery, du Pont exercised on Anne "a certain ascendancy by his communicative gaiety, his verve, his unorthodox ideas."[9] And so an affair of many years of du Pont and Anne did not alter the Lavoisier marriage. It can be dated to 1781, based on two letters of du Pont to her. In one du Pont evoked "17 years of intimacy."[10] A scholar who has studied the documentation in depth came to the opinion that the intimacy was courtly and not with a physical dimension, while generally they are assumed to have been lovers.[11] Pierre, with his sons, first quit France for America after narrowly missing the guillotine before settling there permanently. His son Irenée du Pont studied chemistry with Antoine and founded in Delaware the chemical manufacturing plant, which would have borne the name Lavoisier except that Anne negated it. After Lavoisier's execution, Pierre du Pont proposed to Mme. Lavoisier but was rejected. She referred to him in letters as "mon père," even when the letters palpitate with intimate feelings, probably vestigial from when Lavoisier, frequently away at his farms or doing his tax collector's rounds, tolerated her affair. A critical apercu of Anne in love comes from du Pont just before he left for America: *"Il faut bien vous aimer d'amour, avec une nuance ou avec l'autre. J'ai l'experience que vous n'êtes pas proper à l'amitié. Vous n'avez ni épanchements, ni son intérêt, ni ses consulations, ni ses conseils, ni ses caresses, ni ses discours, ni son doux silence. Ou cess votre tendress, tout cesse. Vous devenez froide, dure, querelleuse, et c'est l'expression désobligeante qui arrive d'elle-même sur vos lèvres"*[12] [You have to be loved with passion, with one nuance or the other. In my experience you aren't capable of friendship. You don't have its outpourings, its interest, its consolations, its advising, its caresses, its speeches or its sweet silence. When your tenderness ends, everything ends. You become cold, hard, quarrelsome, and it's an unkind expression that comes spontaneously on your lips].

Du Pont might have warned Thompson that if he had lost his bride's favor there would be no means to recapture it. Just after du Pont had left definitively for America, Anne wrote him a long letter expressing her wish he would return, dangling her affectionate regard. Conducting a salon on her own had paled and she was ready for a new compelling interest, predictably a suitor in the field of economics or science. Many years later, Pierre du Pont would virtually throw his cape before Anne that he had vowed affection to her 34 years before and never wavered. Two realities must be factored in. First of all, he wrote flowery letters to people, including Thomas Jefferson, assuring inviolable affection; it was his elegant style. Second, du Pont was in debt to Lavoisier, hence to Anne. Whether the debt hanging between them reinforced his posture of courtly devotion cannot be guessed.[13]

Sir Charles, who had introduced the Palmerstons and Thompson in 1793, seems an enduring peripheral figure in Anne's life and a sort of perpetual lackluster suitor. The social scientific network of these scientific notables continued to include Anne throughout her life; they honored her and she entertained them. The chemist Claude Louis Berthollet would ask Sir Charles to pay Anne his respects in 1816 and the next year was expecting a visit from Sir Charles and Madame de Rumford.

Thompson's pursuit wore Anne down. He had the assets of a prepossessing (good features, athleticism) appearance and prestige. He wrote her 300 letters when they were apart, beginning discreetly during the winter of 1801 and building to a crescendo of rapturous epistles that addressed her a "chérissime amie" and "la plus digne femme de l'univers" (the most exemplary woman) and called himself a "belle ame." Perhaps from the day he left Paris after visiting her for the first time, as he took a carriage from his lodging on the rue St. Dominique at 9:00 and went across the Seine to breakfast with her and left at 11:00 for England, he was determined to have this woman whose intellectualism combined with her fortune bowled him over.

Anne was hedging her bets. Writing on March 1, 1802, she implored du Pont to return to France. He did come back to Paris in June but it was at the behest of Napoleon, who involved him with Talleyrand in the sale of Louisiana to America. At this juncture, however, du Pont got little of Anne's time. Thompson reappeared in Paris. He mingled with the powerful while enjoying the relationship with Anne. On July 14 he was invited to the Tuileries Palace and the next day sat two seats away from Napoleon at the opera.

Thompson went to concerts, ballet, and theater, marveled at the Louvre and the Invalides, and, in a departure from the rounds of most tourists, visited institutions for the blind, mute, sick, indigent, aged, insane and orphaned. He was highly interested in whether the conditions were humane and recorded his impressions briefly. At the insane asylum he was mystified and made curious by a man who insisted on being dressed as a female. At the boys orphanage he complimented the facility and program but commented that he thought the boys, ages ten to 14, would be "happier and more useful" if the establishment were in the country.[14] By now the count and Anne were engaged but French authorities would take about the same time to scrutinize Thompson as they would, at the end of the decade, hedge over giving Aaron Burr a passport.[15]

On a Saturday in late summer 1802, Anne invited Pictet to lunch as her sole guest. They spent four hours together in the laboratory that had been Lavoisier's, "*au milieu d' instruments de son mari et comme environné de son ombre.*" They experimented together on the effects of a gas scarcely known at the time, nitrous oxide, or laughing gas.[16] Anne was an independent woman who did not require a chaperone, and her free and easy friendship with Pictet continued for many years. The picture of the two of them getting high in the great Lavoisier's laboratory is very funny.

If Thompson was instrumental in replacing Lavoisier's caloric theory of heat with the mechanical theory (friction), and thus somewhat in opposition to Anne, he admired Lavoisier, as did all scientists of the time. But her worship of the memory of her departed first husband would have been tiresome eventually. Had he lived, Lavoisier might have evolved and changed his caloric theory. For an intelligent and prominent widow to create a monument to her husband that others would admire had a precedent in the Necker family. Jacques Necker governed the finances of the French state based on his wife's deference to his brilliance, which she promoted at her salon. Anne came to prominence at the same time. She had no children to distract her from her quest to promote her husband to fame and prestige.

It is clear that Anne kept up with her who's who of scientists. On Christmas Day 1802 she gave a reception for Lady Edgeworth, and on January 15, 1803, she received among the guests at a small party Rumford, Pictet and du Pont. They went together to visit the chemist Claude Bertollet, who had discovered the bleaching effect of chlorine gas and had also gone with Napoleon's expedition to Egypt. Pictet heard of the arrest of the Duc d'Enghien at Madame Lavoisier's. The duke's execution was an atrocity to the French people and a major tactical blunder by Napoleon, as the Duc d'Enghien was not involved in politics and his arrest for spying for Britain was bogus.

At the end of 1803 Thompson was in Munich and he wrote hundreds of missives to his fiancée. According to Suzanne Blatin, a scholar who read these elusive letters, many of them were sexually explicit, or as Blatin said, "at the brink of indelicacy." For example, one reads, "I can conceive of nothing more tender than living with you, working with you all day and then sleeping in your arms." How modern to court her with the idea of good sex at the end of a shared workday! Thompson in these letters "mixes admiration, passion, heartache (dépit amoureux), and even a certain lyricism."[17]

In the summer of 1893, when Pictet was guiding Anne and Thompson on a mountain holiday in Switzerland, she wrote du Pont (July 26) not to forget her, as she had not forgotten him. The letter conveyed her intrepidness and the fact she kept a nun's hours. She did not mention Thompson: "My heath is quite all right, but I am visibly losing weight—I'm leading the life of a traveler. I get up every day at five and go to bed at night at eight. It was black bread or cheese for dinner." But she praised the purity of the mountain air, the 12 hours a day of walking or riding horseback, and how the Alps raised her spirits—*"les affections de l'âme sont moins triste."*[18]

Thompson wanted to select his wife not as he had at nineteen but with maturity. He had entwined emotionally and physically with beautiful young aristocrats, where Anne was of the haute-bourgeoisies and near his age. Before she would marry her suitor, he had to get the documentary proof that his first wife was dead (which took a year) and she needed to gather and organize the sheets of the scientific memoir that had been sitting in the attic for ten years.

Politics had created an uneasy backdrop for moving ahead to marriage. Thompson was Anglo-American. Many British flocked to Paris when temporary peace was signed between Britain and France in 1802. For a peer of the realm or a member of parliament it was de rigueur, and Napoleon was delighted at all the tourists going through the Exposition des Produits Français in September and the Louvre, expanded with loot from Italy and the Low Countries. Britons were journeying to enjoy their previous haunts on the Continent: "Over eighty members of Parliament and more than sixty peers of the realm spent part of 1802 once again enjoying Paris."[19] But, understandably, it was questioned that Thompson could see anything to admire in Napoleon. Britain and France were, except for the truce from early 1802 to the spring of 1803, continually at war from 1793 through the whole time the count lived and died in France.

His daughter was the only family member Thompson likely told of his impending marriage. In late January 1804 he was looking forward to making a tour of Italy with Anne and said, "She appears to be most sincerely attached to me, and I esteem and love her very much."[20]

Anne girded her courage and forged ahead.

16

A New Method of Spending Time (October 1805)

> For some reason or other, the European has rarely been able to see America except in caricature.—James Russell Lowell, *On a Certain Condescension to Foreigners* (1869)

Britain declared war on France in 1803, ending the Peace of Amiens. For the next decade, during which the two countries were at war, Thompson held a trickier position in the shifting sands of nations than before. Moreover, the mood of Paris itself was tattered. Napoleon's aggressions in northern Italy and elsewhere, and his military successes such as his momentous victory at Austerlitz didn't counterbalance for Parisians a sharp economic decline. Luxuries that elite persons in Anne's social set had counted on became very dear after bad harvests, blockades, and bank collapses, and the human casualties of war, though at a distance, cast a pall which parades and circuses, monuments and fountains did not dispel. The count was in a sense a man of four countries and Napoleon, crowned emperor in December 1804, would no longer tip his bicorn to an English knight. On the other hand, since Maximilian had fled to Mannheim when the Austrians marched into Bavaria, he released Rumford from the requirement that he spend half each year in Munich, now saying the count could live where he pleased.

Despite the inexorable military campaigns, few soldiers were visible except on parade or furlough. The scene in Paris was of everybody related to government jockeying for position and access to power. Whereas Pictet sought favors on behalf of his Protestants and was run ragged, Thompson was more detached and had a niche. He saw Madame Lavoisier was acquainted with everybody who counted. She had endured a summer in jail after Antoine was executed then, like many other elites, disappeared for a while, and returned to a society where old nobility was being integrated with new. Thompson didn't need to be a courtier and curry favor. *Good riddance to that*, he clearly thought, forgetting he would have to continue to court a demanding spouse! Sally commented in her abstract of her father's letters from this period: "Without being entirely free from a sense of self-consequence,—more generally known by the name of vanity,—he must have thought himself superior to anything he was before. In Germany he was naturally smiled upon for his ingenuity and his good works. But here [Paris] he was always addressed with a very peculiar grace, that was flattering, while he had nothing to do but to listen to sweet tones.... Who, without being different from every one else, could stand all this?"[1]

The chemist's widow and the physicist-courtier had traveled together over several years. The year before Lady Palmerston died Thompson wrote with concern about her health while also reassuring her about his own situation: "This climate [of Paris] agrees with me, and I am very happy."[2] According to Pictet, in the spring of 1805 the new house of Madame Lavoisier at 39, rue d'Anjou-Saint Honoré (today 49 and at the top of Rue Lavoisier), Faubourg Saint-Honoré was the talk of the town. Madame Gautier Delessert (to whom Jean-Jacques Rousseau addressed his *Letters on Botany*) reported that Thompson's cooking device contributed to Anne's table: "The cuisine was excellent. We had a formal dinner with the lamb cooked in a rotisserie oven. People speak of it a lot at parties."[3]

Thompson personally went about making their abode comfortable and attractive to his specifications, from the color of the walls and upholstery to central heating and, of course, the kitchens and fireplaces. Stimulated by all the entertaining, he became intent on improving lamps. Of this he wrote in an essay, "My next attempt was to light a large dining-room in my house in Paris, by a single luminous dome suspended over the middle of the dining-table; and, in order to prevent cross-lights, I ventured to place a cluster of burners on Argand's principle, in the axis of this dome, and so near together as to touch each other, and to feed them with oil from a circular reservoir, in the form of a hollow flat ring on which the dome was supported."[4] He was more absorbed in imprinting his genius on the house by his innovative inventions than he was in Anne. Could sexual incompatibility have been what caused the marriage to fail? They so quickly would loathe each other that such would be a first guess except that the relationship went south gradually, not precipitously after the wedding night. It took a while for Anne to decide she had married a social deviant and for Thompson to view her as a "female Dragon."[5]

Sir Charles was *en froid* with the count, who hadn't helped defuse the accusation in 1803 of Sir Charles being a British spy. Lady Palmerston was still the safe repository for Thompson's thoughts. He explained, vis-à-vis his friend's umbrage, that he could not "expose myself by taking up the cudgel for him in this country." For his part, Sir Charles, who kept Sally up on her father's love life, wrote, "They are now living together in Paris, and, as far as I can learn, very happily. I know nothing of it from your father himself, which is not surprising as I some time since intimated to him my wish that our correspondence should cease."[6]

The relationship of the couple, which had been harmonious during the four years of their acquaintanceship, went south within two months of tying the knot. They could not have been more paradigmatic of the couple that tries to change each other. Several issues of conflict emerged: temperament, territoriality, mores, her keeping her first wedded name, his servants, and their lifestyle. These hit their daily reality so fast that, having married in October 1805, by October 1806 this couple that had traveled together and bought a house together revealed themselves to be intractably at swords' points, and Thompson felt Anne had stolen his peace.

When historians take account of fault, they usually point to both parties, although the marital misery has provided the occasion to defame Thompson's personality. Duveen, for example, declared that Thompson was "a self-opinionated and conceited individual who had been used to living a self-indulgent and extravagant bachelor lifestyle for years."[7]

The marriage certificate of October 22, 1805, shows Anne kept the name Lavoisier. She did this expressly, as the painter Elisabeth Vigée Le Brun kept her father's name, Vigée. Anne considered this an obligation, "as a religion." She had provided great support for Antoine but did not incarnate the Rousseauean ideal of a gentle and modest woman. She had grown up in the course of managing her father's socializing, and participating in the scientific endeavors of her first marriage, into a woman who needed to rule. The feminization of power of the 18th century salonists was in twilight and the feminism of the revolution was short-lived. The ideal woman of the Corsican ruler, the homemaker, didn't work for a woman without children. Napoleon loathed the type of the strong-willed Madame de Staël and loved the frivolous Josephine. Napoleon declared, "If there is one thing that is not French it's a woman who does what she wants."[8]

Anne provided for the count generously in the marriage contract but insisted that she retain the name and signed her letters "Lavoisier Rumford." This grated on Thompson because it indicated she was locked into the renown of Antoine—a posthumous monomania that disadvantaged the second marriage. What did the count not have? He lacked the social bonhomie, the refined education, and the stature among members of the French intelligentsia of her father and Antoine. Once she lived with the count she realized this fully. Her anticipated pleasure curdled into scalding words and steaming hauteur, and emotionally there was no turning back. Her contempt for her American husband echoes du Pont's words (albeit written when he was feeling rejected) that if she wasn't passionately in love there was no love in her. When questioned about keeping her name, Anne said, "*M. de Rumford n'a pas su que, si les lois donnent toute suprématie au mari, les moeurs donnent aux femmes les avantages de la politesse; ainsi, M. de Rumford croyait exercer un droit de suprématie en montant en voiture le premier; il ignorait que la politesse exigeait qu'il n'y montât qu'après moi. Il prenait ma voiture fermée lorsqu'il pleuvait pour me laisser la barouche qu'il ne me laissait jamais quand il faisait beau.*"[9] [Monsieur de Rumford did not know that, if the law gives all supremacy to the husband, custom gives to women the advantages of polite behavior. This, Monsieur de Rumford thought to exert a right of supremacy in getting first into the coach; he didn't realize that politeness required him to mount only after myself. He took my closed carriage when it rained, leaving the barouche to me, when he never left me that when it was clement].

A woman should be educated but not scientific; this view of Julie de Lespinasse, whose salon had intellectual chic during the prerevolutionary period, endured into the new century. Although Anne mastered much science and mathematics to aid her husband, on her own she was a hostess with no mission. But Thompson did not renew the mission she had carried out in her first marriage. Only nature, things, and books could teach him. He had no patience for lengthy discussions of philosophy and speculation that might or might not end up stimulating his mind. However, Anne would call herself Madame de Rumford after the divorce, possibly to acknowledge that period of her life but more likely for a new application of luster. It is unlikely that the count took exclusive umbrage at her keeping Antoine's surname, but it may have added fuel to the fire.

A reckless but fascinating comparison of temperaments was made by the botanist De Candolle: "Rumford was cold, calm, obstinate, egotistic, prodigiously occupied with the material element of life and the very smallest inventions of detail. He wanted his chimneys, lamps, coffee-pots, windows, made after a certain pattern, and he contradicted his wife a thousand times a day about the household management. Madame Rumford was a woman of resolute wilful character. Her spirit was high, her soul strong and her character masculine."[10] Surely the idea of compromise in marriage was inimical to both spouses. This stemmed from the point they had reached in their lives, not their ages per se. Having been subjected to authority since he was a boy, Thompson felt he was marrying a wealthy woman who shared his passion for science, so he could now proceed unhampered in the lines of investigation he chose. Anne saw remarriage as the final step in rectifying and maintaining her position in society.

Thompson tolerated society to a point but his mind was on the plane of research, penetrating the problems that preoccupied him. In the terms of sociologist Irving Goffman, previously discussed, the count needed again to co-shift. Social interaction required him to be in the "front room" in Parisian scientific and intellectual circles at a time when they were politicized; Napoleon looked at science to realize his imperial goals. The newlywed Thompson escaped to his lab. This was a period when many women found intellectual satisfaction in translating for their husbands, but there is no indication he brought his wife into his work. His theories of heat made Lavoisier's caloric theory passé, adding insult to injury. Thompson sequestered himself and in so doing infuriated Anne. If the count was monomaniacal about his work, Anne Lavoisier was considered a difficult personality. According to François Guizot, a man who was a friend to each, "his spirit was lofty, his conversation was full of interest and his manners were marked by gentle kindness," whereas Anne treated others with "a singular mixture of rudeness and courtesy, a bluntness of language and disdain of authority."[11]

The greatest clash between them was territorial. They were at complete variance for lifestyle and they would not have experienced this in the period leading up to the marriage but only after they shared space. Factor in that the rootless Thompson repeatedly enthused over settling down, and the marriage to Anne signified his achieving a posh status quo. In Munich he occupied a palatial building's second floor for years but rhapsodized about a vacation home on Lake Starnberg. He and Anne settled on the house they bought together after they bid on two other houses. Real estate seemed to promise a new lease on life!

The house was a paradise, he exclaimed to Sally: "I have the best-founded hopes of passing my days in peace and quiet in this paradise of a place, made what it is by me, my money, skill, and directions. In short, it is all but a paradise. Removed from the noise and bustle of the street, facing full to the South, in the midst of a beautiful garden of more than two acres, well planted with trees and shrubbery. The entrance from the street is through an iron gate, by a beautiful winding avenue, well planted, and the porter's lodge is by the side of this gate; a great bell to be rung in case of ceremonious visits."[12] Sally annotated this letter at a later date, saying with chagrin, "It seems that there had been an acquaintance between these parties of four years before marriage. It might be thought a long space of time enough for perfect acquaintance. But, ah Providence! thy ways are past finding out."[13]

It was the year before the marriage that Anne moved out of the apartment on the Boulevard de la Madeleine where she had last lived with Antoine (they had lived longer at the Arsenal) and went to live at the house on the rue d'Anjou. From her point of view, fussing over a house was done; now she wanted to entertain her friends in it. By December, though, Thompson was directing his focus on the house, changing it to make it his own, similar to what he had done in his Brompton Row house in London, upgrading the heating, kitchen, lighting, and so forth. Before Christmas, the count regaled Sally with where he and Anne were living:

> I gave up my lodgings on quitting Munich, and managed so as to settle all concerns of business. I flatter myself I am settled down here for life, far removed from wars and all arduous duties, as a recompense for past services, with plenty to live upon, and at liberty to pursue my own natural propen-

sities, such as have occupied me through life,—a life, as I try to fancy, that may come under the denomination of a benefit to mankind. You will wish to know what sort of a place we live in. The house is rather an old-fashioned concern, but in a plot of over two acres of land, in the very centre and finest part of Paris, near the Champs Elysees and the Tuileries and principal boulevards. I have already made great alterations in our place, and shall do a vast deal more. When these are done, I think Madame de Rumford will find it a very different condition from that in which it was, that being very pitiful, with all her riches.[14]

The location was in a neighborhood that Napoleon's civic renewal had given wide streets, good lighting and water. Their dwelling dated from the late Renaissance. While she was rich, Anne was disinclined to make changes that disrupted her domestic life, but her new husband wanted it to be a showplace. Naturally it was the use to which each thought to put the house that conflicted. In the same letter of December 20, Thompson went on:

> Our style of living is really very magnificent. Madame is exceedingly fond of company, and makes a splendid figure in it herself. But she seldom goes out, keeping open doors; that is to say, to all the great and worthy, such as the philosophers, members of the Institute, ladies of celebrity, etc.
>
> On Mondays we have 8 or 10 of the most noted of our associates to dinner. (Then we live on bits for the rest of the week). Thursdays are devoted to evening company, of ladies and gentlemen, without regard to numbers. Tea and fruits are given, the guests continuing till twelve or after. Often superb concerts are given, with the finest vocal and instrumental performers.[15]

When he wrote Sally of the constant company, she interpolated, "Just what the Count hated." It is humorous to hear him deplore what a more sociable person would like, e.g., "Conversation their amusement, a new method of spending time."[16]

Antoine Lavoisier had compartmentalized his scientific activities, administration, property management, and social self as few people manage. Thompson's expectation that in a marriage to a woman who understood him he could push society away was sheer error. Antoine, for instance, was interested in music and wrote a paper on harmony, and Anne played the piano. But there is no record of Thompson getting out his violin to play duets. He may have liked a sparkling ballet or opera on occasion but once he delved into technical issues and personal projects he was in his own world. Indeed, it has been suggested that Rumford's interest in floriculture, carried to extremes, was a contributing factor to the breakdown of their marriage. When Anne married a titled man she must have assumed a greater measure of social ease and attention to etiquette: the count liked a ball or a hunt, the leisure activities of aristocrats, but he loathed long parties, affected manners, and artifice generally.

Moreover, Thompson liked to have his work recognized. It authenticated his status in applied technology. For instance, the changes he made in lighting as he sought to solve problems of illumination and invent new lamps were crucial to display to the elite public that otherwise heard his papers only at the institute. Apparently Mme. Lavoisier acknowledged compliments for improvements in her house without giving credit to Thompson. In fact, she let on that improvements were her own—and competitiveness between spouses is an inexorable killer of their affections.

The count may have used equipment of the first husband, whose praises Anne continued to sing at her salon, in his laboratory, which might have offended her. His accusations that she was frivolous—quite unfair, as she entertained rather frugally—must have irritated her. Above all, instead of having an elegant equilibrium between his work and social lives, and including Anne in both, he preferred to withdraw with his experiments and inventions and literally and figuratively close the door, whereas she felt he had usurped the governance of her own house. Thompson was writing many papers to submit to the institute. He was clanging in the house while developing steam boilers, and his soap making gave off a putrid smell of oil mixed with lye that was offensive to guests. Faced with the wit and persiflage of an evening of conversation, Thompson apparently went on and on about his interests, while his wife fumed. Thompson began to lock himself into his laboratory and workshop and not, furthermore, having the kind of pas de deux the Lavoisiers had with each other.

Anne confided her agony to du Pont and there is extant, revealing letter about her suffering, which she wrote to Thompson, where she analyzed their incompatibility:

"Lorsque la plus parfait intimate ne produit pas une succession continuelle de bon sentiments qui sont la base du Bonheur, il en résulte un effet contraire, bien triste et bien affligeant; ce n'est alors que de la familiarité, qui souvent porte a s'oublier a tel point que l'homme qui se dit le mieux élevé se permet des propos qui ne sont jamais sortis de la bouche d'un homme poli, qui des serviteurs n'entendrait pas sans demander leur congé. Et c'est a votre femme que vous les prodiguez! Les supporter serait d'avilir. Je soutiendrai ma dignité de femme"[17] [When the most perfect intimacy doesn't produce a continual succession of positive sentiments, which constitute the basis of happiness, a contrary, very sad and afflicting, effect results. Then all that is left is familiarity, which often carries to the point when the man who considers himself entirely well raised permits himself expressions that never come out of the mouth of a polite man, whom servants wouldn't hear without quitting. And it's to your wife on whom you lavish this! To withstand these expressions would be to be debased. I will keep up my dignity as a woman]. Politesse marked class if birth determined it; money and attire were secondary to language and couth. Language marked politesse above all. (Living in Paris, I linked with a number of young bankers who wanted to improve their English conversation. After some time, one came representing the three and said they liked me and I was a good teacher but the American accent would not be helpful to them as the British accent was more classé.)

Anne wanted a gallant husband. Antoine must have treated her like a princess, still a child, and along came a man who had gallant looks but was wrapped up in his own pursuits. External manners were what she wanted, all she wanted, from him. More than that would scrape her wounds from the trauma of the murder of the two men she loved and trusted. She continued in the same unique document where she calmly told the count what was wrong with him as a husband: *"Je vous demande d'avoir pour moi la même politesse que vous accordez, je ne dis pas aux femmes qui vous plaisent, mais à celles qui vous sont parfaitement indifférente"*[18] [I ask from you the same degree of politeness that you accord—I don't mean to women who please you—but to those women who are utterly indifferent to you].

Alas, the moment the count no longer looked like a prince to Anne, she taunted him and vilified him to others. She sang praises of Antoine at her salon. When she sat at the table and Thompson carried on about his inventions she whispered to her guests that he was a "veritable sample card."[19] One contentious issue that grew up between the newlyweds concerned the German servant family (of six) whom the count had brought with him from Bavaria. The elder Aichner had served him from the first when he came to Bavaria two decades before. The Third Coalition, formed in 1803 of Prussian, Austria, England Russia and Sweden, became very active at this time, creating messy relations at the individual level. Were the Aichners to return to Munich, Thompson maintained, they would be in danger. Mme. Lavoisier would have none of his excuses. She pointed out, six weeks after their marriage, that the crisis of Austrians conceivably taking Munich was over. Napoleon had defeated the Austrians on December 2 and the Aichners had to be dismissed (she retained one daughter as a maid). The count wrote Sally, "I was obliged to hire a place for them some time before they went away. They did not agree with Madame de Rumford's servants, though mine were not in the least to blame, for never were there more honest people than Aichner and his wife. It would have been a great comfort to me to have kept them to the end of my life."[20]

Thompson's affection for the Aichners came across in complaints to Sally that "the whole family of Aichners ... are so good, and those of an age to work so industrious, they cannot be considered a burden, and will ever be a comfort to me, being as it were my family." It seems at least one member lived with Thompson as a dependent beyond working years. After the beloved servant family had been banished to Munich, he confided in Sally: "Between you and myself, as a family secret, I am not at all sure that two certain persons were not wholly mistaken, in their marriage, as to each other's character's. Time will show. But two months barely expired, I forbode difficulties. Already I am obliged to send my good Germans home,—a great discomfort to me and wrong to them."[21] Madame Lavoisier liked the little girl, who bore the names of the count's daughter and of the Countess Nogarola: Mary Sarah. She kept her in Paris when the parents were dismissed. Mary Sarah trained as a milliner and eventually was married to a young French merchant, receiving a dowry of 20,000 francs from Madame Lavoisier.

Entertaining was Anne's lifeline, whereas for Thompson people were an interruption. He could do without them for the most part, after decades of pleasing patrons and others to advance himself. He was nonplused that people would want to spend so much energy and time being witty. In France, in the marriage to Madame Lavoisier, Thompson felt like a victim—but then so did she. A reasonable surmise is that after her father and husband were guillotined she became somewhat unhinged.

Once the split occurred Thompson did not object to his ex-wife and his daughter Sally having a friendship. The rupture, unlike the marriage, was cordial. J.G. Ruelland limned the personalities of the pair as a contrast. Anne's character after her traumas in 1796 "transformed imperceptibly. She became brusque, authoritarian, choleric." As for the count, "The new husband had a difficult character and above all very different from Lavoisier's. Arrogant, irascible, unpredictable, egoistic, condescending with women."[22]

The duc de la Rochfoucault once said English husbands and wives were always together. Cultural collision seems to have been one factor, and when this couple were together they apparently railed at each other and withdrew, like two magnetic poles. Had the count engaged Anne in his work, might they have been a nouveau scientific power couple? But even Voltaire didn't want the Marquise du Châtelet to outshine him; and to Anne science was done with calculations in a laboratory, while the count was an experimenter who was practically oriented. His gift to her was to make her better soap, coffee and lighting. She rejected his gifts. Anne expected the count to be a passe-partout to restore her status instead of an outsider pulling her centrifugally from the center of *tout Paris*. The relationship combusted in the home and in society.

17

Boiling Over (1806–1809)

> Thus come to their Senses, and the Mask thrown off, they look at one
> another like utter strangers, and Persons just come out of a Trance; he finds
> by Experience he fell in love with his own Ideas, and she with her own Vanity.
> —Benjamin Franklin, *Reflections on Courtship and Marriage* (1746)

Newspapers were heavily censored during Napoleon's regime and an underground press of broadsheets was ready to seize on scandals. Thus the misery of the carping widow Lavoisier and her outlandish American husband was public knowledge. Apparently both Thompson and Anne applied to the police commissioner, Joseph Fouché, to condemn each other. As they were coming apart the couple became not only notorious but also isolated as former social acquaintances backed away from their scene of distress and the salons languished. A mocking song about her marriage that was circulating in Paris upset Anne when she heard it. She complained to du Pont and asked him to recall the copies that were in the public.[1]

For his part, the count was mocked not only as an eccentric American but also as unfashionable in supposing a husband could or should arrogate all the power rather than share it with his wife. Being nonplussed and angry, he babbled publicly about his patriarchal rights, causing mirth in the sophisticated milieu of the Parisian bourgeoisie. It was foolish to want his wife to bow down to him as her god, all the more so because she was French! Growing up without the influence of someone a child views as a rightful father, that child looks to a multiplicity of father figures. Thompson did this in a way that made him happy and the men he looked up to happy, being almost obsequious to Governor Wentworth, Lord George Germain, and Duke Karl Theodor, rather than competing with them for their luster. Later, when a head of household, the person who had no father to bounce the concept of father against can only operate on the societal belief system and philosophical ideas of fatherhood, rather than a more desirable complex of experience, observation and belief. What the count sputtered was that he was head of their "family" (of two) and therefore she ought to obey him.

Ironically, Thompson's string of affairs had caused no scandal, but his second marriage did, as Parisians derided the poor results of a high-profile transnational marriage. A bystander wrote, *"J'ignore combien dura le mois de miel dans ce lieu de délices: ce qu'il y a de certain, c'est que la philosophie, qui devait mettre l'harmonie dans le ménage, y mit le feu très promptment. Quand le comte américain eut fini d'exercer son empire sure les pôeles et les fourneaux de la maison, il se mit à vouloir l'exercer sur sa femme, qui, avec ses quarante-cinq ans d'indépendance, s'attendait à maitriser plutôt qu'à être maitrissé. Il en portait ses plaints à tout le monde et il était fort pleasant pour des Parisians, parce qu'il prenait les lois conjugales au plus grand* sérieux.² [I can't say how long the honeymoon lasted in this delightful place. What is certain is that philosophy, which ought to have brought harmony to the household rapidly, ignited a fire instead. When the American had finished exerting his empire on the cooking implements and fireplaces of the house, he set to exerting it on his wife, who, with her 45 years of independence, expected to master rather than be mastered. He complained widely of her, which only amused the Parisians, because he took the conjugal laws with the greatest seriousness.]

During one squabble, the count was rumored to have locked Anne in an attic or, some said, in the basement of their house. Pictet, the sober Geneva Protestant who was a friend to both husband and wife, shuddered at the display of *linge sale* of their scandalous marriage. And wasn't their personal strife an aftershock of larger political conflicts? The English were the enemy from 1807 on, after the collapse of peace talks, when successive British governments faced up to Napoleon. Anne, who had been at the apex of European intelligentsia, now was saddled with an Anglo-American. Pictet was still attending soirées at the rue d'Anjou in 1808, but in the interval before 1810 he was on poor terms with Madame Lavoisier, possibly siding with the count. Not until a year after the marriage ended, in 1810, did Pictet note in his diary that the haggling was over, amicable relations were restored between the feuding couple and he was managing to be a friend to each. Some tried to arbitrate in the quarrels. Robert de Crévecoeur mentioned in this capacity the Bavarian minister and Monsieur de Marbois, but stated, "These quarrels were carried out with such a degree of violence that M. le compte Fouché, the Chief Investigator for the state, felt obliged to take notice of them, and on one occasion, except for the intervention of the Bavarian Minister, the Count might well have bent an iron bar over the head of his wife."³

In the meantime, Thompson was making observations about light, roasting coffee beans, boilers, and so on. Recalling the count's experiments on heat, light and ballistics, Sanborn Brown, a physicist assessing him on a lofty scale, said he was "outclassed by the brilliant French intellectuals around him" and "did not have much to do but to putter around his laboratory, and he began to spend more and more time with his flowers and his garden."⁴ But then, the count's investigations had always tended to be on the quiet and ingenious side rather than dazzling. He had in particular an argument over Laplace's theory of capillary action. A great mathematician and deft politician who, like Talleyrand, survived the series of French governments through to the Restoration, Laplace participated in exiling Napoleon, who had given him political favors galore, and became a peer when the Bourbons returned to power. He was a leading intellectual of the day.

By the first anniversary the pair were enemies. To a contemporary, Baron de Frenilly, the marital strife was like Boulevard Theater. They outdid the stage. Thompson's second grand passion after fireplaces, wrote Baron de Tourelle, a noted art collector, was gardening, and he was too avid in his hobby to suit Anne. It was a publication of the Royal Society of London that pointed to the count's private greenhouse in Paris as a contributing factor to the ultimate separation of the couple: he "became further interested in floriculture, and carried his hobby to extremes,"⁵ which is hard to grasp as being irritating to the point of inciting a feud.

The baron recalled an incident in which M. de Rumford went out of the house one morning and found his greenhouse ravaged. Monsieur de Tourelle (possibly a noted art collector) paid a visit, learned the cause of the count's distress, and inquired of madam. She had blamed the cat, so Thompson seized and measured the cat but it was too large to have passed through the keyhole, so madam was locked in her room. Rumford told the visitor that she was "doing penance and not receiving anybody." Visitors were being discouraged. However, it was a Sunday and a relative came by but found the house empty, and the maid said Madame was in the cellar.[6] Whatever validity the story has is up in question by how the baron describes Rumford as "a tyrant out of tragi-comedy," Anne as "the poor countess, the innocent unhappy, persecuted woman," and the house as a "castle of Udolpho," conjuring up the Gothic novel Jane Austen parodied in *Northanger Abbey*.[7]

With punctiliousness and irony Thompson wrote Sally his woes on a number of anniversaries of the marriage. On October 24, 1807, he had this to say:

> This being the first year's anniversary of my marriage ... I am sorry to say that experience only serves to confirm me in the belief that in character and natural propensities Madame de Rumford and myself are totally unlike, and never ought to have thought of marrying.... Very likely she is as much disaffected towards me as I am towards her. Little it matters with me, but I call her a female Dragon,—simply by that gentle name! We have got to the pitch of my insisting on one thing and she on another.
>
> It is possible that, had the war ceased raging, and had we gone into Italy, where she is dying to go, and with me too, she having heard me speak much of the delights of that country,—she having been very happy, too, in travelling with me in Switzerland, it might have suspended difficulties, but never have effected a cure. That is out of the question. Indeed, I have not the least idea of continuing here, and, if possible, still less the wish, and am only planning in my mind what step I shall take next,—to be hoped more to my advantage.[8]

Just as marriage counseling is so often futile, at the one-year mark the count thought that they might patch it up. If only they could agree long enough to go on a trip! He must have been looking back at happier times with Anne. A further plaint to his daughter continued the description:

> I can do no more, my dear Sally, than simply give you the latest news upon this the anniversary of my marriage, for I am still here, and so far from things getting better they become worse every day. We are more violent and more open, and more public, as may really be said, in our quarrels. If she does not mind publicity, for a certainty I shall not. As I write the uncouth word *quarrels*, I will give you an idea of one of them.
>
> In the first place be it known that this estate is a joint concern. I have as good a right to it as Madame,—she having paid rather more in the beginning, but I an immensity of money in repairs and alterations, &c &c, besides a great deal of my own time and care spent while we have been here.
>
> I am almost afraid to tell you the story, my good child, lest in future you should not be good; lest what I am about relating should set you a bad example, make you passionate, and so on. But I had been made very angry. A large party had been invited I neither liked nor approved of, and invited for the sole purpose of vexing me. Our house being in the centre of the garden, walled around, with iron gates, I put on my hat, walked down to the porter's lodge and gave him orders, on his peril, not to let any one in. Besides, I took away the keys. Madame went down, and when the company arrived she talked with them,—she on one side, they on the other, of the high brick wall. After that she goes and pours boiling water on some of my beautiful flowers.[9]

Thus one reason tout Paris knew that the newlyweds fought was that it was carried outdoors, a "war of the roses."

This was far from the measured and rational behavior that is the stereotype of Enlightenment elite. Anne was out to castrate her husband, who tended, and was devoted to, his flowers and not to her needs. What he had spent on the house was no doubt a small portion of her contribution but again the core of the strife was the house and its shared use. Thompson, who cherished order, is out of his element when chaos has to be dealt with. His wife is upset and he steps back and watches her emotions burn. At this time Sally is a grown woman, yet he is thinking of her in absence as a china doll that might be tainted by knowledge of her father's involvement in low behavior for which he himself feels contempt.

Even the King of Bavaria heard of the misery of his courtier, and Thompson wrote Sally, back in New Hampshire, "He speaks most kindly to me, and encourages me to bear my misfortunes like a man of firmness who has nothing to reproach himself with." Sally commented that her father and his wife disagreed on nearly everything and that this alienation began from the first flush of friendship, which is incredible, as they "dated" for four years: "One wanted this, the other wanted that. Madame loved company, the Count loved quiet. One was lavish in money for entertainments; the other had no objection to spending money, but wished to see something come of it, in short, *improvements*. The lady said, calling him still by tender names, 'My Rumford would make me very happy could he but keep quiet.' The Count, on his side, says, 'I should not mind entertainments, but I hate to live on the scraps of them ever after.' With occasional grumblings they got on for a while. The Count, still engaged on his favorite subjects—light and heat,—invented a lamp."[10] This was the source of the joke that circulated in Paris of the workman who took the "Illuminator" lamp home and became so blinded he could not see his way and had to stay out all night in the Bois de Boulogne (the lamp was six times as bright as the Argand lamp).

Anne's coterie had complaints of the count. He was a picky and abstemious eater, partly from theory, partly on account of his poor health. He eschewed meat and drank only water. His table was frugal in an era when plenty was the rule for the well off. His very indifference to cuisine irritated people. He would put the tiniest piece of a dish to his mouth and then forget about it and he appeared ridiculous. Sally noted that her father could make himself agreeable in society but, even so, eating meagerly at a banquet and preferring not to drink alcohol at all alienated people. When everybody else was eating with gusto, said the count's friend Baron Cuvier, "he discoursed upon the breadfruit."[11]

The astute Emma Gannell Burgum in her notes (at the New Hampshire Historical Society) passed on half a century later, what she had heard: that Rumford preferred broiled chicken to French recipes and liked to experiment with flowers; also that he wanted a son and Madame Lavoisier could not give him one.

Sally extracted and copied from a letter of April 12, 1808, the following update from her father: "There are no alterations for the better. On the contrary, much worse. I have suffered more than you can imagine for the last four weeks; but my rights are incontestable, and I am determined to maintain them. I have the misfortune to be married to one of the most imperious, tyrannical, unfeeling women that ever existed, and whose perseverance in pursuing an object is equal to her profound cunning and wickedness in framing it.... Little do we know people at first sight! Do you preserve my letters? You will perceive that I have given very different accounts of this woman, for *lady* I cannot call her."[12]

The couple wrote each other letters while living together. Thompson wrote Anne that she scorned his authority (even Rousseau believed women should act with submission). For two years she had refused to have her servants wear his livery and she frequently went out in a carriage without being followed by a valet. He scribbled: he was the head of the household and his orders were to be obeyed. One can picture Anne's being unspeakably angry when she wanted to go out when it was raining and Thompson himself had the closed carriage. Other images are more in the nature of gossip or comical scenes from *Taming of the Shrew*. To Anne's dismay, for instance, Thompson summoned the police to help him chase a coachman who displeased him.

Anne appealed to the minister of justice to help her. In retaliation Thompson addressed complaints to the prefect of police, Dubois. Both hoped the emperor would listen. The count wrote Dubois: "I hope the emperor has too high an opinion of my taste to believe me capable of passing the rest of my life in intimacy with a woman as venomous as her, but I consider my honor at stake, and I cannot abandon the field of battle." Three weeks later he wrote Dubois again: "I was cruelly calomnied! I have nothing to reproach myself and I do not want to believe that His Majesty the Emperor would permit a foreigner who was given asylum to be persecuted vilified, oppressed and chased from court and city by the cabals of a woman who is haughty, scheming, and implacable who wants at any cost to do away with her husband."[13] This was just before the Battle of Wagram, and the warring couple had lost perspective if they imagined Napoleon would care about their squabbles.

The count wanted Sally to join him as soon as he was settled in the house that he leased in Auteuil. The last three months he and Anne lived together he was ill, bedridden before he moved out in early 1807. In October Loammi Baldwin died in his house in Woburn. This must have rung out "you can't go home again" in the count's heart. (From this time on, the son, James F. Baldwin (d. 1862), would be Sally's advisor and support).

Sex for the sake of it (without love) doesn't seem to have held interest for Thompson. All his intimates seem to have been emotive and passionate about their friendship. A friend was a confidant, a person missed when absent, a support, and someone to go to for fun and in duress. When Thompson was a teenager (about 17) Baldwin and he had a falling out over Baldwin's being left behind to carry boating gear. The friendship meant so much that Thompson wrote a serious apology to Baldwin begging forgiveness and hoping to repair the rift. One senses he did this because of the high value he put on friendship. People didn't just pass in and out of the life of the peripatetic count, he made strong friends—with Lord Germain, Charles Blagden, the Palmerstons, scientists from various countries, and the Italian countesses. The caring was mutual and, alas, it seems that Thompson was spoiled in expecting it to come easily. He stated repeatedly he thought the marriage to Anne would give him peace to do science and follow his inclinations. He was expecting another intimate friend; she was seeking a carbon copy of what she had with Antoine. Neither wanted the type of new life the other offered. In the union there was no caring or trust, only competitiveness, territoriality and temper.

Thompson had regulated his front and back stage selves, kept them in balance, and now he was 50 and wanted to be independent of the set of behaviors of the politics of elite circles and employment. Anne, to the contrary, strove to operate entirely on the front stage, as the back stage had been torn from her. She had grown up in the laboratory, more or less. It was a stage set that she even drew as if it were a stage, with herself on a chair in it being secretary and assistant. She had an extraordinary social tool kit for dealing with this milieu, which Thompson could take or leave, preferably leave. Antipathy replaced the nascent connection between them as soon as they married because in all the ways they interacted relating to science, money, house-holding, and daily life they didn't trust each other a whit.

The physical separation occurred politely on June 9, 1809, and the marriage ended June 30, by which time Thompson had already moved out. It is of interest, placing the events in the context, that just when Thompson and Madame Lavoisier were straining at the bit to be done with each other, rumors were circulating of an impending divorce of Josephine by Napoleon. That same summer of 1809 the Polish mistress of Napoleon, Marie Walewski, had become pregnant, so Napoleon had a strong indication he was not infertile. He told Josephine of his intention two weeks before the annulment on December 15 of the same year. The word divorce would be in error. Such an act would have contravened the Code Civil. Article 277 of the 1806 statute stipulated that mutually agreed divorce could not take place if the wife had reached 45 (Josephine was 46 by this point). The legal dissolution of Thompson and Anne's marriage had to halt at a formal separation and not a divorce, as the Code Civil was in effect, because Madame Lavoisier was 51 years old.

Soon after, the count wrote Sally from Auteuil: "I find myself relieved from an almost insupportable burden. I cannot repeat too much how happy I am, gaining every day in health, which from vexations had become seriously deranged. I am persuaded it is all for the best. After the scenes which I have recently passed through I, realize, as never before, the sweets of quiet, liberty, and independence.... O! happy, thrice happy, am I to, be my own man again!"[14] He experienced his relief at singlehood as a kind of resurrection of the dead. In the second half of the year, he again wrote Sally: "Madame de Rumford is well. I see her sometimes, though very seldom. After what is past a reconciliation is impossible. She now repents of her conduct, but it is too late. The less I see her the better. I now enjoy peace and tranquility, and my health improves every day."[15] The rupture might have been avoided had they gone to Italy on vacation, or if he had waited until his angry wife came to her senses, typical post-divorce ponderings. On October 24, 1809, six months after the separation, the count told Sally it was better she hadn't come while he was at the rue d'Anjou, despite his often wishing for her to have been there: "I am recovering my health and spirits fast. I am like one risen from the dead."[16]

18

Single Again (1809)

> What hope have we to know our selves, when wee
> Know not the least things, which for our use bee?—John Donne,
> *Of the Progress of the Soul: The Second Anniversary* (1633)

"Heaven hath no rage like love to hatred turned," wrote the 18th century poet William Congreve. Anne had Count Rumford ostracized from fashionable society and tried to get Napoleon to declare him persona non grata at the Tuileries. She tried various approaches, based on Thompson's being British, and sought the collusion of Madame de Rémusat, lady in waiting to Empress Josephine. A dinner was organized with Talleyrand, then Napoleon's Grand Chamberlain, and Joseph Fouché, minister of police, but they were busy plotting against Napoleon. When the emperor heard of the dinner from his secret police he figured it was a conspiracy. Years later the son of the Rémusats recalled his parents discussing this dinner, citing it as an example of how some fortuitous and trivial incident could have unexpected and large importance: "They would say, smiling, that Madame de Rumford did not know what that dinner had cost them."[1]

Just when Anne belittled Thompson at home for experiments like building a boiler for soap manufacture in their house, he was having hard times at the French Institute. He had already presented a paper on diffusing lampshades the year before and in August 1807 gave another paper proposing that roughened glass panes would light rooms better than transparent ones. He gave the very room in which the academicians were sitting as an example, saying that if ground glass were used for outside windows there would be more and more pleasant light. This was too much for the audience, which dissolved in laughter. For over three years after this embarrassing incident he presented no more papers at the institute's podium.

In November 1808 Thompson was ill and took his meals alone and received few visitors. He wrote Sally how Madame continued to give evening teas three times a week, while he was determined to not adopt "this strange manner of living." He continued: "A separation is unavoidable, for it would be highly improper for me to continue with a person who has given me so many proofs of her implacable hatred and malice."[2] He had been poorly for several months. When he was convalescing in the winter of 1808–1809 he focused his attention on coffee makers. Using his typical methodology he first studied roasting the beans and then the design of the apparatus. Coffee had to be treated with care as its price went up when France lost coffee-growing colonies in the Caribbean. (Napoleon recommended the alternative of domestic chicory but he himself was a coffee drinker). Thompson devised a drip pot with a heated water jacket to maintain a constant temperature and the use of an alcohol lamp to make the pot portable. He did all this because of his conviction that drinking coffee was a healthier stimulant than alcohol. In Paris, he would do a range of investigations, from studying the radiation of heat to the power required to drive a carriage.[3]

In April 1808, after five years in France (during which he contributed 20 papers to the French Institute), Thompson bought his last home, Number 59, rue d'Auteuil, in the west of Paris, now the southern part of its 16th arrondissement. Auteuil and Passy were two villages side by side on a hill, between the Seine and the Bois de Boulogne, then known for intellectual chic and popular with expatriates. Ben Franklin lived at the eastern limit of Auteuil from 1777 to 1785 and Molière had lived at number 2. Number 59, rue d'Auteuil was a fine house with two acres of garden. Some months later, Thompson moved in. There he could isolate himself, become an island,

"Caffetiere" pour 1. 2. 3. 4. 5. ou 6 Tasses. **Auteuil. April 10, 1812 (Houghton Library, Harvard University).**

renew. When he wrote Anne henceforth, how he addressed her, as "Mme. La comtesse," reveals attitude, an element of jocularity about titles, including his own.

In the history of old houses, 59, rue d'Auteuil holds a prominent place because of the people who lived there. It was built in 1770 by Quentin de La Tour, a master of pastels and Louis XV's court painter. He could not afford the money he owed for it, due to his charities—a school and foundations for indigent women and old artisans. Next the alluring mistress of Benjamin Franklin, Madame Helvétius, purchased and lived in the house. Before the French Revolution, Madame Lavoisier had herself done a picture of Benjamin Franklin in the house when visiting her friend Anne-Catherine (Madame Helvétius). When the audacious widow Madame Helvétius asked Franklin why he hadn't come to her for the night, he had replied that he was waiting until the nights were longer.

Madame Helvétius was called "Notre-Dame d'Auteuil" because, like the artist de La Tour, she was uncommonly charitable. She also held a salon of such chic that Napoleon came to it after his return from Egypt. The worthy husband, Claude-Adrien, whom she outlived by almost a decade, was the only *fermier-général* to voluntarily give up his lucrative position. His death in 1771 prompted her move to Auteuil, where she kept a menagerie in the house including dogs, cats, chickens, and canaries. When she died in 1800 she was at her request buried in the garden.[4] Thompson bought the home from a banker named Monsieur Osiris, who owned it for the intervening six years after Madame Helvétius. A copy of Michelangelo's statue of Moses stood in the front yard, which Monsieur Osiris had intended as a tombstone for his own grave.

In July and August 1808 Rembrandt Peale painted Thompson's portrait and in 1810 Napoleon's. Peale was fatigued with portrait painting, so this one of the count was among the last batch. The artist added it to the Apollodorian Gallery of portraits of famous Americans, by then in the gallery that his father had in Philadelphia; thereafter Peale turned to historical subjects. When the painter was 80 years of age, in a letter to someone who had inquired about the portrait, he noted Thompson's garden at the rue d'Anjou, and with political shading the fracas of the count and countess: "His Garden, in the heart of Paris, was distinguished by possessing a great number of American Trees—and, by the lamentable fact that they were destroyed by the malice of his wife, (the widow of the celebrated Lavoisier), who professed to hate every thing that was American."[5] Peale recalled the year as 1812. The count would no longer have been in the house at rue d'Anjou in that year as he was already settled at 59, rue d' Auteuil; therefore Peale was mistaken in either the year or the garden but accurate about the level of strife.

A law permitting divorce had been instituted in 1792 in France; but as Anne's union with Thompson took place beyond the age when divorce was legal, they were a square peg and could only have the legal separation. Few European countries sanctioned divorce, and even in France the law permitting legal divorce would be revoked in the nineteenth century. In any event, property and propinquity were over on June 30, 1809, which was equivalent to divorce. The count's finances presumably improved but he had been marrying for security not money. His daughter said that if her father "had shown himself mercenary or avaricious on this occasion, it would have been for the first time."[6]

On October 24, 1809, the first anniversary of the dissolution of their marriage, Thompson wrote his daughter and said how glad he was to be in Auteuil away from Madame Lavoisier and how miserable their marriage had been. The count set out from Paris in August 1810 for Germany—first to Munich and then to Salzburg at the behest of Prince Ludwig. In Munich terrible news greeted him. Countess Nogarola, he wrote his daughter, had died and her sister was very ill. He now wanted Sally to visit him in Paris. He also told her that Sophie was married and now had the name Madame de Miltez, which removed her a few degrees from the count, something perhaps gratifying to Sally.[7] The next "anti-anniversary," in 1810, keeping wryly and methodically to the accounts to Sally, Thompson wrote as follows: "You will perceive that this is the anniversary of my marriage. I am happy to call it to mind, that I may compare my present situation with the three and a half horrible years I was living with that tyrannical, avaricious, unfeeling woman. You can have no idea, my dear Sally, what I had to suffer during the last fourteen months—indeed, during the whole three and a half years I lived in that house; but the closing six months was a purgatory sufficiently painful to do away the sins of a thousand years."[8]

The count was continuing to send his mother money and letters from Paris as the marriage with Anne disintegrated. He wrote his mother that his life appeared to him like a dream and assured her that he never forgot her. One of the Baldwins must have relayed that his mother was proud of him, as it was clear that her satisfaction in his doings and enterprises meant a lot to him. A letter of February 1812 concluded, "I shall never cease to be, my Dear Mother, your dutiful and affectionate child, 'BENJAMIN.'"[9] Ruth, Sally's grandmother, died the next year. Her children by Josiah Pierce would now receive the annuity that had been hers, betokening warm feelings on the count's part towards the distant family.

Sally sailed from New York on July 24, 1811, on a ship called the *Drummond*. A British brig named *Cadmus* captured the *Drummond* off Bordeaux as a suspected blockade runner. The *Cadmus* was taken to Plymouth, England, and Sally reached her father's house about five months after she had sailed from New York. She once again embraced the adventure of a transatlantic voyage during the whole trip. Once at her father's, not until December, she soon met and liked the "separated lady," i.e., Anne Lavoisier Rumford.

In Auteuil, the count worked in his laboratory and raised a garden of 50 varieties of roses. Like Montaigne, who it was said could barely distinguish a cabbage from a lettuce, the count discarded the nonessential and didn't bother with botanical names. He saw friends like Lagrange and Cuvier, permanent secretary of the French Institute, while becoming less connected to le beau monde. The neighborhood had been fashionable since the time of Louis XV. Thompson's house was already one with a history, and the count added to its luster.

Scarcely a year after being miserable in his domestic situation, Thompson was comfortably settled in Auteuil. While Laplace was put out with the count for contesting his capillary theory, Thompson had a coterie of other brilliant French scientist friends such as the chemist Claude Louis Berthollet, who isolated ammonia and, being interested in technological application, as was the count, worked at how to manufacture it. Thompson also advised John Armstrong, Jr., the U.S. ambassador to France, on how to clean his iron pots.[10] Armstrong (1758–1843) had just won a seat in the U.S. senate when four months later Jefferson appointed him ambassador to France, a post he held until 1812. Under James Madison, Armstrong served as minister of war but was removed from the post when he made the poor judgment call that the British would not attack Washington, D.C. Armstrong was the last surviving delegate to the Continental Congress and the only one to be photographed.

Sally, who seems to have in her life had more perception about others than herself, wrote in her diary a canny opinion regarding what had gone wrong between her father and his French wife: "I had not been many days at Auteuil before we had a visit from his separated lady, for they seemed to be on good terms—at least on visiting terms. The lady was gracious to me, and I was charmed with her, nor did I ever after find reason to be otherwise, for she was truly an admirable character. Their disagreements must have arisen from their independence of character and means; being used always to having their own ways. Their pursuits in some particulars were different. He was fond of his experiments, and she of company."[11] Sally continued to be friendly with Mme. Lavoisier and ignored the animosity that had built up in the marriage. Reports are that the exes were convivial and maintained an acquaintance until his death. "Sally can hardly have been predisposed to form or rather have a good opinion of Marie after the long series of letters from her father.... If she gave such a favorable account of Madame Lavoisier, we may believe that it is likely fairly to represent the lady in question."[12] Her father had declared, "You have no idea what a fiend she is to live with," and yet Anne remained an important acquaintance in Paris. He found his new home through Anne's contacts, and when he had a pair of horses too spirited for his coachman he asked his ex if she would like to buy them. She agreed and said complaisantly, "I will trust you not to cheat me, for you know I am no judge of horses."[13] Anne, might, he wrote her, stay in his London house with Sally as companion. This speaks for its not being comme il faut for a proper woman to live without a man. He also offered to sell Anne "real moka coffee at 44 sous a pound," which at the distance of two centuries sounds like the slap of a glove—i.e., why not give her the coffee?—but it was possibly from friendly intention.

In this era, aristocratic titles still signified wealth and power and thus mattered a great deal. Anne rebuked Thompson as a person but in later years called herself Madame Rumford or Comtesse de Rumford. In 1841, in his *Mélanges biographiques et littéraires*, Guizot wrote as follows: "After domestic agitations, that Monsieur de Rumford with more tact could have rendered less fiery, the separation became necessary, and took place amiably on June 30, 1809." The chronicler continued that Anne lived agreeably from then on, staying in the milieu of friends and society, whom she received "with a singular mixture of rudeness and politeness, always showing mosts companionable qualities and full knowledge of the world, not withstanding her brusque speech and imperious whims (*"fantasies d'authorité"*).[14]

According to Sally, who had been her father's companion in London and Munich, he was leading a rather secluded life. In the fashion of the day, to say the most important things in a letter as if casually in allusions, she wrote to James Baldwin and folded in mention of a mistress who made her father happy and provided singing birds in the dining room:

> The first salutations over, his hat being called for, we took a walk in the extensive garden which he had laid out with great care, and made very beautiful. He had written to me about it, but I found it much finer than I had expected. It covered over two acres, with tufted woods and winding paths, with grapes in abundance, and fifty kinds of roses [it being winter, this fact was told to her]. A gardener was constantly employed, with a laborer under him. My father was exceedingly fond of flowers, and, in order to gratify him in making things as agreeable as possible to him, a young person—either housekeeper, companion, or both—put them in every place where he was likely to set his foot or turn his eye.[15]

Returning to the house in Autueil we get to look back as if in a time machine, or, say, a feature accidentally perceived when looking at details in a photograph. The room that served as a laboratory for Thompson in his house at Autueil appeared in the *Illustrated London News* of January 22, 1870, fifty-six years after his death. Prince Pierre Bonaparte, a cousin of Louis-Napoleon (Napoleon III), arrived at this appointed place to duel with a revolutionary journalist. Two seconds were present but the nobleman refused to deal with them, as they were beneath his rank. In the altercation, Pierre shot and killed one of the seconds, Victor Noir. (Perhaps the duel took place in a room where Benjamin Franklin flirted with Madame Helvétius amidst her longhair cats.)

The populace rose up in anger at the tragedy. One hundred thousand people followed Noir's funeral procession to Neuilly. Violent demonstrations at Pierre's acquittal (obviously because of his being in the family of Louis-Napoleon) were a factor in the fall of the Second Empire. During the Commune of 1871, communists burned the house down because of its association with Pierre Bonaparte.[16] In the picture it appears that the room was not a science laboratory as we now picture it but rather had some sort of rococo dec-

"The Murder of Victor Noir," *Illustrated London News,* **January 22, 1870.**

orated panels on its walls. Imagine that a blistering duel of political import took place where Thompson was perfecting the drip coffee pot and wide carriage wheel, not to mention where Ben Franklin flirted with his favorite French mistress. The house was destroyed purportedly to avenge the murder of Victor Noir. Antoine Lavoisier's own laboratory is largely, and tranquilly, in a science museum in Paris.

Thompson continued to do experiments and did the drawings of his own inventions. He was mocked for riding around Paris in an experimental carriage, built for comfort and efficiency. It was bordered by ornate springs and dynamometers and had wheels wider than the norm (he tried two- and four-inch rims). He parked the carriage in front of the institute and told people to get a good look at it. He wore white clothes and hat in the winter in a mistaken belief he would thereby absorb sunshine. For leisure he walked, landscaped and gardened flowers and vegetables. He played some chess but became impatient with it and said his feet became icy and his head feverish when he sat immobile so long. He played billiards, often against himself.

Politics still determined his whereabouts. If he returned to England or America, he might lose his pension from Bavaria, as Bonaparte would not have allowed his vassal, Maximilian (having become the king of Bavaria), to have paid the count. An English visitor might see Thompson as a prisoner of France, but he had never had a true home and liked this one. Sally wrote home to Concord: "I have seen little of Paris as yet, therefore cannot say much about it, but my Father's situation at this place, which is about two miles from Paris, I find very pleasant, and I see nothing to prevent me from being very happy here. My father is in excellent health, I never knew him better."[17]

The friends who visited the count had at least seen his housekeeper and realized he had a mistress. They would have been discreet, i.e., they would not likely have commented.

It was polite to stay on Parnassian conversation and Victoire Joseph Lefebvre must have been an attractive young woman who gave her feminine charm to the house. The visits were repeated and the visitors few: a next-door neighbor who was a senator; Mr. Underwood, associated with the Royal Institution, and Pierre-Simon Laplace, the mathematician. The other visitor whose name crops up, a Mr. Parker, was an American businessman in Paris with agricultural interests, likely on uncommon ground vis-à-vis cohabitation. A friend or perhaps physician whose identity has not been uncovered visited Thompson almost daily in Auteuil at the end of his life and did refer to Victoire. This person, a "Marquis Chansener, asked the Count if he expected an addition to his family," an indirect reference to Victoire's condition. The count replied politely, "No, I only expect to go away myself."[18] It was typical for a bachelor or widower to have an unofficial union with a woman of lower status. How Thompson handled this type of liaison and how he treated Victoire are the crucial points, which clues from the past disclose.

An account by Rousseau of what he liked so much about the simplicity of dalliances with his paramour Thérèse, a half-century before Thompson and Victoire sat down to their meals, evokes a picture that could be Thompson and Victoire in the house at Auteuil. Rousseau recalled a meal while looking down from a fourth floor apartment in Paris: "The windowsill served as our table, we were breathing fresh air.... Who could describe or feel the charm of these meals, composed entirely of a quarter loaf of bread, some cherries, a bit of cheese, and a half bottle of wine that we shared between us? Friendship, trust, intimacy, sweetness of soul—what delicious seasonings you contribute."[19]

A Woman in a Garden (1793), **miniature by Billot** (Walters Museum, Baltimore).

Unlike Rousseau, it will be seen that Thompson did not put his progeny by his mistress into a foundling hospice but, rather, looked out for her and their child's future. She also had her housekeeping tasks alongside his gardening and projects and didn't have to help support her man by hiring out as a laundress. Additionally, being in his late fifties when the liaison with Victoire began, and burned by marriage to a totally correct lady, Thompson was not going to abandon Victoire to marry up. Yet the desire of a worldly, creative philosophe for a basic kind of union with a woman where they enjoy simple pleasures was surely identical for both these famous outsiders to Paris of the Enlightenment era.

Sally was in Le Havre, sent by her father on an errand, when he was seized by a "sudden violent fever" on August 18, 1814. It is recounted that his abstemiousness had been so severe that he could not fight off the fever and died after three days. Yet it was also reported that he was in good form and supervising additions to buildings on the grounds. A letter from Baron Delessert reached Sally with the news of her father's death on August 22. She did not attend the small funeral three days later. The tombstone remains in the Auteuil cemetery today. Years later Sally jotted down, right after this series of sad dates, that both the Countess Nogarola and Lady Palmerston were no longer living, thus validating them as her father's cherished women friends. It's no wonder, if Sally was accurate, that the count packed her off on a trip to Switzerland when Victoire was showing the pregnancy, promising to join her. In her absence the count's housekeeper Victoire gave birth to his son. On top of that, when Sally was back from Switzerland he whipped up the Le Havre junket. The birth certificate, witnessed by a *rentier*, or person of independent means and a wine merchant, was filled out hastily and the child's surname was misspelled. In its corrected version, the mother is Victoire Joseph and the child Charles François Robert Lefebvre. It says of the father "not present."

A macabre postscript to Thompson's death casts a peculiar light on his daughter. He had not actually died, she insisted. Rather, disgusted with the world and seeking absolute privacy or wishing to wander away among strangers, he had enacted burial rites as a farce. Sally was now officially a countess upon the death of her father, although she had been addressed as such in Bavaria. In the days following her father's death, Sally accepted an invitation to dine with Anne. When the dessert was served and the servants had left the room, Anne remarked, "Your father died young and in a very sudden manner." "Died!" cried Sally. "I do not believe him to be dead, no more than I am at this moment."[20] Madame de Rumford, maintained Sally, shared her opinion, to the extent Anne made three trips to London, where she had never been before, with the hope of tracing her late husband. As late as 1831 Sally held to her fantasy that her father died "in the eyes of the world." In a letter from Brompton Row to a sympathetic James Baldwin, who found time when not doing engineering feats to help manage her affairs, she wrote the following: "Of one thing I am certain, that Madam de Rumford, his supposed widow, did not believe it, any more than myself. In short there never was anything to equal the mystery of his apparent death, the details of which quote too numerous to relate here. He was a very strange man & quite equal to a thing of the sort, in my opinion."[21]

Two of Thompson's friends acted as his executors, the polymath banker and naturalist J.P. Benjamin Delessert and the American businessman who had long lived in Paris and got immense wealth from being a supplier of arms and financier of the American Revolution, Daniel Parker. Buying a beautiful retreat is a time-honored way of showing respectability and in this case Parker had a chateau at Draveil, about 12 miles south of Paris on the Seine. Parker, who bought Draveil in 1803, kept to the Louis XV interior décor: mirrors, carved gilded panels, and the like. As a consequence, in 1936 when the property was being sold the Philadelphia Museum bought its Grand Salon. Given Thompson's sense of panache, the fact that the will was executed in the opulence of the chateau seems perfect. The extent to which the gentlemen had forgotten what side they were on during the American Revolution is evidenced by the fact that the Marquis de Lafayette acted as one of the witnesses to Thompson's will.

The eulogy at Benjamin Thompson Count Rumford's small funeral was given by Baron Cuvier, secretary of the Institut National, and was odd and politically shaded. He began with how it was an honor for France that Thompson lived his last years there and that he did so because France was where celebrity was awarded to the great. Cuvier continued that the deceased, despite his successes and the good he did, appeared to have been indifferent to, and embittered towards, his fellow man and he believed that democracy to be a "fictitious fancy born of false notions of enlightenment." With condescension Cuvier alluded to how the count approved of a Chinese-style government, "*which makes so many millions of arms the passive organs of the will of a few sound heads.*"[22] Four months before Thompson's death, Napoleon had abdicated and the Allies were rejoicing that the despot had departed from the European political scene.

Sally stayed in Auteuil through the following spring and then moved to her father's house in London. She was back in France in 1817 and at last returned to America. She took under her wing an English child, Emma Gammell, who lived with her and called her "Aunt." In 1852 Emma married John Burgum of Concord, who also had come from England. As an older person, Sally would wear fine jewelry and laces that Madame Lavoisier had sent after the marriage to her father. Her writings are a major source of material on the Lefebvre family. An elaborate stone was erected for Thompson in the cemetery at Auteuil. According to the guardian of the cemetery, the tombstone was destroyed by exploding shells during the war of 1870 and restored by Harvard University in 1876 and then by the American Academy of Arts and Sciences in 1925.

After his influence and privileges at the Bavarian court, his prestige founding the Royal Institution in London, and seeing his societal innovations and inventions celebrated in many lands, being an outsider in Napoleon's capital and generating science that was judged there as minor might have been sorrowful indeed for Thompson had he been an egomaniac. To be consistent with their view that he was a self-absorbed show-off, biographers mostly jump on the bandwagon of proclaiming his misery in Auteuil. Yet Sally said that when she came to visit she had never seen him happier. He was totally busy with his projects, no more than a little frustrated by the politics of science, and supremely engagé. Gardening, thinking, a modicum of socializing and occasional contact with other scientists suited him utterly. My favorite overview comes from a short article by French historian of science Robert Champeix: "The ten or so years remaining to him to live were for Rumford a happy period, without worldly receptions, only receiving a few carefully chosen friends that he would invite for a potluck meal. He profited from this semi-solitude to throw himself into the joy of research on physics, which, if it fell somewhat into the category of tinkering ['bricolage'], was interesting nonetheless."[23]

19

Victoire (Circa 1809)

> Labor when she dealt with it had the easy and spontaneous charm of play.
> —Nathaniel Hawthorne, *The House of Seven Gables* (1851)

About Thompson's mistress Victoire Lefebvre, the little that is known is almost all conjectural but fascinating and testifies to her many positive traits. Victoire was strong and resilient, independent and capable, life loving, and an indomitable matriarch. She can be seen through others' eyes—lines from a letter of Thompson to her, remarks bridging about 30 years by Sally, and the few sketches by Sally's "adopted" daughter, Emma Gannell Burgum. As the sources are unique documents in all Rumford-related personal papers they will be laid out here at some length.

Lefebvre is a common name in the north and west of France, and Count Rumford would have wished a housekeeper who was not encumbered with local family, thus reinforcing his solitary penchant and the privacy of the sexual relationship that developed. There is no reason to interpret that she was hidden just because little about her is known. Being from afar would explain why Victoire lived in the porter's lodge instead of coming in by day from the environs. The count had a workman from Germany, an instrument maker, living at Auteuil as well. Whereas Ben Franklin had a son out of wedlock, whose mother has never been identified, Victoire was a real part of the count's household and daily life over years, when he was mostly alone except for her company.

The relationship had no hypocrisy. It was consensual. A housekeeper was "somebody," not a servant. She had youth and energy and he had fire and means. It was important what Victoire was not. She was not going to criticize him for soap-making in the house or what clothes he wore when he went to town or his not giving a hoot about keeping up with notable people who did not interest him. It will be seen in this chapter and the next that Victoire was adaptable and practical but also warm. The great devotion she demonstrated to her son and his family, while laudable, is less surprising than how she brought Sally, become an orphan, into their lives. Some people, Benjamin Thompson among them, find their lasting friendships among strangers who share their interests. Others go forward onto life's pond on the stepping-stones of their earliest family, hometown, and schoolmates. That was Sally, who trusted only the stepping-stones her father had laid down (and in fact Victoire also, it seems).

Sally in 1827 was back in London living at her father's old house, 45 Brompton Row, and lonely. The Palmerstons, Sir Charles and her father had passed on, and she decided on a strategy to fight loneliness: in effect she would borrow a baby. This was the second time she was lonely and she found a rather lordly remedy. The first time, after the count's death, she asked Mr. Grove, the man who managed her father's house, to look around for a young girl to live with her as a companion. He offered Mary, his eight-year-old daughter, who lived and traveled with Sally for years. After Mary married she lived with her husband, Henry Gannell, a silversmith, and was raising her children. Sally was alone again. Emma Gannell was the 18-month-old first child of Mary and Henry, whom they "lent" to Sally. Everywhere Sally went Emma went and their passport read "The Countess of Rumford and her niece Emma Rumford." Sally, like her father, could self-invent!

Emma would go with Sally to England, France and the U.S., where she met and married another Britain-born individual, John Burgum. It is important to understand that Emma was truly integrated into the lives of both Sally and the Lefebvres. To take a prime example, the Burgums' six children were rocked in a cradle made from a bread trough that had belonged to Sarah Williams Rolfe Thompson and which John fitted out with rockers (and of course painted).[1] The information and episodes of Emma Burgum's days as a young child "adopted" into a glamorous cross-Atlantic life and written down much later are credible. They are, moreover, an apercu into the real lives of Thompson's mistress Victoire and their son, Charles Lefebvre. The style Emma chose resembles a storybook but the facts were intended to be exact, by contrast to Sally's more fanciful autobiographical tales she signed "Serafine" (or "Serafina").

Emma's own love story would be rocky. Sometimes people were invited to the Rolfe-Rumford mansion in Concord to admire the Rumford collection of portraits and landscape paintings. John Burgum (1826–1907) was an ornamental painter who had apprenticed to a clock dial painter in England and in 1850 emigrated to America, where he painted designs on horse-drawn coaches. When John came to the mansion to view the pictures, he and Emma were drawn to each other and a romance ensued. He wrote in Emma's autograph book (September 1851), "Thou hear this fervent wish, love / Of my full soul to thee; That on some blissful day, love. / Thou'lt be the world to me."[2] Their attachment for some time was secret. When Sally Thompson found out, she disapproved vehemently of the match, likely having dreamed of a husband of higher rank for Emma. Sally wrote her friend George Pierce on June 21, 1852: "You can hardly have an idea how much I have suffered for the last months, owing to Emma's intimacy with this man."[3] She was outraged that for months John had been placing secret letters to Emma in the fence of Sally's home—sometimes two or three in a day! The couple was married October 30, 1852, in Old North Church in Boston. Sally Thompson did not attend the wedding, saying her health did not permit, but she allowed John and Emma to live in her house until they found a place of their own.

John Burgum did all the paintings on the doors of wagons and coaches of the Concord Coach Company for 25 years, as well as taking out patents for a number of associated inventions. The Long Island Museum in Stony Brook, New York, has a highly decorated horse-drawn omnibus, *Grace Darling*, which operated in Berwick, Maine, in the 1880s and 1890s. It was named after a famous Victorian heroine, a lighthouse keeper's daughter who rescued survivors of a shipwreck off the coast of England. On an exterior door panel of the omnibus Burgum put a stag, a dog, and Diana with bow and quiver. The Concord Coach was modeled after the coronation coach of George III, demonized in the previous century.

At eleven, Emma spent a month away from Sally in Paris with Victoire, when Sally was in London. And from 1838 to 1845, when Sally and Emma lived in Paris at 20, rue

Miromesnil (8th arrondissement) across from the widow at 25, they saw Victoire frequently. Victoire herself likely told Emma episodes from her life, unless Emma overheard the remarkable tale in dinner conversation or when the adults were at the whist table. Victoire was one among many poor people who took the *grande route royale* from the region of Normandy to the capital, a journey discussed in the following pages. Emma wrote a number of little pieces about the Rumfords and cleaved to the facts, but only this one leaps out as an account found nowhere else that sheds light on Thompson's housekeeper and the future of his son. The precious record of Victoire follows:

> In the spring of 1810, three young girls started to walk from Normandy to Paris to seek their fortune. They were daughters of well to do farmers. One, Victoire Lefebvre, aged 22, and her sister Sophia, four years younger. They had another elder sister and brother, who were to remain at home and help their parents.
>
> They had a young friend, the daughter of a neighbor, who had accompanied them on their journey: she was only sixteen years old. Theresa was very pretty, small, and delicate of figure, a blonde, with bright blue eyes and a small face.
>
> The two sisters were good looking healthy country girls. They each carried a small valise and were dressed in traveling outfits. They went along for some miles. At last, being somewhat weary, and hungry also, they sat down on the grass, under the trees, which shaded the roadside.
>
> It was about noon, and while they were eating their frugal repast, there came along a man in a wagon, he looked like a farmer; on seeing the three young women sitting by the roadside, he stopped his horse, for he thought they looked like travelers. He asked them where they were from and where they were going, and when they had answered these questions, the young man in return, informed them that he was from Linas near Paris, he being the gardener of Mr. Cabot; and added, if they liked he would take them in his cart, and drive them the rest of the way to Paris, or from Linas.
>
> Of course, the girls were only too glad to have the chance to ride. They having found that walking many miles in the hot sun in the month of May, was rather fatiguing.
>
> So on the road, in the course of conversation, they learned that Mr. Cabot had a nurse for a little boy who was an invalid, but the maid was obliged to leave soon, to go and take care of her mother. And this meant that perhaps one of these girls might like to go there and be nurse for the little boy. So when they arrived at Linas, he took the three of them to his mother's house, nearby.
>
> The next day, the young man went for the girls, and introduced them to Mrs. Cabot, who was well pleased with their appearance, all three of them, but the youngest looked as she thought too frail and young for a nursery maid in the country. The eldest looked very nice and capable and so did her sister Sophia. And while Mrs. Cabot was making up her mind, the young sister whispered to Victoire, "Oh! How I should love to live here. What a beautiful place it is!"
>
> "What did you say young woman? Really would you like to come and live here?"

Sophia Baumgarten (circa 1795) attributed to J.G. von Dillis. The miniature is said to have hung in all places of abode of Sally (Countess Rumford) and on the wall of the chamber in Concord, New Hampshire, where she died (New Hampshire Historical Society).

"Yes, Madame."

"Well I will take you on trial," said Mrs. Cabot.

And "on trial" ending in the long run, to her [Victoire's little sister Sophia's] marrying the gardner, Dechassur, that being his name and living in the Cabot family all the rest of their lives; and the son always lived at home, never married, was an invalid all his days, and died before he was forty years old.

In the mean time, in some way Count de Tauzier having heard of Theresa, engaged her as waiting maid for his wife, who was in need of one. And where she remained, being liked very much by both the Count and the Countess, and at the end of two years the Countess passed away, after a lingering illness. There were no children. And in less than a year after his wife died, the Count married Theresa.[4]

In the course of time, they had two children, Pauline and Leonel.

A Search for a Better Life
by Mrs. Brigitte Muller Konrad, Normandy

Apropos of the travels of the three girls who left Normandy to "go up" to Paris, there was nothing extraordinary about it, the most illustrious example being that of La Dame aux Camélias (*La Traviata*), whose real name was Alphonsine Plessis. This celebrated courtesan was born in Nonant-le-Pin in 1824, and lived until the age of 23. The story of those years, transfigured first by Alexandre Dumas Fils (who wrote the story in 1848) then by the composer Giuseppe Verdi, created the myth of an irresistible and magical woman.

The famous courtesan's trajectory began like that of many girls from the Normand countryside who set out on the Grande Route Royale. At fourteen she was working for an umbrella seller when she departed from her home village of Gacé, a simple, uneducated, poor orphan. Four years later she had transformed into the most elegant woman in Paris, who received in her salon the most influential men of her time and had as lovers the richest dandies as well as artists like Alexandre Dumas Fils and Franz Liszt.

Normandy was very prosperous at that time. Its fertile lands provided the capital, Paris, with most of its food. After the Napoleonic Wars, trade with overseas countries resumed and was soon in full swing through the ports of Le Havre, Rouen, Dieppe, Fécamp, Honfleur, and Granville. Plenty of famous people were born in Normandy, or lived and worked here including Gustave Flaubert, Guy de Maupassant, Eugéne Boudin, and Jean-François Millet. Honoré de Balzac, Alexandre Dumas, and Victor Hugo traveled there every year as did most of the Impressionists, and many British were buying lands in Normandy too: Benjamin Franklin wrote home on his trip from Le Havre to Paris, "but beware of Normandy, it is full of English people." (For example, Lord Stuart of Rothsay, twice British Ambassador to France, escorted Louis XVIII to Paris at the restoration of the monarchy and bought the Renaissance cloister of Jumièges Abbey).

Throughout the 19th century, many maids in Paris came from Normandy or Brittany. Sometimes they left their farms by necessity, other times because they wished to live in Paris and find work other than agriculture. Lefebvre is a very Normand and very ancient name. For these three girls to travel together, *pourquoi pas?*

Sally, in letters and the bits she recopied from her own diaries, never referred to Victoire by her first name. At first, in fact, having lived in Auteuil for over two years and being aware of her father's and Victoire's relationship, she merely said that the woman who lived in the porter's lodge (Victoire) supported her fantasy that her father lived on. The woman in the porter's lodge demurred that the count had died so suddenly. Sally attached great significance to the fact that "not even this person was allowed to view the body."

Someone must badly need corroboration of a narrative to bring in someone else not otherwise desired in the story of one's life. There is no reason to think that Victoire did not continue to have sexual relations with the count. It is Sally's wording that implies something undefined. Sally disparaged Victoire by nonchalantly calling her the woman in the porter's lodge and would have overlooked the existence of her father's mistress except for getting Victoire on board with the fantasy that her father had not really died. This was on the one hand because she wished Victoire would disappear but on the other it was customary. In the stately house of Broadlands Sally had visited in England, servants were expected to be invisible, neither seen nor heard, and the principle of the concealment of the help was the same, if lesser.

The burial was arranged before Sally's return to Auteuil. For practical reasons regarding the household, and to share grief, Sally would have briefly drawn close to Victoire. She asked Victoire questions and imagined "that person" did not view her father's body because there was no body. This was because Victoire was not family and it was not tradition to have other than immediate family parade through. As people will do, Victoire was giving details to assuage acute grief and Sally ran with this detail. It fit in with belief in the supernatural, ghosts and other hovering spirits. Sally did not suppose her father had taken a packet ship to China but that he was only half-gone, a person of such genius that he could appear and disappear. Her view would have seemed odd but not really crazy, due to the fashion of metaphysics.

Having barely got to know her father's ex-wife, Anne, Sally had to assimilate that, while she herself was back in Concord, her father had taken up with a new woman, a person much beneath him socially. The inferior status of Victoire must have seemed egregious because Thompson's previous mistresses were titled nobles. To Sally's mind Victoire pulled down her own rank as well just when the Holy Roman Empire had in 1804 been ended by Napoleon, making her rank of countess immaterial.

Thomas Underwood, an Englishman who lived in Paris at that time, wrote an article in the *Gentleman's Magazine* about what was on the count's drawing board, work interrupted by his death: "One object of his later occupation was a work—not yet finished … 'On the Nature and Effects of Order', which, had he been spared to finish it, would probably have been one of the most valuable presents ever made to domestic society. No man in all his habits had more the spirit of order; everything was classed; no object was ever allowed to remain an instant out of its place the moment."[5] This praising description also gives insight into how living with Thompson would not have been easy. Victoire had a personality that could take the bad and not be riled.

Thompson lived for a longer time with Victoire than with either of his wives, from 1809 to 1814. He lived with Victoire for five years. Living in the same premises also went on for a long time, five years in Auteuil versus two years with Sarah Rolfe Thompson in Concord, three years with Anne Lavoisier in the 8th arrondissement of Paris and a very intermittent if protracted residence in Munich's Swabing Gasse. Sally never used the name Victoire in any letter she wrote to the Lefebvre family, whom she treated as importunate poor relations. She would have culled mention of Victoire from anything the count wrote about, or received from, her. A Rumford scion was one thing but an ex-mistress of one's father practically one's own age was another.

That Thompson had married up, a widow from a socially prominent family at 19, was an unsurprising path for an ambitious young man. It meant that his daughter was aware of being of higher birth on her mother's side. Thompson was 50 when he married a woman whose prestige by association with her husband and wealth made her lovable according also to the conventions of the day. This would not injure Sally's sense of right. What's more, Anne Lavoisier bowed out personally, leaving Sally as the most important of Count Rumford's relatives. It is of importance there were five letters from Rumford to Victoire that Professor Scott from Wagner College saw. He did not reveal their contents in any publication and the letters are nowhere to be seen today. All the same, Rumford wrote to Victoire as he had to other mistresses. After the count arrived in Munich in the late summer of 1810 he wrote a homely, touching missive to "my good Victoire" even in just the excerpted snippet in the Sanborn C. Brown biography of Rumford. It begins: "I send you a few lines, my good Victoire, to tell you I have arrived here in good health." Brown left out the body of the letter, giving the end: "Adieu, my good Victoire, take care of everything I pray you. Write to me from time to time to let me know how everything is going at home." There comes through in the letter a warmth that Thompson did not seem to have had toward either of his two wives.[6]

Where is the letter from which this segment was published? Brown gave the "Rumford Family Collection in Paris" as the source. Brown could have known where it was when he researched his book, with the help of a son and future daughter-in-law, doing some of the research in Europe. Brown published shortly before his death in 1981. His son Stanley W. Brown says that neither he nor his mother or siblings think that "Rumford Family Collection" was a cache that Brown saw personally, rather that the author, who spent decades on his study, would have had reliable secondary sources.[7]

It is the bouquets all over the house that give the strongest proof Thompson had feelings for Victoire. Desire had to be mutual for him. He was not given to conquests. The relationship was consensual and must have been entered into with good nature on both sides. He was, nevertheless, acting out an inveterate tradition in sleeping with the help. In his European journal Aaron Burr describes the attentiveness towards him of a Swiss servant, Julie Huguenin, who was about 30 years younger than he, in 1810 and 1811. He faulted himself when another servant appeared on the scene and he had sex with her, thereby offending "so good a creature" as Julie. It was permissible for him, as an elite male, to enjoy the sexual favors of a devoted servant and overstep the line between employer and employed. That is because he was single. It was not approved in Europe or America when a wife discovered such a "folly," as Burr called throughout his journal his sexual encounters with lower-class women. Thus, when English diarist Samuel Pepys groped a servant girl, Mrs. Pepys kept her husband up for the next twenty nights remonstrating against his sexual activity. Burr noted that Julie was upset to see that Burr turned his sexual attentions on a rival.[8]

Contrarily, for Thompson to have sexual relations with his housekeeper was exceptional. To bed a servant was not his habit; if it had been, some hint would emerge in letters or his diary from his first, several-month visit to Paris. He had benefited from the affection of cultivated women who were in tune with him. He would only have been lonelier in Napoleonic France if a purely physical relationship was all Victoire provided. Also, to Thompson servants were people, not possessions. Not merely from kindness but also because he gave supreme value to his various homes as refuge from his active life, he had ties of friendship with servants. The Aichner family included six children, of whom several accompanied their parents to Paris to work for Thompson after he married Anne Lavoisier. To him this never seemed too much. Their departure to Germany was unwanted and traumatic, and Thompson subsequently made at least one visit to his old friends in Munich and made sure Maximilian would look after their welfare. He gave his housekeeper at Brompton Row thoughtful gifts and expressed concern for her when he was away from London, as well as giving her time off when her sister was ill. The employees were individuals to him beyond the functions they performed. He did not take the service of others for granted, one reason for this his having been an employee himself most of his life.

A friend, perhaps someone Madame Helvétius had known in Auteuil, likely found Victoire as a table maid for Thompson. The position of housekeeper was more responsible. The count entrusted Victoire with housekeeping and she became a mistress. She would have had composure and a gentle character, because he would have sought these attractive qualities, not merely competency or prettiness, after the debacle with a strident wife. He loved being offstage and would not have associated with Victoire unless she and he were well suited. She was a subordinate, but balanced by that formal reality was the fact she was younger and healthier and shared the common interest of gardening with him.

Victoire brought flowers, light and birds into the count's cerebral life and devoted herself to his comfort. He was a great man who appreciated her efforts and worked side by side with her in the garden and on projects in the house. They shared the realms of the house and the garden, neither surrounded by family, and their attraction encountered no taboo. A connection was ineluctable. Victoire's job was especially responsible because she connected Thompson with the outside world of the adjacent villages of Auteuil and Passy, as she did the shopping and managed the house.

Count Rumford now had a lively companion who shared abiding interests right at home. Gone were the days of his having to be furtive, as he was in Munich with Countess Baumgarten, whether in Schwabing, north Munich, in his rental palace or her family's house, or elsewhere. He and Victoire didn't have to be clandestine to be proper, as it was accepted that a single man had a housekeeper/mistress. He didn't have to tear around Germany and Italy to meet his beloveds either. A woman who gratified his sexual needs was at hand and he had feelings for her. Because life was good he stayed home more and socialized less. From Auteuil he went to the institute once a week, but otherwise he did his experiments on the like of teapots, coffee pots, carriage wheels, lamps and double-pane glass and spent time in his garden, where he had an easy heart. He attended weekly meetings at the Institute and had printed a thousand copies of most of his private scientific papers from this fecund period.[9]

Whatever the source of Thompson's frequent and prolonged illnesses, he said, and others opined, that they had a nervous component. In the five years cohabiting with Victoire, he did science, enjoyed tranquility and was happy in relative retreat. As is best for any couple living together, they were equals in regard to their interaction in the course of a day. Victoire had the superior knowledge of Paris and other household practicalities while the count modernized, though not as extensively as when he was trying to impress and make things good with Anne Lavoisier. Very much like the gardening pair—sunny Phoebe and the protean intellectual the daguerrotypist—in *The House of Seven Gables*, Victoire and Thompson worked together in the garden, which flourished from their combined skill. The relationship had less of a power differential than those with previous mistresses due to the shared and complementary activities of the couple.

It is probable that when Thompson had a bout of sickness he sensed that he might die. As he had always been concerned to provide for his mother and daughter he was now concerned for the future of the woman under his protection and mother of his child. According to Emma Burgum's account, "before Victoire left the Count's house, he had her married to his gardener; a good steady young man by the name of Bonnet. And he had a cottage with a good garden, and gave it to them." At some point he may have suggested a marriage between her and the gardener, Monsieur Bonnet; there is one slender source of a note by Sally Rumford's adopted daughter that suggests it. According to

Emma, "The Count put into the bank a large sum of money divided into three parts, one in the name of Bonnet, another in the name of Victoire Lefebvre Bonnet, and the other, though double, in the name of Victoire's baby Charles. Bonnet continued to be the Count's coachman and gardener as long as the Count lived, for his cottage was near." Otherwise, how would Victoire have fared without her lover?

Putting a veil over a veil, the 19th century writer the Reverend Ellis makes an observation that suggests Victoire received a bequest from the funds of the count, who was of course a rich person: "In a sealed letter to his executors the Count commits to them, in trust, certain funds assigned for the benefit of persons having 'sacred claims' upon him. As it was his declared wish that his directions in this matter should not be made public, I, of course, withhold them."[10] That "sacred claim" would likely refer to Victoire and the child Charles, to whom Thompson would not have been permitted to leave a bequest by the Napoleonic Code. Only two were named in the "Succession": Anne Lavoisier, his second wife, according to the terms of their marriage contract, and Sally, to whom funds were dispersed from banks in Paris, London and Munich.[11] The house in Auteuil had been leased.

Charles François Robert Lefebvre was born an hour past midnight on October 11, 1813. Two days later the birth certificate was registered, which made corrections both in the spelling of Lefebvre (from the error that weaves in and out of all identifications of the family, "Lefevre") and in the mother's name (Victoire Josephy instead of merely Victoire). The first document probably was done in a hurry in the wee hours. The witnesses appear to be the husband of the midwife and a Passy wine merchant. The father of the count's natural son was marked "not present" on the birth certificate. Presumably it would have been indiscreet to identify the patrician father. The birth was liable to present two legal complications. First, Thompson was separated formally but not divorced from Anne Lavoisier. Second, if he did plan to adopt the baby at some point the child could not be known to be his issue, i.e., his bastard.

In any event, Amédée Joseph, son of Charles, did not doubt that Charles was Thompson's son. There is a portrait by Hippolyte Holfeld of Charles as a toddler at the New England Historical Society. The child has a striking similarity to Benjamin Thompson— red hair, blue eyes, and crested eyebrows. It is unknown who commissioned this portrait. One hypothesis is that Sally requested it, as she had it with her in all the rooms where she lived and in the room where she died, and she cherished portraits of loved ones. She had three copies made of the picture of Charles when he was a military officer, very tall, upwards of 6' 3" and slender like his father. Furthermore, it

Miniature of Charles Francis Robert Lefebvre at age five (1813–1855), original artist unknown; copied by Charles in the 1840s from an 1818 portrait (New Hampshire Historical Society).

was not a custom in France to have paintings done of one's small children, possibly a miniature but not a painting. Any mother would like to think her child had great expectations and if Sally requested the picture be done that would have confirmed her continuing interest in her half brother. Despite the fact the count was not present at the birth of his son, he and Victoire loved Charles very much. Charles, artistic like his father, copied the painting in 1842 when he was 29 years of age in 1843, this being the oval portrait in the collection of the New Hampshire Historical Society.

Sally made a few oblique remarks about having encountered in her father's house someone who occupied the porter's lodge, not a servant, "a young person, either housekeeper, companion, or both" who was "then agreeable to him" and put flowers at every turn. "The singing birds which greeted our entrance to the table made it a perfect enchantment." This unfixed human presence "seemed to take charge of the flowers, the illuminations and the singing birds of the dining-room. Her curiosity was roused, and her feelings were alternately excited and quieted as she asked one or another of the domestics about this additional member of the family. At times she seems to have acquiesced in the arrangement as an excusable one, considering the circumstances of her father and the usages of the country where she was. At other times she felt as if she had a right to interfere and remonstrate so as to assert her own dignity. She describes two stratagems, in which she had an accomplice in one of the servants, amounting to practical jokes played upon her father, to let him know that her eyes were opened."[12]

The garden had aristocratic flowers and plebian vegetables. The visionary count concentrated his greater effort on the flowers. The indication in Ellis's commentary is that the flowers were part of the décor within. At Brompton Row Thompson had created features for houseplants and flowers, such as tables constructed with recesses and bay windows. A person who puts bouquets in a house is cheering. Putting singing birds in the house seems whimsical, possibly countrified, and all the more cheering. Victoire added her touches to the count's rule of order and made the house a home.

Thompson tried to play down his union to Victoire when his daughter came from America. Victoire was a positive force and Sally may have liked her, but when Sally's mood darkened she wanted to punish her father. She portrayed herself in a diary of traveling with her father in Germany and living in Munich as a prankster. Ellis commented that she played pranks on her father in the house at Auteuil with regard to demonstrating that she knew Victoire was his mistress. Over the 21 months from the time Sally arrived from America (December 1, 1811) until her father's death (August 21, 1814) she had to share being the woman of the house with his concubine and she wasn't going to make that easy for him.

Even the existing letter of Victoire's comes through Sally, who did not keep the original but translated it for the Baldwins. The translation is in the Massachusetts Historical Society. Victoire wishes for legitimization of her son. She says that Charles, the count's son, would return to Paris from Africa (he was stationed in Algiers and perhaps elsewhere) to visit Sally if she came. (Victoire may have meant Morocco). Sally would have a very good room in the apartment with conveniences and a water closet.[13] Victoire's son was fond of (*attaché à*) Sally. Sally knew Charles as a tot because she stayed at Auteuil for a while after her father's death (then went to stay at Daniel Parker's until May). She saw Charles frequently when she lived in Paris from 1820 to 1823 and for seven years from 1838. She at least credited Victoire as being a good housekeeper.

Victoire stayed with her husband in their cottage in Auteuil as long as her husband lived. Monsieur Bonnet died in 1820. Some time after that she sold her cottage and moved to Paris with Charles, who was about seven or eight, and sent him to school. Charles, according to Emma Burgum's account, worked "with great progress and assiduity, so much so, that at the age of eleven years, he was taken down with brain fever, and was out of his mind for some time, and his life was in danger for nearly a year; but with the greatest of care, he did recover, and then resumed his studies and soon went to the Polytecnic [sic] school."

Sally blew hot and cold towards her half brother and his family. She comes across as a tightly wound individual, never more so than vis-à-vis the Lefebvres, whom she saw as interlopers. Sometimes she liked having the wider family. Mostly she seemed suspicious of their motives, unwilling to acknowledge that what Charles craved was a connection to the father he never knew and about whom, presumably, he had heard positive things from his mother. Charles was free to seek the privilege of his father's name later; the mechanics were there. This was often the case with a natural son, who had to earn what a legitimate child got at birth. Charles would have to go through lawyers over a period of time.

How was a bastard perceived? Being the natural child of a noble was an entirely different order, and to be legitimized would have bounteous results either of wealth or position. The father not being present had inevitably some slight emotional imputation as a child born out of wedlock was a nonentity. This dismal reality often led a young man to distinguish himself or at least set out like a picaro. It explains why as an adult Charles did a copy by his own hand of the painting of himself as a tot.

Victoire seems only to have had the one child. A note on the back of Charles's portrait as an adult says that Victoire married a "man of fortune," Monsieur Antin, in 1839, at which time she was "the widow Bonnet," and that Monsieur Antin died in 1841. Thus Victoire was married twice, both times after her liaison with the count. Whether it is true that Thompson arranged for her to marry his gardener, Bonnet, cannot be determined, but Emma, a good reporter but basing this on hearsay, attested it in her notebook of vignettes.

Victoire kept the memory of the father of her child alive with mementos and anecdotes. She lived a comfortable existence, Thompson having given her gifts and money. Perhaps sensing his illness, or simply providing for her and their child as he had done from an early stage for Sally out of concern for the future of his dependents, he left her and Charles a bequest. It was mysterious, as he liked to do things, and no information survives about it but it was referred to after his death. Victoire also sold the cottage she shared with the gardener when she took Charles to Paris so he could have a good education.

Charles earned an adequate living as a military officer to support his little family, and the mother had what Thompson gave her, which she would have handled frugally. The first marriage was to a young poor man but the second was to a man who was old and well off. Victoire and he moved to Linas, a beautiful small town of just over a thousand residents 12 miles from Paris. Sally repeatedly said flat out that Victoire married both husbands for money. She also implies (in a veiled and acid anecdote) that they had a lovely home and gardens, and maneuvered to inherit from not only Mr. Antin, but also a maiden aunt relative of his. It seems that Sally was out to get the Lefebvres once she had lived in close relations with them in Paris. Having "the widow Bonnet" remarry—carrying on the family line plus having two husbands when Sally had none—was too much for her. She began to think all French people wanted was money and she would in a peevish moment discredit Victoire's second marriage: "I call the Antin business nothing short of robbery."[14] But how could marriage to a gardener be perceived as being entered into from greed?

Sally was a foreigner living in Paris for her third, and longest, time—from 1838 to 1845—and finding falseness at the society's surface (Honoré de Balzac's Cousine Bette of the eponymous novel vividly comes to mind). Sally meddled less but absolutely gave out that the Lefebvres were "family," for instance sending her maid over to Victoire to show her the ropes of Paris in preparation for Sally's arrival from England in the summer of 1822; moving in on the street in Paris exactly opposite Victoire in 1838; and leaving her adopted daughter, Emma (who spoke no French), for a long spell in Victoire's care.

The little Lefebvre family—first Victoire and Charles, then Charles's wife Pauline and their son and daughter—were never in the kind of duress that would create strong resentment against either Thompson or Sally. Sally felt their equal for a long time and then she felt their victim when she fostered the idea that all Victoire (and Charles) wanted was her money, and she had to block contact with Victoire, Charles and Pauline Lefebvre and seek the protection of the men she trusted most, Loammi's son James Baldwin and her banker Delessert, from her French "biological" relatives. Her pique seemed to begin when Victoire married Monsieur Antin. The new couple encouraged Sally to move to their neighborhood after they married. She liked to be asked but then they took back the offer when they moved out of the city to Linas (where Sally was an occasional guest).

Grief hung over Charles, whose renowned father remained present in the public realm due to fame, yet vanished from the son's life. Moreover, whereas Sally was plain, the count's two children fathered out of wedlock both resembled him in face and coloring and were very good-looking (Charles also had his height). Every time Charles looked in the mirror he saw a person whose appearance—features, build and reddish hair color, mirrored his father's. This note accompanies Charles's portrait, presumably written by Emma Burgum: "Charles Lefebvre was said to have been extremely bright and an accomplished pianist and artist. After studying for the priesthood, he chose instead the army as his profession and was stationed at various locations in Europe and North Africa. He was killed in the Criea [sic] during the Battle of Sevastopol."

Inheriting his father's ability at math and technical subjects, Charles studied engineering to prepare for the army. Both for pragmatic reasons and to honor his father, his son Amédée too became, and remained all his life, a military officer. Charles's goal was to become legitimized. It took years to accomplish, until past his youth. In the process, it seems that his nerves became shot. The uphill battle for his mass of pottage is likely to have been one factor and the violence he experienced as a soldier another in his suffering a nervous breakdown. This development is known because Sally wrote to James Baldwin (one of Loammi's sons) that Charles was in a "madhouse" and it was successfully hushed up. Sally wrote from Paris to James Baldwin a series of letters on various topics, newsy letters that relayed Charles's sad predicament when he was 30.

In the spring and summer of 1844, Sally poured her heart out over her distress that Charles was locked in the madhouse, to correspondents who didn't know him and had no reason to care about him. He was a military officer, unmarried (he would start his married life soon after recovering from his breakdown), and when not with his regiment living at home. He was acting in such a way in the military that he was punished. He was thus deranged. How did he become unhinged?

Charles was the son of a famous man who was venerated for doing good, if also mocked as a loony. The count was understood in his time to be a benefactor of humankind, a selfless person, and the boy could match the father on all these points—spirituality, brilliance, running off the rails. What Emma Burgum heard was that Charles had brain fever at eleven that kept him out of school and under home care for a year. Charles prepared for the priesthood. However, because he had no established family connections or modeling after his father, who had held high military rank as a British colonel and general of the Bavarian regime, the young man changed tack and became an officer in the imperial French army. In his late twenties the recessed identity often asserts as the received identity no long holds. Like a chrysalis of no use, being the child left by a parent's death was unsatisfactory and the conflict with the deceased parent had to be resolved.

Charles groped for identity as he re-created his father's path. It was a painful process to find himself while a military officer. He can't have been a natural soldier. His proclivities were for music, painting and engineering. No matter, he felt worthless because he could not resurrect his father to demand the will to live. If he was held down and made to feel like nothing as a soldier, the unfortunate side effect was that he was driven to distinguish himself in his vocation and thus have a sort of fame. The tomb inscription in Linas said he was very brave. He also went after legitimacy as if his life depended on it, because his whole life, in different ways, he was shown he was nobody. The military provided only a temporary mask, assuaging his inferiority complex but leaving him hollow.

Others who cared about him might feel guilt and responsibility—mea culpa. Sally said she thought it was the inheritance matter (she probably meant regarding Mr. Antin's property but perhaps it was the legitimization issue) that drove him round the bend and that he was acting out because he was very angry. She agreed with Victoire that Charles was not crazy, saying the rest of his family thought he was. A letter wouldn't have unhinged him but a money squabble, never letting the matter rest, might have. This was a constant whirr in the house and an agitation, as in the novels of Balzac describing this period, over Charles's quest for legitimacy. He craved identity as the natural progeny of the self-made famous scientist. Sally stressed how angry Charles was and was behaving. That Charles's upset might have had to do with the inheritance is hinted at by Sally's mention that a Delessert put him into the "madhouse" and this prefect of police could get him out. Delessert was her banker and had been her father's banker and friend who likely did assist in Charles's release at the end of the summer 1844.

Sally called Charles only by his last name—distancing him just as she did Victoire, whom she identified as "Mrs. Antin" or "the mother." Yet she is preoccupied and concerned. Empathetically, she hated the thought of him in the strait jacket in a room with no chair. She told one of the Baldwins ("Dear Friend" often makes it unclear which one) how urgent the situation was with Charles in late spring 1844. Her state of mind and the turmoil of the family show in the letter. That Sally curiously shows a disregard for the spelling of their name also shows in the letter, where she leaves off the "v" and towards the end slips in a random acute accent:

> Poor Lefebre is still in his prison, or mad house, as one likes to call it. It is a terrible thing for him, for he keeps himself in a constant state of fomentation from anger, which they consider derangement. Most of his family say he is actually crazy, but his mother the contrary, which is my opinion. Various methods have been adapted to get him out of Charendon, without success. The mother now request me to write to Delessert, which I did yesterday, I think it will have affect. I do not believe he can get over the letter I wrote him. One of the Delesserts, (there being three Brothers) is Préfecture de Police.

> Through him it was Lefebre was put there, and who has equal power to have him liberated. His mother insists upon it, that though his senses are not gone yet, they certainly will be if he is suffered to remain where he is. They treat him scandalously. Since they have no Bastile, I should never think that there was so disagreeable a place in all France. At the least resistant, they put the strait jacket on Lefébre, leave him in a room without even a chair, order him to do things whether he wishes it or not, in short treat him like a criminal instead of a young militaire.[15]

Sally thought a letter (not extant) from her might have sent him over the edge and she wanted him out of the "prison." She felt the pressure of time to get him out as his mother feared that, while Charles was not insane, if he stayed there he might become insane. Sally called Charles an innocent and took the opportunity to accuse Victoire of not only being the grasping one but also of being a fortune hunter who married old Monsieur Antin just for his money. In Sally's view, the mother and family had pumped Charles up over the inheritance issue, overtaxing his weak mind.

Sally felt reviled that the Lefebvres suggested she write to one of Charles's generals that she would take him to America (as a ploy to get him released). She often suspected the Lefebvres of trying to get her money; but in connection with Charles's being in the madhouse, during clearly a difficult period for Sally as well as for Victoire, she displayed bitterness laced with paranoia. A visit from Thérèse, the girlhood friend with whom Victoire and her younger sister walked from Normandy and who was now the Countess of Tauzier (or as sometimes Sally spells the name, "Tosia"), provoked Sally's sullenness: "She is, in my opinion sent for by the widow [Victoire], to make one more bold stroke with me to see if there be no possibility of drawing me out to do something towards the Capt's getting a nice little wife with whom to take his comfort. This gentleman ... this Parisioner, is highly educated. He plays the piano & paints! It is natural he would rather amuse himself with these things than work; & my property would be convenient."

Charles had a restless and wandering soul. He had dreamt of becoming a priest but changed his mind given the stern reality of commitment to the priesthood. Likely he dreamed next of military glory and his mother, at wit's end, bought him the officer's commission. He was tied to his mother to the extent that he did not look outside her intimate circle for his wife. Thus, although Sally was so ambivalent towards Charles, she felt protective of him and wanted him to "grow up," recognizing in him the danger of being an eternal boy, a *puer aeternus*, arty and unfocused and bound to his mother.

Charendon, where Charles had been committed and was being held against his will, was the asylum where the Marquis de Sade's family had him committed in 1801 to avoid Napoleon's prison sentence. This was De Sade's second time being committed there and he remained in Charendon, permitted to write his works, until his death in 1814. Charendon was established to be humanitarian so was less grisly than French mental asylums that preceded it. Music, art, and theater were encouraged: express don't repress. De Sade staged several plays and Charles must have done paintings. It likely was Charendon that Benjamin Thompson visited when he was touring the hospitals of Paris in 1801.

The fact that Charles was said to be excellent at art and to play the piano well connected with his confinement in Charendon. In this era it was expected that a gentleman would draw and sing or play music or at least dance, yet Charles's abilities were singled out, so they must have been better than average. The picture by Charles of himself as a young boy in the collection of the New Hampshire Historical Society is dated 1842, a date based solely on what Emma Burgum wrote on the back of the picture, according to the archivist who told me it "might be best to say 'probably 1842.'" The "paper board" on which the watercolor was done is a humble material that might have been available at the asylum. The child is unsmiling and his eyes have a penetrating, wistful look.

The milestone of age 30 is a time for looking back and a threshold. There are no other paintings known by Charles, only the mention of his talent. His father also was known to draw well and he put cartoons of people, some sketched during a church service, in his commonplace book. Possibly the reason Charles did this careful picture was that he was idle and reflecting on his life so far and his identity while in the asylum. To render a copy of a picture of oneself as a child is a curious thing to do, perhaps something a person would do who didn't have a lot of subjects at hand to choose from or who was trying to find himself, with the help of the redheaded, blue-eyed boy he once was. Someone would, of course, have had to have brought him the portrait from home. Who was the miniature for? Did he intend it as a gift to Sally or to his mother? He was in the madhouse because he had gone off the handle; otherwise the prefect of police (a relative of the banker Delessert) would not have got involved. Surely, whether the portrait was done in 1842 or 1844, this little boy's solemn affect hid a person who felt anything but calm inside.

Poor Charles must have been a wreck to get to Charendon but he became composed, possibly helped by the confinement and despite the scary restraint that Sally spoke of to James Baldwin. He was there at least from the winter of 1844 through the autumn, possibly longer. The Te Deum from Sally when she could tell her friends in America that Charles was out of Charendon commented that she agrees with his mother that "he must have been put there for fault" and that she did "not think he will go there again very soon. I think he has had enough of it."[16]

Thus Charles was out by the fall and by February 1845 he was engaged. He went back into military service and soon had a child. Pauline's being 30 before the marriage suggests she waited for Charles to establish his career or to be stable. There is no suggestion he was miserable after that point, only that he was obsessed with getting legitimate status and perplexed about what Sally would effect for his inheritance. He was in active duty but also spent time with his family. In her Journal Extracts, Emma Gannel Burgum singles out going with Charles and "her aunt" Sally to the Théâtre de la Renaissance to see the opera *Shipwreck of the Meduse* and other outings including to the Champs-Elysées and Versailles.

Since Sally had stayed with Emma Burgum for seven years in Paris and had constant social interactions with the Lefebvres, perhaps relations had been amicable and then gone sour by the time she left Paris in July 1844. Or perhaps the life there was no fun given the distress over Charles. At least she didn't mention him "in the madhouse" after that spring of 1844 and left for America, a few months short of age 70, in July. In April 1847, back in New Hampshire, she wrote James Baldwin acridly: "I am often troubling you with my letters, and it troubles me to write them, but I could not well help answering these. I do not think I shall be troubled so much in future, these answers will cool off some people...."[17] Sally had been asked several times to become a godmother and her reaction was to make no answer to such requests from Europe. Who desired Sally to be godmother and whom she was putting off was unsaid. It did not signify to Sally that the Lefebvres or Thérèse Tauzier (who, given her close friendship with Victoire, likely visited Auteuil while the count lived and had sold her husband's chateau in Bordeaux and moved to Paris) were proud of and wanted to continue their association with the famous man. Mistrust overwhelmed her.

A very limited appearance of the Lefebvres occurs in the correspondence with Sally over the legalization issue. Sally's irritability towards the Lefebvres surfaces in letters to them and to her several American confidants. Now the address she is writing to is on the rue du Colisée. This address was in the 8th arrondissement, very central, running from the Champs-Elysées to the Faubourg-Saint-Honoré—a desirable area but with smaller apartments than on the newer boulevards. It seems that Victoire had returned from Linas.

In the early and mid–19th century one what one's father was and Sally, who had never felt that her father had compensated adequately for his being absent in her childhood, remained hurt. The fact of a half brother piled on more hurt. Jealousy blighted her relationship with the sibling. Letters from her side exist about inheritance and Charles's taking of the name Rumford. In them she feigns forbearance and they contain a note of her sense of supremacy. Her father would have been delighted to see Charles grow up, just as he was by his other natural child, only he would have had more time and freedom to express affection for Charles compared to the muted situation of fathering Josepha Baumgarten's daughter Sophie in Munich. For Thompson's daughter the Lefebvres were probably a reminder that she did not carry on the line.

Two years before Sally died she made a will in Concord, New Hampshire, that had one of those types of bequests intended to control the beneficiary: "Upon condition that Capt. Lefebre's Son Amédée Lefebre, now about three years old learns English, takes the name of Rumford, Lives at least a part of his time here ... I give ... to said Amédée Lefebre, Two hundred Thousand Dollars." James Baldwin drew her attention to the fact she didn't have this much money so the amount was reduced once and then again to a small fraction of the original figure; her intention was to recognize the lineage. The final bequest to Amédée was that he "now or hereafter ... be called Joseph Amédée Rumford," "Joseph" being the name added to Victoire's when the birth certificate of Charles was revised. Amédée asked James Baldwin whether a formal act would be required to change his name and James said not, that using the name Joseph Amédée Rumford was good enough.[18] Amédée took the name informally but did not follow the wishes of Sally Thompson that he come to America. The greater portion of her estate went to the New Hampshire Asylum for the Insane and a projected Female Charitable Society. Sally Thompson's will left to Maria Louise Pauline De Tauzia (Charles's wife) "my gold watch set round with pearls and the Venetian chain with various trinkets attached and belonging thereto."[19] This was hand delivered by a Francis Lowell, Esq., to Madame Lefebvre de Rumford.

Significantly, Pauline, not a blood relative, was the only Lefebvre towards whom Sally's feelings were mild. By the summer of 1852 her resentment of and irritation at the Lefebvres had hardened to virulent animosity, for which letters to the Baldwins continued to be an outlet. The prospect that Charles would get a title, possibly become a count, if his son became a Rumford incensed her: "What! My Fathers respectable name and title to be disgraced and lowered by a Frenchman born and one of that description!"[20]

Amédée-Joseph Lefebvre de Rumford obtained, like his father, the rank of major and died at age 29. Amédée corresponded with Thompson's biographer George Ellis. He lived in the town of Auxerre and wrote on February 21, 1883, thanking Ellis for his book and sending "quelques souvenirs." These were a decorative plaque given to Thompson by the prince of Bavaria, a portrait of his grandfather on vellum done just before his death and given to Charles by Sally; and a box with the initials BT containing Benjamin Thompson's early compass and instruments. Amédée apologized, saying that he had wanted to meet Ellis at the Universal Exposition of 1878 (which had exhibited the completed head of the Statue of Liberty) but that he was ill at that time. He spoke of a wife (records show he was married in 1872 under the name Amédée Lefebvre Rumford) and three "fillettes." The letter is signed "A. de rumford, 27, rue Joubert, Auxerre."[21] In Auxerre town records, Amédée does not show up. When Amédée sent Ellis mementoes of his grandfather in the 1880s there was no mention of Victoire, his grandmother, who was probably no longer living and these mementoes had passed to him.

The fine portrait of Charles as an adult, which Sally left to a Walker cousin, who gave it to the New Hampshire Historical Society, has four labels on the back and in her hand is written (on June 3, 1852, at Concord): "This is a fine likeness of Charles R. Lefebvre of Paris by Oldfeld, of Paris—a natural Son of the late Count Rumford's. Certainly not favored as it respects illegitimacy but in other respects good, a character that bids fair for some considerable renown. Has already two beautiful little children—a Son a daughter.

The resemblance to his father is striking—slender, blue eyes, reddish hair, tight jaw, slender, even the medal on his chest has a Maltese Cross like the one Thompson was awarded by Joseph II, Holy Roman Emperor." Psychically, Sally felt superior for being the one and only legitimate child and had ambivalence at the continuing line of her father going through Charles and not herself. When she died in 1854 Victoire may have been about 66.

After using his grant from the American Philosophical Society to investigate materials in Europe on Thompson, Professor Kenneth Scott, in the APS Year Book for 1950, noted 29 pages in the French Archives Nationales on the application of Charles Lefebvre to assume the name of "de Rumford," a request that was granted. He also noted "the present Comte de Rumford, a grandson of Charles Lefebvre, owns four letters written by Rumford to Victoire Lefebvre. Sanborn Brown was acquainted with Professor Scott's research but did not indicate what he saw of it."

It was Thompson's character to prefer to stay at home quietly rather than socialize or get into mischief in Paris. He didn't gamble, get intoxicated, or go to brothels. Once a week he went to the institute, sometimes presenting a paper, but eventually he printed the results of his experiments separately from the establishment and just went to listen. As a man estranged from his wife, living in London and Munich, he had several long-term romantic and sophisticated, not necessarily sexual, liaisons, which he worked in with his employment. If the Princess of Taxis, Baroness de Kalb, and Josepha Baumgarten's sister, Mary, slept with Thompson when they welcomed him to their homes these affairs would have been seen as peccadillos. These aristocrats' marriages were arranged for them when they were very nearly children. So long as the affairs were discreet, elite women were in general spared censure in the social scene if they strayed from their marriages.

Victoire was Thompson's choice of a partner in his mid–50s. As soon as she was in his employ, in his first months in Auteuil, he asserted that "the most faithful, honest people, attached to me, without dissension, bribery, or malice" formed his household[22] and clearly he would have said the same, that Victoire was devoted to him, five years later. Predictably, their relationship was as private as his with Anne Lavoisier had been public. He wasn't a courtier anymore, having been released from that social sphere. He still would have chosen not only a mistress but also someone to take an interest in his gardening and his projects. When his old scientist friends visited, they did not mention Victoire. Her invisibility derived from her being not of their same status.

Every invention and scientific experiment the count was involved in, except the cannon-boring and bullet velocity, he shared with a woman. Often this was Lady Palmerston but also Mary Countess Nogarola, and probably when designing the park that was not built in Mannheim he shared his plans with the Baroness de Kalb. With Victoire he shared first his passions for gardening, efficient cooking, and home improvement, and then the delight of a son.

20

Children on Both Sides of the Atlantic (Mid–19th Century)

Children begin by loving their parents; as they grow older they judge them; sometimes they forgive them.—Oscar Wilde, *The Picture of Dorian Gray* (1890)

This chapter looks more closely at the lives of Sally, Victoire and Charles after Benjamin Thompson's death. Sally's life was unsettled (until the end she was thinking of moving back from New Hampshire to Paris); Victoire was happy in the bosom of family and under the protection of a husband most of her life; and Charles had successes but was beleaguered by mental problems and wrestled with being rendered fatherless by the death of a famous man.

Charles not only looked like his father but also had similar traits. His first choice of vocation was the priesthood, but he changed his mind and went into the military, was promoted to major in the 138th regiment in 1850 and made a chevalier in the French Legion of Honor. As he grew up, he liked to paint, landscapes and portraits, and played the piano well. His other talent, engineering, lined up with his father's too.

The facts about Charles Lefebvre's nervous breakdown come from Sally, who didn't think Charles was insane and worried about him the six months he was institutionalized.[1] He was therefore prone to breaking down under pressure for weeks or months and then rising phoenix-like, like his father—although Charles was identified as having mental illness and, one time, boils that kept him out of commission, and Thompson was described as having stress-related gastrointestinal issues.

It was during the spring and summer of 1844 that Sally poured her heart out over her distress over Charles's being "in the madhouse" to correspondents who didn't know him and had no reason to care about him. He was a military officer, unmarried (he would start his married life soon after recovering from his breakdown) and living at home.

As discussed earlier, perhaps during Sally and Emma Burgum's stay in Paris for seven years, and the constant social interactions with the Lefebvres, relations among them had been amicable and then soured. Although Sally preferred to leave Autueil after a year of mourning her father and move to London, the Brompton Row house was ever a burden on her spirit. She had the house on leased land and it seemed to need repairs and her attention. In Paris she stayed in apartments, which was so much easier. Perhaps on a visit to Paris in 1822 she imagined remaining there, the indication being that she gave a ball at her own lodgings (her painted fan adorned with shells and ribbons is in the New Hampshire Historical Society).

Charles's thirties found him recovered from his mental breakdown, married, and then a father. He married the daughter of his mother's old friend Thérèse, who had walked with Victoire and her sister from Normandy. Charles and Marie Pauline Louise de Tauzier had two children, Amédée Joseph Lefebvre and Marie Sarah Lefebvre, born respectively in 1846 and 1848. A namesake of Charles's daughter was, of course, his half sister Sarah, a French Catholic name preceding it. Major Lefebvre went many places with his regiment, including Algiers, Strasbourg, and St. Germaine-en-Laye. He took up and reclaimed the name Rumford at his own request, made in January 1853 and authorized on January 28, 1854.[2]

Emma got to know Charles well after going to live with Sally in Paris. Around that time, Victoire bought his commission as a military officer and he would come home on leave. Emma relayed in her two anecdotes about the Rumford line that Charles demonstrated the promise he showed as a child. Her storytelling has all the marks of being "as told to" by Victoire:

> Little Charles was a bright child, and quite a genius like his illustrious Father. When he was but five years old, and still living at Auteuil, he would dig in the garden trenches and take straws and lay them in a row together, and then cover them over with earth, as he had seen some men do the day before, who were laying pipes for a drain in the street in front of the house.
> At another time, he had a carpenter's bench, with tools he carved out with his pocket knife, such as toy square, a plane, hammer, and handsaw, and then glued them onto the bench: the bench was only five inches long, two wide, and two high, and the tools were of the size to match the bench. I saw the toy in 1840, for his mother had it always under a glass case, she felt so proud of her little boy's work.[3]

The child's artifact on display is one that will strike a chord with many people about their own families. Not only did Victoire see being a mother as a most important part of her identity but also she connected being at Auteuil when raising her young son with happy memories. Charles was a brilliant and sensitive person his loved ones worried about. He was, Emma Burgum wrote, subject to "brain fever" from working so hard in school, after his mother moved to Paris so he could benefit from an education there. The last full year Sally lived in Paris with Emma she wrote Charles at "the madhouse."

Victoire's sole extant letter only exists in Sally's translation[4] and is an encouraging invitation to Sally to visit:

> You know that you have only to occupy yourself to seek my apartment … whenever you wish it. You shall have a beautiful chamber water-conveniences cabinet. I will have also a place where you will put Emma who will be near you. There is here a good girl that you shall have in your service. She has not left me and is very … I wish that Amédée and Sarah knew you and you loved as well, they are very pretty both of them. Mr. Lefebvre will be very happy to see you also. He is generally in Constantine but if you come to France he easily [will obtain] permission … how he attached to you. In all his letters he speaks to me of your near arrival. I repy to him always that I have heard no news. While that the weather is fine—come then and we will meet. Do not occupy yourself with … as you will live here as in your house. You shall rise when you wish.—You will take your meals comme at any hour which will be convenient for you. I have a very pleasant apartment…. My dining hall and my kitchen are both very large. My husband carries himself always very well.

Victoire also alludes to a name change to Rumford for the count's son and grandson. She could aid this by sending her grandson Amédée's birth certificate from Paris to Sally, who had proposed a name change for him. Obliquely yet warmly Victoire pays her respect to the deceased count: "Charles will be very happy if he can bear even the name of his

Father and he will transmit it to his children. He labors always in hopes of being worthy of it and he will bring up his son in a manner that he will bear it nobley … who is very dear to us all."

Sally attached notes to pictures, as was a Victorian Age custom. Besides the painting of Charles as a young man of 26 in his army uniform, Sally had pretty pictures of Victoire's grandchildren, done by Charles, as babies, which are now in the collection of the New Hampshire Historical Society. Victoire was a family-oriented person, domestic, a proud mother, and proud of what she had achieved in life, starting from nothing. She wanted her son legitimized. She did not mention her former lover by name, as she was always private about their relationship. If she had created a shrine to the great man no one would have married her.

In Sally's unsettled lifestyle (relative to the age in which she lived) she continued to have fleeting romantic attachments. One was around the same time as her father courted Mme. Lavoisier, and her father let her know he only wanted her happiness. However, nothing came of it. Regarding the "Northampton gentleman," Sir Charles warned Sally about confessing to either her father or her "lover" how she could play "forever" at billiards and whist: "If the latter be really a man of sense, and were to judge that such is unalterably

Watercolor painting of a harpsichord recital at Sally Rumford's home in Concord, New Hampshire, circa 1800. According to Doug Copeley of the New Hampshire Historical Society, the house, built in 1764, was at 15 Hall Street and was demolished about 1956—"The recital is said to have been at this house." The National Gallery of Art attributes the painting to Benjamin Thompson, with the title *Harpsichord Recital at Count Rumford's, Concord, New Hampshire.* **He was not known to be a painter, however. and never returned to America after he fled Boston (National Gallery of Art).**

your character; he would avoid you as the most dangerous person with whom he could form a connection. But no doubt he believes, as I do, that your dissipation is not natural, and that if your affections were once properly fixed, if you were fulfilling the duties of your sex as the mother of a family, you would feel much more real pleasure in the occupations which would result form that situation than play, or company, or any kind of dissipation ever afforded you. The latter always end with the feeling of which you so justly complain, that 'nothing delights.'"[5]

There are disparate reasons that might explain why Sally did not do what most young women did and get married. She was very well off so didn't need to depend on a man financially. She had a romantic temperament, which meant that she might have had dreams that a man interested in her could scarcely fulfill. Her father sent a few men away, which is always pointed out in biographical writings to Thompson's discredit. But that was only two or three men in her early twenties, and after she returned to America he wrote explicitly to Loammi Baldwin that she was free to marry whomever she wished. In her sixties in Paris Sally found her fun in parties and cards. It was a shade of what Sir Charles had warned against, although hardly dissipation, only, rather, very mild. A former suitor ten years younger than Sally, Monsieur Letort, came often to call and played whist with her and the Lefebvres. Emma sensed the gentleman had a tendre for Sally as of 25 years before. Sally, said Emma, had never had looks but she had an appealing vitality. In any event, Sally was more than skittish about being courted.

Overall it was Sally who loved portraits and found comfort and reassurance in surrounding herself with them. Thus she wrote this note about a portrait of her father, that William Lane of London drew the picture and she had it copied three times in paints by Oldfield [sic] of Paris: "This Painter, likewise painted for me, Lefebvre, likewise Emma; excellent likeness's of both, and beautiful copy of my father."[6]

After most of a year at Auteuil, Sally then lived in London, Paris, and Concord, New Hampshire, between 1814 and 1845, and until her death in 1852 in Concord. She was active in philanthropy, her sympathetic impulse being a reminder of her father. She established the Rolfe and Rumford Asylums in Concord and bequeathed her mansion to this institution. She gave to charitable societies in Concord and Boston for needy children, orphan girls, widows and the mentally ill.

During the seven years from 1835 in France, Sally seemed happiest. She said it was easy to make acquaintances. Emma was about ages 11 to 18 and so more malleable than she would be when deciding her future with a man (Sally wrote that Emma was happy relatively, writing ambiguously, "I really think the child was perfectly happy for a little while; or is much otherwise ever").[7] Sally had a built-in social life with people who recognized her status and she characteristically had a handy stag male. The first week after Sally and Emma arrived from London they stayed with Victoire. That must have been a trial for Sally, who went to London for a month and left Emma with Victoire. Emma did not speak a word of French but was conversing well when Sally returned, both averred. In one of her diary extracts, Sally wrote she had taken a French servant "but Mme. Bonnet was exceedingly useful to me; she is a very fine house-keeper and acquainted with French ways."[8] That suggests Victoire was communicating between Sally and the outside world in some way, perhaps shopping for her provisions and having her *bottines* resoled. Such a relationship would have been condescending and gives insight into the fact that for all the socializing back and forth when Sally and Emma lived in Paris, Sally continued to see Victoire in the role of her father's housekeeper.

Captain Charles Lefebvre (1839) by Hippolyte-Dominique Holfeld. Sitter has red hair and moustache and wears a gray coat, red medal pinned to chest of military uniform, red trousers, and white gloves. From note on painting: "This written at Concord 3d June 1852./This is a fine likeness of Charles R. Lefebvre of Paris/by Oldfeld, of Paris—a natural Son of the late Count/Rumford's. Certainly not favored as it respects illegiti/macy, but in other respects good, a character that bids/fair for some considerable renown. Has already two beautiful little [children—a son a daughter]" (New Hampshire Historical Society).

The chief friends of Sally, the Baldwins, Sir Charles, and the Lefebvres, were "inherited" from her father. As for her relations through, and including, her half brother, Sally felt gingerly about them, from jealousy and because of the awkwardness of the sexual relations of Victoire and the count by which he begat his son. Her notes, rewritten from some unseen diary, mention one or two events each for the years 1838 to 1845 predominately connected to Victoire and her family. Their events were key for her as well and she noted how many months Victoire had been married when she and her second husband, Monsieur Antin, moved out of Paris.

Monsieur Antin was someone Victoire had met living in a good neighborhood with her family, who were rising on the social ladder, or through her close friend Thérèse, who had set out to walk from Normandy to the capital with her. Victoire was a person who inspired confidence and had prospered through hardships, out-of-wedlock motherhood and caring for a sick son being paramount among the obstacles in her life that are known. Monsieur Antin and Victoire decided to live near Victoire's friends in the country, or he was a Linois or had connections and land with the town already. Sally was glad she didn't move in with them—the couple must have asked—given that they soon left the city.

Sally at some point made a list of important events in her life in Paris. In the chronology of these events Sally chose to extract from her diary, all but one date, her return from a trip to England, related to Victoire and Charles, proving how central they were to her emotional life during that period:

1839
14th March—the widow Bonnet was married to Monsieur Antin.

1840
11th July—the family moved to Linas, 30 miles from Paris (16 months married)
22 Nov.—Went with Mme Lefebvre and Emma to pay a visit to Lias

1841
14 April, Mr. Lefebvre sent to Toulouse
16 August [Charles] ought to have stayed month instead of four
26 August—I returned from England.
12 October—went in company of Mrs. Antin and Son, to pay a visit to Linas, found Mr. Antin with the dropsy.
25 Oct. Mr. Antin died (31 months married)
17 December. Went again to Linas to see the widow. The Capt. Was still there suffering much with boils.

1842
16 Feb. Mr. L. went to Poitier, rather better.

Sally rented an apartment (or as Sally said "apartments") on the opposite side of the street, the rue Colysée, from the Lefebvres, where Sally and Emma lived from 1838 until July 6, 1845, when they went to London to take a ship for America, thereafter to live in the estate Sally inherited from her half brother.

Sally wrote a flowery 8-stanza poem, rhyming a careful ABAB, called "Leisure Hours" to celebrate Charles's marriage to Pauline de Tauzia. She dedicated the poem to Charles, detailing the fact that Pauline was the daughter of a Count de Tauzia "in the time of Louis XVIII under government but since that time living on an estate of his at Bordeaux, and where still the widow Madame de Tauzia and a son reside." She identifies herself as "by a lady and friend" and mentions the relations of mothers, fathers and offspring, ending in the next to last stanza with a reference to her father's being in one of the seats of honor with the family in the hereafter:

> At a day of jubilee [sic] all meet,
> Children with wonders to relate;
> Papa, mamma, in-honored seat;
> If not in youth, in mellow joys partake.⁹

Emma described the kind of socializing with the Lefebvres they had in Paris:

> Always when Mr. Lefebvre would have a furlough from his regiment and come home to his Mother's, he would often be invited by his half sister the Countess of Rumford to take breakfast with her and her little Emma, and some times to have dinner; when to dinner, his Mother, Mr. Letort and the Countess of Delmase would always be invited also. So one day in particular, we were all six together for the little dinner party, which generally took place at four o'clock. After dinner there would be a table of four at a game of whist, Mr. Lefebvre at the pianoforte with his music, for he was a first class musician, among all his other accomplishments. All had passed a very pleasant evening, soon after nine the party began to break up. All had left together except Mr. Letort, who was the last to leave, seeming in no hurry—perhaps he was thinking of the twenty five years that had gone, never to return, when he had first made the acquaintance of the Countess while she was residing at the Baths of Tivoli with her maid Mary Grove. Mr. Letort had then Proposed to her as her future husband, though ten years younger, he deemed that no drawback she was still young looking and very prepossessing in manners, even if not very handsome. And even once in my hearing he had made the same propossial [sic] to her. That be as it may, it was plain that he still lingered. I noticed that the Countess looked tired and was pale. While in London she had purchased false teeth at her dentist there, she had them made to order, and did think at the time that they fitted her mouth all right. And did....

By the time Sally and Emma returned to Paris in 1838 Charles was a military officer. Victoire had purchased his commission and he was launched in his career. Charles was 30 when he married, as was his bride. If this represents a delay, that might have to do with Charles's mental health issues. His choice of a bride shows he was close to his mother and must have pleased her, as Pauline Tauzier was the daughter of Victoire's close friend Thérèse. It also must have been of some satisfaction to Sally that Pauline's father had been a count of the ancien régime, a fact Sally put in the front of the wedding poem she wrote to honor Charles and had saved. Let us return to Emma's storytelling, the source of this knowledge: "Count de Tauzier had a fine chateau in Bordeaux, at the time of Louis XVIII, in whose cabinet he was employed. And he owned a large collection of fine paintings. But the one he prized the most, was a full sized portrait of his most honored and beloved King, who sat expressly for the count's pleasure. The same as the Elector of Bavaria did for Count Rumford. But, alas, in 1830, when Louis XVIII had to vacate the throne of France, for Louis Philippe, the count lost his high position also, and most of his property." Emma continues with the fairy tale story of the friend of Victoire's from farm country in Normandy who rose to the rank of countess:

> The Count married, for his second wife, a peasant girl for her beauty, Theresa, from Normandy. They had two children, a daughter Pauline born in 1814, and a son Leonel, born in 1816.
> After the death of the Count in 1836, the widow with her two children moved up to Paris, after she had sold her chateau, and collected what money her husband had in the bank at Bordeaux, and invested it in the bank in Paris. And hired apartments in the Rue de Chamre, near the Champs Elysées, where they resided until the daughter was married to Charles R. Lefebvre in January 1845, and in 1846 [Oct. 18] they had a son, Joseph Amédée, and two years later a daughter [Marie Sarah, born Dec. 6, 1848].

In Paris there were evening get-togethers of Victoire, Charles (if not with his regiment), Pauline, Sally, and a man who was sweet on Sally, also recounted in Emma's passages.

Curiously, the younger two of Thompson's children, Sophie Baumgarten and Charles Lefebvre, may have had afflictions of the spirit, where emotional overload led to physical failure; "may have" because that information comes by way of Sally, Sophie's half sister, who would have been as glad to have Sophie melt into an angelic wax figure as not.

In the wake of unremitting and intense labor, Thompson would get sick. His career kept him among people but in ritualized situations. If informal human contact became aggravated by bickering, he experienced weakness and pain. Whatever type ailment, generally gastritis, he suffered chronically he kept at bay by rigid diet, spas, and sometimes a medication and treatment, like drinking milk or the beer he took in draughts that astonished Lord Palmerston (Thompson was usually a non-drinker). Count Rumford acknowledged the psychological component of these sieges of sickness that laid him up for a month or several months. That the people of Munich lit candles in their churches for him indicates how serious these bouts could be.

Sophie was said by her aunt Mary and Sally to have a frivolous character. It piqued Mary that the niece only came to visit when she had nothing better to do, and Sally wrote that Sophie suffered from "the peculiarly light, trifling character of her mother."[10] Certainly Josepha's sister Mary said so to Sally Thompson. Thompson was concerned about Sophie, enough so that he attempted for quite a while to make a change in her life, apparently to have her live with her aunt and uncle, the Count and Countess Nogarola. What to do about Sophie's deportment? Her Aunt Mary (Nogarola) in Verona discussed this with Sally in Munich, only the remarks on the Countess Nogarola's side being extant. The discussion was approached in a desultory fashion as a minor topic but clearly was one that Mary considered paramount to Sally's father.

According to a plan Thompson had proposed to the countess sisters, Sophie, age ten, would live with Mary to acquire a solid foundation for life. Josepha had agreed but showed her control by equivocating. The plan also counted on the consent of Mary's husband, who rather than say a clear yes or no, was inclined to put off a decision while generally showing displeasure at the idea. Mary let Sally know that she would do anything for the count because she was devoted to him but did not see the plan as germinating when it was raised in the first half of 1798. In fact, Mary pointedly leaves out mention of her sister in the correspondence with Sally, though did disclose that her daughter, Teresa, went to a ball with Sophie, as children.

Would Thompson have championed this idea merely because Sophie was frivolous? He observed well. He observed she was musical and bought her the pianoforte. He may have felt she was slightly unstable and wanted Sophie to live in Verona away from the Bavarian court, an idea rejected by Mary's husband and Sophie's mother, it seems, based on correspondence from Mary's side. When Thompson went to Munich in 1810 for the last time Sophie was ill. A note at the lower left margin of one of Emma's diary pages says that Sophie was disappointed in love and was put into a mental asylum in Geneva, where she died quite young. Asserting the causality between romantic calamity and physical decline, Sally put it more poignantly: "She marries a nobleman by the [name] of Milteese, but who proved so unfeeling ... first to destroy her health then her mind ... dying in a mad-house at Geneva in Switzerland."[11] Yet if Sophie lived until 1828, to the age of 44, and had already been very ill (physically, it seems) in 1810, she may have been unwell with physical infirmity for a long time. In any event, what Sally told Emma is theatrical and suggests some level of distortion.

Charles Lefebvre was described by Emma (hearsay, since this was before she was born), as having "brain fever" at age eleven from excessive study. In his late twenties he was out of the army for a season with an attack of "boils" and then Sally wrote letters to and about him in "the madhouse." Lest that be seen as a building that had changed purpose, like, for instance, the Invalides, Sally noted to James Baldwin she didn't think Charles was actually crazy.[12]

Sally Rumford had a sensitive point, an inner conflict about whether to shut out or to open her arms to her biological brother, and an ambivalence of attitude towards his family who were her social support in Paris. On August 31, 1852, from Concord Sally wrote James Baldwin: "You will read Madam Lefebvre's letter if you please which I have written in English, too much fatigued with the whole business to write it in French, and then it may deaden down their dreadful inclination to be writing, but I think my letter may pretty well do the business for that. You cannot think what a mess I had of it this last time. The French are sickening for that, where they think there is the least prospect of gain, they are disgustingly persevering."[13]

On August 3, 1852, Madam Lefebvre had written looking forward to Sally's arrival, offering a room with water cabinet and conveniences and saying she would engage a servant during Sally's stay and a place for Emma nearby. Mr. Lefebvre was generally in Constantine [Constantinople] but would get permission to visit if she came. The son and daughter were Amédée and Sarah. "You know madame how he [Charles] is attached to you. In all his letters he speaks to me of your near arrival." She said that her son was "in Africa" and continued that he "does nothing immoderately as he is of good temperament."[14]

It was the very quality of expansiveness that disturbed Sally's Yankee sensibilities. Charles seems openhearted on his side of the correspondence. He would share that he missed his children, longed to be home and that his mother was not as blithe-spirited as she had once been. After Sally's death he wrote the Baldwins that he had a feeling of affection for her since childhood. He signed the letters to his half-sister with flourishes such as "Aimez-moi comme je vous aime" and "Votre tout affection." Sally probably frowned if not recoiled. On occasion she asked after the family's health but no more.

Sally wrote from Concord on September 1, 1852, to Charles' wife, Madame Pauline Lefebvre, at an apartment in Paris as follows: "If my father had wished to give Mr. Le Febvre his name and title he could have done it—besides he has a very pretty name and is himself, as I think, doing honor to it. And Amédée needs nothing more than his father's examples for instruction to render him according to what you say of him, all you could wish. Thus I decline all further proceedings towards changing his name, but the gift of the 10,000 dollars will hold good registered on my will."[15] Sally appended regards to the person's mother, Victoire. She really was thrashing around about what to do regarding her father's grandson. It seems as though Sally feared that Amédée, while a nice child, might metamorphose into a snarly youth. Even at his birth she disparaged to the Baldwins his peculiar name. She wrote, in answer to a September 30 letter, to Pauline that she wanted "no more to do with the business.... I am besides informed by high authority that there was evil in it. That often the child came upon the parent with claims at an adolescent age."[16] Sally had for a while the conceit of educating Charles in America, in order to banish the French in him and have him grow up culturally American.

Illegitimates and the Napoleonic Code
by Nicholas Dames, professor of humanities, Columbia University

Illegitimate sons could not, under the Code Civil adopted in France in 1804, inherit unless legally recognized, and accomplishing this required a court procedure. Even in that case they could inherit only a third of the hereditary portion that went to legitimate sons. The inheritance laws gradually evolved but only in 1972 was full equality provided to all children, natural and legitimate. But those were legal limitations and in societal terms being a bastard seems not to have been socially disabling in the way that it was in Britain. Thirty percent of births in post–Revolutionary France were illegitimate; and certainly in aristocratic circles, bastard sons were married off to families (usually of a slightly lesser rank or station) to cement various alliances. The best fictional example is Julien Sorel from Stendhal's Red and the Black. At one point, late in the novel (before Madame de Renal sends her accusatory letter to the Marquis de la Mole), an arrangement is made to pass him off (falsely) as the natural son of a nobleman, in order to make his marriage to the Marquis's daughter Mathilde possible. Illegitimacy, that is, in certain circumstances, could enable a social rise.

Honoré de Balzac himself had at least one, possibly more, illegitimate children. While the major novels do not have a bastard as a central character, two of the four "inheritance novels," *Ursule Mirouet* and *The Black Sheep* [*La Rabouilleuse*] have plots involving illegitimacy in the bourgeois social world. In each, Balzac shows his sympathies with the illegitimate figure, and the obstacle in the plot is not social stigma so much as the specifically legal disabilities faced by a bastard. While these figures don't face the strong social exclusion they might have had in Britain, certainly not being able to inherit would create subsidiary social obstacles, particularly in regards to marriage. It might also script certain professional outcomes—the army and the clergy most prominently.

Honoré de Balzac set *Ursule Mirouet* in 1829–1830 (and published it in 1841), the time that—for his career, status, and peace of mind—28-year-old Charles Lefebvre wanted to establish his legitimacy. In Balzac's novel, the old Dr. Minoret strives for a means to give his angelic godchild, Ursule, his wealth. Ursule is the legitimate daughter of the doctor's deceased brother-in-law; however, that person was illegitimate and the stigma perdured. The plot revolves around how to sidestep the contemporary law's bias in the favor of intact families and legitimate offspring. As an attorney tells the doctor, "The law is so strict ... that by the terms of a judgment of the Court of Appeal of 7 July 1817, a natural child can claim nothing from its natural grandfather, not even maintenance."[17]

Charles lost his life at Sebastopol in the terrible last major battle of the Crimean War in which the French took the fortified position of Malakoff and the Russians lost their presence on the Black Sea. When Charles was killed (September 8, 1855) he had gained to right to use the name Rumford. There is record of a military pension to his wife, Marie-Louise Pauline. His final resting place is in Linas. On his tomb, maintained by an association called "le souvenir français," is a crown formed of vines and bunches of grapes, a symbol of rebirth.

Sally died at age 78, on December 2, 1852, in the same southwest bedroom of the Rolfe mansion in southern Concord where she was born. Her friends and relatives donated many of her personal effects to the New Hampshire Historical Society. They include silk slippers, a watercolor paint set, a fan (ribbon, shell and paint), detached sleeves, cotton stockings, an English sewing kit, and a gros point carpetbag. *SR* was worked into the weave of the stockings' lacy tops and a crown insignia surmounted the *R* on her carpetbag.

At the end of her life, Sally Thompson divided the letters from her father into two parcels, a small packet of those relating to the Royal Institution and a large one that she called "the scolding letters," containing advice and reprimand for her or references to his unhappy second marriage. She made extracts from the second group and then instructed Emma to burn both packets of letters. The extracts were last accounted for in the hands of the Reverend Ellis when he wrote his biography. According to Sanborn Brown, Ellis also tipped letters he had in with presentation copies and to his friends.[18]

Sally Thompson spent her life fighting her romantic nature, moving from place to place, and in a general state of discontent: Parisians were too concerned with luxury, the

London house was hard to keep up, and Concord was boring. Others commented on her ups and downs. Her romantic yearnings came to naught as men never came through for her except the ones handling her finances or being the wise old counselor (Loammi Baldwin and Sir Charles while they were alive, then James and George Baldwin). Her staying

Charles Lefebvre's grave. Linas, France (courtesy Michel Petit).

single wasn't really by choice, not what she would have liked. It had to do with having had the absent romanticized father when she was young. She identified her relationships sometimes as infatuation, yet they were her own and cannot be explained away. In terms of individuation the story is sad yet she had her own power, thanks to financial security, and could rely on Thompson's own nexus of intimate friends to act as her friends. They cheered her and told her to keep her chin up, of which examples, excerpted, follow:

> I got your letter of the 6th & was very surprised of the story you told there. You are certainly completely innocent my dear friend and don't merit the pain ["chagrin"] it caused you, but it's a new proof of the danger of liaisons and above all strangers—although it is certain sad to have to be cautious to the point of not risking taking a walk with someone without being compromised.... Everything confirms in me the satisfaction to be proud of my friend; and I hope to merit always on my part the esteem that she inspires in me.[19]
> —Mary Nogarola

Then from Sir Charles:

> I really know too little of the people with whom you live, and of the gentlemen who address you, to judge what it would be best for you to do. After the adventure of the gentleman who married so unexpectedly, had drawn upon you the public attention, I am sorry that you were placed in so conspicuous a situation at Middleton, and that you appear to take so much delight in the attentions of another gentleman, whom you own you had no intention to marry.
> Exuberance of spirits [is fine for a 20-year-old but] your character ought now to be remarked for steadiness, prudence, and good sense.[20]
> —Charles Blagden, March 8, 1806

Being rich, Sally on the one hand didn't require a man but on the other hand being a spinster did bring with it prudishness. She left *Pretty Extracts* (circa 1836–1845) that she made from her own travel diaries and wrote in a tiny hand over the menu of an elegant Parisian food purveyor called Bidault & Co. Here she fulminated against the naked statuary in the fountains of the Place de la Concorde, "which they call sea goddesses, but no matter, they are naked females placed in a most conspicuous manner. They have long and naked figures of men in gardens, but these are of females in the centre of Paris, in short facing the Palace! I do not know where their modesty, or their taste can be. I am sure no modest woman wants to stand anear [sic] the place."[21]

Sally indulged her romantic feelings in poetical writings. One long poem called "Rumford Villa" looked back: "The first morning in Eden! When sin was not there ... and all is harmony-melody." More affecting is a stanza, cut out from something else she wrote when her handwriting had deteriorated from shaky hand or poor eyesight:

> Tell me babling echo why,
> Thou returnst me sigh for sigh?—
> When I of slighted love complained
> Thou delights to make my pain.[22]

Anne Lavoisier Rumford continued to live as a social, wealthy, and proud lady who liked stimulating company. The popular English novelist Maria Edgeworth wrote from Paris on November 15, 1820, that she was going to the theater, had seen the star performer Mademoiselle Mars three times, was meeting duchesses and princesses and discussing le bon ton, and that Anne had invited her to her house: "We have seen a great deal of our dear Delesserts, and of Madame de Rumford, who gave us a splendid and most agreeable dinner."[23] Baron Delessert was Thompson's banker, who had continued to visit him at Auteuil. He was an old friend of Anne's, and Sally, who trusted her friendships with her father's friends (indeed all her important friends derived from him), relied on him to clear up her father's estate, calling him in verse "the Perfect Man."[24]

When peace was restored with England, Sir Joseph Banks remembered Anne with a lovely gift. He wrote Sir Charles Blagden that there was coming from England by night coach to Paris a scented Climbing Air Shire rosebush and Irish Ivy, "both well rooted in a basket," for the Countess Rumford. Later that fall of 1819, Banks sought Sir Charles's help with another similar gift to her. Banks wrote, "By this Evenings Paris diligence I Send Two Pacquets of Strawberries the one for The Countess Rumford the other for Madame Bertholet they are Roseberry Strawberries the Kind I most approve both for Quantity of Produce & for Flavor they are a Seedling Variety Raised at Aberdeen I have them yet in Pots in my hot house which yields me about a good Dish a Week I have directed them to you to the Care of MM Delessert as it would not be fair to make Either Lady Pay for both Pacquets be So good as to Put the Carriage to my account & Let me Know how much I am in your debt the next Parcel Shall bring you Whites Ephemeris as you desire."[25]

These elite scientific circles of Britain and the Continent had provided friendships and intellectual concourse to Benjamin Thompson and continued to do so for the gentlemen of science of the 19th century. Sir Joseph's gallant horticultural gifts were his way to connect with the memory of Benjamin Thompson and perhaps also Lavoisier, Banks's contemporary. It was Thompson who had thrown his energy into the garden at his and Anne's house a little over a decade before.

Anne contributed both to a charity for poor children and a charitable organization of which Lavoisier himself had been an early member. She trusted those who had been with her for a long time, so perhaps Thompson had been too new an element! After he moved out, she continued her Monday dinners, the parties, concerts, and open houses at the rue d'Anjou for the next 27 years.

A curious anecdote relates to Madame Lavoisier and her favorite niece, the Countess de Gramont. The Countess de Gramont was fond of cake and when she was coming to tea Madame Lavoisier had a special cake baked for her. Madame Lavoisier had a maid wrap up the remains of the cake and carry it out to the niece's carriage. After good-byes were said, the niece went out to the carriage and, seeing the buttery package on the satin-covered seat, threw it into the street. Anne spied this from an upstairs window and thereupon disinherited her niece.[26]

Sally's will is the one place it is documented that she asserted unequivocally, after mention of Madame Antin, the descendancy of the line. As to her father she used the present tense to allude to his death, as it was still in the present for her in emotional terms: "She Mr Lefebre's Mother; the Count Rumford's Son, Amédée Lefebvre his Son, consequently, Count Rumford's Grand Son. So Count Rumford dies not without some one to come after him, & glad am I. S. Rumford"[27]

Amédée Lefevre gave memorabilia to George Ellis around 1878, in honor of the biography of his grandfather Benjamin Thompson Count Rumford.[28]

Epilogue: "The Most Sublime of All Affections"

> What is commonly, in a popular sense, called reason is nothing
> but a general and a calm passion, which takes a comprehensive
> and a distant view of its object.—David Hume, 1739

The Elector-Prince Karl Theodor did not censure his courtier for having a child by the royal mistress. Thompson was discreet and not boastful about his intimacies with women. By all accounts, he was physically attractive: tall, blue-eyed, with reddish-brown hair, slender, a nice smile and good teeth, and fastidious. He liked to hear music, attend balls and wear elegant clothes. He liked to have fun and included women in picnics, boating, hikes, horseback riding, attending horse races, and going on carriage jaunts. He was interested in interior decoration and beautiful landscapes. He was a romantic figure because he was so smart and an adventurer and liked women too.

He gravitated to the women he bonded with. He missed them when absent from them. He sought them out to recreate. He was a man of the Enlightenment who treated women as intelligent and he had impeccable manners. He had affairs with friends' wives and yet his social behavior was such that no one called him on this, even if occasionally a husband curbed his enthusiasm, as when Countess Nogarola's husband reminded her she had a duty to leave Munich (and Thompson) with him for Verona.

Thompson's whole sexual and intimate personal story is unlike what Americans like to identify with. His associations with women were deep and sincere and yet at the same time plural or sequential. Sex mattered very much and his women friends mattered a great deal, but he was bonded by affection with a number of women, in relationships overlapping. They fulfilled his sexual, social and aesthetic needs and conformed to liberal Enlightenment thinking. For example, Mary Wollstonecraft called friendship between men and women "the most sublime of all affections," a hypothesis implying that friendship outlasts passion. As Count Rumford matured he preferred educated, intellectual or sophisticated women, specifically three mistresses: Josepha Baumgarten, Laura de Kalb, and Princess Taxis, and two intimate friends, Lady Palmerston and Countess Nogarola. This maturation transpired easily and without suffering. Assuming the best, he was not watchful. He was not prepared for a woman, Anne Lavoisier, who caved in to his pursuit of her and then corroded his spirit by demanding he change.

Biographers have claimed Thompson was dishonest because he was a spy; a selfish

Pierce family graveyard (courtesy Kathleen Pierce).

father because he did not approve two matches for his daughter; homosexual because Lord Germain spent much time in his company; a social climber because he made his way up in society; dishonest because he exaggerated about his ancestors very slightly; and perhaps above all a false lover, a womanizer, and a rake. Thompson did strategize his ambitions, but did he lie? He only can be fairly accused of some "theological lying" where he inserts a creator God into writings to prevent zealots in Bavaria from persecuting him, feigning some interest in religion, which he did not have. Of all the notable people whose lives you have read about there is no one who is treated more like a Rorschach test than Benjamin Thompson. He organized the American Dragoons to avoid being drawn and quartered in the la Motte spy ring? He had a son by his French wife's gardener? If his contemporaries purveyed such gossip, current historiography has gobbled their inkblots up to tell tales like these.

History is swinging back to counterbalance the legends and the preceding story has disputed these accusations. Now I focus on the last. His biographers to a man (literally) praise his achievements in science and condemn his sexual story. They do not recognize that Thompson in his years in Europe was an outsider to whom friendship with men and women meant a great deal; they were like his family, and his best friends were women. Sexual intimacy could be engendered by, or result from, these friendships. That, additionally, Thompson had a practical versus religious view of the marriage vow, i.e., it had an exit door, has been struck down as immoral. Yet, who better exemplifies Margaret

Tombstone of Ruth Pierce, widow of Josiah Pierce, mother of Count Rumford.

Mead's anthropological insight about her own several marriages that she led "successive lives"?

Decorum, including hiding one's sexual follies, was the watchword of the social set Thompson circulated in and he obeyed that perfectly and until his death. Husbands often accepted their wives having love affairs or even—as a doctor with an invalid wife did when the Calvinist friend of Thompson's, M.A. Pictet, fell in love with her—invited the lover to live with them in Paris. The adoring Pictet would have absorbed some of Julie Charles's emotional attention and permitted the doctor to catch his breath and work at his passion, chemistry. Yet this fact would have been private, not advertised. Being in Europe meant the cultivation of a trans–Atlantic self; a front stage coping while the core individual might remain unchanged. Regarding distinguished Americans when they visited Paris in this same era as did Thompson, the similarity is that they all had different sexual lives than back in America. Libertinage was not, points out Thomas Foster, the doyen of the Founding Fathers' sexual practices, anti-marriage. Writing about Gourverneur Morris, Foster observed how "the discourse of eighteenth-century libertinism could be taken up by individuals and applied in ways not intended by the authors of didactic literature. Although set in opposition to one another in print culture, individuals could, of course, combine libertine principles with the affective sentiment of companionate marriage and sentimental friendship in ways that were unexpected and that do not produce a neat character type."[1]

Sally Hemings became Thomas Jefferson's concubine while he indulged in serious flirtation with Maria Cosway; Gouverneur Morris romped with little forethought once he identified a woman's sexual desire, while having one married French lover for years; and Aaron Burr for the most part was paying (fairly) ladies of the night to avoid entanglement at a fraught period of life. Meanwhile, Thompson, like Benjamin Franklin, had

Taking Water for Vauxhall. Text: Be cautious my love, don't expose your leg! **One of a series of "Drolls" by Isaac Cruickshank (Lewis Walpole Library, Yale University).**

affairs that modeled the Enlightenment vision of sexual desire as a salubrious force. It's not in the scope of this book to discuss the sexualities of these famous men but it's interesting that Morris, when he returned home, finally married at 58, and Thompson tried to move from illicit sexual activity to a marriage that would combine romance and friendship.

Seen in the context of the mores of his time, both in the American Revolution and later in England and Napoleonic Europe, Thompson had a lively but not crazed sexual life. He liked women. He was in America a prepossessing youth on his way up and subsequently a young officer in the king's army; in Europe his sexual identity reflects his status as a gentleman, his world as a courtier, and his definitive separation from his wife, and, ipso facto, living in a context more sexually open than in America, during a long pause in any expectation of a companionate marriage. When he entered into a sexual relationship with Victoire he was worldly and unconcerned about social strata.

In America he, like George Washington, married money. To overlook how common this was and praise Washington for his choice of an older, wealthy wife but mock Benjamin Thompson belongs to a pervasive political point of view, that of the winners of the war, distinguishing Americans from Europeans. Being close to, spending time with, and enjoying the company of women who were members of the patrician society where

Kitchen with Rumford roaster, Rundlet-May House, Portsmouth, New Hampshire, photograph by David Bohl (Historic New England).

Thompson carved a place for himself hardly made him a knave or a rake. Lady Palmerston mourned her adored husband and was Thompson's confidante; yet she is described as his mistress who resented his other mistresses, with no proof that she and Thompson had an affair. Thompson surely had a sexual liaison with the married Princess of Taxis and the married Laura de Kalb. Aristocrats were permitted what was unwise for ordinary folk. But so was Maria Cosway married and that did not stop her and Jefferson from indulging in a serious flirtation.

We come to Thompson's having romances, one he called a dishonorable person due to his being implicated in an affair with two sisters. The countesses Nogarola and Baumgarten seemed marginally *en froid* but they got along. Discretion was the rule of the day. When Mozart mentioned in a letter that Countess Baumgarten was the mistress of the prince elector Karl Theodor, he wrote it in code. Unlike our times, men and women typically gushed sentiment when fond of members of the same sex without being thought to be sexually involved with them. From the time Rousseau published *Emilie* to the mid-Victorian era, showering one's friend with words of affection was natural. Thompson expressed his feelings in his letters and was very sensitive, even falling ill when stressed, and very rococo in loving to dress beautifully and have a beautiful woman in his arms at a ball. Therefore, there is no way to know how far Thompson carried relations with the Parisian ladies who dazzled him as they had dazzled Benjamin Franklin 15 years before.

Some writers of history have disliked Thompson for abandoning his native country and having foreign ways. For example, when offering charity in his daughter's name in the form of a fund for clothing to poor children, he is derided for not understanding they wouldn't want a uniform. In fact, the town fathers of Concord, New Hampshire, accepted the spontaneous gift of a fund graciously and no serious faux pas was committed. Moreover, high officials in America asked him to serve as the head of West Point.

Thompson transgressed against monogamy, the norm of American society, by leaving his wife behind. She was not in financial duress and when she died he formed an attachment as a good father to their daughter. His relationship life passed through stages. First he was the young husband almost yanked into maturity (without the muscles) going to bring his wife home to his mother when spring came. Then he was the knave in the big cities of Boston and London, fooling around with married women but inclined to one partner and not a range of partners. Then he had the shadow marriage and could not have a full-fledged life with any woman, which he turned to advantage in being a sexual "stag" for beautiful young aristocrats in lackluster marriages. They were the age he had been when he would have fallen in love naturally had Sarah Walker Rolphe not plucked the callow youth to be what she wanted, a husband.

He was no threat to the husbands. The affairs did not distract him from his agenda of bringing greater comfort and efficiency to the world and making his mark in science. He faced forward to the sun and left yesteryear in shadows. At one moment he was buying a summer house near the Princess of Taxis's and the next he was convincing Karl Theodor to buy these and a third adjacent property to make a park. Josepha Baumgarten asked more of him. It is unknown what that was, not more involvement in the upbringing of Sophie, which he would have liked but some more attention, connection. He self-consciously avoided Josepha and experienced her as oil on his wings. Then in France, a widower nearing 50, at last he had something to bring to the table: himself, an available man. It infused him with hope that he could backtrack and recapture the state of a young man wooing. But Anne Lavoisier cleaved to memories and wished for someone more like Pierre Du Pont, who knew her world and her needs (but was in his mid–70s).

In his marriage to Madame Lavoisier, Thompson was befuddled and he provokes pathos. The last thing Anne wanted was newness. She struck out angrily at his best self, the active man who at once in the marriage commenced tearing apart and modernizing their home. No oppressor, he was a scientist who needed space and time to do his work. Her emotional clock had stopped, causing her to become somewhat unhinged after her father and husband were guillotined. What seems to have shocked biographers is how Thompson shouted out, e.g., to his daughter in America, how miserable he was and how little he liked his wife. Once the split occurred, he did not object to Sally's and Anne's being friendly and on occasion dined in Paris with his ex-wife.

Perhaps some have a suspicion of a scientist who loved fine clothes, looked great on a white horse, and lounged with aristocrats at estates in the English countryside, on Bavarian lakes and in Italian towns for weeks or months. Could it be that this man who accomplished almost more to advance society than any other person of his generation didn't struggle or work enough and was a turncoat? For instance, the author of a French biographical article, Robert Campeix, is one of several who made Thompson into a curmudgeon, in this case as he entered into matrimony with Marie-Anne: "Having put aside for the time being his rotten [*humeur de dogue*] moods, they decided to get married."[2]

One author commented that Thompson's funeral was a plain and modest affair and how he who reveled in pomp would have hated that.[3] This offensive critique does not match up with what those who knew Thompson and lived in the context of his world and time thought of him, that he had the directness of a man of action and enlightened progressive. The critique does line up, however, with the calumny that Thompson has received from biographical writers, the same ones who laud his science. Moreover, he complained to friends like Lady Palmerston that court protocols were so hard to endure he was tempted to leave the Bavarian court.

It appears that when Thompson had flings with the wife of the printer, Mary Dill Thomas, and Susan Jeffries, the wife of the doctor and hospital administrator, he made the first move or initiated a liaison. Such may have been the case with Victoire, his housekeeper in Auteuil. In contrast, the noble ladies may have approached him, that is, the seduction could have been on their part. It cannot be known if his visits to the castles of Viscountess Palmerston, Countess Nogarola, Princess Taxis, and Laura were lovers' meetings. There was certainly opportunity. His correspondence, however, suggests friendship was the keynote in his romances with the first two of these women and that he was no Casanova. He wrote a most impassioned letter to Lady Palmerston explicating why to him she represented "home."

It is known that his noble women friends were close to Thompson apart from their marriages, through letters, visits and acts they did for him, e.g., networking, befriending his daughter, and translating. Their relations with him were not backstairs affairs. Such a romantic friendship had a different emotional value than marriage, and at this time Rousseau had validated male-female friendship. Among the elite it was a popular concept of transformative experience. For aristocrats it was relatively easy to have a romantic friendship because they traveled, had more than one home, and it was accepted for the husbands to have mistresses, as marriage was firmly about property. The 18th century aristocratic marriage in Europe did not require a companionate relationship.

The woman in an arranged marriage, if she found a soul mate and the relationship was discreet, could connect with her intelligence and emotional self with this secondary figure, her intimate and abiding friend, the man who brought some exquisite nuance to her life.

That Thompson was close to a number of educated, well-bred women can be interpreted as a testimony to his being a caring friend and thoughtful person, whatever the sexual aspect was. The typical description of biographers of his character is seen in Duveen's potshot, that Thompson, by the time at about 50 he married Madame Lavoisier, was "a self-opinionated and conceited individual who had been used to living a self-indulgent and extravagant bachelor lifestyle for years."[4]

Being close to, spending time with, and enjoying the company of women in the patrician society in which Thompson was a sort of guest member did not make him a knave or a rake. Had he been a knave he would have been gossiped about as one. It's striking that scholars have tended to judge the count's intimate life as evidencing flawed character, whereas his contemporaries in several countries thought he was quite all right. His whole sexual and intimate personal story is unlike what Americans like to identify with, as sex mattered so much and his women friends mattered a great deal. But there was never one woman but a number of women, concurrently and serially. He was indifferent to the marriage vows of himself and the women he bedded, yet he was not a seducer like Gouverneur Morris, his acquaintance, and several times remarked in diary or letter that he restrained himself.

The women admired him and yet there was a sense that he was a pet, controlled; as Lady Palmerston wrote her husband, "we mustn't expect him, he's a man of service." He wasn't really serious about remarriage until he met Anne Lavoisier, who seemed "made to order," and joked, in his mid–40s, about asking Lady Palmerson to find him a wife since there was a vogue for young women to like older men like him. At an age when he might have been expected to find peaceful companionship with a woman, as a widower, he had nothing but rows and was incapable of self-control or of resolving things himself.

He was idealistic in his social ideals and in private he was pragmatic. His longest sustained sexual relationship was with his housekeeper Victoire. Notably, the lifestyle he chose when in his mid–50s showed he had only appeared to be absorbed into the ruling elite. Perhaps had the count lived he would have married Victoire, but he died when their son, Charles, was but 10 months old. As mentioned, the count died without Sally's being present. He had encouraged her to take a trip to Switzerland for possibly as long as a year while his mistress was carrying and bearing his child. Whether this was more his idea or Sally's it was within convention of the day for dealing with such a situation. There is irony in the fact that the count found his happy garden and a compatible mistress in Auteuil, and, characteristically, did not force the matter on his daughter, instead sending her away on an errand when Victoire was due.

The criticism that can aptly be applied to Thompson for his relations with women is that he calculated. Even when he told Lady Palmerston he was falling in love with her (by letter) he made it clear this was a perversion of the friendship he cherished. When Thomas Jefferson saw Maria Cosway and her husband a final time before they returned to England in October 1786 and he to Paris, he wrote a dialogue of heart and mind in a letter to her. The same admonishments Jefferson levied at himself seemed to come naturally to Thompson:

Auteuil 5 June 1809

Dear General,

The mode of preventing cast-iron Pots employed in Cookery from rusting and communicating to the food cooked in them a disagreeable taste of iron is to first to wash them well and dry them and even heat them pretty hot over a fire of live coals, and while they are still hot to put into them a quantity of grease of any kind into which, when the grease is boiling hot a quantity of green herbs as spinnage for instance, or what would be still better sorrel. After these green herbs have boiled for half an hour in the boiling grease, the inside of the pot is to be well rubbed with them, and with the liquor in the pot, by means of a small mop, and even the outside of the pot may be rubbed over in the same manner.

The cast iron which was before of a brown colour becomes of a deep shining black, and it will be found to be much less liable to rust than cast iron which has not undergone this operation.

The heat of the boiling grease being much greater than the heat of boiling water all the moisture in the pores of the rough surface of the iron is forceably expelled under the form of steam and the grease taking its place is not afterwards easily dislodged even by boiling water; and to this we may add that it is very probable that the acid of the vegetable united to the hot grease may form with the iron an oxide at its surface not soluble in water, which if the conjecture should be well founded the single fact would alone be sufficient to account for all the appearances and fully establish the utility of the process.

A most effectual method of preventing iron Guns from rusting on the inside surface that is to say in the bore of the Piece, is to grease them well with hogs fat or butter quite free from salt and keep them well closed at the muzzle by a fit tompion air-tight and at the touch hole by a plug likewise air-tight. The outside of the Gun may be preserved from rust either by being painted, or being now and then well rubbed over with oil of any kind or grease.

I think it very probable that the method practiced in this country for preventing the rusting of iron pots might be advantageously used for preventing the rusting of Iron Artillery which by the bye I am persuaded is preferable on many accounts to Brass Guns which cost four or five times as much as Iron Guns of the same calibre internally and of the same length strength and weight.

This opinion, which is the result of a great number of very decisive experiments, was announced to the Public near ten years ago in the first Vol. of my Philosophical Papers.

You will pardon me for sending you an open letter, for the fact is that I have not at hand either sealing-wax or wafers, being not yet established in my new habitation tho' I am here almost every day from morning till night.

Accept the assurance of my perfect esteem and very sincere attachment.

Rumford.

His Excellency
General Armstrong
&c. &c. &c.

Letter Rumford to General Armstrong, June 5, 1809 (George E. Ellis papers, Massachusetts Historical Society).

Everything in this world is a matter of calculation. Advance then with caution, the balance in your hand. Put into one scale the pleasures which any object may offer; but put fairly into the other the pains which are to follow, & see which preponderates. The making an acquaintance is not a matter of indifference. When a new one is proposed to you, view it all round. Consider what advantages it presents, & to what inconveniences it may expose you. Do not bite at the bait of pleasure till you know there is no hook beneath it. The art of life is the art of avoiding pain: & he is the best pilot who steers clearest of the rocks & shoals with which he is beset. Pleasure is always before us; but misfortune is at our side: while running after that, this arrests us. The most effectual means of being secure against pain is to retire within ourselves, & to suffice for our own happiness. Those, which depend on ourselves, are the only pleasures a wise man will count on: for nothing is ours which another may deprive us of. Hence the inestimable value of intellectual pleasures.[5]

Afterword: Experiments and Inventions

> As their highnesses traveled, they were almost making discoveries, by accident and sagacity, of things which they were not in quest of.
> —Horace Walpole, letter to Horace Mann, January 28, 1754

Columnist and author Pagan Kennedy writes in *Inventology: How We Dream Up Things That Change the World* of the ways in which inventors' creations are expressions of themselves. Benjamin Thompson liked warmth, pleasant lighting, efficiency, comfort, speed, simple food, and color and wished for peace and to improve social conditions. Consequently, he applied his studies in physics to the practical, often homely realm.

At the beginning of the 19th century people dubbed his style of fireplace and his device of the first convection oven "Rumford," literally making him a household name. But he was the silent inventor of all kinds of things, most of them having a link to heat and light. They include the thermos bottle, insulated clothing, the wider tire, the double boiler, the drip coffee pot, a smoke-free fireplace, the convection oven, central heating, and the double-glazed window. He has some claim to discovering the fundamentals of photography through his investigation of the chemical effects produced by light, such as the deposition of metallic gold and silver film on a ribbon or slip of ivory that had been dipped in a solution of salts. He studied the theory of color and discovered blue shadows. He improved signal systems for ships and proposed an advance in the balance of a ship armed with cannon. His oil lamps were safer and not as messy as the Argand lamps, and they served as desk lamps or over a big table to great improvement. By diplomatic ingenuity he saved Munich from being devastated by the armies of Napoleon and the Austrians. He turned the Prince of Bavaria's army into a useful civil service, created Munich's great park, the Englischer Garten, and while in Bavaria solved the problem of indigent and homeless people by giving them food, shelter and viable work first, as opposed to, say, religion.

But the image of Thompson in his spare time going around with a Midas touch is inaccurate. His inventions tended to result from experiments and reflection over a long period of time. He said that wondering why, when he was a child, apple pie stayed so hot stimulated his study of heat and convection. Each cannon was different in the 18th century and there were many gunner's myths, such as how cannons operated better in wet weather. At Lord Germain's country estate, Thompson and some of his military friends were discussing a notion that putting moisture in gunpowder increased the cannon's firepower (by adding the expansion of steam to the explosion). To check this out, Thompson, over nine days, conducted 123 experiments in Germain's coach house and concluded that dry powder was better. His published paper on his gunpowder experiments led to his membership in the Royal Society.

Described in this chapter are some of the experiments and inventions Thompson undertook. According to "Scientific Drawings of Count Rumford at Harvard," published by Houghton Library, he wrote 30 papers on heat, six on light, seven on the formation and operation of scientific and charitable institutions, and seven on other inventions. His collected 64 scientific papers were edited by Sanborn C. Brown and published in Cambridge, Massachusetts, by Harvard University Press. Most of his papers were written before 1800 but he read 20 papers before the French Institute in Paris or the Royal Society in London during the time he was in Paris before separating from Anne Lavoisier. Believing himself a benefactor of human progress, Thompson never patented an invention.

Fireworks, the Softer Side of Gunpowder

An undated entry in the keepsake book Thompson kept while an apprentice gives directions for various kinds of "rockets," with the proportions of powder, sulphur, saltpeter, and charcoal:

> When you have filled the Rocket within about two inches of the top, thrust down a piece of leather about the bigness of the hole of the Rocket, and punch it full of holes in the middle with a bodkin, then strew a little dust of powder ground fine, and fill the rest up with unground powder, and stop up the remaining part with leather or paper, and stop it up.

In the fashion of a keepsake book, the instructions for firework displays closes with a reflection whose relevance was known only to the writer: "Love is a Noble Passion of the Mind. LOVE."[1] Fooling around with gunpowder in 1769 Benjamin injured himself so badly he had to leave his apprenticeship in Salem and go home to Woburn.

Fireworks were much appreciated in early America and their dangers and misuse understood. In 1721, a penalty of 5 shillings was levied for setting off fireworks without a governor's special license; not paying up resulted in two days in jail. The colony of Rhode Island enacted laws forbidding fireworks altogether, with substantial fines against firing "any gun, pistol, rocket, squibs, or other fire-works, in any road, street, lane or tavern or other public house, after sunsetting and before sunrising." Benjamin was not disobeying the law in Massachusetts, where gunpowder laws imposed fines related only to firearms. It is known how thrilling fireworks were at this time. John Adams wrote Abigail from Philadelphia on July 3, 1776, before the signing of the Declaration of Independence, envisioning gleefully the day in the future being marked "with Pomp and Parade, with Shews, Games, Sports, Guns, Bells, Bonfires and Illuminations from one End of this Continent to the other from this Time forward forever more." The actual celebration in Philadelphia on July 4, 1777, closed with a spectacular exhibition that began and ended with 13 rockets going off on the commons, illuminating the city.

The making of sophisticated fireworks outside of China dated from around Benjamin's birth. A Jesuit priest conveyed formulas from China to the Paris Academy of Science, and his writings were translated to English in 1765. At the time Benjamin was crafting his fireworks he would have seen displays of fireworks and black ash as well as perhaps a range of pyrotechnics from China on sale from Salem merchants.

A Fight Against Poverty

The workhouses, described in Thompson's essay *An Account of an Establishment of the Poor in Munich* (1796), were a sweeping corollary of his reform of the Bavarian military. Soldiers were assigned to garrisons near where they came from and each soldier was allotted a plot of land and the wherewithal to cultivate a garden. The military force was subservient to the public good, so, working as paid laborers and with music playing, the soldiers were to maintain roads, drain marshes, and repair riverbanks.

Meanwhile, unarmed mounted police rounded up Bavaria's beggars, then estimated at 5 percent of the population in Munich. Over two thousand individuals were given nice shelter in a former monastery, food and schooling. Adults and children made clothing—performing tasks from carding wool to sewing on buttons—for the soldiers. A sign outside what was called the Workhouse read in gold letters on black, "No alms shall be received here." Most of the people stayed with the program, earned wages, and were integrated into society. The costs were lower than before to the government for the military force, and private donors gave to a socially affirmative program instead of just handing out money. Meanwhile, the soldiers, now stationed permanently in garrisons instead of being moved around, were farming their newly assigned garden plots with free seeds, planting unfamiliar vegetables—turnips and potatoes—that became very popular, and learning crop rotation and the use of clover as fodder. Unlike the Englischer Garten, though, the Workhouse was abandoned, in 1800.

Rumford Soup

Wholesome fare at low cost was Thompson's goal for public nutrition. To achieve this, he created the dish that became known in Europe as Rumford soup, its major ingredients pearl barley and dried yellow peas. Minor ingredients were vegetables, salt, sour beer, and, later, potatoes. Because he invented it for the poor (around 1790), Thompson has been credited with originating the first modern soup kitchen.

One portion was the measure of a Bavarian pound, or about 22 ounces, which was served with a ration of seven ounces of rye bread. A 20th century analysis showed that the soup's caloric count would have been 960. Thompson also suggested adding minced red herring and grated cheese when possible. At the hour of dinner a large bell was rung in the court of the first workhouse, in Munich, and those at work in the different parts of the building repaired to the dining hall, "where they found a wholesome and nourishing repast." This consisted of "a very rich soup of peas and barley, mixed with cuttings of bread; and a piece of excellent rye bread, weighing seven ounces, which last they commonly put in their pockets, and carried home for their supper."

Potatoes were not an accepted food in 1790 Bavaria, so Thompson had them boiled behind a screen, out of sight of the workers, until the potatoes had disintegrated enough to be unrecognizable. Potatoes, like other members of the nightshade family, Solanum genus, were considered inedible prior to the 19th century, given that some varieties were so toxic. They also were a reminder of the grim "Potato War" (1778–1779) and starvation in Bohemia. Austria and Prussia desisted from hostilities only when they had eaten all of Bohemia's potatoes.

In making Rumford soup, water and peeled barley are put together in a saucepan and brought to a boil. Peas are then added, and the boiling continued for two hours. Then raw, peeled potatoes are added and boiling continues for another hour while the contents of the saucepan are stirred frequently with a large wooden spoon. Slow, long cooking makes the recipe palatable and thickens the barley. Finally, some vinegar, salt, and, immediately before serving, pieces of fine wheat bread are added. Alternately, the soup is poured atop the bread prior to serving.

The soup had a high protein content from the dried peas, starch from the barley and the potato, and simple carbohydrates for energy from the beer. Thompson viewed meat as an added ingredient not contributing very much. His essay "Of Food" also drew attention to his preferred healthful grain of Indian corn, and he gave a recipe for it in pudding. Saying, "I own I am old-fashioned," he had an officer lead the inmates at the Munich workhouse in a short grace.

Rumford Soup is a traditional offering at Oktoberfest in Munich still today.

The Englischer Garten

Thompson created, in northeastern Munich, one of the most extensive and beautiful urban parks in the world. This was not the formal garden of a chateau but an idealized landscape where the populace could mix. He convinced the Duke of Bavaria that this would endear his sovereignty to the people of Munich and thus be worth the sacrifice of the royal hunting ground. Friedrich Ludwig von Sckell, a peerless landscape gardener of royal gardens and scenic parks, collaborated with him and had charge of the Englischer Garten after Thompson moved to France. Wrote Ellis in the *Memoir*:

> Sir Benjamin conceived the project of converting this region, with the permission of the Elector, into pleasure-grounds, a park, and fields for making improving experiments in agriculture. He surrounded it with a road or drive of a circuit of six miles, on which, at proper intervals, were erected cottages and farm-houses for laborers employed on the grounds. Walks, promenades, grottos, a race-course, and other attractions, diversified the extensive stretch of territory. With the earth scooped out in preparing a small lake, he built up an elevated mound. A refreshment saloon, handsomely furnished, and a Chinese pagoda, were among the conveniences and adornments; and Sir Benjamin exercised all his ingenuity in perfecting the details of his plan so as to render the Garden attractive as a place of resort to the higher classes, and a place of carefully guarded amusement to the common people.[2]

The order was that Thompson work on the Englischer Garten before he initiated building gardens for vegetables by the soldiers in Munich and other German cities. He looked to China as the model for an economy having farming as the highest value and paid Asia tribute by several imitations of Chinese buildings in the park, including a bridge and the beloved Chinese Tur. The exoticism was also a pleasing touch. The Grand Pagoda in the Royal Botanic Gardens at Kew dated from a quarter-century before (1762). The Munich pagoda is half as tall but has much charm.

The Rumford Fireplace

I can't have been the only person, when my husband and I bought a house dating from the early 19th century, to be disappointed by a fireplace. It was narrow and shallow. How could anybody have hung a cast-iron kettle in it? My favorite features of the Chambord chateau were the over two hundred walk-in–type fireplaces, but in our house somebody had apparently skimped. But we saw the virtues of our peculiarly designed fireplace when we had perfect fires in it. Thompson wrote two essays, in 1796 and 1798, that conveyed his improvements to fireplaces based on his knowledge of heat. His fireplace was smaller and shallower, with widely angled sides so they would radiate more heat. He streamlined the throat of the chimney, which drafted better than those of existing fireplaces, and also invented the damper. All these changes could be retrofitted. For almost a year before the Prince of Bavaria called him back to his military post, Thompson lectured about his improvements and created a stir. The following ditty appeared in the London press in 1796:

> Lo, every parlor drawing room, I see,
> Boasts of thy stoves and talks of not but thee,
> Yet, not alone my lady and young misses,
> The cooks themselves could smother thee with kisses.
> Yes, mistress cook would spoil a goose, a steak,
> To twine her greasy arms around thy neck.[3]

His mission was to reduce the dark cloud of smoke over London as well as provide more efficient and cleaner heat in the room. Rumford fireplaces were built from the late 1790s until cast-iron stoves came into use.

Kitchen Ranges and Roasters

Thompson invented the kitchen range to streamline cooking "and consequently to put the cook in good humour, which is certainly a matter of serious importance." By the time he published *On the Construction of Kitchen Fire-places and Kitchen Utensils* (1799–1800), he had installed kitchen ranges in institutions, such as two hospitals in Verona, and in private residences. This is from his *Description of a Kitchen in the House of Baron de Lerchenfeld at Munich*, which was the house of the parents of the Countesses Baumgarten and Nogarola.

> The mass of brickwork in which the boilers and saucepans are set projects out into the room, and the smoke is carried off by flues that are concealed in this mass of brick-work, and in the thick walls of an open chimney fire-place, which, standing on in, on the farther side of it, where it joins to the side of the room is built up perpendicularly to the ceiling of the room. At the height of about twelve or fifteen inches above the level of the mantel of his open chimney fire-place, the separate canals for the smoke concealed in its walls and in the larger canal of this fire-place, which last-mentioned larger canal, sloping backward, ends in a neighbouring chimney which carries off the smoke through the roof of a house into the atmosphere.

His companion invention, the Rumford Roaster, was a round iron pot with a door, built inside a masonry oven. Flues conveyed hot air around the food in the oven so that several dishes could be cooked at once and the cook was spared the hot flames. He invented it around 1800. A description of his invention was published in America in about 1804; within a few years it was popular in both England and New England. There were not so many of Thompson's designs for "roasters" as for the fireplaces because the masonry stove had to be built into the original kitchen, unlike the fireplaces, which were retrofitted. Then, in the mid-19th century, cast-iron stoves came into vogue.

The first person to have a Rumford Roaster in Salem was the minister who succeeded

Dr. Barnard, who had taught Thompson mathematics and astronomy when he was an apprentice with John Appleton. The Rundlet-May House in Portsmouth, New Hampshire, has a fine example. James Rundlet became wealthy importing textiles and after the War of 1812 he began manufacturing textiles (President Madison honored him with a visit and admired his woolens). Between 1806 and 1808, Rundlet built his house with the latest conveniences, including forced-air heat and three sources of water; the house and grounds were virtually self-sufficient for his large family. Rundlet was one of the first Americans to use Count Rumford's roaster. Descendants of James Rundlet lived in this beautiful home until 1971. At some point the family stopped using the roaster, presumably mid–19th century when cast-iron stoves came into vogue.

It can be seen that the roaster was the latest thing from the fact that the Federalist mansion Gore Place in Waltham, Massachusetts (now a historic landmark), had one. Christopher Gore was Thompson's contemporary, a prominent Massachusetts businessman who was governor in 1809 and 1810. Recorded in Christopher Gore's account book is that on May 22, 1806, he paid for setting the Rumford kitchen and for copper for a bath laundry. In the ledger of Tomas Barnes it is recorded that in January 1818 Gore paid for "repairing Rumford Roaster." So it is known that Christopher and Rebecca Gore had a Rumford kitchen, although it does not survive.

Industrial Furnaces

By the logic of separating the burning fuel from limestone, Thompson improved the design of kilns used to produce quicklime; the furnace produced lime not adulterated by the ash from the fire. His innovation was to separate the combustion changes for limestone and fuel, connecting them by a transverse channel that carried the hot air. Previously the wood or charcoal fuel was mixed with the limestone; the process was discontinuous and the product had to be cleaned. Rumford's furnace worked by a continuous operation in which the limestone was preheated by the jacket of heat from the fuel flowing upward and the ash waste fell to the bottom and could be removed. One of the original Rumford furnaces is still found in the Museumpark Rudersdort, near Berlin.

Thermal Clothing

Clothing was of great interest to Thompson. When leaving American shores, he wrote a Boston minister and asked him to take care of a scarlet coat he owned but had left behind. When in the employ of Lord Germain Thompson rose to have charge of the supply of clothing to the British forces in America. He wore white clothes and hat in Paris in his fifties because he thought them warmer (a mistake). But his study of the insulating properties of materials such as fur, wool, and feathers came when he had charge of modernizing and reorganizing the Bavarian army. He saw clothing the army as its greatest expense and turned his attention to the physics of insulation so more practical protective clothing could be designed for the soldiers. To do this he invented a new type of thermometer, which he called the cylindrical passage thermometer because a liquid surrounded the bulb. He used this to find out that the insulating properties of cloth came from air trapped in its interstices. Physicist Sir John Meurig Thomas explained that in the process of using his cylindrical passage thermometer Thompson discovered convection currents and this resulted in the invention of thermal clothing. From experiments on the relative thermal conductivity of various fabrics he concluded that trapped air was the best form of heat insulation and that materials insulated the convection of air. Thus he advocated cotton uniforms for summer and wool for winter. They were rather pared down, e.g., no tails on the coats, which brought some complaints, as such uniform modifications had during the Seven Years' War when he was a small boy and his maternal grandfather was in the Anglo-American forces.

Shadow Photometer

Wishing to discover an inexpensive method of lighting, Thompson developed a photometer that could compute and compare the intensity of lamps and candles. The instrument had two rods placed a few inches from a screen. A separate light source illuminated each rode separately and directly. A pulley device adjusted the distance of the light sources without the observer's having to break his attention. Each rod had a wing, and the observer made the two shadows touch by rotating the rods. Besides measuring the intensity of light, Thompson used the instrument to make rather accurate measurements of the reflective power and transparency of glass. After he could scientifically compare light sources, he built an improved version of the widely used Argand lamp with linseed oil.

Differential Thermometer

A Scot in Edinburgh, John Leslie (1766–1832), and Thompson began to use this type of device at about the same time and are both credited as its inventors. It has two thin spherical bulbs connected by a U-shaped tube. The closed system is filled with dry air, and the two segments are separated by a slug of mercury in the horizontal part of the tubing. In use, the two bulbs are placed the same distance from two sources giving off radiant energy at different rates. The thermometer gives a differential reading.

Illuminators

To make the rooms in the poorhouses of Munich and Mannheim bright and airy, for the cheer and to better see the clothes as they were being made, Thompson began experimenting with illumination. As a first step, he invented a photometer to measure the intensity of light various fuels—whale oil, tallow, vegetable oils, and beeswax—emitted. Concluding that the purest light and most beautiful illumination was from lamps, he then constructed over a hundred versions. He was interested in the most pleasant diffusion of light, for which a screen on an oil lamp created the best effect, using a substance like ground glass or thin silk or paper (referring to the Chinese lamps). This obviated shadows and did not lessen the light.

He also improved on the mechanism of the Argand lamps, patented in 1780 by Aimé Argand, which dazzled Benjamin Franklin. The Argand lamp operated on the principle of a hollow cylinder within a circular wick. It was revolutionary in its brightness but it spattered and dripped and the oil reservoir had some trouble rising inside the wick.

In 1800, the same year B.G. Carcel patented a new lamp with a pump for the oil and the oil reservoir under the burners, Thompson was putting the oil reservoir under the burners. In 1800, he lit large rooms of the Royal Institution in London with Argand lamps suspended from ceilings or elevated on stands and covered with flat domes or truncated cones of white gauze. He began to develop fixtures like the Argand, but using just one burner with several wicks. He wrote of lighting the large dining room in Madame Lavoisier's house in about 1806 by "a single luminous dome ... and, in order to prevent cross-lights, I ventured to place a cluster of burners, on Argand's principles, in the axis of the dome, and so near together as to touch each other, and to feed them with oil from a circular reservoir, in the form of a hollow flat ring, on which the dome was supported.... All the dishes and plates on the table were illuminated by the direct rays from the burners, but the eyes of those who were seated round the table were defended from those direct rays by the hoop of gauze."

His big light fixtures for ballrooms and billiard rooms had multiple burners and cut-glass globes. All had a circular, horizontal reservoir for the oil, and clustered burners at the center.

The Drip Coffee Pot

The essay *Of the Excellent Qualities of Coffee and the Art of Making It in the Highest Perfection* (1812) proposes to make coffee drinkers of the bibulous. It offers three styles of coffee pots—for the rich, the middle class, and the poor person, the latter of whom would make but a cup:

> The pot sits snuggly on a lamp flame or portable heater (another invention). Water is boiled in a reservoir inside the jacket. From it a quantity of the boiling water is removed by a cock at the lower side and used to pour into the cylinder, which is filled with ground coffee and has, suspended by a brim, a strainer at the bottom through which the liquid passes. A rammer weighs down the coffee to further prevent air entering. There are three strainers that fit inside the pot, largest to smallest, for making six, four or two teacups of coffee. All three can be employed to make 12 cups.

A larger, urn-shaped version used in Paris was of gilded tin or ornamented silver.

The "public advantages" derived from coffee, pointed out after the design description, include a "pleasing flow of spirits ... accompanied by a consciousness of ease, contentment and good-will to all men, which is very different from that wild joy and unbridled licentiousness which accompanies intoxication. A simple breakfast of coffee with milk or cream accompanied by unbuttered bread is recommended."

Wide Wheels for Carriages and Coaches

Freight wagons rolled well with larger wheels. Thompson found that broadening the tires of pleasure coaches increased comfort of the ride and reduced the amount of force required of the horses to draw them. He rode in Paris on his new wheels, which were twice as broad as ordinary coach wheels. They slid less from side to side, wore more evenly because they didn't tumble into the spaces between the pavement stones, and the holes pierced to attach the tires to the wheels didn't weaken them as much as with ordinary wheels. To test his theory he studied the relation of the force required to the increase of speed. His apparatus had a needle that measured the amount of force used by the horses.

A foreign inventor had to be patient for the resistance to his invention to die down, and meanwhile weather machinations or derision. Another foreign scientist, Giuseppangelo Fonzi, makes a just comparison. An itinerant dentist born in Abruzzo, Italy, Fonzi came to Paris to refine his knowledge. After much experimentation, he published in 1808 his discovery of durable false teeth custom fit to a person's jaw. These were clearly superior to anything that had come before. At first he was praised but soon his enemies set out to discredit him, beginning with potshots at his French. Fonzi became best friends with former U.S. vice president Aaron Burr and artist John Vanderlyn. Burr was a lucky patient whose false teeth Fonzi carefully constructed. Fonzi offered to give every dentist his type of "terro-metallic" prostheses to try them out for themselves.[4]

This was like Thompson's parking his broad-wheel carriage in front of the French Institute and inviting the academicians to take a ride. This was a very nationalistic period in France and the way the count and Fonzi sought to have their inventions given a fair review was to disassociate somewhat personally from them.

An anecdote about Antoine Lavoisier suggests how entrenched in theory the brilliant scientific circle of Paris could be at the end of the ancien régime and during the First Empire. On Tuesday, September 13, 1768, villagers in Lucé near Chartres saw a rock fall from the sky after a thunderstorm. The rock was sent to Paris for chemical analysis and Lavoisier reported to the Academy of Science that it was no thunderstone but merely iron-pyrite–rich sandstone from earth which had been hit by lightening. "Stones can't fall from the sky," he told his fellow academicians; therefore the witnesses were mistaken or lying. Not until 1803 did the academy accept the reality of meteorites. Coincidentally, one of Thompson's last papers demonstrated that meteorites came from beyond the Earth's atmosphere.

American-born Thompson was polite but not a bona fide member of polite society by birth, education or marriage. Yet, even if cliquey, the French scientists were patently famous for good reason. Thus Joseph-Louis Lagrange, the Italo-French mathematician who had an enduring friendship with Thompson, said of Lavoisier, "It only took them a moment to drop that head, and a hundred years may not perhaps suffice to replicate another like it."

Et cetera

Benjamin Thompson Count Rumford was perhaps the first to insulate windows with double-glazed panes. He also invented the folding bed. Other experiments include building an electrostatic machine, an electrometer, and a Leyden jar for storing static electricity. But, as he may have almost electrocuted himself if he were involved (as he likely was) in repeating Franklin's kite experiment with his friend Loammi Baldwin, he ventured into electricity as a sideline and carefully. Thompson was an early person to use baking soda but in 1859 a former Rumford Professor at Harvard, Eben Norton Horsford, patented its formulation.

Chapter Notes

Preface

1. Anne O'Hare McCormick, "At 60 He Is Still a Happy Warrior," *New York Times Magazine*, Jan. 26, 1942, 3.
2. George E. Ellis, *Memoir of Sir Benjamin Thompson, Count Rumford: with Notices of His Daughter* (Boston: American Academy of Arts & Sciences, 1871), 217.
3. Harriet Monroe and Alice Corbin Henderson, eds., *The New Poetry: An Anthology* (New York: Macmillan, 1917); Bartleby.com, 2002, www.bartleby.com/265/.
4. Ibid.

Chapter 1

1. Ellis, 13.
2. David Freeman Hawke, *Everyday Life in Early America* (New York: Harper & Row, 1988), 45.
3. John Ayrton Paris, *The Life of Sir Humphry Davy*, vol. 1 (1831; New York: Cambridge University Press, 2011), 11.
4. M.A. Pictet, *Bibliothèque Britannique Sciences et Arts* 19 (August 15, 1801) in Sanborn C. Brown, *Benjamin Thompson, Count Rumford* (Cambridge: MIT Press, 1979). 2. Marc-Auguste Pictet was a scientist just a year older than Thompson who became his personal friend after 1800 and recorded conversations with him.
5. Baron Cuvier, *Récueil des Eloges Historiques lus dans les Séances Publiques de l'Institut de France*, vol. 2 (Paris: Firmin Didot), 26ff.
6. Francis M. Abbott, "Count Rumford and His Daughter," *New England Magazine: An Illustrated Monthly*, Sept. 1893–Feb. 1984, 464.
7. Roy Porter, *English Society in the 18th Century* (New York: Penguin, 1991), 38.
8. *Essex Gazette* [Salem, MA], Dec. 20–27, 1768, n. pag.
9. Lyman C. Newell, "Count Rumford: Scientist and Philanthropist," *Science* 68, no. 1752 (July 27, 1928), 67.
10. Edwin E. Slosson, "Benjamin Thompson," *Leading American Men of Science*, ed. David Starr Jordan (New York: Henry Holt, 1910), 9.
11. Benjamin Thompson [BT] to Loammi Baldwin [LB], Aug. 15, 1769 in Ellis, 24–25.
12. *Essex Gazette*, May 9–16, 1769.
13. George E. Street, *Mount Desert: A History* (Boston: Houghton Mifflin, 1905), 124.
14. Egon Larson, *An American in Europe: The Life of Benjamin Thompson, Count Rumford* (New York: Philosophical Society, 1953), 19–20.
15. Memorandum Book of Benjamin Thompson, Oct. 14, 1766, Massachusetts Historical Society (hereafter MHS).
16. Ellis, 23.
17. Hopestill Capen to John Appleton, Oct. 11, 1769, George E. Ellis Papers, MHS.
18. Samuel Adams Drake, *Historic Fields and Mansions of Middlesex* (Boston: James R. Osgood, 1874), typescript, 3, Woburn (MA) Public Library.
19. Stacy Schiff, *A Great Improvisation: Franklin, France, and the Birth of America* (New York: Henry Holt, 2005), 8.
20. John C. Hamilton, ed., *The Works of Alexander Hamilton, Micellanies, 1774–1789*, vol. 2, "A Full Vindication." (Nabu Press, 2010), 46.
21. Hawke, 156.
22. Ellis, 34.
23. David McCullough, *John Adams* (New York: Simon & Schuster, 2001), 35.
24. Frederick E. Brasch, "John Winthrop (1714–1779), American's First Astronomer, and the Science of His Period," 28, no. 165 (Aug.–Oct. 1916), 157.

Chapter 2

1. Ellis, 35.
2. Sherri Morrill, whose family owns 278 North Man and has a farm on adjoining lands. The foundation of the stockade is still visible.
3. Diaries of Rev. Timothy Walker, 1922–1923, 46336, New Hampshire Historical Society, Concord, New Hampshire (hereafter NHHS).
4. Count Rumford notebook, 1769–1772, Rumford Papers, Burgum Collection, NHHS.
5. Ellis, 45.
6. Ellis, 8.
7. A solid interpretation by one biographer is that by the remark Thompson was "implying that the enthusiasm was not on his side. This may well be partly true; his motives were probably mixed and not clear even to himself." W.J. Sparrow, *Knight of the White Eagle, Sir Benjamin Thompson, Count Rumford of Woburn, Mass.* (New York: Thomas Y. Crowell, 1964), 23.
8. BT to Rev. Timothy Walker, Jan. 11, 1775, Rumford Papers, Folder 2, 1974–1947, NHHS.

9. Calendar of Home Office, Papers of the Reign of George III, 1899, 1020 in Sparrow, 261.
10. BT to John Wentworth, Dec. 13, 1774, Clements Library, University of Michigan, Ann Arbor.
11. BT to Rev. Timothy Walker, Dec. 24, 1774, Rumford Papers, 1974, 47, Folder 2, NHHS.
12. Nathaniel Bouton, *The History of Concord: from its first grant in 1725, to the organization of the city government in 1853, with a history of the ancient Penacooks* (Concord, NH: B.W. Sanborn, 1856), 272–273.
13. Thomas Hutchinson to Chief Justice Oliver, *The Diaries and Letters of His Excellency Thomas Hutchinson, Esq.*, ed. Peter Orlando Hutchinson (Boston: Houghton, Mifflin, 1884) 450.
14. Miscellaneous Observations upon the State of the Rebel Army, Benjamin Thompson, Nov. 4, 1775, Clements Library, University of Michigan, Ann Arbor.
15. BT to Rev. Timothy Walker, Aug. 14, 1775, in Ellis, 88.
16. BT to Samuel Williams, Oct. 7, 1775, in Brown, 44.
17. John A. Nagy, *Invisible Ink: Spycraft of the American Revolution* (Yardley, PA: Westholme Publishing, 2009), 298–299.
18. Note in cipher, Nov. 1, 6, 7, 1771, Rumford Collection, NHHS.
19. BT to Rev. Timothy Walker, Aug. 14, 1775.
20. George Baldwin to George Ellis, Feb. 2, 1870, George E. Ellis Papers, MHS.

Chapter 3

1. Henry Wadsworth Longfellow, *Tales of a Wayside Inn* (1891; Boston: Houghton Mifflin, 1906), 170.
2. Substantiation of the affairs comes from the diary of Lieutenant William Dyott, unofficial aide to the prince while in Halifax in 1787. Philip Young examined the evidence in his *Revolutionary Ladies* (New York: Alfred A. Knopf, 1977), 94–141 passim.
3. Brian Cuthbertson, *The Loyalist Governor: Biography of Sir John Wentworth* (Halifax, N.S.: Petheric Press, 1983), 41.
4. Benjamin Thompson, "Address of Inhabitants of Concord to Governor J. N. O. Wentworth," 1773, in Nathaniel Bouton, *Two Sermons Preached 21st November 1830: In Commemoration of the Organizing. Nov. 18, 1730* (Concord: Asa McFarland, 1831).
5. N.H. Prov. Papers 7, 418,, in James O. Lyford, ed., *History of Concord, New Hampshire*, vol. 1, prepared under the supervision of the City History Commission (Concord, NH: City Government, Jan. 14, 1896), 253–254.
6. Kenneth Baumgardt. ResearchGate. https://www.researchgate.net/publication/235165803_The_Royal_Army_in_America_During_the_Revolutionary_War_The_American_Prisoner_Records.
7. John Wentworth to Tristan Dalton, July 31, 1775, in Cuthbertson, 4.
8. Maya Jasanoff, *Liberty's Exiles: American Loyalists in the Revolutionary World* (New York: Knopf, 2011), 353.
9. Cuthbertson, 37.
10. Rumford Papers, 1974–1947, NHHS.
11. Paul Wilderson, *Governor John Wentworth and the American Revolution: The English Connection* (Lebanon, NH: University Press of New England, 1994), 273.

Chapter 4

1. As there are many names that are similar in this chapter I will call individuals first, last or both names to keep the narrative clear.
2. Quoted in Sir George Otto Trevelyan, *The American Revolution, Part 1, 1766–1776*, 2d ed. (New York: Longmans, Green, 1899), 121.
3. Mary A. Favret, *War at a Distance: Romanticism and the Making of Modern Wartime* (Princeton: Princeton University Press, 2010), 63.
4. Christopher Anstey, *The Poetical Works* (London: T. Cadell, 1808), English Poetry Database, http://gateway.proquest.com.
5. Clifford K. Shipton, *Isaiah Thomas: Printer, Patriot and Philanthropist, 1749–1831* (Rochester: Leo Hart, 1948), 19.
6. GC3/Series 1710X, Governor's Council, Divorce Files, 1774–1788. Case of Isaiah Thomas and Mary Thomas, 1777. Courtesy Commonwealth of Massachusetts, Archives Division, Boston.
7. Brown, 321n8. Sanborn Brown gave compelling circumstantial evidence for Major Thompson's being Benjamin Thompson, then of Concord, NH.
8. Tony Horwitz, "The True Story of the Battle of Bunker Hill," *Smithsonian Magazine* (May 2013), http://www.smithsonianmag.com/history/the-true-story-of-the-battle-of-bunker-hill-36721984.
9. Shipton, 28.
10. Amanda Vicery, *Behind Closed Doors: At Home in Georgian England* (New Haven: Yale University Press, 2009), 41.
11. BT to Sam Parker, March 1776, in A. French, *General Gage's Informers* (Ann Arbor: University of Michigan Press, 1951), 129.
12. Shipton, 39.
13. Shipton, 76.

Chapter 5

1. W. Howe to BT, March 10, 1775, Clements Library, University of Michigan, Ann Arbor.
2. Brown, 50–51.
3. Paul David Nelson, *General Sir Guy Carlton, Lord Dorchester: Soldier-Statesman of Early British Canada* (London: Associated University Presses, 2000), 22–23.
4. Brown, 51.
5. *The Diaries and Letters of His Excellency Thomas Hutchinson*, vol. 2, 289, entry of Oct. 18, 1779 (New York: Franklin, 1971), 289.
6. Alan Valentine, *Lord George Germain* (New York: Oxford University Press, 1962), 472.
7. George Atkinson Ward, *The Journal and Letters of Samuel Curwen* (New York: C.S. Francis, 1842), 316.
8. Francis Bickley, ed., *The Diaries of Sylvester Douglas (Lord Glenbervie)* (London: Constable, 1928), entry for Sept. 6, 1801, in Brown, 51.
9. Sparrow, 64.
10. Sparrow, 44.
11. Diaries of John Jeffries in his papers. Related to April 2, 1779, through departure for New York early July. Houghton Library, Harvard University, Cambridge,. All Jeffries quotes are from these diaries.
12. Hutchinson, vol. 2, 337–338.
13. Ward, Letters of Curwen, 316.
14. Brown, 64.
15. Brown, 54.

16. *The Collected Works of Count Rumford: Devices and Techniques III*, ed. Sanborn C. Brown (Cambridge: Belknap Press of Harvard University Press, 1968), 442.

17. Brown, 71.

18. Richard Holmes, *The Age of Wonder* (New York: Random House, 2008), 152.

19. The letter is at Amherst College.

20. BT to George Germain, Jan. 12, 1782, Clements Library, University of Michigan, Ann Arbor.

21. Edward McCrady, *The History of South Carolina in the Revolution, 1780-1783* (New York: Russell & Russell, 1897), 600-601.

22. *Ibid.*

23. BT to George Germain, Aug. 6, 1782, Clements Library, University of Michigan, Ann Arbor.

24. "Old Burying Ground (17th Century) & Fort Golgotha (1782)," https://www.huntingtonny.gov/filestorage/13747/13817/16499/Old_Burying_Ground_%26_Fort_Golgotha.pdf.

25. Brown, 89.

26. BT to Guy Carlton, March 14, 1783, in Brown, 90-91.

27. BT to Daniel Murray, Sept. 10, 1783, in Brown, 93.

28. Brown, 307.

Chapter 6

1. He would remain for 30 years.

2. Charles Francis Adams, Sr., to George Ellis, Dec. 24, 1869, George E. Ellis Papers, MHS.

3. John Meurig Thomas, "Sir Benjamin Thompson, Count Rumford and the Royal Institution," *Notes and Records of the Royal Society of London* 53, no. 1 (1999), 11.

4. *The Autobiography and Correspondence of Edward Gibbon, the Historian* (London: Alexander Murray & Sons, 1869, rpt. Nabu Press, 2013), 301.

5. Sparrow, 75.

6. "Wenzel Anton Kaunitz," *Encyclopedia Britannica*, 9th ed.

7. Cecil Hartley, *British Genius Exemplified in the Lives of Men: Who by Their Industry or by Scientific Inventions...* (London: E. Wilson, 1820), 183-184.

8. Ellis, 157.

9. *Ibid.*

10. Herbert J. Redman, *Frederick the Great and the Seven Years' War, 1756-1763* (Jefferson, NC: McFarland, 2014), 27.

11. Eric Nelson, *The Royalist Revolution: Monarchy and the American Founding* (Cambridge: Belknap Press, 2014), 25.

12. Chester Penn Higby, *Religious Policy of the Bavarian Government during the Napoleonic Period*, Studies in History, Economics and Public Law 85, no. 1 (New York: Columbia University; Longmans, Green, 1919); re. AMS 1967, 22.

13. Brown, 96.

14. Brown, 97.

15. E. Winslow to W. Chipman, April 26, 1784, in *The Winslow Papers*, ed. W.O. Raymond (St. John: New Brunswick Historical Society, 1901), 195.

16. Key to his approach as a social reformer was that "visible example" and practicum would improve the lot of the populace.

17. Stephen E. Ambrose, *Undaunted Courage: Meriwether Lewis, Thomas Jefferson, and the Opening of the American West* (New York: Simon & Schuster, 1996), 62.

Chapter 7

1. "A Meeting of Genius: Beethoven and Goethe, July 1812," Gramaphone. http://www.gramophone.co.uk/features/focus/a-meeting-of-genius-beethoven-and-goethe-july-1812.

2. Adam Kirsch, "Design for Living," *New Yorker*, Feb. 1, 2016, 69.

3. Harvey J. Kaye, *Thomas Paine: Firebrand of the Revolution* (New York: Oxford University Press, 2000), 56.

4. Brown, 297.

5. Robert Rothschild, *Two Brides for Apollo: The Life of Samuel Williams* (1743-1817; New York: iUniverse, 2009), 150.

6. Of these exchanges in 1786 and 1787, Thompson may have feared his letters would be opened in America as they were in Bavaria. Brown, 109.

7. Loammi Baldwin to BT, Dec. 1, 1788, Clements Library, University of Michigan.

8. J.C. Easton, "Charles Theodor of Bavaria and Count Rumford," *The Journal of Modern History* 12, no. 2 (June 1940), 146.

9. S.M. Toyne, "Dr. Struensee: Dictator of Denmark," *History Today* 1, no. 1 (Jan. 1951). http://www.gramophone.co.uk/features/focus/a-meeting-of-genius-beethoven-and-goethe-july-1812.

10. BT to R. Keith, April 13, 1785, in Brown, 102.

11. BT to George Germain, Aug. 16, 1785, Clements Library, University of Michigan, Ann Arbor, in Brown, 107.

12. Benjamin Thompson, *Essays Political, Economical, and Philosophical* 1 (1796; Memphis: General Books LCC, n.d.), 5.

13. BT, *Essays, Political Economical and Philosophical* 1 (London: J. Cadell and W. Davies, 1796; rpt. Ecco Print Editions, n.d.), 34.

14. Ellis, 233.

15. A scientist who did not share his open approach was James Watt. Thompson sent a Bavarian engineer to England to study the mechanism of the steam engine at the Birmingham factory of Watt and his business partner Matthew Boulton. When rebuffed, the engineer made secret sketches which he brought home. Thompson was in trouble over this for years. Brown, 136-137.

Chapter 8

1. In his *Letters of a Travelling Frenchman to his Brother in Paris* (1783), Kaspar Risebeck limned the Bavarian court as a "glittering swarm" eating, drinking, whoring, and gambling as the life style of the noblemen, and "many ladies of the court do not now any other way of occupying their time, apart from the bed, but to play with their parrots, their dogs or cats." Larson, 52-53.

2. Hinrich Sievekind, Fuseli to Menzel, *Drawings and Watercolors in the Age of Goethe from a German Private Collection, Munich* (New York: Prestel, 2000), 52.

3. Quoted in New Hampshire Statesman, Jan. 17, 1845, from Concord Herald March 21, 1792.

4. *Memoirs of a Lady* was begun in Paris circa 1842 and ended May 1845. Sally took the pen name "Serafina." It was unpublished and only exists in excerpts by George Ellis in his Rumford biography.

5. ST, Miscellaneous Note, June 25, 1852, NHHS.

6. BT to Lady Palmerston, Sept. 7, 1794, Rauner

Special Collections Library, Dartmouth College [hereafter Dartmouth].

7. BT to Lady Palmerston, June 4, 1795, Dartmouth.
8. BT to Countess Nogarola, Jan. 4, 1795, AAAS.
9. Countess Nogarola [Countess N], to Sally Thompson [ST], March 22, 1798, Rumford, Nogarola, Mary, Vingt-deux lettres de la comtesse de Nogarola à la comtesse de Rumford 1972–73.
10. Countess N to ST, April 15, 1798, NHHS.
11. Burgum Papers, NHHS.
12. BT to Lady P, Feb. 25, 1797, Rauner Library, Dartmouth.
13. Amadeus Mozart to Leopold Mozart, Nov. 13, 1780, in Wolfgang Hildesheimer, *Mozart*, trans. Marion Faber (New York: Macmillan, 1991), 134.
14. Daniel Heartz, *Haydn, Mozart, and the Viennese School, 1740–1780* (New York: W.W. Norton, 1995), 698.
15. Luisa Ricaldone, *A History of Women's Writing in Italy*, ed. Letizia Panizza and Sharon Wood, trans. Peter Brand (New York: Cambridge University Press, 2000), 102.
16. Ricaldone, 103.
17. Rodolphe Apponyi, archive.org, *Vingt-Cinque Ans à Paris (1826–1850)* (Paris: Plon-Nourrit et cie., 1913), https://archive.org/details/vingtcinqanspa01appouoft.

Chapter 9

1. Kirsch.
2. Andrew Cayton, *Love in the Time of Revolution* (Chapel Hill: University of North Carolina Press, 2013), 19.
3. Cassandra A. Good, *Founding Friendships: Friendships Between Men and Women in the Early American Republic* (New York: Oxford University Press, 2015), 7–9.
4. Lady Palmerston [Lady P] to Lord Palmerston [Lord P], June 23, 1792, in Brian Connell, *Portrait of a Whig Peer* (London: André Deutsch, 1957), 286.
5. Lady P to Benjamin Mee, June 28, 1792, in Connell, 287.
6. "Henry Temple, 2nd Viscount Palmerston (1735–1802), Politician and Traveller," *Oxford Dictionary of National Biography*.
7. Lord Palmerston's diary, October 10, 1782, in Connell, 138.
8. Connell, 287–288.
9. These were the good, wise and educated that Jefferson believed that the citizenry would elect.
10. Connell, 288.
11. For instance, Brown, 147, which states that in Florence in October 1793, the Count's attraction toward Mary Mee had "ripened into a full-fledged love affair."
12. Ivan Sergeevich Turgenev, *Faust: Novels of Ivan Turgenev* (New York: Macmillan, 1906), 12, 163.
13. MS 62 Broadlands Archives BR 13/7, Journal of Henry Temple, second Viscount Palmerston, describing excursions around the Rome area, including Pompeii, 18 Dec. 18, 1793–Feb. 21, 1794, Hartley Library, University of Southampton.
14. *The Journal of Elizabeth Lady Holland (1791–1811)*, ed. The Earl of Ilchester, vol.1 (New York: Longmans, Green and Co., 1908). Sanborn Brown made a point that Thompson tended to unrelieved disquisitions on his interests and was egotistical. However, Brown cited the subject of the count as "mortality" whereas Lady Webster used the word "morality," less a quirky topic of discussion but one that might make a woman peeves when she is thinking of leaving her spouse.
15. BT to Lady P, Nov. 29, 1793, Dartmouth.
16. BT to Charles Blagden, July 27, 1793, in Brown, 146.
17. BT to Lady P, Sept. 28, 1783, Dartmouth, in Brown, 146.
18. BT to Lady P, Nov. 29, 1793, Dartmouth.
19. Brown, 156.
20. Brown, 154.
21. Connell, 276.
22. Julia Peakman, *Emma Hamilton* (London: Haus Publishing, 2005), 69.
23. BT to Lady P, June 13, 1795, Dartmouth.
24. BT to Lady P, July 30, 1795, Dartmouth.
25. *Ibid.*

Chapter 10

1. Ellis, 495–496.
2. BT to Lady P, Sept. 7, 1794, Dartmouth.
3. BT to Lady P, June 4, 1795, Dartmouth.
4. Brown, 164.
5. BT to Lady P, Nov. 7, 1795, Dartmouth.
6. For instance, G.I. Brown, E. Slosson and S. Brown (see bibliography). An absurd coup de jarnac came from Stephen G. Brush, who wrote of Thompson, "he was the most unpleasant personality in the history of science since Isaac Newton" ("Marvelous Bedtime Reading for Physicists," *Physics Today*, Nov. 1979, 55). Yet the worst Sally conjured up about her father was that "he was fond of having his own way, even, as I fancied, to despite me" (Larson, 91), and that "when quiet and happy himself, he was like others, or, in other words, agreeable; but when perplexed with cares or business, or much occupied, there was no living with him" (Bence Jones, *The Royal Institution: Its Founder and Its First Professors* [London: Longmans, Green, 1871], 60).
7. Sanborn C. Brown, *Count Rumford: Physicist Extraordinary* (Garden City, NY: Anchor Books, 1962), 166. Similar allegations are that "he was hard, brittle, self-centered from first to last" and "the women in his life meant little to him" (James Alden Thompson, *Count Rumford of Massachusetts* [New York: J.J. Little & Ives, 1935], 262); and "except for his work in science, he was a man without principles, without standards, without regard for others, or for his own character" (Duane Bradley, *Count Rumford* [Princeton: D. Van Nostrand, 1967], 169).
8. BT to Lady P, Dec. 23, 1795, Dartmouth.
9. BT to Marc-Auguste Pictet, Oct. 1796, University of Geneva.
10. Lady P to Lord P, Feb. 18 and Feb. 22, 1796. Lord P had also complained to her, Feb. 24, 1795, in Connell, 347.
11. Jane Austen, *Northanger Abbey*, ed. Claire Grogan (London: Broadview Literary Press), 265.
12. Allan McLane Hamilton, *The Intimate Life of Alexander Hamilton, based chiefly upon original family letters and other documents* (New York: Scribner's Sons, 1910), 342–343.
13. Typically an enslaved person did not have a surname. The master replaced the African first name with one thought appropriate for a slave. "Slavery in New Hampshire," posted by Maggie MacLean, *History of American Women*, Dec. 16, 2007, http://www.womenhistoryblog.com/2007/12/slavery-in-new-hampshire.html.

14. James Otis Lyford, Amos Hadley, Will B. Howe, Concord (NH), City History Commission. *History of Concord, New Hampshire from the Original Grant in Seventeen Hundred and Twenty-Five to the Opening of the Twentieth Century* (Concord: Rumford Press, 1903), 248.
15. BT to ST, Aug. 1, 1792. in Brown, 335n22.
16. BT to Lady P, March 17, 1796, Dartmouth.
17. Ellis, 226.
18. Slosson, 41.
19. ST to Loammi Baldwin, Oct. 24, 1798, in Brown, 173.
20. ST to Margaret Baldwin, Oct. 24, 1798, SCD01: Rumford Family Collection, 1775–1870, Vol. 1, American Academic of Arts and Sciences [AAAS], Cambridge, Massachusetts.
21. ST to Mrs. Baldwin, June 13, 1796 in Ellis, 217.

Chapter 11

1. Laura's brother-in-law, the Major von Kalb, came to America to fight in the revolution, survived and returned to Europe.
2. BT to Loammi Baldwin, Feb. 15, 1797, in Ellis, 281–282.
3. Ellis, 304.
4. Ellis, 299.
5. Note on back of the portrait by Kellerhoff. Sally gave the Kellerhoven portrait to Joseph B. Walker in 1852, Joseph B. Walker Papers, NHHS.
6. Countess N to ST, Aug. 15, 1798, George E. Ellis Papers, MHS.
7. Ellis, 311.
8. Ellis, 612
9. Amada Vickery, *The Gentleman's Daughter: Women's Lives in Georgian England* (New Haven: Yale University Press, 1998), 149–150.
10. Ellis, 230.
11. Ellis, 310
12. BT to Lady P, May 22, 1795, Dartmouth.
13. BT to Lady P, Aug 28, 1797, Dartmouth.
14. Ellis, 315.
15. Ellis, 318.
16. BT to Lady P, Oct. 26, 1801, Dartmouth.
17. Dorothy Wordsworth to Mrs. Clarkson, Oct. 9, 1814, in Emie Legouis, *William Wordsworth and Annette Vallon* (New York: Dutton, 1922), 95.
18. Ellis, 321.
19. Ellis, 325.
20. Ellis, 324.
21. Brown, 191.
22. Larson, 98.
23. Countess N to ST, July 16, 1797, Rumford Papers, Countess Rumford 1977–73, folder 3, NHHS.
24. Ellis, 309.
25. For instance, Countess N to Sally, July 16, 1799, NHHS.
26. Countess N to ST, March 11, 1798, Rumford Papers, folder 2, NHHS.
27. *The Diaries and Letters of Gouverneur Morris* 2, ch. 39, ed. Anne Cary Morris (London: Kegan Paul Trench & Co., 1889), 333.
28. *Diaries and Letters of Gouverneur Morris*, 340.

Chapter 12

1. Brown, 190.
2. Ellis, 538.
3. Rumford, *Complete Works*, 345.
4. Ellis, 209.
5. BT to Loammi Baldwin, Sept. 28, 1798, AAAS.
6. Charles R. King, *The Life and Correspondence of Rufus King* (New York: G.P. Putnam's, 1895), vol. 2, 252.
7. He wrote Lady Palmerston that a fortnight before he received a letter from the new president John Adams and another from George Washington. She must be thinking, he quipped, "what the deuce could they have to write you about," and gave his answer: "Why, to thank me for my most interesting Essays … Sally was so delighted to see a letter from her God Washington that she kissed it for half an hour." BT to Lady P, Feb. 25, 1797, Dartmouth.
8. Alexander Hamilton to Col. Ogden, Sept. 28, 1799, New York Historical Society in Brown, 209–210.
9. Brown, 209.
10. *Complete Works*, vol. 5, 439.
11. Brown, 223–224.
12. ST to Mrs. Margaret Baldwin, Oct. 24, 1798, AAAS.
13. Burgum Papers, Emma Gannell Burgum, 1913, NHHS.
14. Ellis, 367–369.
15. ST to LB, Aug. 24, 1799 in Ellis, 363.
16. Countess N to ST, 1800, NHHS.
17. Countess N. to ST, March 18, 1800, NHHS.
18. G. Cuvier, *Récueil des éloges historique* (Paris: Didot Frères, 1861), vol. 2, 52 in Brown, 100.
19. BT to Lady P, Mar. 17, 1796, Rauner Library, Dartmouth.
20. Ellis, 375.
21. Ellis, 368. The author's farmhouse also looks out on that portion of the Saint George. A reconstruction of the Knox mansion today has the name that Henry Knox gave it, Montpelier.
22. BT to Pictet, Aug. 27, 1800, AAAS.

Chapter 13

1. BT to Lady P, Nov 1, 1801, Dartmouth.
2. Alfred Cobban, *History of Modern France* (New York: Penguin, 1961), vol. 2, 19.
3. Ellis, 433.
4. Personal communication with Neil Chambers, May 6, 2016.
5. Journal of Sir Benjamin Thompson, unpaginated, Special Collections, University of Birmingham. Future references in the text to his journal are to this unpaginated, unpublished document.
6. BT to Lady P, Oct. 3, 1801, Dartmouth.
7. Journal of Sir BT.
8. BT to Lady P, Oct. 26, 1801, Dartmouth.
9. Francis J. Grund, "Reminiscences of Germany," *Graham's American Monthly* 24, no. 167 (Philadelphia: George G. Graham, 1844).
10. BT to Lady P, Oct. 26, 1801,Dartmouth.
11. Jane Merrill and John Endicott, *Aaron Burr in Exile: A Pariah in Paris, 1810–1811* (Jefferson, NC: McFarland, 2016), 87.
12. BT, Journal from Paris.
13. Roger Hahn, *Pierre-Simon Laplace, 1749–1827: A Determined Scientist* (Cambridge: Harvard University Press, 2005), 264n.
14. David Bodanis, *Passionate Minds* (New York: Crown, 2006), 164.
15. Claude-Anne Lopez, *Mon Cher Papa: Franklin*

and the Ladies of Paris (New Haven: Yale University Press, 1966), 20–21.
   16. Journal of Sir BT.
   17. Jean Rilliet and Jean Cassaigneau, *Marc-August Pictet ou le rendez-vous de l'Europe universelle, 1752–1825* (Geneva: Editions Slatkine, 1995), 448.
   18. Pictet, 528–529.
   19. George E. Ellis Papers, 1759–1897, Loose Papers, 1769–1897; subsection misc. papers, Count Rumford Papers, Box 21, Folders 1–6, 7–15; bound 32 pp. Brompton Inventory, May 9, 1802, MHS.

Chapter 14

   1. Bence Jones, *The Royal Institution: Its Founder and Its First President* (London: Longmans, Green, 1871), 76.
   2. Suzanne Blatin, "Un Amour Physique et Chimique," *Historia* 106 July 1976), 106.
   3. Sparrow, 269.
   4. Jane Merrill, "Thirst for Enchanted Views in Ruskin's 'King of the Golden River,'" *Children's Literature* 8, no. 198, 68–79. Ellis, 541.
   5. Ellis, 541.
   6. Charles Blagden to ST, Aug. 8, 1803, in Ellis, 521.
   7. Charles Blagden to ST, Dec. 5, 1803, in Ellis, 522–522.
   8. Ellis, 542–543.
   9. Sparrow, 245.
   10. Roger Hahn, *Pierre-Simon Laplace, 1749–1827: A Determined Scientist* (Cambridge: Harvard University Press, 2005), 264.
   11. Charles Coulston Gillispie, *Pierre-Simon Laplace, 1749–1827: A Life in Exact Science* (Princeton: Princeton University Press), 178.
   12. Journal of BT.
   13. Brown, 248.

Chapter 15

   1. Denis Ian Duveen, "Madame Lavoisier, 1758–1836," *Chymia* 4 (1953), 13–14.
   2. Lavoisier, le parcours d'un scientifique revolutionionnaire—sur le CNRS, Oct. 11, 2011, www.cnrs.fr/cw.
   3. Vera Lee, *The Reign of Women in 18th Century France* (Cambridge: Schenkman, 1975), 129–30.
   4. Diary of Gouverneur Morris, Sept. 25, 1789, in Jean-Pierre Poirier, *Lavoisier: Chemist, Biologist, Economist*, trans. Rebecca Balinski (Philadelphia: University of Pennsylvania Press, 1993), 245.
   5. Fara, 172n2.
   6. Fara, 72.
   7. Benjamin Franklin to Marie-Anne Lavoisier, Oct. 23, 1785, in Edouard Grimaux, *Lavoisier* (Paris, 1888), 43.
   8. Judith Brady, "Behind Every Great Scientist," *New Scientist* 1592/1593 (Dec. 24–31, 1977).
   9. J.J. Peumery, "Marie-Anne Pierrette Paulz, épouse et collaboratrice de Lavoisier," *Vesalius* 6, no. 2 (2000), 109.
   10. Dupont to Anne-Marie Lavoisier, Oct. 23, 1798, in J.J. Peumery, 109.
   11. J-G Ruelland, *Marie-Anne Pierrette Paulze-Rumford, comtesse de Rumford (1758–1836): Lumière surgie de l'ombre*, 10.

   12. DuPont to A-M Lavoisier, Sept. 16, 1799, in J.J. Peumery, 112.
   13. The debt was for a printing press that Dupont was going to set up in 1791 when the French Revolution ruined him financially. His son Eleuthère Irénée Dupont de Nemour, who had made a success of his factory in America, paid the debt.
   14. Journal of Sir BT.
   15. Merrill and Endicott, 182–186.
   16. J. Cassaigneau and J. Rilliet, *Marc August Pictet ou le rendez-vous de l'Europe universelle, 1752–1825* (Geneva: Slatkine, 1995), 203.
   17. Blatin, 106–107.
   18. Anne Lavoisier to P.S. DuPont, July 26, 1803, Winterthur Manuscripts, Hagley Museum and Library.
   19. Linda Colley, "Facing Napoleon's Own EU," *The New York Review of Books*, Nov. 5, 2015.
   20. Jones, 88.

Chapter 16

   1. Ellis, 542.
   2. BT to Lady P, May 10, 1804, Dartmouth.
   3. Jean Rilliet and Jean Cassaigneau, *Marc-August Pictet, ou le rendez-vous de l'Europe universelle, 1752–1825* (Geneva: Slatkine, 1995), 261.
   4. *Collected Works of Count Rumford*, vol. 4, 106–107.
   5. Ellis, 543.
   6. Sir Charles to ST, Mar. 8, 1806, in Duveen, 24.
   7. Duveen, 23.
   8. *Revue Bleue, politique et littéraire* 8 (July 3, 1897), 32.
   9. Suzanne Blatin, "Un Amour physique et chimique," *Historia* 356 (July 1976), 107.
   10. Slosson, 46.
   11. M. Francois Guizot, *Memoirs to Illustrate the History of My Time*, vol. 2, trans. J.W. Cole (London: Richard Bentley, 1859), 392.
   12. BT to ST, Oct. 25, 1805, in Ellis, 548–549.
   13. *Ibid.*
   14. Ellis, 549–550.
   15. BT to ST, Dec. 20, 1805, in Duveen, 23.
   16. Ellis, 558.
   17. Poirier, 214–215.
   18. Blatin, 106–107.
   19. Sparrow, 250.
   20. Ellis, 551.
   21. *Ibid.*
   22. Ruelland, 11.

Chapter 17

   1. Madame Lavoisier to P.S. Du Pont, Jan. 9, 1809, Winterthur Manuscripts, W2 3749, Hagley Library, Delaware.
   2. *Souvenirs du Baron de Frénilly, pair de France (1768–1828)*, published with introduction and notes by Arthur Chuquet, new ed. (Paris: Plon-Nourrit, 1909), 283.
   3. *Robert de Crévecoeur, sa vie et ses ouvrages* (Paris: Librairie des Bibliophiles, 1883), 414.
   4. Brown, 303.
   5. C. Harrison Dwight, "Count Rumford," *Notes and Records of the Royal Society of London* 11, no. 2 (March 1955), 197–198.

6. Frénilly, 283–284.
7. Frénilly, 283.
8. Ellis, 559.
9. Ellis, 560.
10. Ellis, 562.
11. Ellis, 563.
12. BT to ST, Apr. 12, 1808, in Ellis, 561.
13. BT to Dubois in Blatin, 107.
14. Ellis, 564.
15. Jones, 97.
16. Jones, 98.

Chapter 18

1. Paul de Rémuset, ed., *Mémoires de Mme. De Rémuset, 1802–1808* (Paris: Calmann, Levy, 1881), vol. 1, 43–45.
2. BT to ST, Nov. 2, 1808, in Ellis, 562.
3. *Collected Works*, vol. 5, 265.
4. Antoine Guillois, *Le Salon de Madame Helvitius* (Paris: Calmann Levy, 1894), 240.
5. R. Peale to N.J. Harrison, October 1858, AAAS.
6. Ellis, 534.
7. Ellis, 570.
8. Ellis, 571.
9. *Ellis*, 600.
10. BT to John Armstrong, Jr., June 5, 1809, Simon Gratz Collection of the Historical Society of Pennsylvania.
11. Ellis, 602.
12. Duveen, 26.
13. Blatin, 107.
14. Guizot in Ellis, 579–580.
15. Ellis, 609–610.
16. Herbert Demory, president délégué de la Société Historique d'Auteuil et de Passy, and his website, histoire-auteuil-passy.org, contributed information on the house.
17. ST to James F. Baldwin, Dec. 7, 1811, George E. Ellis Papers, MHS.
18. Ellis, 610.
19. Leo Damrosch, *Jean-Jacques Rousseau: Restless Genius* (New York: Houghton Mifflin, 205), 207.
20. Larson, 166.
21. ST to James F. Baldwin, March 10, 1831, AAAS.
22. Brown, 100.
23. Robert Champeix, "Le comte Rumford, aventurier et physician," *La Revue* 14 (March 1996), 42.

Chapter 19

1. Elizabeth Hoyt Stevens, "Emma Gannell Rumford Burgum," *The Granite Monthly: A New Hampshire Magazine Devoted to History*, ed. Henry Harrison Metcalf and John Norris McClintock, vol. 50, 124.
2. John Burgum's Autograph Book, NHHS.
3. ST to George Pierce, June 21, 1852, NHHS.
4. "Three Young Girls. Chapter One," Burgum Papers, Emma Gannell Burgum, 1913. All references to Emma Burgum's writings come from the Burgum Papers, NHHS.
5. Ellis, 624.
6. BT to Victoire Lefebvre, Aug. 21, 1810, in Brown, 295.
7. "As you will know from Dad's culminating Rumford biography, 'Almost nothing is known about Victoire Lefèvre....' That remains the case, and is also true of her family, including her descendants and their papers presumably housed in the Rumford Family Collection, whatever and wherever that might be.

"You write that you think SCB 'would have been in touch with the descendants,' a reasonable enough assumption except that there is no such evidence, and even if he was for some reason obliged to suppress that connection or information, he would have mentioned it to his immediate family, longtime supporters and confidants of his enthusiastic research. Having searched my own mind and that of my siblings I yesterday discussed the question in depth with our mother ... and she has no memory in this regard.

"I am in fact the son who helped with some of the research in Europe. After checking references in Munich and Geneva I was headed for Paris but was advised that it would accomplish nothing. (I forget the precise details, but they were clearly insignificant). This was in 1967.

"It seems clear that Dad tapped reliable secondary sources for what information he gleaned about the Lefèvre/Rumford connection without ever finding the Rumford Family Collection."
Stanley Brown is Curator of Rare Books, Emeritus, at Dartmouth College.
Stanley W. Brown to Jane Merrill, email July 25, 2016.
8. Jane Merrill and John Endicott, *Aaron Burr in Exile: A Pariah in Paris, 1810–1811* (Jefferson, NC: McFarland, 2016), 178–182.
9. Brown, 298.
10. Ellis, 635–636.
11. DQ14/1984.101, no. 405, Succession directe et maritale de Benjamin Comte de rumford décédé à Auteuil le 20 aout 1814. His will made in 1812 besides military designs to the U.S. government and money to Harvard bequeathed personal gold objects were bequeathed to four me, a watch to Davy, a snuff-box to Delessert, and a gold tipped cane to Daniel. That Lafayette was the one of three executors not named suggests he may have been present at Parker's when the will was signed as a guest not because of a close friendship with the Count.
12. Ellis, 609–610.
13. Victoire Lefebvre to ST, Aug. 3, 1852, George E. Ellis Papers, MHS.
14. ST to James Baldwin, May 5, 1844, AAAS.
15. ST to Dear Friend, May 15, 1844, AAAS.
16. ST to Dear Friend, Sept. 16, 1844.
17. ST to James Baldwin, Apr. 25, 1847, AAAS.
18. Charles Lefebvre to James Baldwin, Aug. 9?, 1853, and James Baldwin to Charles Lefebvre, Aug. 2, 1853, AAAS
19. My Will of Paris, June 16, 1844. Sally identified Charles' wife Pauline as "Madame Lefebvre de Rumford." MHS.
20. ST to James Baldwin, July 16, 1844, MHS.
21. Amédé Lefebvre to George Ellis, n.d., MHS.
22. Ellis, 564.

Chapter 20

1. Burgum Papers, NHHS.
2. January 28, 1854, was the official authorization of the surname Rumford.
3. Burgum Papers, NHHS.
4. Victoire Lefebvre to ST, Aug. 3, 1852, George E. Ellis Papers, MHS. Napoleon III had earlier in the year demanded that Abd-ul Mejid, the sultan in Constan-

tinople, restore Roman Catholic rights to shrines in Turkey while Russia insisted on the rights to protect all Christians in the former Ottoman Empire.

5. Ellis, 525–526.
6. Note on back of portrait of BT (1798–1800) by William Lane, NHHS.
7. ST, "Pretty Extracts 1836–1845," "Pretty Extracts, 1836–1845," Countess Rumford Papers, NHHS. All passages from her non-epistolary writings are from this source.
8. Sally did acknowledge two accords in their thinking, that her father's death strange and that Charles wasn't insane and would be better off released from the asylum.
9. Charles Lefebvre file, NHHS.
10. Ellis, 311.
11. Her married name is given by George Ellis as Madame de Milteese and Sanborn Brown as Madame de Miltez. The painting with the note about Sophie's fate is at NHHS.
12. ST to James Baldwin, May 15, 1844, AAAS.
13. ST to James Baldwin, Aug. 31, 1851, MHS.
14. Victoire Lefebvre to ST, Aug. 3, 1852, George E. Ellis Papers, MHS.
15. ST to Pauline Lefebvre, Sept. 1, 1852, MHS.
16. St to Pauline Lefebvre, Oct. 15, 1852, MHS.
17. Honoré de Balzac, *Ursule Mirouet*, Project Gutenberg.
18. Brown, viii.
19. Countess N to ST, Apr. 15, 1798, NHHS.
20. Sir Charles to ST, Mar. 8, 1806, NHHS.
21. ST, "Pretty Extracts 1836–1845."
22. "Rumford Villa," NHHS.
23. *The Life and Letters of Maria Edgeworth*, ed. by Augustus J.C. Hare, vol. 2 (Boston: Houghton Mifflin, 1895), 360.
24. ST to Benjamin Delessert, n.d., NHHS.
25. Neil Chambers, ed., *Scientific Correspondence of Sir Joseph Banks, 1765–1820*, vol. 6 between Charles Blagden and Joseph Banks (Abingdon-on-Thames: Routledge, 2007), Sept. 6, Nov. 9 and Nov. 16, 1819.
26. Duveen, 29.
27. Rumford Papers, Countess Rumford, "Directions and Extracts," NHHS.
28. Amedé gave memorabilia of his grandfather to Ellis, as mentioned in a letter of Feb. 21, 1883, from Auxerre (Yvonne), France. George Ellis Papers, MHS. Besides the plaque from the Elector of Bavarian is a typical memento but the other two may have had special significance. The case with the initials BT from the count's early years were probably either given to Victoire for her son or something she was allowed to have because of Charles. The portrait on vellum was done, according to Amedé, just before the count's death, meaning around the time of Charles' birth. MHS.

Epilogue

1. Thomas Foster, "Reconsidering Libertines and Early Modern Heterosexuality: Sex and American Founder Gouverneur Morris," *Journal of the History of Sexuality* 22, no.1 (Jan. 2013), 67.
2. Robert Campeix, "Count Rumford, Adventurer and Physicist," *La Revue* 14, Musée des arts et métiers (March 1996), 41.
3. It has been remarked that the count spent much of his life in realms of pomp and circumstance so several biographers have judged that he would have been disappointed not to have a pretentious funeral. For example, a mid-20th century biographer wrote, "Of all the misfortunes that befell Benjamin during his lifetime, the reaction to his death would have seemed the most terrible to him" (Duane Bradley, *Count Rumford* [Princeton: D. Van Nostrand, 1967]). It would be the rarest person to aspire to a "big" funeral, and a practical, economical person would not be among them.
4. Duveen, 23.
5. M. Andrew Holowchak, *Dutiful Correspondent: Philosophical Essays on Thomas Jefferson* (Lanham, MD: Rowan & Littlefield, 2013), 83.

Afterword

1. Brown, 6 and 10.
2. Ellis, 195.
3. Sanborn C. Brown, *Count Rumford, Physicist Extraordinary* (New York: Anchor Books, Doubleday, 1962) 111–112.
4. Merrill and Endicott, 50–51.

Bibliography

The trail of research I pursued was earmarked by Sanborn Brown's seminal biography of 1979. As I have, he based much of his information on the Reverend Ellis's one-volume *Memoir*, while giving a roadmap of archives, which I gratefully followed, my slant being more the personal life of the inventor. I have also drawn considerably, as indicated in the endnotes, from archives of the American Society of Arts and Letters, the Massachusetts Historical Society, the New Hampshire Historical Society, and the Rauner Library of Dartmouth College.

Abbott, Francis M. "Count Rumford and His Daughters." *New England Magazine, An Illustrated Monthly*, Sept. 1893–Feb. 1894. Boston: Warren F. Kellogg.

Adams, John. *The Works of John Adams*. Ed. Charles F. Adams. Boston, 1856.

Atkins, Diane C. *The Glorious Fourth of July: Old-Fashioned Treats & Treasures from America*. New York: Pelican, 2009.

Bernier, Olivier. *Pleasure and Privilege: Life in France, Naples, and America, 1770–90*. Garden City, NY: Doubleday, 1981.

Bouton, Nathaniel. *The History of Concord, from its First Grant in 1725, to the Organization of the City Government in 1853, with a History of the Ancient Penacooks...* Concord: Benning W. Sanborn, 1856.

Bradley, Duane. *Count Rumford*. Princeton: Van Nostrand, 1967.

Bradley, James E. "The Reprieve of a Loyalist: Count Rumford's Invitation Home." *New England Quarterly* 47 (1974).

Brown, G.I. *Count Rumford: The Extraordinary Life of a Scientific Genius—Scientist, Soldier, Statesman, Spy*. London: Sutton, 1999.

Brown, Sanborn C. *Count Rumford*. Cambridge: MIT Press, 1962.

Brown, Sanborn C. "International Informers." *New England Quarterly* 21 (1948).

Brown, Sanborn C. "Scientific Drawings of Count Rumford at Harvard." *Harvard Library Bulletin* IX.

Campeix, Robert. "Le Comte Rumford, aventurier et physicien," *La Revue* 14 (March 1996).

Cayton, Andrew. *Love in the Time of Revolution: Transatlantic Literary Radicalism and Historical Change, 1793–1818*. Chapel Hill: University of North Carolina Press, 2013.

Connell, Brian. *Portrait of a Gentleman*. Boston: Houghton Mifflin, 1958.

Connell, Brian. *Portrait of a Whig Peer: Viscount Palmerston, 1759–1802*. London: André Deutsch, 1957.

Crosland, Maurice. *Society of Arcueil*. Cambridge: Harvard University Press, 1967.

Cuthbertson, Brian C. *The Loyalist Governor: Biography of Sir John Wentworth*. Halifax, Nova Scotia: Petheric Press, 1983.

Delbanco, Nicholas. *American Heritage* (Sept. 1993).

Dolan, Brian. *Ladies of the Grand Tour: British Women in Pursuit of Enlightenment and Adventure in Eighteenth Century Europe*. New York: HarperCollins, 2001.

Domberg, John Robert. "Count Rumford, the Most Successful Yank Abroad, Ever." *Smithsonian* 25, no. 9 (Dec. 1994).

Duveen, Denis I. "Madame Lavoisier, 1758–1836." *Chymia* 4 (1953).

Dwight, C. Harrison. "Count Rumford: His Majesty's Colonel in Carolina." *South Carolina Historical Magazine* (Jan. 1956).

Dwight, C. Harrison. *Sir Benjamin Thompson, Count of Rumford*. Cincinnati, 1960.

Easton, J.C. "Charles Theodoree of Bavaria and Count Rumford." *The Journal of Modern History* 12, no. 2 (June 1940).

Einstein, Lewis. *Divided Loyalties*. London: Cobdens-Sanderson, 1933.

Ellis, The Rev. George E. *Memoir of Sir Benjamin Count Rumford*. Published in England by Macmillan & Co. (London, 1876); in America by Claxton, Remsen and Haffelfinger (Philadelphia, 1870).

Fara, Patricia. *Pandora's Breeches: Women, Science and Power in the Enlightenment*. London: Pimlico, 2004.

Foster, Thomas. "Reconsidering Libertines and Early Modern Heterosexuality: Sex and American Founder Gouverneur Morris." *Journal of the History of Sexuality* 2, no. 1 (Jan. 2013).

Fraser, Flora. *Beloved Emma: The Life of Lady Hamilton*. London: Bloomsbury, 1986.

French, Allen. *General Gage's Informers*. Ann Arbor: University of Michigan Press, 1932.

Gillispe, Charles Coulston. *Pierre-Simon Laplace, 1749–*

1827: A Life in Exact Science. Princeton: Princeton University Press, 1997.

Good, Cassandra A. *Founding Friendships: Friendships Between Men and Women in the Early American Republic*. New York: Oxford University Press, 2015.

Hahn, Roger. *Pierre-Simon Laplace, 1749–1827: A Determined Scientist*. Cambridge: Harvard University Press, 2005.

Hale, Richard W. "Some Account of Benjamin Thompson: Count Rumford. His Romantic Career in Statesmanship and Science." *New England Quarterly* (October 1928).

Higby, Chester Penn. *The Religious Policy of the Bavarian Government During the Napoleonic Period*. New York: AMS Press, 1967.

Hutchinson, Thomas. *The Diary and Letters of his Excellency Thomas Hutchinson, Esq., by Peter Orlando Hutchinson*. Vol. II. Boston: Houghton Mifflin, 1886.

James, Ioan. *Remarkable Physicists: From Galileo to Yukawa*. Cambridge: Cambridge University Press, 2004.

Jeffries, John. *Diary and Papers*. Houghton Library Harvard. Oct. 24, Nov. 1, 1780, etc.

Jones, H. Bence. *The Royal Institution, Its Founder and its First Professors*. London, 1871; rpt. BiblioLife LCC.

Kaldenbach, Robert. "Lord of the Flues." *Yankee Magazine* (Jan. 1998).

Kaye, Harvey J. *Thomas Paine, Firebrand of the Revolution*. New York: Oxford University Press, 2000.

Kleppner. D. "About Benjamin Thompson." *Physics Today* (Sept. 1992).

Larson, Egon [pseud. for Egon Lehrburger]. *An American in Europe: The Life of Benjamin Thompson, Count Rumford*. London, 1953.

Larson, Egon [pseud. for Egon Lehrburger]. *Graf Rumford: Ein Amerikaner in Munchen*. Munich: Prestel Verlag, 1961.

Lee, Vera. *The Reign of Women in Eighteenth Century France*. Cambridge, MA: Schenkman, 1975.

Lyford, James O., ed. *History of Concord, New Hampshire*. Vol. I, prepared under the supervision of the City History Commission. Concord, NH: City Government, January 14, 1896.

Marshall, James F., ed. and trans. *De Staël-Du Pont Letters; Correspondence of Madame de Staël and Pierre Samuel du Pont de Nemours*. Madison: University of Wisconsin Press, 1989.

McCrady, Edward. *The History of South Carolina in the Revolution, 1780–1783*. New York: Macmillan, 1902.

Morris, Gouveneur. Diary. Library of Congress.

Nagy, John A. *Invisible Ink: Spycraft of the American Revolution*. Yardley, PA: Westholme Publishing, 2011.

Nelson, Eric. *The Royalist Revolution: Monarchy and the American Founding*. Cambridge: Belknap Press, 2014.

Nicolson, Colin. *The "Infamas Governer": Francis Bernard and the Origins of the American Revolution*. Boston: Northeastern University Press, 2000.

Norton, Mary Beth. *The British Americans: The Loyalist Exiles in England, 1774–89*. Boston: Little, Brown, 1972.

Orton, Vrest. *The Forgotten Art of Building a Good Fireplace*. Dublin, NH: Yankee, 1969.

Oxford Dictionary of National Biography. Henry Temple, second viscount Palmerston.

Paris, J.A. *The Life of Sir Humphry Davy*. London, 1831, vol. II.

Peumery, J.J. *Marie-Anne Pierette Paulze, épouse et collaboratrice de Lavoisier*. Vesalius VI, no. 2 (2000).

Pictet, M.A. *Bibliothèque Britannique Sciences et arts* 19 (Aug. 15, 1801).

Poirier, Jean-Pierre. *La Science et l'Amour*. Paris: Pygmalion, 2004.

Porter, Roy. *English Society in the 18th Century*. New York: Penguin, 1981.

Renwick, J. "The Life of Count Rumford." Library of American Biography, conducted by Jared Sparks, Vol. XV (Boston, 1845).

Ridley, Jasper. *Lord Palmerston*. New York: E.P. Dutton, 1971.

Rilliet, Jean, and Jean Cassaigneau. *Marc-Auguste Pictet ou le rendez-vous de l'Europe universelle, 1752–1825*. Geneva: Editions Slatkine, 1995.

Rothschild, Robert Friend. *Two Brides for Apollo: The Life of Samuel Williams (1743–1817)*. New York: iUniverse, 2009.

Ruelland, Jacques G. *Marie-Anne Pierrette Paulze-Lavoisier, comtess de Rumford (1758–1836), lumière surgie de l'ombre*.

Rumford, Benjamin Graf von. *The Complete Works of Count Rumford*. London: Macmillan, 1876. (The numbering of the volumes is different in the American and English editions. In the English edition the Memoir is Vol. I, followed by vols. II, II, IV, V.)

Rumford's Journal of His Stay in Paris in 1801 (Lady Palmerston's Copy). Library of the University of Birmingham MS481.

"Scientific Drawings of Count Rumford at Harvard." *Houghton Bulletin* 9, no. 3 (1955).

Shipton, Clifford K. *Isaiah Thomas, Printer, Patriot, and Philanthropist, 1749–1831*. Rochester: Printing House of Leo Hart, 1948.

Sieveking, Hinrich. *Fuseli to Menzel: Drawings and Watercolors in the Age of Goethe from a German Private Collection*. Munich: Prestel, 1998.

Slosson, Edwin, E. *Benjamin Thompson, Count Rumford. Leading American Men of Science*. Ed. David Starr Jordan. New York: Henry Holt, 1910.

Sparrow, W.J. *Count Rumford of Woburn, Mass*. New York: Thomas Y. Crowell, 1964.

Taylor, Alan. *American Revolutions: A Continental History, 1750–1804*. New York: W.W. Norton, 2017.

Thomas, Sir John Meurig. *Notes and Records of the Royal Society of London* 53, no. 1 (1999).

Thomas, Marvin Edward. *Karl Theodore and the Bavarian Succession, 1777–1778*, vol. Lewiston, NY: Mellen Press, 1997.

Thompson, James Alden. *Count Rumford of Massachusetts*. New York: Farrar and Rinehart, 1935.

Tyndall, John. *Count Rumford: A Brief Biographical Account of this Outstanding American, born Benjamin Thompson*. Whitefish, MT: Kessinger Legacy Reprints.

Valentine, Alan. *Lord George Germain*. London: Oxford University Press, 1962.

Vickery, Amanda. *Behind Closed Doors: At Home in Georgian England*. New Haven: Yale University Press, 2009.

Weidner, Thomas. *Rumford: Rezepte für ein besseres Bayern: Eine Ausstellung des Münchner Stadtmuseums*. Munich: Hirmer, 2014.

Wilderson, Paul W. *Governor John Wentworth and the American Revolution: The English Connection*. Lebanon, NH: University Press of New England, 1994.

Williams, Kate. *England's Mistress: The Infamous Life of Lady Hamilton*. New York: Ballantine, 2006.

Young, Philip, *Revolutionary Ladies*. New York: Alfred A. Knopf, 1977.

Ziegler, Philip, *King William IV*. New York: Harper & Row, 1971.

Index

Numbers in ***bold italics*** refer to pages with photographs.

Acton, John 66–67
Adams, Abigail 54, 110, 224
Adams, Charles Francis 59
Adams, John 13, 14, 27, 34, 67, 225
Adams, Sam 18
Aichners 85, 108, 131, 133, 140, 166–167, 188
American Revolution 13, 19–20, 28–29, 66
American Royalists in London 30, 45–48, 111
Antin, Monsieur 192–195, 205
Apollodorian Gallery 176
Appleton, John 10, 226
Apponyi, Count Antoine 88
Apponyi, Countess Therese 88, 124, ***125***
Armstrong, Gen. John, Jr. 177
Austrian attack on Munich 83
Auteuil 31, 175–180, 183, 189–191, 220

Baldwin, George 24, 83, 210
Baldwin, James 57, 181, 379, 415, 440
Baldwin, Loammi 7–14, 20, 24, 67, 69, 106, 108, 132, 135, 151, 172
Baldwin, Margery 83
Banks, Joseph 48, 91–92, 212
Banks, Lady 116
Barnard, Thomas 10
Bastille Day 137
Baumgarten, Countess Josepha 71, 80–87, 91, 102–103, 116, 119, 134, 176, 218
Baumgarten, Sophia "Sophie" 81, 83–85, 102, 121, 140–141, 176, ***185***, 206–207, 218
Bavaria 60–88, 102, 112–126
Beethoven 66–67
Belknap, Jeremy 28
Berthollet, Claude 158, 177

Bibliothèque Britannique 9, 106, 131
Bigelow, Timothy 42
Blagden, Sir Charles 88, 91, 97, 114, 130, 145, 150–151, 158, 162, 183, 202, 205, 210–211
Blanchard, Jean Pierre 54–55, 93
Bonaparte, Prince Pierre 178
Bonnet, Monsieur 189–192
Boston, evacuation 44, 48, 57
Boston massacre 13
Boston Tea Party 77
Bow, New Hampshire 17
Bradford, Massachusetts 15, 17, 25, 67
Broadlands 76, 93–95, 105, 141, 187
Brompton Row 75, 139, 147, 164, 183, 191, 200
Brown, Capability 92
Brown, Sanborn Conner 2, 23, 36, 46–47, 95, 104, 127, 148, 169, 198, 209
Brown, Stanley 139 ch19n
Burghausen, Heinrich Otto von 61–62
Burghausen, Mrs. 61–62
Burgoyne, General 60
Burgum, Emma Gannell 171, 182–209 passim
Burgum, John 182, 184
Burr, Aaron 105, 154, 159, 188, 231

Calais 60
Canada, Eastern 16, 30, 45, 56
Candide 74
Candolle, Augustin de 163
Capen, Hopestill and Patience 12–14
Carleton, Maj. Gen. Guy 46, 56, 57
Caroline Mathilda, Queen 71

Catherine of Russia 131
Chambers, Neil 139
Chamonix 150
Chaptal, Jean Antoine 143
Charenden 194–196
Charles, Julie 146
Charleston, South Carolina 34, 55
Charlestown, Massachusetts 29, 34, 77
Charlotte, Queen 118, 120
Châtelet, Marquise Emilie du 144, 167
Chinese rule 77–78, 181
Chopin 86
Christian VII, King 70
Church, Benjamin 22
Common Sense 45
Committees of Safety/Correspondence 21–22, 29, 40
Como 91–92
Concord, New Hampshire 16–22, 26, 34, 69, 106, 184, 202
Concord Herald 82
Congress of Vienna 127–128
Continental Congress 21, 29, 177
Cook, Captain 92
Copley, John Singleton 18, 26, 27
Cosway, Marie 216, 218, 220
Curtoni, Versa Silvia 86–87
Cuvier, Baron George 9, 77, 133, 171
Curwen, Judge Samuel 22, 47, 52

Dames, Nicholas 208–209
Dartmouth College 2, 26–28
David, Jacques-Louis 149, 156–157
Davy, Humphry 9, 131, 138, 152
Deane, Silas 12
Deerfield Raid 15

243

Delessert, Mme. Gautier 162
Delessert, J.P. Benjamin 180, 181, 193–196
Dickens, Charles 93
Diderot, Denis 4, 156
Die Räuber 113
Dillis, Johann Georg von 64, 82, 83, 87, 123, 132–134
Dinah 106, 133–134
Don Carlo 141
Dorner, Johann-Jakob 73
Dover, England *55*, 60
Dover, New Hampshire 18, 19
Drummond 177
Dublin 78, 105, 110
Du Pont, Pierre 145, 157–166, 219
Durand, Asher B. 82

Edgeworth, Lady 159, 212
Elliott, Charles William 1
Ellis, the Rev. George 57, 59, 106, 108, 212
Empire style 4, 111, 120, 128, 144
Enghien, duc d' 159
Englischer Garten 75–77, 120, 140, 226
Este, Isabella d' 135

Farmer Refuted 13
Federal Spy 44
Fenton, Col. John 29
Fergusen, James 22–26, **23**
Fogg Museum 58, 125
Fontaine, Pierre
Fontana, Felice 97
Fonzi, Giuseppangelo 231
Fouché, Joseph 168–169, 174
Foundling Hospital, London 70, 78
Fowle, Mary 44
Fowle, Mary (of Londonderry, NH) 39
Fowle, Zachariah 34–35, 44
Franklin, Benjamin 2, 10, 13, 34, 54, 78, 89, 156, 175, 186
Franklin, William 34
Freedom Trail 12
French and Indian War 11, 13, 19, 55
French Institute (Paris) 89, 143, 174, 224, 151
French Revolution 66–67, 96, 113, 185
Frick Museum 82

Gage, Gen. Thomas 21, 23, 29, 31
Gainsborough, Thomas 58
Gallina, Madame 92
Garrick, David 92, 95
George III 13, 47, 50–51, 114
Germain, Lord 43–71, 104, 214, 223, 228

Ghost of Minden 46
Gibbon, Edward 60, 96, 104
Glenbervie, Lord and Lady 47, 96
Godwin, William 90
Goethe 66–67, 69, 90, 118
Good, Cassandra A. 91
Gore, Christopher 228
Gore, Rebecca 228
Gore Place 228
Gotthard Pass 92
Gramont, Countess de 212
Greenland, New Hampshire 37
Guy Fawkes Day 11

Halifax, Nova Scotia 29–32, 49, 52
Hamilton, Alexander 13, 109, 130
Hamilton, Lady Emma 82, 95–98, 111
Hamilton, Sir William 94
Hancock, John 34, 41, 51
Hardy, Sir Charles 52
Harvard College 14, 22, 68
Hawthorne, Nathaniel 9
Hay, Dr. 14, 15, 69
Helvétius, Anne-Catherine 6, 175–178
Hemings, Sally 216
Henry VIII 95
History of Printing in America 44
Holfeld, Hippolyte 190
Holy Roman Empire 76–77, 118, 127, 135, 187
Horry, Col. 56
Hospital of Mercy, Verona 99
House of Seven Gables 8
Howe, Gen. William 23, 37, 48
Hunt, Hannah 54
Huntington, New York 57
Hutchinson, Gov. Thomas 22, 47, 51–52

Idomene 82
Illuminati 64, 81–82, 122
In Promptu 35
Ingres, J-A Dominique 88, 126, 157
Intervention of the Sabine Women 157

Jefferson, Thomas 78, 106, 110, 143, 216, 220
Jeffries, Dr. John 48, 55, 93
Jeffries, Susan 49–53, 219
Johnson, Dr. 95
Jollien, Madame 153
Joseph II 61
Joséphine, Empress 97, 163, 173
Julie, ou la nouvelle Héloïse 157

Kalb, Baroness Friederike Eleonore Sophie von 81–83, 90
Kalb, Johann, Baron von 112, 113, 131
Kaplan, Paul 137
Karl Alexander 120, 128
Karl Theodor, Elector 61–104 passim, 112–139 passim, **114**, 213, 218
Kaunitz, Wenzel Anton 61–62
Keith, Sir Robert 61, 63, 71, 104
Kellerhoven, Moritz 70, 80, 103, 118
Kindred Spirits 82
King, Rufus 130, 132, 138
King's American Dragoons 28, 54, 56, 57
King's Woods 26, 30
Knox, Gen. Henry 138
Konrad, Brigitte Muller 186
Kroncke, Jedidiah

Lady Chatterley's Lover 93
Lafayette, Andrienne 45–46
Lafayette, Marquise de 45–46
Lagrange, Joseph Louis 14
Lamartine, Alphones, de 146
Laplace, Pierre Simon de 143, 144, 153–154, 169, 177, 189
La Tour, Gen. Louis de 114
La Tour, Quentin de 175
Laurens, Henry 59
Lavoisier, Anne-Marie Paultz 16, 144–145, 148–190 passim, 198, 211–213, 219–220
Lavoisier, Antoine 94, 152–153, 157, 165, 179, 231
Lawrence, Thomas 95
Lee, William 143
Lefebvre, Amedée Joseph 190, 197, 201, 212
Lefebvre, Charles Francis 190, 195–199, 205- 210
Lefebvre, Marie Sarah 201
Lefebvre, Pauline 186, 196–197, 201, 205–209
Lefebvre, Victoire Joseph 179–189, 199
Lerchenfeld family 80–81, 121
Leslie, General 56
Leslie, John 229
Lespinasse, Julie de 163
Lessing 69
Long Island, New York 56–57, 111
Longfellow, Henry Wadsworth 19, 26
Loyalists 13, 30, 46, 54–57

Madison, James 177
Maison d'Arrêt 157
Mannheim 64, 68, 69, 74–76,

97, 112–113, 141, 150–151, 161, 113
Maria Carolina, Queen 67
Maria Theresa, Empress 61
Marion, Gen. Francis 56
Massachusetts Spy 12
Mather, Cotton 14
Mather, Increase 16
Maximilian, Count of Lerchenfeld 128
Maximilian Joseph (duc de Deu Ponts) 60, 62, 131, 140, 148, 150, 161, 179
Medford, Massachusetts 10
Melbourne, Lady 131
Melville, Herman 9
Memoirs of a Lady 83, 108
Memoirs of a Woman of Pleasure 45
Merrimack River 16–17
Metternich 128
Middlesex Canal 9
Militias 17, 19, 29, 32, 34, 54, 56
Minutemen 21, 34
Mohawks 16
Montaigne 177
Morison, Samuel Eliot 22
Morris, Gouverneur 6, 124–135, 156, 216–217
Mother Osgood's Tavern 22
Mount Pleasant 28
Mount Vernon 13, 31
Mount Vesuvius 94
Mozart, W.A. 81, 83, 85–86, 218
Munich 61–167 passim, 176, 187–190, 207, 223, 230
Munich State Museum 84
My Fair Lady 110

Naples 67, 86, 89, 92, 94, 98
Napoleon Bonaparte 87, 96, 97, 127–128, 137, 142–143, 146, 148, 151, 159, 160, 163–164
Napoleon Collection, McGill 51
Napoleonic Code 208–209
Necker, Jacques 159
Nelson, Eric 62
Nelson, Horatio 90, 98, 139
Newburyport, Massachusetts 38, 41
Nogarola, Countess Mary 81–102 passim, 111–134 passim, 140–141, 150, 167, 176, 181, 211
North, Lord Frederick 12, 47, 57
Nova Scotia 30, 32–34, 40, 48, 57, 63

Onderdonk, Henry 57
Osiris, Monsieur 176
Ottoman Turks 61, 239ch20n4

Paine, Joshua 68
Paine, Thomas 45, 67
Palmerston, 3rd Viscount 90

Palmerstons, Lady (Mary Mee) and 2nd Viscount (Henry Temple) 78–183, **88**, passim, 207, 213, 218–220
Paris: Benjamin Thompson in 139–182; Sally Thompson in 184–197
Parker, Daniel 180–181, 191
Parker, Sam 42
Patterns (by Amy Lowell) 4
Paulze, Jacques 155–157
Peace of Amiens 161
Percier, Charles de 144, 154
Perrault, Charles 76
Petit Arsenal 157
Pickering, Timothy 130
Pictet, Marc-Auguste 9, 19–20, 104, 139, 145–146, 159–162, 169, 215–216
Pierce, Josiah, Jr. 7–9, 177, 215
Pierce, Ruth Thompson 7–8, 18, 34, 68–69, 107, 136, 177, **215**
Piscatuqua River 29
Portsmouth, England 109, 111, 112, 118
Portsmouth, New Hampshire 16–17
Pounall, Thomas 50
Pride and Prejudice 109
Priestley, Joseph 9, 98

Québec 46, 53

Rémusat, Madame de 174
Revere, Paul 34, 42
Reynolds, Sir Joshua 92, 95
Riesbeck, Kaspar 118, 235 ch8n1
Robinson Crusoe 77
Rochfoucault, duc de 167
Rockingham, Marquis of and Lady 27–29
Rolfe, Col. Benjamin 16–18, 21, 31, 106
Rolfe, Paul 135
Romford, England 95
Roosevelt. Franklin D. 1
Rosenborg Castle 70
Rotterdam 55
Rousseau, Jean-Jacques 89, 162–163, 171, 180, 218
Royal Institution 130–131, 138–139, 148, 182, 209, 230
Royal Society 48, 52, 145, 150, 169, 224
Royalists 21, 30, 45, 47–48, 111, 242
Rumford, New Hampshire 16, 76
Rumford roaster 102, **217**, 227–228
Rumford soup 72, 74, 225–226
Rumford stove and fireplaces 78, 102, 105–106, 162, 169, 226–227
Rundlet, James 228

Rundlet-May House **217**, 228
Rutland Herald 69

Sadler's Wells 50
Saint John's River 57
Saint Lawrence River 56
Saint Paul's Cathedral and Churchyard 50, 78, 103
Salem, Massachusetts 10–13, 75, 224
Saxony 76, 83, 113–114, 141
Scarborough 23
Schiller, Friedrich 113, 140, 141
Schwabingerstrasse 67, 189
Sckell, Friedrich Ludwig von 75–76, 226
Seeau, Count 85
Seven Years' War 62
Sign of the Cornfields 12, 13, 15, 34
Simmons, Dr. Levi 44
Springfield, Massachusetts 44
Stamp Act 11, 28
Starnburg Lake 85, 119
Struensee, Dr. Johann Friedrich 70–71, 77
Switzerland 64, 85, 150–151, 160, 181, 207, 220

Talleyrand 66, 128, 136, 143, 147, 159, 174
Tallien, Madam 145, **145**
Taming of the Shrew 172
Tasso family 127
Tauzier, Countess Therese of 86, 195–196, 201, 206
Taxis, Count 120, 122
Taxis, Princess Theresa of Mecklenburg-Strelitz 119–128 passim, 139–140, 198, 218
Terray, Joseph-Marie 155
39, rue d'Anjou-Saint-Honoré 151, 162, 164, 169, 173, 176, 212
Thomas, Isaiah 34–44
Thomas, Mary Anne 44
Thomas, Mary Dill 35–45
Thomas, Mary Fowle 44
Thompson, Ebenezer 20–21; house **8**
Thompson, Hiram 7, 10
Thompson, Ruth 8, 21–22, 146–148, 198, 229, 289
Thompson, Sarah Rolfe 16–21, 25, 31, 33–34, 59, 82, 95, 133, 152, 184, 187, 218
Thompson, Sarah "Sally" 20, 21, 67, 82–212 passim
To the Lighthouse 93
Tower Armory 50
Treaty of Paris 59
39, rue d'Anjou-Saint-Honoré 151, 162, 164, 169, 173, 176, 212

Trinity Church 42
Trumbull, John 54
Turgot, A.R.J. 157

Union Oyster House 12, 35
University of Michigan 22
University of Southampton 2, 100
Ursule Mirouet 209

Vallon, Annette 121
Vanity Fair 116
Vauxhall 49, 50, **216**
Vermont 44, 69
Verona 84–102, 123–124, 133–135, 207, 213, 227
Vienna 61, 104, 118, 120, 129
Vigée Le Brun, Elisabeth 162
Vindication of the Rights of Women 116
Volta, Alessandro 9, 97, 143
Voltaire 69–72, 78–79, 92, 144, 155

Walewski, Marie 173
Walker, Sarah 16–18; thimble **17**
Walker, Timothy (of Bradford) 16, 28
Walker, Col. Rev. Timothy, Jr. 16, 21
Walker-Woodman House 16
Wallmoden, Madam 114
Walpole, Horace 46, 104, 223
Warren, Dr. Joseph 34, 36, 42
Washington, George 1, 19, 22, 34, 54, 106, 130–131, 217, 237ch12n7
Washington, D.C. 177
Watertown, Massachusetts 42
Webster, Lady Elizabeth 96–97
Wedgwood, Josiah 143
Weidner, Thomas 84
Wentworth, Gov. Benning 16, 19, 21, 26–29
Wentworth, Charles Mary 29, 30
Wentworth, Francis ("Fanny") 25–32, **26**, 57
Wentworth, John 17, 19, 23–31, 57
Wentworth-Coolidge Mansion 19
West, Benjamin 50
West Indies 53
West Point 132, 136, 138
Westminster School 30
White Mountains 21, 28
Wieland 69
Willard, Dr. Joseph 107–108
William Henry, Prince (later William IV) 30, 56
Williams, Eunice 15
Williams, Jonathan 138
Williams, the Rev. Samuel 15, 16, 22, 26, 67–68
Williams, Warham 15–16
Wilson, Peter H. 76–77
Winslow, Edward 63
Winthrop, Gov. John 7
Winthrop, Prof. John 14, 22, 68
Woburn, Massachusetts 2, 7–24, 34–35, 42, 67–69, 135, 172
Wolfboro, New Hampshire 28
Wollstonecraft, Mary 89, 91, 116, 213
Woodman, Timothy 16–17
Worcester, Massachusetts 36, 42, 44
Wordsworth, William 121–122

www.ingramcontent.com/pod-product-compliance
Lightning Source LLC
Chambersburg PA
CBHW081549300426
44116CB00015B/2810